(UN)THINKING CITIZENSHIP

*For my mother, Johanna Maria Gouws, who taught me
the value of struggle*

(Un)thinking Citizenship
Feminist Debates in Contemporary South Africa

Edited by

AMANDA GOUWS
University of Stellenbosch, South Africa

Published by
Ashgate Publishing Limited
Gower House
Croft Road
Aldershot
Hants GU11 3HR
England

Ashgate Publishing Company
Suite 420
101 Cherry Street
Burlington, VT 05401-4405
USA

Ashgate website: http://www.ashgate.com

British Library Cataloguing in Publication Data
(Un)thinking citizenship : feminist debates in contemporary
    South Africa. - (Gender in a global/local world)
    1.Women's rights - South Africa 2.Citizenship - South
    Africa 3.Women - Government policy - South Africa 4.Women -
    South Africa - Social policy 5.Women in politics - South
    Africa
    I.Gouws, Amanda, 1959-
    305.4'2'0968'09049

Library of Congress Cataloging-in-Publication Data
(Un)thinking citizenship : feminist debates in contemporary South Africa / [edited] by
Amanda Gouws.
        p. cm. -- (Gender in a global/local world)
    Includes bibliographical references and index.
    ISBN 0-7546-3878-2
    1. Women's rights--South Africa. 2. Women--Government policy--South Africa. 3.
Women--South Africa--Social conditions. 4. Women in politics--South Africa. 5.
Citizenship--South Africa. 6. Feminist theory--Political aspects. I. Gouws, Amanda,
1959- II. Series.

    HQ1236.5.S6U68 2004
    305.42'0968--dc22

                                                                            2004020044

ISBN 0 7546 3878 2

Printed and bound in Great Britain by
Athenaeum Press Ltd., Gateshead, Tyne & Wear

Contents

List of Contributors

Danwood Mzikenge Chirwa

Danwood Mzikenge Chirwa is a lecturer in the Law faculty at the University of Cape Town. He was admitted to practise law in the High Court and Supreme Court of Malawi on 8 January 2001. He is the holder of a LLM in Human Rights and Democratization in Africa from the University of Pretoria, and a LLB (Hons) from the University of Malawi.

Between May 2002 and December 2004 he worked as a doctoral researcher in the Socio-Economic Rights Project of the Community Law Centre. He also worked as a research assistant for Prof. Jeremy Sarkin of the University of the Western Cape, South Africa, from 2001–2003. In addition, he has practised law with the firm of Savjani & Company of Malawi from March 2000 to April 2002.

He is published in the field of socio-economic rights, children's rights, privatization, and corporate social responsibility.

Daniel Conway

Daniel Conway, BA (Hons) (Exeter) MSc (Bristol) is a PhD student at Rhodes University studying masculinities, citizenship and political objection to compulsory military service in the South African Defence Force (SADF) between 1978–1990. This research built on his Master's research at the University of Bristol, focusing on gender and the militarization of apartheid South Africa.

He is primarily interested in interconnections between political and personal identities that are particularly apparent in the context of military service and 'manhood'.

Louise du Toit

Louise du Toit teaches Philosophy at Rand Afrikaans University in Johannesburg, South Africa. She obtained her degrees in Philosophy and Literature from the University of Stellenbosch. The topic of her PhD dissertation is on the normative implications of sexual difference. Her research interests include Feminist Ethics, Theories of Embodiment, Women and the Law, Hermeneutics, and Ancient Greek Philosophy.

Gertrude Fester

Gertrude Fester has been involved in anti-apartheid politics since an early age and was part of women's mass-based organizations. She is a founder member of various organizations, e.g. United Women's Congress, Federation of South African Women and Women's National Coalition. She is a board member of the Gender Advocacy Project and initiated Women's Education Artistic Voice and Expressions in 1997. She has lectured at Hewat College of Education and was an ANC member of National Parliament, serving on the *Improvement of Quality of Life and Status of Women* Portfolio Committee. She is currently a Commissioner on Gender Equality. Her publications include chapters in *From Amazon to Zami: Towards a Global Lesbian Feminism* (1996, edited by Monika Reinfelder), *Sisters, Feminism and Power* (1998, edited by Obi Nnaemeka) and *Belonging: Contemporary Feminist Writings on Global Change* (2000, edited by Ali, Coates and Wangui wa Goro).

Beth Goldblatt

Beth Goldblatt BA (Hons) LLB LLM (Witwatersrand) is a Senior Research Officer in the Centre for Applied Legal Studies at the University of the Witwatersrand. She has been involved in research, advocacy, litigation and teaching on gender and the law for the past seven years. She has published in the areas of human rights, family law and gender.

Amanda Gouws

Amanda Gouws is a professor of Political Science at the University of Stellenbosch where she teaches Gender Politics and Feminist Theory. She is one of the coordinators of the Gender Studies Programme. Her research focus is on women and citizenship and she has published widely on the National Machinery for Women in South Africa. She has also published on social welfare policy and the ethics of care as well as issues of representation. In this book she develops her arguments on the National Machinery for Women. She and her co-author Jim Gibson of Washington University, St Louis, Missouri recently received the Alexander L. George Award for excellence in research from the International Society of Political Psychology for their book *Overcoming Intolerance in South Africa: Experiments in Democratic Persuasion*, Cambridge University Press, 2003.

Shireen Hassim

Shireen Hassim is a Senior Lecturer in Political Science at the University of the Witwatersrand. She has researched and published in the area of women, state and policy-making. She was the co-author of *South Africa: A Country Gender Analysis* (with Sally Baden and Sheila Meintjes) which was commissioned by SIDA and published by the Institute for Development Studies, Sussex University. In addition, she was part of a team that assessed the extent to which the South African state has been engendered, commissioned by the United Nations Institute for Training and Research on Women (INSTRAW). For this study, she reviewed the National Machinery for Women.

Sibonile Khoza

In 2003, Sibonile was appointed as coordinator of the Socio-Economic Rights Project of the Community Law Centre at the University of the Western Cape where he is also a researcher. He obtained his Master's Degree in Law (LLM) and Bachelor of Laws (LLB) at the University of Natal, (UND). He also completed a six month practical legal training course with the School of Legal Practice there.

From 2001–2002, Sibonile held a position of a Provincial Coordinator of Street Law/Democracy for All Programmes of the Centre for Socio-Legal Studies, UND after being a human rights educator/trainer in the Programme since 1999. In 1999 and 2000 he worked as a Research Assistant at the Qualitative Research Unit of the Centre for Socio-Legal Studies, University of Natal (Durban) and in 2001–2002 was the convenor of the Provincial Forum for Democracy and Human Rights Education in Kwa-Zulu Natal.

He has presented papers at international and national conferences, published and taught on socio-economic rights, the right to food, nutrition and health. Sibonile is also a member of the Board of Directors for Street Law Incorporated and RAPCAN (Resources Aimed at the Prevention of Child Abuse).

Cheryl McEwan

Cheryl McEwan is a Lecturer in Human Geography at the University of Birmingham, UK. Her interests are in post-colonial and feminist theories and how these inform cultural and political geographies, with a specific interest in gender and citizenship in South Africa. She has recently completed a research project (funded by ESRC) entitled 'Engendering citizenship: gendered spaces of democracy in South Africa'. She is also the author of several journal articles on gendered citizenship in South Africa (published in *Agenda*, *Political Geography*, *South African Geographical Journal*, *Geoforum*).

Linzi Manicom

Linzi Manicom has been working on a doctoral dissertation on gendered political subjects and state formation in post-apartheid South Africa over many years. Her publications on this topic include 'Globalizing "gender" in – or as – governance? Questioning the terms of local translations', *Agenda*, No.48, 2001; '"Afastada" Apprehensions: The Politics of Post-exile Location and South Africa's Gendered

Transition' in *Emigre Feminism: Transnational Perspectives*, edited by Alena Heitlinger, University of Toronto Press, Toronto, 1999, and 'Ruling Relations: Rethinking State and Gender in South African History', *Journal of African History*, Vol.33 No.3, 1992, pp.441-465. Recent conference presentations and talks that address the issue of gender and citizenship in South Africa are *'Gender' in the New South Africa: Exploring the implications and ironies of 'women' and 'gender' as national political subject categories*. Linzi is currently teaching courses on globalization, transnational feminism and transcultural feminist understanding at the Institute for Women's Studies and Gender Studies at the University of Toronto.

Anneke Meerkotter

Anneke Meerkotter completed her BProc and LLB degrees at the University of the Western Cape. She was then employed at the Community Law Centre at the University of the Western Cape in both the Gender and Children's Rights Projects where her work focused on child justice, reproductive rights and the rights of commercial sex workers. Whilst there, she also coordinated a diversion programme for young offenders. She is currently practising as an attorney in the AIDS Law Project at the Centre for Applied Legal Studies at the University of the Witwatersrand. She is a volunteer for the Treatment Action Campaign, and has done research on women and HIV/AIDS.

Mikki van Zyl

Mikki van Zyl was an activist in the anti-apartheid struggle from the late 1970s until democratization in the 1990s. Since 1993 she has run her own business for gender and capacity development, *Simply Said and Done*. Mikki comes from a background in gender studies with degrees in Communication and Media Studies, and an MPhil in Sociology. She has done extensive qualitative research on a variety of topics such as gender and media, gender-based violence, sexualities, gender and land reform, sustainable development, identity-based gender social movements, institutional culture and exiles in the anti-apartheid struggle. She has lectured in Media Studies, Sociology, Criminology and Diversity Studies. For the last fifteen years she has worked as a trainer, writer and consultant in gender and development and participatory research methodologies. *Simply Said and Done* is an associate of iNCUDISA (the Institute for Intercultural and Diversity Studies of Southern Africa) at the University of Cape Town. Besides her academic publications, she has also published short stories and poetry in both Afrikaans and English.

Preface

On 27 and 28 April 1994 the liberation election turned all South Africans into citizens. Men and women stood in long lines to cast their votes and claim their citizenship. But did men and women really gain the same citizenship on those two days? Being actively involved in the transition process as a political scientist peaked my interest in citizenship. I was particularly interested in how the inclusion of women into citizenship was unfolding – from being able to vote, to gaining representation in government, to presence in policy-making and to being able to utilize the National Machinery for Women. Couched in a liberal rights discourse citizenship opens a space for women's agency but leaves many inequalities caused by women's relationship with the private sphere and the state intact.

It is the aim of this book to stimulate debate on a theoretical level on issues of citizenship, whether it is poverty, HIV/AIDS, political representation or violence against women. There is a dearth of feminist theoretical literature in South Africa. While books with a feminist perspective on different aspects of politics such as rights, voting behaviour, representation, and policy making have appeared, very few deal explicitly with theory. This book aims to make a contribution to theory building.

Even though this is a theoretical book the theory is illustrated with empirical evidence and it is written in an accessible style so that practitioners, students and politicians may find it useful. Scholars from different disciplines such as political science, law, philosophy, geography and gender studies as well as the voices of activists have been included. The difference in training and epistemological approaches is evident in the different chapters and lends texture to the theoretical perspectives explored in the different chapters.

During my sabbatical in 1999 I spent three months at the Beatrice Bain Centre for Research on Women at Berkeley University in California where this book was conceptualized. However, it took another four years to complete due to a heavy teaching load on my part and that of some of the contributors, as well as the brutality of administration that has become part of the changing terrain of universities in transformation in South Africa. During this time the shifting contours of citizenship required some of us to rewrite our contributions.

During the time at Berkeley I had helpful conversations about this project with Daiva Stasiulus and Radha Jhappan, also fellows at the Beatrice Bain Centre. It made my stay in Berkeley a memorable one.

I want to thank The Beatrice Bain Centre for Women's Research for the opportunity to be a Fellow in the Centre. I also want to thank all the contributors for their patience with this unfolding project. A special thanks goes to Mikki van Zyl for language editing and preparing the camera ready copy. Without her this project would have taken much longer. A word of thanks also goes to Jane Parpart for her encouragement and support. I want to thank Marthane Swart for research assistance, and Marleen van Wyk, subject librarian for Political Science at the J.S. Gericke Library for tracking down references. I am grateful to my partner, Louis de Lange for bearing with me and to my two beautiful daughters, Frankie and Simone for keeping me grounded. I dedicate this book to my mother whose citizenship has been confined to the private sphere but who taught me to follow my dreams and never to give up on what I believe. I owe my feminism to her.

Series Editor's Preface

This series critically engages debates on globalization through focusing upon gendered processes and identities at the intersections of global and local sites. *(Un)thinking Citizenship: Feminist Debates in Contemporary South Africa*, edited by Amanda Gouws, provides new perspectives and insights about women's lived experience of citizenship. It is a view from the South, from a developing democracy that is to a large extent viewed as one of the great success stories of democratic transitions. The book theorizes women's citizenship from the uniqueness of the South African context, while also acknowledging the similarities of women's conditions globally. It is designed to contribute to an emerging comparative body of feminist scholarship on citizenship that has begun to challenge Anglo-American dominance in feminist and political theory. It seeks to un-think the past, to free existing knowledge from its limitations and to create new liberating knowledge.

South Africa is unique for its high level of gender awareness and activism during the transition period to democracy, for its gender sensitive constitution, its advanced National Machinery for Women and its considerable number of women parliamentarians. Yet achieving gender equal citizenship has been a challenge for a nation faced with addressing the inequalities and injustices of a highly racialized past in an increasingly competitive world economy. The AIDS pandemic and high levels of violence between women and men further complicates matters. *(Un)thinking Citizenship* addresses these complexities, particularly their global-local articulations, by examining citizenship and gender around five themes: moving beyond the inclusion/exclusion debates; deconstructing discourses of citizenship; extending the boundaries of the law; citizenship as agency; and an exploration of the crucial and often ignored connection between sexuality and citizenship. This approach offers exciting new perspectives, grounded in Southern realities but placed within a broad global perspective. *(Un)thinking Citizenship* thus enriches theory and practice aimed at strengthening gender equitable citizenship practices in a highly competitive and often patriarchal global/local world.

Jane Parpart
October 2004

Introduction

Amanda Gouws

Why (Un)thinking Citizenship?

We decided to title this book *(Un)thinking Citizenship: Feminist Debates in Contemporary South Africa* on the grounds of what Corlann Gee Bush (1983, p.152) has argued, that the great strength of the women's movement (and of feminism) is the 'twin abilities to unthink the sources of oppression and to use this analysis to create a new synthesizing vision'. The strength of feminist scholarship is the dynamic process of unthinking, rethinking, energizing and transforming. To be able to unthink is to free existing knowledge of the assumptions that limit it and to create new liberating knowledge.

The aim of this book is to do exactly that – to bring new perspectives and insights about women's lived experience of citizenship to the body of existing literature on citizenship. This book is a view from the South, from a developing democracy that is to a large extent viewed as one of the great success stories of democratic transitions. We theorize women's citizenship from the uniqueness of the South African context. Yet, at the same time we want to acknowledge the similarities with women's conditions globally. The articulation of the local with the global informs many of the arguments in this book, contributing to a comparative body of feminist scholarship on citizenship that has begun to challenge Anglo-American dominance in feminist and political theory (Siim, 2000, p.9).

The uniqueness of South Africa is related to the conditions of a developing state where women have expressed a great gender awareness and activism during the transition period to democracy and have managed through their activism to enable women to enter parliament in large numbers. Post-1994 (the period following the first democratic election) the complexity of building a nation out of the racialization of the apartheid past and the increasing engagement of the South African economy with a global economy have challenged the gains that women have made. Conditions particular to South Africa are extremely high levels of gender based violence such as rape and domestic violence, combined with one of the highest increase of HIV/AIDS infections in the world and varying levels of poverty among at least 40% of the population. Our theorization tries to capture the complexities of these adverse conditions in a situation where large-scale law reform has managed to create very women friendly legislation to promote gender equality. These conditions are enhanced by one of the most advanced National Machineries for Women in the world as well as one of the most liberal constitutions.

One of our main concerns is whether a liberal democratic rights-based democracy can really deal with the complexities that these conditions create for women on a grassroots level. Under the conditions we discuss, what does it mean to claim rights? In the face of large-scale law reform gender activism has dwindled and changed shape from its former robustness. A discourse of gender mainstreaming has contributed to depoliticizing gender activism and to turn gender into a technocratic concept. While theorization of some of these issues has taken place in a Northern context we are trying to develop new theoretical insights from the vantage point of a developing state.

The book also aims to contribute to a very small body of indigenous feminist theory that exists in South Africa. In developing countries it is often the case that feminist theory and practice are situated as binary oppositions, where theory is connected to the 'ivory tower' of abstract ideas and practice is viewed as projects that change women's lives.[1] Posing them as binary oppositions is however not helpful since we need both. Theory informs practice and practice shapes theory. Very often the radical nature of feminist theory opens new avenues for activism.

Feminist social and political theory provide invaluable conceptual tools to re-examine liberal democracy and to interrogate the master narratives on citizenship (Dillabough and Arnot, 2000, p.37). Theorizing women's experience places it on the level of the abstract that enables us to make generalizations. While we do not want to lose the particularity of women's experience we find generalizations necessary for theory building. We concur with Anne Phillips (1992a) that 'the impulse that takes us beyond our immediate and specific difference is a vital necessity in any radical transformation' (p.28). Of course using women as an analytical category opens us up for the critique of essentialism. While we are aware of this danger we show where possible in our analyses that women in South Africa are not a homogeneous group. Linzi Manicom's excellent theorization of this problem in this volume produces new theoretical vantage points.

What makes theory feminist as Jodi Dean (1997) has argued is that it is 'always a complex combination of their author's interests and intentions, their ability to provide insights and solutions to feminist problems and issues and their potential for improving women's lives' (p.3). It is the ability to connect feminist discourses rather than a single aspect of, or approach to, or interpretation of these issues. Many of the authors of this book are also gender activists and their theory is inspired by their activism and the transformative potential of their scholarship.

The theme that runs through the texts is one of women's subjective experience of citizenship and the limits of rights and law, creating an intertextuality among the different contributions, opening up multiple readings and interpretations, even conflicting ones. The authors approach citizenship from their different disciplines – political science, law, philosophy, gender studies and geography, as well as from the perspectives of practitioners and activists. These multiple approaches lead to a rich texture of meanings and authenticity of scholarship. It is the contestation of readings that opens up new perspectives on existing literature and produces new meaning.

A reconceptualization of citizenship should include status (ability to claim rights on all levels – political, social and civil), participation that would include activities in a number of political arenas such as national and local government, civil society such as social movements and formal and informal organizations, and discourse (the discursive construction of citizenship), as well as locales (or sites of struggle). This book attempts such reconceptualizations. What comes under scrutiny is the complexities of the implementation of liberal democracy in a developing state where procedural equality often takes priority over substantive equality.

Feminists Theorizing Citizenship

Citizenship is a contested concept for many reasons but from a feminist perspective specifically, because of its gendered nature. Feminists concern themselves with the exclusion of women from citizenship, due to their relationship with the private sphere and the problematization of their inclusion in the public sphere. For example, without the vote women are not citizens but when they gain the vote, are they truly citizens when they have no access to water, electricity or housing? The discourse of citizenship itself is gendered and feminists want to provide an alternative discourse through the inclusion of the embodied citizen into the public sphere (Jones, 1990, p.785).

From a liberal democratic perspective citizenship is limited because according to this perspective justice is viewed as equal access to rights and opportunities. Liberal democracy concerns itself with formal rather than substantive equality because the individual is abstracted from his/her social conditions. Inequality is therefore intrinsic to the politics of liberal democracy rather than extraneous as Phillips (1992b) points out. The distinct drawbacks of women's location in the private sphere where they lack rights need to be accounted for in the concept of citizenship. But rights in the public sphere alone are not enough to deal with political issues that undermine the exercise of citizenship such as the gendered nature of poverty, violence and a lack of health care etc. To comprehend these inequalities, feminist scholars have tried to extend the concept of citizenship to make it more comprehensive and to give meaning to the idea of substantive equality.

Citizenship is a status and a practice (or form of agency) (Lister, 1997). Citizenship as a status refers to the relationship between the individual and the state and between individual citizens regulated through rights. Here the focus is on the individual citizen (Lister, 1997, pp.14-15). Citizenship as agency draws on the civic republican tradition of participation and relates citizenship to the wider society. The focus here includes civil, political and social rights as conceptualized by Marshall (1950). For the inclusion of women the challenge is to transform the practice of citizenship from an isolated practice of juridically defined individuals with rights to the recognition of participation, even on a local level (Jones, 1994, p.268).

Kathleen Jones (1994) extends the concept to include issues of identity and locale (p.260). For her citizenship is a boundary project where citizens share a common identity in relation to the state. This common identity is often contingent upon the ultimate subordination of specific particularized identities of gender, race and class. It is very often the case in societies in transition that the forging of common identities negates women's struggles for gender justice.

Feminists object to the false universalism of citizenship, which treats all citizens as ungendered, abstract, disembodied individuals (Lister, 1997, p.70). The ungendered political subject can be related to the assumptions of liberal individualism, for one, that rationality is the root of equality and not embodiedness. The issue that feminists grapple with is whether the inclusion of women into citizenship should be related to their difference from or their sameness with men. The liberal model of rights includes women through the extension of rights on the grounds of equality as sameness. The differences between women and men, and between women are often ignored because liberalism constructs a unified/universal political subject.

Women's inclusion into citizenship or their entry into the public sphere, however, always takes place as embodied individuals (for whom reproduction, for example, often leads to discrimination) (Lister, 1997, p.71). Women should be incorporated *as women* (Voet, 1998, p.15). In this regard Young (1989) has argued that people are not included into citizenship as individuals only, but in dealing with difference we need to consider the inclusion of people as members of groups such as women and minorities. She calls this the 'politics of group assertion' through which members of oppressed groups such as women organize themselves separately, according to their own interests.

Lister (1997) makes the very important argument that equality and difference are misrepresented as opposites because it is actually difference and sameness that are opposites (p.96). As she argues the opposite of equality is inequality and to pose it as difference disguises relations of subordination and hierarchy. Ignoring women's difference with men reinforces or reintroduces inequality into the concept of citizenship.

As Siim (2000) rightly points out citizenship becomes 'a central problematic for the analysis of discourses about gender in modern democracies because it expresses a contradiction between the universal principles of the *equality* of men and the *particularity* or *difference* of women and other excluded groups' (p.3, emphasis in original).

While it is assumed that rights apply universally to everyone many groups of people with particular identities feel excluded from citizenship. The perceptions as well as the lived realities of exclusion created the space for identity politics through which different groups of women assert their identities and make political claims. This development led to the fragmentation of women as a single category, theorized very well by post-structuralist theorists. The contributions of African American feminists and black women in developing countries contribute to the nuances of this debate.

Using women as an analytical category has led to criticism of essentialism when theorizing women as a homogeneous group. Difference is also present among women. Ignoring these differences could lead to another form of exclusion through which non-dominant groups, or groups within non-dominant groups, such as black women, for example, became 'othered' or excluded as subjects within the feminist citizenship debate. In relying on post-structuralist thinking excluded groups of women demanded a consideration of fluid and multiple identities, and of voice and agency (Lister, 2003, p.75). One solution through which multiple identities could be accommodated is a notion of 'feminist pluralistic citizenship' that would recognize the differences between women as well as the different sites of their participation (Sarvasy and Siim, 1994).

The domain of the private sphere is still one important site of women's agency as well as their oppression. Changing the divide between the private and the public sphere but also understanding the fluidity of its boundaries and the interconnectedness between the two spheres are some of the greatest challenges for creating a more egalitarian citizenship. How the private sphere is constructed, and its interrelationship with the public arena has profound implications for women's citizenship. Lister (2003) correctly argues that '[T]he struggle to control its meaning and positioning is central to the project of re-gendering citizenship' (p.124). The sex/gender system together with the division of labour in the family in which care is a central labour burden, often determines to what extent women are free to exercise their citizenship as a rights based notion or as practice.

Sevenhuijsen (1998) has demonstrated the profound implications for women of the exclusion of care as a dimension of citizenship. Women perform most care work in society. Care work often relies on time as a resource and determines the amount of time and energy women have to spend on political participation and other types of political involvement. It also highlights the collective dimension of politics because care is not an atomized activity, and as she argues, if the values of the ethics of care such as attentiveness, responsiveness and responsibility are included in citizenship, the importance of care as a social value will be acknowledged (Sevenhuijsen, 1998, p.15).

Care as a dimension of citizenship has been preceded by the debate about motherhood as a basis for citizenship. Maternal feminists such as Ruddick and Elshtain have argued that values of mothering such as care, nurturance and morality should be projected into political life (Lister, 2003, p.97).

In a critique of maternal thinking Dietz (1998) argues that maternalists (what she calls socialist feminists) have distorted the meaning of politics and political action by embracing a one-dimensional view of women, as only able to deal with the values of the private sphere (p.46). She argues that Elshtain's values of mothering – that of intimacy, love and attentiveness are exclusive and not the values of citizenship. As she puts it, women as mothers can 'chasten arrogant public power; they cannot democratize it' (Dietz, 1998, p.59). If women do not engage the values of citizenship they cannot develop an adequate understanding of the way in which politics determine their own lives and it will be difficult for them to transform political conditions that conflict with maternal values. For her politics is about engaging other citizens in order to determine individual and common interests in relation to the public good. Women will have to realize that they are not just mothers but women who share a common political situation whether they are mothers or not.[2]

This view of mothering is revisited and retheorized in this book from an African perspective, a continent where motherhood has formed a basis of political power for African women and has led to the politicization of women engaging in political struggles, often leading to a feminist consciousness. These arguments underline the importance of contextualizing theory and the need to pay attention to the specificities of particular cultures, political economies and historical trajectories. While motherhood has often necessitated political activism, in developing countries entry into institutionalized politics demands different strategies from women.

Women's inclusion into the public sphere means that women have to negotiate inequalities in power hierarchies between women and men in the political sphere as well as the labour force. The most difficult is entry into government as political representatives. In order to gain equality women also have to represent their own interests in the public sphere. Women have to be empowered to be involved in decision-making and policy-making processes. But women also have to be represented in large numbers in order to gain parity with men. This entry into positions of political authority very often has to be enabled by mechanisms such as quotas or special representation highlighting the difficulty of changing existing structural relations of power as well as attitudes and prejudices of voters. Representation has, however, to be extended to the exercise of influence as well. If women cannot influence the policy making process representation becomes limited. The relationship between the public and the private and relationships between women and men in the private sphere are often the outcome of the very policies shaped in the public sphere (Phillips, 1991, p.95).

Women's participation is often associated with the local level. But is local government women friendly? Representation and influence on this level is often more crucial for women who know the needs of their constituencies and the impact of deficient service delivery on gendered household relationships. Locales of participation need to include both formal and informal politics on local level.

Citizenship is, however, not only embedded in structures but as Siim (2000) points out it would be difficult to understand women's citizenship without understanding how it is constructed through political discourse. Siim (2000) argues that equal citizenship includes the dynamic relationship between agency, political institutions and political discourse (p.8).

This book is divided into five broad themes – 'inclusion/exclusion and the constitution of the subject', 'deconstructing the discourse of citizenship', 'extending the boundaries of the law', 'citizenship as agency' and 'sexualizing citizenship'. In the first theme of inclusion/exclusion we draw on North American and European literature to theorize women's exclusion from citizenship and the ways they have been included in South Africa. But we also critique the in/exclusion debate by arguing that we need to understand how women as subjects are constituted through citizenship. There will always be degrees of inclusion and exclusion and that in/exclusion is not a stable condition but dependent on the constitution of the subject in different political/economic conditions.

The second theme is a deconstruction of discourses around citizenship. The discourse that constructed the subject under nationalism shifted to a discourse of democracy where the rights of citizenship became paramount. Discursive shifts have the power to shape identities and interests, or to depoliticize gender projects as the deconstruction of the gender mainstreaming discourse will show. The changing discourse of masculinities from apartheid authoritarianism that demonized homosexuality to present day constitutionalism that protects gay rights shows that men have the agency to choose the gender identity they perform so that masculinity is never truly achieved.

While law and law reform have been the most successful tools for creating better conditions for gender equality the law has its limits. With regard to issues such as poverty, childcare and HIV/AIDS the boundaries of the law need to be extended in order for citizens who live in these conditions to truly become citizens with the rights and privileges of citizenship. This constitutes the fourth theme.

In 'citizenship as agency' we interrogate women's participation on a local level and the conditions that prohibit them from exercising their agency. The contested issue of motherhood as a platform of action in the African context as opposed to motherhood as a form of subjugation in the private sphere has been the subject of many debates and an issue that has divided South African women from time to time. This is a theme that attempts to destabilize the boundaries between the public and private sphere.

In South Africa, if one wants to be cynical, you could argue that gender based violence is probably the greatest equalizer among women. Rape and domestic violence know no boundaries of race, class, age (girl children as young as three months have been raped) or even disability. In the face of the very high HIV/AIDS infection rate rape very often carries a death sentence. In sexualizing citizenship we look at the meaning of rape in the South African context and the devastating effects it has on women's citizenship. We also interrogate sexual identities in the context of heteronormativity. While the constitution protects gay rights citizenship is often a very exclusionary device for gay people, especially lesbians. The theme of sexualizing citizenship exposes the very often unarticulated sexual nature of citizenship.

Citizenship in Post-1994 South Africa

Citizenship in South Africa under the apartheid regime was mainly a history of exclusion of many different categories of people, of black Africans, of coloureds (mixed race) of Indians, of the Khoi and San and of women. When white women gained the vote in 1930 it was not because they were considered valuable citizens but as part of the quest for white domination by countering the limited voting rights of African men in the Cape.[3] Under the apartheid government the coloured and Indian populations were represented through male dominated representative councils not as citizens in their own right. In 1983, in an attempt to include the minority populations, coloureds and Indians were included in separate chambers of the tricameral parliament, but still in terms of their racial identities, while Africans were completely excluded from this parliament.

The liberation election of 1994, ushering in South Africa's democracy for the first time awarded all South Africans the first two categories of Marshall's (1950) rights – namely civil and political rights. The very progressive Bill of Rights that also protects the third category of socio-economic rights provides for an equality clause that includes seventeen grounds on which no discrimination may take place. This clause also allows for the redress of past disadvantage and thus opens the door for affirmative action, that will also benefit women. It can therefore be concluded that the constitution also provides for substantive equality and not only procedural equality.

The meaning of politics and membership in a community is embedded in the struggles over citizenship (Werbner, 1999). Prior to 1994 the authoritative discourse of opposing nationalisms, primarily Afrikaner and African nationalism, dominated the political terrain. These discourses constituted women as mothers, as the biological reproducers of the nation and the transmitters of its values, not as rights bearing individuals.[4] As Werbner (1999) has expressed so well – '[t]here is a constant leakage between the passions of nationalism and the moral sentiment constituting human rights and the rights of citizenship' (p.221). Nationalism denies the agency and identity of women – women become the bearers of a collective identity, they do not have to act. They are the embodiment of the nation through gender constrained definitions of nationalism (Yuval-Davis, 1997, p.45). The democratic transition in South Africa became a 'shape shifting' experience where women's citizenship shifted from assumptions embedded in nationalism to assumptions embedded in a liberal rights discourse.

Post-1994 the discourse of rights and liberal democratic individualism has become the prevailing discourse in South Africa. The focus on human rights, law and engagement with the state brought welcome law reform that benefited women, particularly in regard to personal empowerment such as reproductive rights (the legalization of abortion), the reform of customary unions, addressing violence against women, sexuality and the inclusion of women in the workplace through labour law. However, while legal gains improved women's lives, many aspects of conditions in the private sphere remained unchanged.

The liberal rights discourse frames citizenship in South Africa around rights claiming by individuals through their engagement with the state. A lesser value is placed on the community and the collective needs of groups of people, especially defined around interests. Collective needs are taken seriously when they are taken to the courts (for example the Treatment Action Campaign sued the South African government for not rolling out anti-retroviral medication for people living with HIV/AIDS). Many other discourses, such as a discourse about culture, have become muted, consequently leaving the constraining effects of culture on women's lives intact and unchallenged (see in this regard Albertyn and Hassim, 2004).

For a long time, feminists have questioned whether a liberal rights discourse can facilitate social transformation because of the dichotomies that it creates between the individual and society. This view of rights obscures the reality of political choice, particularly for women, and encourages passivity and reliance on the state. It creates an appearance that rights are distinct from politics and imbued with an intrinsic value, while in actual fact rights are part of political struggle (Schneider, 1991, p.319). When a rights discourse becomes divorced from social practice and conditions it loses its liberating power.

The focus on the public sphere creates a situation where the discourse of law, law reform and legal remedy bolsters the discourse of rights and individualism. Law becomes a form of expert knowledge in Smart's (1989) terms. In the contestation over rights, other knowledges become 'disqualified knowledges' (Smart, 1989, p.12). To qualify for attention experiences have to be organized and legitimized through legal experts. What this book however demonstrates, are the limits of the law, because law has a limited ability to transform social conditions, to rectify economic marginalization or to change deeply held cultural values. Women most often bring their everyday experiences of subordination, abuse, poverty and a lack of resources to the sites of state power. Yet, when these conditions are mediated by the law, they often lose the urgency for political intervention and activism.

Women are often criticized for not claiming their rights or accessing the state. The reasons why policies fail or why women are not receptive to these policies may be related to underlying assumptions and gender norms of a rights discourse that go unaddressed (Albertyn and Hassim, 2004, p.150). These gender norms are strengthened by societal attitudes about women's roles and place in society. Where patriarchal norms of traditions are still strong, such as the case in developing societies, attitudinal change can only come through large-scale consciousness raising and education about gender inequality. It is ironic that there is such a strong awareness of racial inequality and discrimination in South Africa but that this understanding is not carried over to gender inequality and discrimination even though gender and race are interrelated identities.

Solutions for material inequality have to be resourced through the economic system. With democratization becoming a global phenomenon after 1989 the global impact of neo-liberal economic policies had a growing influence on South Africa. Apart from having to deal with the particularizing effects of nationalism after apartheid the new South African government had to realign its economic system with global capitalism. As Cvetkovich and Kellner (1997) have pointed out the local is an aspect of the global, rather than a discrete separate space (p.2). The local and global mediate each other.

Gobalization is a shorthand for contradictory shifts in relations of power connected to economic rationalism and neo-liberalism (Pettman, 1999, p.208). It is within this politics of power and material interests that women have to negotiate their citizenship within the nation-state. Pettman (1999) astutely remarks that globalization is characterized by the renegotiation of relations between the state and society as the latter becomes more economic than social, a shift away from state responsibility for social welfare to greater family responsibility (p.211). This reduces the political space for citizenship and social rights for women. These shifts are profoundly gendered in their consequences.

While a strong history of socialist beliefs existed during the liberation struggle on the side of the ANC, the trade union movement and other liberation organizations, increasing globalization caused a shift toward greater neo-liberal economic policies. Evidence of this shift is the government's change in economic policies from the Reconstruction and Development Plan (RDP), with a focus on redistribution to the macro-economic policy of Growth, Employment and

Redistribution (GEAR) with an emphasis on investment, privatization and the relinquishing of trade barriers. As a consequence the delivery of Marshall's third category of socio-economic rights remains problematic with increasing levels of poverty among the poorest 20% of the population (see e.g. Everatt, 2003).

In attempting to remedy women's exclusion from citizenship one of the main foci of policy makers and gender activists has been inclusion through representation of women in decision-making bodies. Gender scholars in South Africa have contributed to developing a large body of literature on women's inclusion through the electoral system and specialized mechanisms such as quotas (see e.g. Hassim, 1999; Goetz and Hassim, 2003; Fick et al., 2002). The challenge for representational inclusion is whether women really make a difference when they get to parliament. Is it merely an issue of representation or do women also gain power?

South Africa has made significant progress with regard to women's representation – after the 2004 election it is eleventh in the world, with regard to numbers of women in parliament with women holding 131 seats. There are ten women ministers and twelve deputy-ministers and four women premiers out of nine provincial positions. One of the main aims of gender researchers is to determine to what extent women in government influence policy making from a gender perspective.

Another dimension of inclusion is the institutionalization of women's machineries – the creation of structures in the state for gender mainstreaming. In South Africa the Women's National Machinery is an integrated set of structures that includes the Office of the Status of Women, gender focal points in each state department, a Women's Empowerment Unit, a multi-party women's caucus, the Joint Standing Committee on the Quality of Life and the Status of Women and the Commission on Gender Equality. These structures together with the Women's Budget Initiative shift the focus on policy influence from individual women in parliament to more coordinated efforts of monitoring and intervention within the state. The outcomes of these efforts are uneven with one of the main areas of concern the access these structures afford to the women's movement (see e.g. Gouws, 2004).

Post-1994 the women's movement in South Africa has changed from a ground-swell movement consisting of hundreds of organizations mobilized around the establishment of a women's charter of rights, the Charter for Effective Equality to a more fragmented appearance of women's organizations, which tend to deal largely with single issues, such as poverty and gender based violence. Activism around HIV/AIDS involve both men and women but most spokespeople on this issue are men. The gendered nature of this activism still needs to be investigated.

With the growing epidemic of HIV/AIDS, care and the ethic of care become central aspects of citizenship in Sub-Saharan Africa. With primary care givers dying of AIDS the gendered nature of care is exposed. Creating a social welfare net for South Africa that presently has a 40% unemployment rate in certain areas, with women bearing the brunt of unemployment has become a priority for government. The 'ethic of care' is included in the preamble of the White Paper on Social Welfare, yet implementing welfare policies that are care focused is a great challenge (see Sevenhuijsen et al., 2003). Often being a caregiver becomes another way of being excluded from the full benefits of citizenship.

In the following section the main arguments of the different chapters inform the different themes.

Chapter Outline

Part I: From In/Exclusion to the Constitution of the Subject

In chapter one Linzi Manicom opens up the analysis of citizenship by moving outside the debate about inclusion and exclusion. She contextualizes and reconsiders citizenship in the South African context. In a similar sense to what Arnot and Dillabough (2000, p.8) have argued, that rather than looking at citizenship as inclusion and exclusion we need new articulations between the universal and the particular in a new perspective on women's citizenship, Manicom argues that citizenship in South Africa must involve more than the analysis of the gender requisites of institutionalizing and substantiating democratic citizenship.

For her the debate about inclusion and exclusion of women as rights bearing subjects of the liberal discourse masks ways in which struggles for realizing particular forms of citizenship privilege some women over other. She shifts the analysis to the making of political subjects rather than the analysis of claims to citizenship. Women are the subjects of the power of the state and also subject to its regulatory aspects. Gendered citizens are produced through the technologies of citizenship programmes and tactics. Consequently citizens as subjects are produced within different discourses through which difference is also created. Difference has to be understood as varying across different sets of power relations.

Manicom poses a different set of questions from asking how women might be fully included in institutions of citizenship or how citizenship can be debunked from its gender assumptions. For her the focus is not on exclusion because she argues that women do not exist a priori or outside the political forms, processes and discourses. Her aim is to determine how women are shaped as different kinds of gendered political subjects. She wants to uncover the political effects of gendered constructs of citizenship, expose how new modalities of power are produced, certain categories of women re-marginalized and new hierarchies among women formed. Citizenship according to her is an important site where racialized and genderized subjects are produced and the gendered nature of citizenship normalized.

Manicom's chapter is very important for bringing new insights to the problem of essentialism that arises in the citizenship literature when women are used as a category of analysis. She poses the question of how the political power of the category 'women' can be retained without misrepresenting women in different social locations, since the category of women is always produced in and through other identity categories. She wants to make us understand women as a historically contingent, politically produced identity rather than a prior ontological category.

Deconstructing the Discourse of Citizenship

In chapter two Shireen Hassim traces the role of the women's movement in shifting a discourse of nationalism to a discourse of democracy. She looks at political discourse as the ideological space that is available to women's organizations. She argues that the universe of political discourse determines what is considered to be political as opposed to private, religious or economic. Discursive shifts in the broad political environment have the power to shape the ways in which interests and identities are articulated within the women's movement. This creates an enabling environment for women's claims to be articulated.

She explores the implications of the shifts away from the authoritative discourse of national liberation to one of citizenship, showing how mobilizing women during the struggle was consistent with gender role definitions inherent in nationalism such as privileging motherhood. This emphasis on nationalism marginalized alternative discourses.

The shift to a discourse of citizenship opened new avenues for thinking about women's political participation in institutions of democracy as well as civil society and social movements. Citizenship participation outside the ideological constraints of nationalism offers political alternatives for women. Within the framework of citizenship women could articulate claims for substantive equality.

She illustrates her arguments with an analysis of the Women's National Coalition that existed during the transition phase to democracy and its campaign for the Charter for Effective Equality (a women's charter).

She argues that 'citizenship broadly conceived, displaced nationalism as the new political ideal and political language through which the aspirations of subordinate groups were expressed'. The shift away from discourses of nationalism was highly enabling for feminist activists by disentangling women's citizenship from that of the nation.

In chapter three Amanda Gouws concerns herself with the limits of the discourse of gender mainstreaming as well as rights in the liberal democracy in South Africa. She argues that the gender mainstreaming discourse that forms part of the institutionalization of the gender machinery in South Africa sets up institutional and discursive frameworks that depoliticize gender and change the political opportunity structure through which women can engage the state.

She also shows how a shift occurs from a discourse of rights to a discourse of needs through which women are portrayed as a vulnerable group in need of state intervention. Being constructed as a vulnerable group limits women's agency.

Moving from a focus on women and citizenship to men's citizenship, in chapter four Dan Conway analyses conscientious objection as an alternative discourse of citizenship to the hegemonic one constructed by the state.

Struggles over citizenship are struggles over the meaning of politics and membership in a community. Looking at military conscription in apartheid South Africa he argues that citizenship and the inscription of identity on individual attributes and normative gender roles was a primary method of political mobilization and control.

Multiple masculinities revolve around the construction of gender identity that varies across time and culture. Men have agency to choose the gender identity they perform so that masculinity is never truly achieved. Masculinity must be proved and men who do not buy into the identity construction of the military are relegated to the bottom of the masculinity hierarchy. There is an interplay between the construction of gender and militarization.

The End Conscription Campaign (ECC) challenged the supposedly natural bonds between masculinity, military service and citizenship, posing a serious threat to the state's ideological foundations. The ECC wanted a citizenship imbued with the values of civic republicanism. Conway shows that the inscription of militarized masculinity into personal identity was challenged by reclaiming concepts such as courage, bravery and duty, thereby challenging the hegemonic construction of masculinity.

Extending the Boundaries of the Law

In chapter five Beth Goldblatt interrogates the public/private divide and what a lack of childcare means for women. She argues that the rights of citizenship in the Bill of Rights should entail assistance for parenting. Lack of childcare often prevents women from entering the public sphere or to exercise agency. She argues that childcare is a necessity to transform the gender division of labour in the household as well as gendered social relations. Since childcare is a requirement for the full participation of women in society, the right to citizenship should be used to ensure state provision.

She argues that the courts are just one limited mechanism to bring about social change. Efforts to get the state to coordinate and develop policy for the provision of childcare need to take different forms in the legal sphere such as the strategic use of the courts, litigation used to create precedent and to raise awareness, the development of a rights framework within which childcare is located.

Also arguing within a legal framework Danwood Chirwa and Sibonile Khoza show in chapter six how poverty, disproportionately experienced by women in South Africa, puts limitations on the full enjoyment of citizenship.

In an analysis of a court case, called the *Grootboom* case they argue that judicial remedies are critical for holding policy makers accountable for duties imposed upon them by the Constitution. The *Grootboom* case laid down important guidelines regarding the discharge of positive obligations engendered by economic, social and cultural rights by the state. Positive obligations, however, do not obligate the state to do more than is permissible by available resources. A balance has to be struck between the duty to attain the goal of realizing rights effectively and the availability of resources.

What they find problematic is that what is 'a reasonable measure' is gender insensitive. In the *Grootboom* case the Constitutional Court failed to include a requirement that a reasonable programme must make explicit provision for vulnerable groups. As they argue, without such requirement inequalities may not easily be eliminated. *Grootboom* offers us a milestone in establishing that economic, social and cultural rights are in certain circumstances capable of being immediately enforced.

Remaining in the legal realm, in chapter seven Anneke Meerkotter fosters an understanding of how citizenship in the context of HIV/AIDS has become increasingly abstract and limited. Concurring with Chirwa and Khoza she argues that citizenship is a contested terrain bound to the social and economic context in South Africa where interaction between institutions and human agency is a crucial factor in the delivery of services that ensure citizenship rights.

She wants to know how we address the lack of citizenship faced by people whose socio-economic positions marginalize them politically. She argues that HIV/AIDS is a perpetuation of the exclusion from citizenship. Women who suffer from HIV/AIDS are excluded from citizenship through marginalization, powerlessness, cultural imperialism and violence. In the face of the South African government's very problematic policy on the roll-out of anti-retroviral drugs she opts for affirming rights through the courts.

She argues that campaigns that use the constitution as a platform to reassert rights are necessary in the absence of concrete government support. The exclusivity of decision-making and the unequal distribution of resources need to be challenged. She points out that these challenges will only be effective if communities organize collectively to achieve a more just dispensation.

Citizenship as Agency

Interrogating the assumptions of agency and sites of participation Cheryl McEwan analyses participation in local level politics in chapter eight. In her examination of the translation of rights at the national level to the local level she comes to the conclusion that citizenship must encompass more than formal political rights. She urges the inclusion of informal politics as part of the definition of politics/citizenship.

Her chapter explores the desire of women to be involved in community development projects and local government at the same time as they face the frustration of not knowing how. One of the main problems is a lack of information and a disregard for women's multiple tasks in the private sphere that limit time for political participation, once more showing how the private limits public agency.

In chapter nine Gertrude Fester argues that motherhood should be viewed as a platform of action around which women become mobilized. She draws on the writing of Temma Kaplan on 'motherism' and how motherism evolves into female and feminist consciousness. The value of analysing motherist movements is recognizing how and when female consciousness transforms into feminist consciousness and how women challenge their limited private roles and involve themselves as political activists in the public sphere. As Werbner (1999) has argued '[p]olitical motherhood in postcolonial nation-states has to be understood … as a process of discovery rather than a specific feminist movement or intellectual "approach"' (p.241).

Women, through organizing themselves, take pride in their identity. They are not necessarily perpetuating their roles in the private sphere as mothers only. On a symbolic level they are also mothers of the community. This contradicts arguments that motherists' actions cannot be seen as indicators of political maturity nor as feminist. She argues that motherhood is a powerful resource in Africa.

In an analysis of the United Women's Organisation (UWO) she shows that they were motherist in origin. Women's consciousness was radicalized over time and many basic needs issues such as bus fares, food and safety were turned into political issues.

Sexualizing Citizenship

In chapter ten Mikki van Zyl argues that claiming citizenship emerges in contexts of deep divisions. Her focus is on sexual citizenship, an issue that is complex and contested. Liberal concepts of citizenship are deeply sexualized and constituted through gendered and racialized discourses. Sexual citizenship's focus on rights emphasizes the embodiedness of citizens and exposes the private in the public, making the sexual nature of citizenship visible. She interrogates sexual identities, relationships and practices, arguing that the notion of intimate citizenship foregrounds the inseparability of the public/private sphere.

Sexual rights shift citizenship to a context of belonging where citizenship can become a powerful exclusionary device. She argues that belonging is a 'thicker' concept than citizenship and transcends membership rights and duties. Belonging is a hegemonic construct that only becomes visible when threatened. Sexuality in the context of intimacy is easily relegated to the private sphere. This reinforces and maintains the public/private dichotomy. As she points out the struggle for equal sexual citizenship has been a history of challenging the terms of privacy and heteronormativity that uphold the gender division of labour.

Bringing gender into a category of sexed citizens tends toward reasserting biological determinism. Sexual citizenship exposes the fluidity of sexuality as well as the socially constructed dimensions of affective relationships.

In chapter eleven Louise du Toit declares rape a citizenship issue. She forces us to look at how the subjective experience of rape (what she calls the phenomonology of rape) devastates women's citizenship.

She wants us to reflect on whether it is possible to maintain a sense of moral outrage in the face of the institutionalization of rape. She makes an analogy between rape and torture where rape instils fear or terror in a clearly defined section of the population. Rape as torture places rape in the realm of political crime. Reflecting on the Truth and Reconciliation process in South Africa she argues that men did not use the word rape when they were sexually violated. Through this denial they turn rape into a women's issue. She poses the question of why rape has become such an accepted, almost banal part of every day life in South Africa.

For her the solutions lie on a political level. She argues that the government's failure to respond effectively to the HIV/AIDS pandemic and to the systemic violence against women forces new loads of caring work onto families where neither boys nor girls are equipped to understand and promote democratic citizenship. Through this lack of responsiveness, on a political level women are forced back into the private sphere.

Notes

1. The North, however, also experiences this dichotomy. In this regard see a discussion on the feminist theory/praxis split that took place in the context of North America by Lisa Yun Lee 'Who's Afraid of Theory?' *In These Times*, (http:www.inthesetimes.com/comments.php?id=692_0_4_0_C).
2. But Dietz is silent on other issues related to the private sphere, such as sexual relations, the subordination of women and domestic violence, which are also not democratic values.
3. See Walker (1990) for a discussion on the suffragist movement in South Africa.
4. See for example Gaitskell and Unterhalter (1989) and Brink (1990).

References

Albertyn, Catherine and Hassim, Shireen (2004), 'The Boundaries of Democracy, Gender and HIV/AIDS and Culture', in David Everatt and Vincent Maphai (eds.), *The Real State of the Nation – South Africa After 1990*, Interfund Special Edition, pp.138-164.

Arnot, Madeleine and Dillabough, Jo-Ann (2000), 'Introduction' in Madeleine Arnot and Jo-Ann Dillabough (eds.), *Challenging Democracy – International Perspectives on Gender, Education and Citizenship*, Routledge, London, pp.1-18.

Brink, Elsabe (1990), 'Man-Made Women: Gender, Class and the Ideology of the *Volksmoeder*' in Cherryl Walker (ed.), *Women and Gender in Southern Africa to 1945*, David Philip, Cape Town, pp.273-292.

Bush, Corlann Gee (1983), 'Women and the Assessment of Technology: to think, to be, to unthink, to free', in Joan Rothchild (ed.), *Machina Ex Dea: Feminist Perspectives on Technology*, Pergamon, New York, pp.151-170.

Cvetkovich, Ann and Kellner, Douglas (1997), 'Introduction: Thinking Global and Local' in Ann Cvetkovich and Douglas Kellner (eds.), *Articulating the Global and the Local*, Westview Press, Boulder, pp.1-30.

Dean, Jodi (1997), 'Introduction: Siting/Citing/Sighting the New Democracy' in Jodi Dean (ed.), *Feminism and the New Democracy*, Sage, London, pp.1-12.

Dietz, Mary, G. (1998), 'Citizenship with a Feminist Face: The Problem with Maternal Thinking', in Joan B. Landes (ed.), *Feminism, the Public and the Private*, Oxford Readings in Feminism, Oxford University Press, Oxford, pp.45-64.

Dillabough, Jo-Ann and Arnot, Madeleine (2000), 'Feminist Political Frameworks – New Approaches to the Study of Gender, Citizenship and Education Introduction', in Madeleine Arnot and Jo-Ann Dillabough (eds.), *Challenging Democracy – International Perspectives on Gender, Education and Citizenship*, Routledge, London, pp.21-40.

Elshtain, Jean Bethke (1981), *Public Man, Private Woman*, Princeton University Press, Princeton.

Everatt, David (2003), 'The Politics of Poverty', in David Everatt and Vincent Maphai (eds.), *The Real State of the Nation – South Africa After 1990*, Interfund Special Edition, pp.75-99.

Fick, Glenda, Meintjes, Sheila and Simons, Mary (eds.), (2002), *One Woman, One Vote*, Electoral Institute of Southern Africa, Johannesburg.

Gaitskell, D. and Unterhalter, E. (1989), 'Mothers of the Nation: A Comparative Analysis of Nation, Race, and Motherhood in Afrikaner nationalism and the African National Congress', in F. Anthias and N. Yuval-Davis (eds.), *Women-Nation-State*, Macmillan, Basingstoke, pp.58-79.

Goetz, Ann Marie and Hassim, Shireen (2003), *No Shortcuts to Power*, Zed Press, London.

Gouws, Amanda (2004), 'The Politics of State Structures: Citizenship and the National Machinery for Women in South Africa', *Feminist Africa*, Vol.2:1 (forthcoming).

Hassim, Shireen (1999), 'From Presence to Power: Women's Citizenship in a New Democracy', *Agenda*, No.40, pp.6-17.

Jones, Kathleen B. (1990), 'Citizenship in a woman-friendly polity', *Signs*, 15(4), pp.781-812.

Jones, Kathleen B. (1994), 'Identity, Action, and Locale: Thinking about Citizenship, Civic Action, and Feminism', *Social Politics*, Fall, pp.256-270.

Lister, Ruth (1997), *Citizenship: Feminist Perspectives*, New York University Press, New York.

Lister, Ruth (2003), *Citizenship: Feminist Perspectives* (2nd edn.), Palgrave, New York.

Marshall, T.H. (1950), *Citizenship and Social Class*, Cambridge University Press, Cambridge.

Pettman, Jan Jindy (1999), 'Globalization and the Gendered Politics of Citizenship' in Pnina Werbner and Nira Yuval-Davis (eds.), *Women, Citizenship and Difference*, Zed Press, London, pp.207-220.

Phillips, Anne (1991), *Engendering Democracy*, Polity Press, London.

Phillips, Anne (1992a), 'Universal Pretensions in Political Thought', in Michele Barrett and Anne Phillips (eds.), *Destabilizing Theory*, Polity Press, Cambridge.

Phillips, Anne (1992b), 'Must Feminists Give Up on Liberal Democracy?' *Political Studies*, 40, pp.68-82.

Ruddick, Sara (1980), 'Maternal Thinking', *Feminist Studies*, No.6:2, pp.342-367.

Sarvasy, W. and Siim, B. (1994), 'Gender, Transitions to Democracy and Citizenship', *Social Politics*, 1 No.3, pp.249-255.

Schneider, Elizabeth, M. (1991), 'The Dialectic of Rights and Politics: Perspectives from the Women's Movement [1986]' in K.T. Bartlett and R. Kennedy (eds.), *Feminist Legal Theory*, Westview Press, Boulder, pp.318-332.

Sevenhuijsen, Selma (1998), *Citizenship and the Ethics of Care*, Routledge, London.

Sevenhuijsen, Selma, Bozalek, Vivien, Gouws, Amanda and McDonald Minnaar, Marie (2003), 'South African Social Welfare Policy: An Analysis Using the Ethic of Care', *Critical Social Policy*, 23 No.3, pp.299-321.

Siim, Birte (2000), *Gender and Citizenship*, Cambridge University Press, Cambridge.

Smart, Carol (1989), *Feminism and the Power of Law*, Routledge, New York.

Voet, Rian (1998), *Feminism and Citizenship*, Sage, London.

Walker, Cherryl (1990), 'The Women's Suffrage Movement: The Politics of Gender, Race and Class', in Cherryl Walker, (ed.), *Women and Gender in Southern Africa to 1945*, David Philip, Cape Town, pp.313-345.

Werbner, Pnina (1999), 'Political Motherhood and the Feminisation of Citizenship: Women's Activisms and the Transformation of the Public Sphere', in Pnina Werbner and Nira Yuval-Davis (eds.), *Women, Citizenship and Difference*, Zed, London, pp.221-245.

Young, Iris Marion (1989), 'Polity and Group Difference: A Critique of the Ideal of Universal Citizenship', *Ethics*, 99, pp.250-274.

Yuval-Davis, Nira (1997), *Gender and Nation*, Sage, London.

PART I
FROM IN/EXCLUSION TO THE
CONSTITUTION OF THE SUBJECT

Chapter 1

Constituting 'Women' as Citizens: Ambiguities in the Making of Gendered Political Subjects in Post-apartheid South Africa

Linzi Manicom

Introduction

> As women, citizens of South Africa, we are here to claim our rights.
> Preamble, *Women's Charter for Effective Equality*. South Africa, February, 1994.

The clarion tones of this opening sentence of the *Women's Charter*[1] herald the questions that instigate this chapter. When read against the preoccupations of contemporary politics and theorizing of citizenship, the statement above and the ones that follow in the Charter's Preamble evoke something like a nostalgia for the clear and unambiguous elements of the modernist, liberal-feminist project they express, namely: the quest for inclusion as equal citizens on the part of all South African women; a sovereign nation-state as addressee of women's political demands; the framing of those demands in an unequivocal language of rights; and a unitary claimant-category, 'women', portrayed as universal on the basis of 'shared oppression'. For it is precisely these elements, so effective in mobilizing women as a collective identity and a political constituency within the gender politics of the political transition from apartheid, that today are being destabilized by the effects of globalization and reproblematized within transnational feminist debates on citizenship. Yeatman (2001), reflecting on the political-conceptual challenges of current feminist citizenship theory maintains that '[c]ontemporary feminism is historically positioned in ways which require it to have a more complex and ambivalent relationship to what we may see as the classical-modern project of citizenship: self-government for individual as citizens, and for the national citizen community' (p.138).

This chapter explores aspects of that 'more complex and ambivalent relationship' as these are pertinent to a critical rethinking of gender and citizenship in post-apartheid South Africa. The period since that particular modernist framing of citizenship for women was encapsulated in the *Women's Charter*, has been one in which an ongoing paradigmatic shift in the institution of citizenship has become increasingly legible.[2] The proliferation of citizenship debates attests to the wide-ranging and profound implications of this reconfiguration (Isin and Turner, 2002). Put starkly, the most significant features of this emergent form are a loosening and realignment of the association of citizenship with, on the one hand, the modern nation-state and its attendant notion of an imagined, culturally-coherent national community linked to a bounded territory, and on the other, with the self-identical individual subject (Comaroff and Comaroff, 2000; 2001; Sassen, 2002; Walker, 1999; McClure, 1992). This shift is being expressed politically in the push for recognition and rights of identities of difference (of culture, region, nation, gender, sexuality, etc.) and in sites of political practice that are not coterminous with the nation-state, but may be trans-, supra- or sub-national.

Feminism[3] has of course played a significant role in bringing about transformations in the 'classic-modern' citizenship project. It has exposed the masculinist and class-privileged normative subject of earlier versions of liberal citizenship; it has questioned and re-drawn the gendered designation of the public sphere, making visible and contestable the political regulation of the private sphere; it has promoted 'women' as an identity of gender difference, pushing the boundaries of inclusion in both the concept and practice of citizenship. At the same time however, feminist conceptions and politics of citizenship have been increasingly challenged for their own exclusionary tendencies, for their implicit heteronormativity (Alexander, 1994; 1997; Carver, 1998), their complicity in racialized subject-making (Dhaliwal, 1996) and for their limited nation-state orientation (Pettman, 1999; Werbner and Yuval-Davis, 1999; McClure, 1992). Crucial to this revisioning of feminist citizenship have been the analytic contributions of post-colonial theorists who have reflected the political voices of black and Third World women living in the metropoles and post-colonies. These are women who are gendered in ways that do not wholly conform to the normative constructions of Eurocentric feminist models of gendered citizenship, women whose cultural, racialized, national, ethnic, religious or communal identities have been central to their exclusion from citizenship and are integral to their strategies for pursuing an inclusive, democratic politics.

It is not just feminism that is confronting this ambivalence and critical self-reflection in relation to citizenship. Thus we can find Yuval-Davis (2002) referring to 'citizenship as the main inclusionary emancipatory discourse of the left' (p.44). The struggle for citizenship and rights clearly continues to provide the narrative frame for those peoples contesting various forms of disenfranchisement and marginalization, notably those under authoritarian regimes and from formerly colonized zones, whether located in the West or in the Third World. Yet, at the same time, Hindess (2002) can convincingly argue that where liberalism earlier regulated populations in the non-Western, colonized world by denying citizenship, today, under neo-liberal political conditions, the institutions of liberal global governance are actively promoting democratic citizenship, intent on regulating the populations of post-colonial states and subordinating them to the imperatives of a global market. In what ways can a feminist politics draw on the democratic and ethical claims of citizenship within anti-hegemonic struggles while remaining alert to ways in which citizenship might work as a modality of subjection, potentially channelling opposition into containable, governable forms?

There are other unsettling questions about the politics of citizenship that feminists in South Africa, as in other parts of the world, are implicitly having to confront today. Why now, when inequalities between citizens in all countries are growing exponentially and when states' capacities to meet the survival needs of their populations are increasingly compromised by market determinations, is such an overarching emphasis placed on constitutionalism and rights (Comaroff and Comaroff, 2000, pp.328-330)? Why, too, have universalist discourses of citizenship and 'women's rights as human rights' assumed global prominence at the point when many Third World women in the post-colonies and metropoles are problematizing binary notions of gender and insisting on recognition of class divisions, of racialized, cultural and national difference in the shaping of 'women's issues' (e.g. Stivens, 2000)? A related contemplation in South Africa is particularly poignant. What does it say about the meaning of the celebrated constitutional guarantee of human rights, gender equality and non-sexism when a huge proportion of the population, predominantly female, lacks the effective right to dignity and bodily integrity?

Though somewhat rhetorical and perhaps morally stultifying, such questions nevertheless contextualize and motivate the critical reconsideration of citizenship in South Africa. They also indicate that such a rethinking must involve more than an analysis of the many gender requisites of institutionalizing and substantiating democratic citizenship. Also required is a critical evaluation of the analytic adequacy of the prevailing (if eroding) modernist conceptual framework which has generally shaped debates on gendered citizenship in the course of the transition to post-apartheid. This would include an examination of the political effects, the limitations and possibilities of that framework, in the light of changes wrought by the transnational processes of late capitalism. Are the politics of inclusion and the extension of citizenship rights to women specifically still the most democratic and effective strategy for realizing an equitable citizenship for all women and men in this later post-apartheid conjuncture?

To forge a selective path through this expansive topic and offer some critical reflections I identify some of the issues and ambiguities – conceptual and strategic – that reside in the central elements of modern citizenship as highlighted in the opening quote. These conversations – on 'women', 'citizenship', 'rights', and 'South Africa' (as the site of political identity and belonging) – both structure the chapter and in turn, are informed by my analytic approach. As signalled in the title of this chapter, I focus on the ways in which 'women' are variously and unsteadily constituted as subjects within discourses of citizenship that have been circulating within academic and policy debates in relation to the political transition and post-apartheid transformation.[4] I argue that 'women' as a political category is equivocal, expressing at times, or even simultaneously, an agentic, rights-bearing subject and subject of national narrative. Moreover, in as much as it elides difference, its effect is to mask the ways in which struggles for realizing particular forms of citizenship for 'women' privilege some women over others within shifting matrices of power relations. The exploration of this ambiguity will make more discernable the different political agendas that might be borne by notions of women's citizenship.

Also in the title, I refer strategically to 'the making of political subjects' (rather than citizens) with a two-fold intention. The first is to draw attention to the freight of associations that comes with that latter term and ensure scrutiny of the various meanings of citizenship, specifically those that cite citizenship within the language of liberal democracy and those that see citizen-subjects of national narratives. The second is to declare my indebtedness to a Foucauldian approach in understanding citizenship as a productive and disciplinary category (Carver, 1998) where political subjects, as citizens, are both *subject of* the powers and potential that attach to that status, but at the same time, *subject to* its regulatory aspects. As Cruickshank (1999) argues: 'The citizen is an effect and instrument of power rather than simply a participant in politics' (p.5). In other words, the women who were claiming citizenship in the Women's Charter campaign in the first democratic elections and through consultations around subsequent policy-making were being produced as specifically gendered citizens in that very process, through 'the technologies of citizenship': 'discourses, programmes and other tactics aimed at making individuals politically active and capable of self-government' (Cruickshank, 1999, p.1).

Citizens are always therefore, subjects.[5] Citizenship, when detached from an assumed individual subject, does not have to be seen as a once-off achievement or status acquisition, or indeed as the only form of political subjectivity available to women. Rather, citizen-subjects are constituted within the different discourses, practices and institutions of citizenship and the various, even disjunctive modalities and temporalities of power that are inscribed therein. This perspective, in allowing for a fragmented and contingent subject, enables appreciation of the different forms of agency and moral grounds for political participation that are available within different constructions of citizenship. Difference – in this case, amongst women – can thus be understood not as affixed to certain social identities but rather as varying across different sets of power relations.

I am posing, therefore, a different set of questions from those which have predominantly informed the feminist literature on citizenship in South Africa. One set has sought to understand how women might be fully included in the institution of citizenship, to identify the conditions necessary in order that women are able to realize gender equality rights and to determine the appropriate terms in which to frame policy so that gender implications are addressed. Another critique has explored the ways in which the actual concept of citizenship needs to be revised to discount its gendered assumptions which have worked, historically, to preclude women and non-dominant men. Rather than assuming that women exist as political subjects a priori, that is, outside of their representation in political forms, processes and discourses, I am wanting to explore how 'women' are fashioned as different kinds of gendered political subjects when they are constituted as democratic citizens with rights, as active participants in democracy, as citizen-subjects within the new nation, or normatively defined as virtuous or entitled citizens. Each of these different constructs of woman-as-citizen contains ambiguities that I am suggesting need to be exposed. My concern here is to start uncovering the political effects of these constructs, to decipher their latent inclusions and exclusions, and to explore how aspects of the distinctly gendered practices and discourses of citizenship might be implicated in national projects, in emergent class and elite formation, in the re-marginalization of certain categories of women, and in producing new modalities of power and forms of hierarchy amongst women in South Africa.

As Siim (2000) has pointed out, the cumulative body of research and analysis on gender and citizenship from around the world has confirmed the uniqueness of feminist citizenship struggles within different nation-states. It has also revealed how the specific travels and traditions of theory have shaped local debates. Feminist debates on citizenship in South Africa, as indicated above, emphasize state-civil society relations, juridical reform and policy-making, and evidence the strong influence of Anglo-American feminist theories of democracy. This profile reflects the formative place in the trajectory of South African feminist politics, of the negotiations towards the transition, the first democratic elections and the constitution-making process. It also reflects the dominance of liberal feminism within international bodies like the United Nations as well as the way in which feminist political theory over the past decade or so has been engaging the transnational effects of the post-Cold War ascendancy of liberal democracy and the rash of constitution-making in newly-, or 're-newly' democratic states around the world. But there is another significant part of the 'tradition' of citizenship studies in South Africa, the one that deals with notions of membership in the national political community, of belonging in the nation. This focus has perhaps been over-shadowed by the constitutional and legislative focus of national gender politics and hence underplayed within feminist writings on citizenship. Certainly, gender has been inadequately treated within analyses about nation-building except in relation to the Truth and Reconciliation Commission (e.g. Wilson, 2001; Ross, 2003). Lewis (1999) rightly argues that discussions of gendered citizenship must 'address how women define themselves in national communities' (p.44). Equally, I would argue, those discussions must explore how women are defined as citizen-subjects within vying conceptions of national political community, and how constructs of women and gender are invoked and implicated in contesting those imaginaries of political community.

The spectre hovering over the achievements of South Africa's women-friendly constitution and state programmes is that of the derailing, even reversal, of the gains made for women in the political arena during the propitious moment of democratic transition. The rescinding of political space and power for women in many post-independent African states is invoked as an eventuality to be rigorously avoided. Adding to this concern is the global trend, evident in South Africa, of reassertions of ethno-nationalisms and communal identity politics as well as a preoccupation with national identity. A question that must be broached, therefore, is whether there are understandings of women's citizenship circulating within official or more popular discourses which are more susceptible than others to being appropriated to a nationalist project or an exclusive conception of political community. Which conceptions of citizenship are more likely to accord women effective political agency that will ensure their access to resources? Are there ways in which rights-based constructs of citizenship might be articulated to apartheid or nationalist notions of maternal citizenship which confer a strong gender identity and moral agency on women even while positioning them asymmetrically vis-à-vis the state?

Opening up to scrutiny and political contestation the various ways in which 'women' are constituted as political subjects within different practices, institutions and discourses of citizenship will, I argue, not only reveal potential complicities between certain kinds of feminism and nationalist or ruling class projects, but will also make apparent new and more refined possibilities for engaging struggles for democratization and equality and for enhancing an anti-hegemonic and anti-racist feminist project in South Africa.

'Women' Claiming Citizenship

A closer reading of the *Women's Charter* and of the struggles for gendered citizenship on the part of activist women around the time of the political transition reveals not so much an ambivalent relationship to the goal of modern citizenship that Yeatman (2001) refers to, but certainly a more complex and differentiated picture, one that implies some challenges to a narrow conception of citizenship as formal juridical membership within a nation-state. The *Charter* gestures, for instance, toward a more profound critique of the masculinist foundations of conventional notions of democracy and citizenship. It also emphasizes throughout, strong social and economic equality claims indicative of a politics of distributive justice. Understandably, as a manifesto for a gender-inclusive and democratic citizenship, its political objectives are unevenly articulated, reflecting both its origins in a broad consultation of South Africa's extremely diversified female population and the varied political ideologies and constituencies of the women's organizations involved in the Charter campaign.

There is one aspect of the gendered politics of citizenship in the transition and post-apartheid transformation process that is both politically provocative and analytically testing, particularly when considered in the light of post-structuralist, post-colonial, black and Third World feminist critiques of 'Westocentric' citizenship theory. Exemplified in the *Women's Charter,* this is the representation of the subject of that politics as 'women'. How was it that an apparently coherent political identity of women could be so confidently and powerfully asserted, given the social and cultural diversity amongst South African women, the vast inequalities in livelihoods and social capital, the array of political-ideological positions and the violently-imposed, racialized fissures of apartheid? It was, after all, the colonialist and apartheid institution of a racially-exclusive national citizenship that specifically and rigidly reproduced the divisions between and amongst South African women, depriving the majority of that fundamental tenet of modern liberal citizenship, the vote. As in other parts of the colonized world, that formal exclusion was made on the basis of a racialized or ethnicized difference, not on the basis of gender (although, as in other colonial histories, gender was thoroughly implicated in the making of racial categories of rule). White women were included, from 1930, in the political community of self-governing citizens, a status which was integral to apartheid constructions of 'whiteness' and graduated varieties of 'non-whiteness'. The setting up of the infamous Bantustan system and related institutionalization of patriarchal forms of governance was a critical moment in the formal constitution of racially- and culturally-defined political subjects. So, too, was the later allocation of black South African nationals to membership, as putative 'citizens', of respective, ethnically-defined, 'independent national states' under the internationally-recognized (if rhetorically condemned) sovereignty of the Republic of South Africa. The 1983 Constitution of 'the Reform state' instituted the tricameral parliamentary system as an attempt to incorporate so-designated 'Indian' and 'Coloured' South Africans as voting, vested citizens within respective, subordinated sub-national political communities. These measures cumulatively provided for – and left a legacy of – complex mediations of racialized, sexual and gendered 'unbelonging' in the national polity. Yet – ironically, given the paradigmatic place of 'race' and indeed of nation and class in theoretical and popular narratives of struggles for democratic citizenship in South Africa – many feminist accounts of women's citizenship de-emphasize or erase the analytic implications of this significant and formative history by focusing on 'women' as the objects of their narrative. 'Women' and/or 'gender' as subject of the gender politics of citizenship seem comfortably assumed and normalized, as both political identity category and analytic point of departure. Relatedly, the definitive democratic concept of 'equality', in both political and academic feminist discourse refers mostly to a notion of *gender* equality, where 'gender' is narrowly defined in terms of sexual difference along a male/female binary.

There are two kinds of conceptual responses to the questioning of 'women' as the subject of claims to citizenship. One tends to take the form of a disclaimer: South African women are not a monolithic group nor is 'women' a universal or essential category. Women, it is argued, are divided by race, class, ethnicity, region, religion, sexuality, generation, etc. or women have multiple identities along these lines. But these qualifiers do not do much to disturb the assumption that 'women' occupies a fixed category of gender or sexual difference, one that is discrete and distinguishable from gender's intersection with other identity categories. The idea of women organising or having interests *as women* implies the notion of gender as an identity that can be extricated from other identities. It suggests that a discrete gender identity cannot ultimately be dislodged, a formulation which allows a gender essentialism to creep back in. The formulaic differentiation of women along the lines of other pre-given identity categories (race, class, etc.), has the effect of re-positing 'women' as a stable and prior political identity, and of assuming gender as analytically primary. This approach deters analysis of social relations and identity categories other than 'gender' as being both significant in structuring the exclusion of women from aspects of citizenship and as relevant to women's struggles for citizenship. Referring to this tendency in feminist scholarship, Joan Scott (2002) notes that ' ... while "women" historically has served to consolidate feminist movements, it has also made race, class, ethnicity, religion, sexuality, and nationality somehow secondary, as if these distinctions amongst us (and the hierarchical positioning that accompanies them) matter less than the physical similarities that we share' (pp.5-6).

The other kind of explanation for the cross-party, trans-racial, trans-community, women-based politics exemplified in the Women's National Coalition and the gender politics of transition is a more historically-located and political one. Again it is maintained that 'women' are not a homogenous identity, but rather that differently located South African women coalesced, and were actively mobilized, as a political identity around a shared place of exclusion from the political process. Women, it is argued, also had in common a shared objective of ensuring a post-apartheid citizenship that did not (re)marginalize women (Cock and Bernstein, 2002; Seidman, 1999). This politics of inclusion is similarly invoked to explain political struggles to secure full and effective citizenship of women, to achieve the recognition of gender equality within the Constitution, to secure representation of women in state structures and ensure gender-cognizance in policy-formulation and governance.

This approach, often working explicitly against essentialist or reductionist arguments, has provided important interpretations of the gendered politics of citizenship in transitional and post-apartheid South Africa (e.g. Cock and Bernstein, 2002; Meintjes, 1998). While it accounts for the differences amongst women in terms of the politics of coalition and the production of a political constituency of women, it also tends, ultimately, to assume 'the abiding existence of a homogenous collectivity called "women" upon which measurable experiences are visited' (Scott 1999, p.78). There is a fine but theoretically significant line here between understanding 'women' as an historically contingent, politically-produced identity and the uncritical take-up of that identity category as an analytical or even ontological one, one that is prone to universal and trans-historical projections. Echoing the language of the Charter, and representing women as bearers of distinctly gendered interests is, for instance, a notion of 'women's citizenship' that has been articulated within South African academic feminism. While this construct of 'women's citizenship' has been useful in highlighting gendered aspects of the inclusion/exclusion from practices, entitlements and conceptualizations of citizenship (Gouws, 1999; Hassim, 1999) it tends to have the effect of stabilizing and reiterating 'women' as inherently and uniformly disadvantaged 'as women' within discourses of citizenship and of reproducing gender as binary and heteronormative. The universalizing implications of a notion of 'women's citizenship' are belied not only by the huge power differentials and very unequal realization and practice of citizenship amongst South African women, but also by the different discursive constructs of women-as-citizen that traverse political and theoretical debates. For example, as I discuss below, the woman-citizen of gender equality policy, or the de-gendered individual subject of rights, are not synonymous with the mother-citizen of the nation even though these divergent constructs are often conflated analytically or intertwined rhetorically in mobilizing women politically or in support of nation-building projects.

This critique can be extended to a particular construction of 'gendered citizenship' at play in academic and policy discourse. As has frequently been noted, in contemporary South African political and development discourse the semantically-overburdened term 'gender', often stands in for 'women' as the subject of gender politics. To the extent that 'gender' is deployed as an identity (rather than analytic) category or that 'gendered citizenship' is used as a synonym for 'women's citizenship', these formulations also work to reproduce gender solely as setting the terms in which to explain the various forms of political and economic marginalization experienced by women. Clearly, the ambiguities in the meaning of 'women' and 'gender' in relation to citizenship, warrant further interrogation.

The implication here is that certain presumptive notions of women's or gendered citizenship – those that assume and designate women as objects of analysis in ways which abstract them from their constitutive social relations and discursive representations – inhibit analysis of the uneven and unequal place of different women in relation to structures, practices and discourses of citizenship in South Africa. Two central questions within feminist political theory are being indexed here: one is the relationship between the universal claims of citizenship and the acknowledgement of difference. Initially the debate was centred on gender or sex difference, but today is much more focused on differences marked by race, nation, ethnicity, religious and community identity. The other refers to the status and stability of 'women' as subject of citizenship politics, an issue addressed by deconstructionist approaches. Previously there seemed to be an impasse between the position that a stable category of 'women', based on gender difference, was foundational and necessary to the feminist project, and an opposing view which saw the categories of 'women' and 'gender' as exclusionary, 'Westocentric' or even racist in implication. A more productive framing of this debate, one that speaks more usefully to contemporary gender politics in South Africa, is captured by the following questions: How is the political power of the category 'women' to be retained without subsuming difference or misrepresenting the perspectives of women in different social locations? How can the category be understood as unstable and contested while also serving as a site for feminist identity and politics? And – importantly needing further exploration in the context of South Africa – what are the political effects of different constructions of 'women' (Gedalof, 1999; Scott, 1999)? Here I want to highlight two aspects of recent theorizing of gender which implicitly address these questions. They indicate the limitations of analysis of citizenship which focuses on women as its object, and show how notions of gender and citizenship are integral to broader political projects.

The first understands the category of 'women' as always produced in and through relations to other political identities and in particular contexts (Dillabough and Arnot, 2000; Brooks, 2000). As Gedalof (1999) argues, 'women' is an 'impure' category; it is not based purely on gender or sex difference and is never innocent of the mediations of other identities. Social categories are not trans-historical or trans-locational, but are marked through processes of contestation that define their boundaries. An analytic or political focus on gender implies not only a diminished attention to race or class, but the possibility of producing 'women' as an exclusionary racialized and class category. When a social category is relatively stabilized or appears 'pure', it usually signifies, according to Fernandes (1997), 'a particular hegemonic representation of the relationship between the category in question ... and other forms of difference' (p.5).

The second point, one that has been elaborated in particular by post-colonial feminists, emphasizes the inherent relationship between constructions of 'women' and the boundaries of political collectivities, whether national or sub-national. This argument, now made familiar in an extensive literature on women and nation, understands the ideological and practical regulation of women's bodies and behaviours as patrolling the integrity of the national culture and the bloodlines of its subjects (e.g. Yuval-Davis, 1997a; Alarcon et al., 1999; Ranchod-Nilsson and Tetreault, 2000). But it applies equally to the regulation of the boundaries of the modern, secular nation-state through its juridical and bureaucratically-organized forms of citizenship. Formal citizenship is acquired through lines of descent and kinship, by being born in the territory to a citizen or permanent resident, or by being 'naturalized', that is, by subscribing to and being legitimized by a 'natural' (kin equivalent) national identity (Klaaren, 2000). This reading of the relationship between women, citizenship and the nation/state does not need to imply a biological reductionism (that is, that women's importance to the nation/state rests on their reproductive capacities). Rather the particular family form that shapes and rationalizes who belongs legitimately as either national subject or state-endorsed citizen is one that is regulated through state processes. In other words, there is a mutual constitution of state and family and hence, gender-mediated belonging as citizen (Stevens, 1999). Seeing citizen status as rendered 'natural' through women, birth and kinship adds another layer of complexity to the contradictory rationales of the current South African government's nation-building rhetoric and its exclusivist immigration policy. As Peberdy (2001) argues, juridical citizenship has increasingly become the basis for residency and entitlement rights. The harsh exclusion of African immigrants from outside of South Africa runs counter not only to the proclaimed inclusive citizenship and human rights culture, but also to the notion of national belonging being based on an all-embracing African identity.

There are two implications of these ways of conceiving the category of 'women' as a political effect implicating other social identities, and as integrally linked to the boundaries of political communities. One is that constructions of 'women' and gender relations are important sites in which the politics of citizenship are played out and constructions of national political community are contested. Ambiguities in the meaning of 'women' within citizenship discourses, therefore, reflect political and discursive struggles that have significance beyond those pertaining to women and gender and the quest for citizenship. The other implication is that citizenship is a crucial site for the production of racialized and gendered political subjects.

This conceptualization of gender and citizenship provides another way of responding to the question posed earlier as to how a unitary political category of 'women' could emerge where differences amongst women were so pronounced. The 'women' of the politics of transition represented a gendered construction that was integral to the building of an emergent discourse of socio-economic and legal equality and rights-bearing citizenship, one that simultaneously worked to marginalize or down-play identities based on race, class, region and nation. That strong emphasis on 'women' expressed the politics of democracy and non-racialism (as actively espoused by the African National Congress) against other contending constructions of women-citizens in relation to ethno-nationalist or communal identities.[6] Yet the explanation for the hegemony of the political category of 'women' at that time – and since – must also reference the ambiguity and multivalence of that category. Resonating culturally in the signifier 'women' is a widely held construction of women-as-mothers or maternal citizens, claiming their rights by virtue of their moral responsibilities in the family, community and to the nation. This maternalist construct of women-as-citizens is powerfully embedded within popular conceptions of the place of women in the South African nation-state and often discernable in public speech of state actors. Another way of putting this is that while women are uniformly and formally interpellated as 'women, citizens of South Africa', there are different representations of and contestation over the meanings of that gendered citizenship that reflects the politics and locations of different women and speaks to different imaginaries of the emergent national political community (Radcliffe and Westwood, 1996). The political category of 'women' covers for or embraces both 'equal citizens' and 'mothers of the nation'. Emergent constructs of women-as-citizens variously draw on the available cultural repertoires of 'women' as activists, as familial subjects, as needing resources and as community carers.

Citizen/Subject

If 'women' and 'gender' are ambiguous or porous concepts, so too is 'citizenship'. The current ubiquity of debates on citizenship, its multiplicity of meanings, its revitalized and contending traditions and its promiscuous use in both ruling and anti-hegemonic political discourse, can make for rather disjunctive conversations.

Contending genealogies of citizenship within Western political philosophy – liberal, republican, communitarian and radical democratic – set up different preoccupations, different ideas about the ideal citizen and his/her relationship to the imagined political community. Significantly, these 'traditions' of citizenship theory also contain vying notions of the place of gender and women as citizen-members. Aspects of each of these can be located in representations of citizenship in contemporary South Africa, tracing the European heritage of the post-colony's political culture and sedimentations of indigenous cultures of governance. South African feminist debates on citizenship map rather unevenly and eclectically onto the local narratives of citizenship, whether the communitarianism implicit in notions of *ubuntu* and African Renaissance, the active, participatory citizenship of republicanism that is embodied in the consultative style and transformative ideals of early post-apartheid governance, or the enhanced role of courts, commissions, and rights-laden individual subjects that resonate with liberal democratic constitutionalism. As mentioned above, South African feminist writings which explicitly address 'citizenship' are predominantly rendered in the grammar of liberal democracy and are significantly informed by Anglo-American feminist jurisprudence.

Compounding the intricacy and indeed the volume of debate have been the various claims on citizenship made by contemporary and transnational identity-based and social movements, which have asserted their politics through the language of rights and citizenship, much as women and feminism have done. I refer here to 'sexual citizenship', 'ecological citizenship', 'cultural citizenship' and 'indigenous' (etc.) citizenships, each one rewriting the parameters and purchase of the concept, highlighting exclusions and obligations, and generating both formative solidarities and new subjects of citizenship. Several reconceptualizations of citizenship speak to the rise of the place of the market in addressing social needs and to the decline of state-provided social rights that were (in a kinder, more progressive era) being read as inherent in citizenship by theorists of the welfare state, like the much-cited T.H. Marshall. Notions of 'neo-liberal citizenship', 'market citizenship' and 'consumer citizenship' now inhabit debates (Hindess, 2002; Schild, 1998). Grappling with the implications for citizenship of transnationalism, of the reallocation of powers of sovereignty between nation-states and supra-national governing institutions, and the transnational or multinational allegiances of citizens, are notions of 'postnational citizenship', 'denationalized citizenship' and 'cosmopolitan citizenship' (e.g. Sassen, 2002). Clearly, citizenship is neither a singular nor teleological narrative (contrary to its representation as such in popular and modernist accounts). It has become the lingua franca of political activism and a core site for the investigation of contemporary transnational and post-modern developments.

Citizenship is variously depicted as a juridical status, a set of obligations, a normative construct, a political identity or, closely related, as defining the terms of belonging within a national community. Sometimes all of these are included as *dimensions* of citizenship. The point I want to emphasize is that each of these dimensions refers to, and is located within discourses of citizenship which position women in different ways as citizen-subjects, each with different and often ambiguous political implications. Take the example of citizenship as participation, a notion which is central to South African women's struggles for effective gender equality. (I discuss rights and belonging, below.) Participation is emphasized in radical democratic notions of citizenship, embracing both the right to participate in self-government and decision-making and the obligation to contribute actively to the democratic process and a vibrant civil society.[7] But participation, like other aspects of citizenship, is subject to various interpretations. Within transnationally dominant liberal and United Nations-orchestrated feminism at this time, participation has been translated into protocols of state-related practices such as quota-setting, the establishment of women's units, gender policy audits, and programmes for gender-training. Such exercises of 'participation' have been embraced for their results in making more favourable the contexts of women's political involvement and for having an impact on policy-making. They have also been met with scepticism by feminists concerned about complicity in ruling projects and about how the depoliticizing effects of institutionalization might, in effect, reduce women's active citizenship. Participation is also stressed in those polities that are following neo-liberal prescriptions to cut back on social expenditure. Citizens are enjoined to demonstrate their virtue by organizing (or volunteering) to provide social services and supplement health care. Some feminists have interpreted the promotion of women's participation as code for their having to pick up the slack in social service provision. Others argue that the practice and ethic of care and of community responsibility, a potent cultural gender norm particularly within marginalized communities in South Africa and one long associated with 'women's work', should be positively incorporated within the concept of citizenship. Also pertinent to the South African context, 'participation' in planning and executing development programmes has become an ethical norm or 'best practice' in this field. It is emphasized particularly as a strategy for women's empowerment in Gender and Development which is a central location of the practice of citizenship for many Third World women. However, some women experience the injunction to participate as only adding more work onto their triple roles, yoking women to the developmental objectives of national states and international development institutions and shaping them as self-reliant and entrepreneurial citizens (Mayoux, 1998; Schild, 1998). This is just one excursion into the equivocality of citizenship discourse. The political rationalities and prospects of different aspects of citizenship are perhaps most ambivalent when considered from the perspective of subaltern women. Their location renders them marginal and disadvantaged in relation to citizenship norms as these are articulated by more elite women, although, as Mindry (2001) has shown, some subaltern women are able to take advantage of their 'grassroots' and 'needy category' designation in seeking access to state and non-governmental resources. Deciphering the ambiguities of citizenship for different women is a critical task for ongoing, situated feminist critique.

Enslin (2003) has recently characterized the emergent official conception of citizenship in South Africa as a combination of elements embodied in the new Constitution (such as equality, social justice, anti-discrimination and a healing of divisions of the past) and elements residual from the anti-apartheid struggle (active and participatory). She notes, too, an emergent popular conception, somewhat in tension with the former, which evidences a preoccupation with the entitlements of citizenship and with access to public goods, and which is accompanied by a decline in levels of public participation. I would argue that the official conception that Enslin (2003) depicts is less coherent when viewed through the prism of gender and the kind of analysis that I have been advancing above. There is an incompatibility between the gender relations of active participation that characterized the anti-apartheid struggles (which were not particularly gender equal) and the gender equality that is officially represented within the Constitution. The *Women's Charter*, for example, in its emphasis on equality, was edging towards this shift in the discursive formation of female political subjects, from more specifically gendered, maternalist, rank-swelling participants in the anti-apartheid struggle to rights-claiming, equal agents within a modernist, democratic citizenship project. Similarly, readings of declining political participation and concern for entitlements must be read by a gauge that is calibrated for gender if those phenomena are to be insightfully interpreted. South Africa's incorporation into the global market via neo-liberal policies has fostered a feminization of labour and of poverty. It is consequently poor, black women in particular who are both most in need of, and therefore oriented toward the entitlements and public goods promised by citizenship. They are also most constrained by temporal, material, and importantly, cultural factors, in the forms and extent of their participation in public politics.

    Enslin (2003) discusses the national education curriculum as one of the most important sites for fostering conceptions of citizenship and national identity. Another site, not generally considered under the rubric of citizen-making is that of the extensive 'gender industry' which comprises gender policy, mainstreaming strategies, women's empowerment programmes, voter education, gender training, masculinity workshops, and gender and development schemes, etc. These can be understood as technologies of citizenship (Cruickshank, 1999) which in a doubled way enhance women's capacity to engage in citizenly activities, but at the same time delimit and regulate the forms of that engagement, and importantly, produce them as specifically *gendered* political subjects in ways that emphasize gender over other contending social identifications and position them as women (as opposed to racialized or class subjects) in relation to the nation-state.

    In conclusion, I would argue that there is, currently underway, a process of reorganization of forms of racialization, class-differentiation, geographical location and gendering of citizenship that needs to be investigated in a more nuanced way, in a way that attends to the different dimensions and uneven effects of citizenship on different women, including those of rights and belonging which I go on to discuss in the next two sections.

Subjects of/to Rights

That South African feminist debates on citizenship are heavily steeped in the language of rights is hardly surprising. In a context in which political rights were restricted or denied to the majority of the population until a decade ago, where human rights violations were commonplace and where a huge proportion of women lacked legal personhood, the discourse of rights has been a primary vector for various forms of anti-colonial, anti-apartheid and now democratic struggle (Comaroff, 1995). Globally, 'rights' has become the 'archetypal language of democratic transition' (Wilson, 2001) and with the impetus of the UN World Conference on Human Rights in Vienna in 1993 (where the maxim of 'women's rights are human rights' was officially endorsed) a global human rights regime has been consolidated. 'Rights' have come to signify the terms of democracy, morality and social justice. Over the past decade or so, the field of Gender and Development which, as mentioned above, is integral to reconfiguring citizenship in the context of post-apartheid reconstruction, has been infused with notions of rights-based development strategies. It is almost impossible to conceive of an emancipatory feminist politics outside of this sometimes rather evangelical discourse. This makes it all the more important to retain a stance of critical distance in relation to rights.

The notion of 'equality' – the rhetorical theme of the *Women's Charter* now phrased more formally as the 'Equality Clause' of the Constitution's Bill of Rights – is a focus and rallying point for feminist citizenship studies in South Africa. Mirroring transnational trends, a whole slew of 'women's issues' and sites of gender discrimination – reproduction, violence, access to land, work, social provision, law, etc. – have been translated into the language of rights. Feminist political critique is framed by questions of whether and how such formal rights might be made substantive and the extent to which civil, political and social rights have been realized – or are realizable – in relation to all women. Much of this work builds – though in revealing gender-inflected ways – on the well-established leftist interpretation of rights as being implemented within inegalitarian fields of power; they tend, consequently, to be more advantageous and viable to the more powerful, but often fairly gestural and vacuous to those lacking power and prospects. With its more social democratic and redistributive objectives, the Reconstruction and Development Programme (RDP) showed more affinity with the concerns for substantive equality espoused by women activists and policy analysts. The market orientation of the subsequent development programme, GEAR (Growth, Employment and Redistribution), undermines the state's capacity to deliver on the social protections and provisions and works against the realization of those social and equity measures which are cast as 'rights'.

The other central issue that has long been of concern for feminists is the question of the subject status of African women living under customary law, specifically the tension between the principle of gender equality and the recognition of this law. In its current institutionalized form, customary or 'traditional' law is deeply patriarchal.[8] Translated into the terms of rights, this tension is sharpened into a juridical contradiction between equality rights and cultural rights, an intricate debate that is being addressed academically and politically within and across multicultural and post-colonial constitutional states around the world. The question of the constitutional status of customary law was fiercely contested in the final days of formulating the principles of the Interim Constitution in 1993, and again in the process of finalizing the 1996 Constitution. The Constitution recognizes customary law but its applications are limited by the fundamental rights guaranteed in the Bill of Rights where the right to equality with respect to race and sex are listed as non-derogable. Yet there is a certain lingering ambiguity fostered by political concessions made to traditional leaders and the apparent juridical irreconcilability between the 'non-sexism' and gender equality promised by the Constitution and the patriarchal precepts of 'traditional' forms of governance. If there is a consensus amongst interested parties such as the Commission on Gender Equality, the recently established Commission for the Promotion and Protection of the Rights of Cultural, Religious and Linguistic Communities, constitutional interpreters and feminist legal reformers, it is around a general orientation to improve women's protection and legal subject status while being sensitive to the politics of culture and processes of cultural change. Deveaux (2003) has recently argued that the tension between cultural and gender rights should be framed in pragmatic, political terms, rather than moral ones.

My intention here is not to revisit these familiar domains of debate on the politics of gender-based rights in South Africa. It is rather to explore a different optic on citizenship rights for women, specifically, the implications of 'women' becoming subjects of rights. I want to look at how discourses of women's rights construct citizen-subjects as gendered and how, in doing so, generate new forms of difference and hierarchy amongst women.

A number of feminist political theorists, drawing on the work of Foucault, have pointed to the paradoxes inherent in the deployment of rights in addressing women's inequality and subordination (e.g. Ahmed, 1995; Brown 1995; 2002; McClure, 1992; 1995). The first paradox is that women's rights reinscribe, rather than challenge the gender-based identity which is being claimed as the basis of injury or discrimination (Brown, 2002). Ahmed (1995) points out similarly that 'the employment of rights functions as a citational act' (p.68). Rights not only bring into being the category of 'women' as their subject, but also stabilize and delimit the meaning of 'women' within that process, in the structural relations and institutional settings (law, courts, etc.) that are involved in rights claims. The notion of women's rights assumes that the lives (and indeed, the subordinations) of females are organized primarily by gender, that they live their lives solely, or mainly, as 'women'. On the other hand, feminists have long been arguing that where women's rights are *not* specified – that is, where a universal notion of rights prevails – the specific exclusions of women from those universal formulations of rights remain invisible and outside the reach of legal and policy redress. The effect of those exclusions is not neutral but in fact enhances the power of those included in the compass of the universal rights, in this case, socially-dominant men.

This same argument applies, however, to the universal notion of 'women' that is constituted within women's rights discourse. The specific discriminations experienced by black, 'traditional' or working class women are buried within that generic notion of women's rights. Because different modalities of power are involved in racialized oppression, discriminations under customary law or working class exploitation, for example, and because the subjects of race, nation, class, sexuality, etc. are created through different processes of regulation, different histories and different discursive formations, rights articulated in relation to the generic identity 'women' can exacerbate the oppression of some women while producing inequalities amongst women. Policies of affirmative action for black South Africans, for example, do not address specific discriminations faced by black women, while they tend to privilege middle-class black women. Women's equality rights tend not to distinguish gender and sexuality, with the effect that in defining the ways in which women are violable and vulnerable to men, they reinscribe heterosexuality (Alexander, 1997; Brown, 2002).

Brown (2002) sums up the difficulties faced by critical legal theorists who have been struggling to address the paradoxical effects of identity-based rights claims in liberal constitutional democracies:

> ... to treat these various modalities of subject formation as simply additive or even intersectional is to elide the way subjects are brought into being through subjectifying discourses, the way that we are not simply oppressed but produced through these discourses, a production that does not occur in additive, intersectional or overlapping parts but through complex and often fragmented histories in which multiple social powers are regulated through and against one another (p.427).

Beyond the different modalities of power that are implicated in the subordinating relations and rights claims of different identities ('women', disabled, blacks, etc.) there are different *kinds* of rights, often conflated under the singular rubric of 'women's rights'. These have developed unevenly and distinctively in different national-political contexts, and have been differently imbricated both with modern state formation and with the modern citizen-subject (Walker, 1999; McClure, 1995). The political subjects produced within the discursive formations of what are generally understood as positive, negative and entitlement rights vary and this has implications for understanding the uneven political agency of women differently positioned in relation to these different forms of rights and within social hierarchies in South Africa. Positive rights, for example, those currently most associated with notions of citizenship that connote active participation in the institutions of representation, constitute a self-determining subject involved in democratic self-governance. The subject of negative liberty rights which refer to protection or defence of self or property, does not necessarily have to be a citizen. Colonial subjects and women under customary law could be bearers of such rights, for example. Finally, the subject of entitlement rights is most characterized by dependence on public support (McClure, 1995). Women who exercise entitlement rights are subjected to normative pressures to be 'good and deserving citizens' and to regulations that define them as 'in need' or as qualifying for categorization as 'the poorest of the poor'. What is suggested here is that although 'women's rights' in South Africa embrace these three kinds of rights, there is a normative privileging of positive rights within the conception of active, participatory citizenship that

Enslin (2003) has identified as the emerging official notion and which is endorsed by many feminist activists. Concomitantly, there is a negative association of entitlement rights with dependency and victimhood. The subjects of these different rights map in very broad strokes but by no means directly onto gendered, racially and class-marked identity categories. Distinguishing them therefore, and discerning the ways in which they are socially evaluated and regulated is useful in thinking beyond the often reductive and blinding categories of race, class, region, etc. to see how new forms of racialization, of class subordination and gender relations are emerging through the different modalities of power and subjectivities associated with different kinds of rights. In other words, these distinctions allow refinement of the more familiar argument which draws a connection between the politics of rights and the political and economic advancement of elites.

There is a further paradox, linked to the previous ones, which helps to reveal how rights might sometimes constrain and sometimes enhance the political agency of women. Rights operate within a universal idiom; conceived as aspirations or as the rhetoric of emancipatory desires, it is their transcendent status, their broad moral register, that can be seen as the basis of their political potency. Yet, rights are always very specific in their articulation, deeply embedded in time and place and always understood and contested in relation to local cultural understandings of justice. A much noted effect of this paradox is the way in which rights, once specified, become depoliticized. While the language of rights addresses and promises equality to a universal subject (in this case 'women') and appeals broadly to a universal or human morality, rights cannot, in themselves, transform the conditions of inequality that actually give rise to the appeal to rights. In the process of legislating and exercising juridical rights, it is not only the formulations of that subject and its injury that are entrenched (as discussed above). Emancipatory politics, too, become re-defined as the practice of exercising of rights at the same time as this practice is rigidified and regulated within legal procedures and institutions. In South Africa, the active promotion of a rights culture as an aspect of post-apartheid nation-building has some ambivalent effects. Where the ethos of post-apartheid transformation has remained forceful and where backed by activist movements (such as the gay and lesbian or, at times, the women's movement) rights politics have been creatively and effectively deployed. At the same time, Wilson found in his research on gender, local justice and morality in Boipatong, a black township, that ongoing local issues of social justice were now being articulated in a language of rights but in a way that was superficial and indicated no real transformation in understandings or practices of justice. He concluded that '[r]ights talk is vague enough to cloak a variety of claims and entitlements which may not be rights-derived at all' (Wilson, 2001, p.217). It is precisely this political ambiguity and malleability of rights that make some feminists wary, for it points to the potential for not only the language of rights but also the legal machinery of rights to be appropriated to conservative and anti-feminist ends, whether cultural nationalism or the re-instating of masculinist privilege.

Opening up some analytic windows through which to review rights is the growing volume of critical accounts of rights politics drawn up by feminists in post-colonial contexts, fundamentalist states and in the former communist regimes. These depict gendered subjects of rights that distinctively reflect their embeddedness within respective political formations, cultural and ideological traditions. They refer to varying interpretations and implementations of gender equality, implicitly cautioning against the universalizing of what are always historically contingent notions of women's rights and gender equality (e.g. Perry and Obiora, 2002). They also show, however, that even while a politics of 'women's rights' can have a constraining effect on struggles for social justice, it also inevitably disrupts hegemonic cultural constructs of gender and reveals the contestability of gender relations (Ram, 2000). This dislocation provides new opportunities and re-charts the political ground for women's struggles, ground that is necessarily configured by communal relations, class, racialized and national relations. Such feminist critiques of rights coming out of non-Western political traditions and contexts are explicitly developed with data-laden categories of analysis – that is, where conceptualizations of 'women', 'equality', and 'rights' etc. are dialogical with debates of modernity as these are situated within local political-cultural histories and conditions. They potentially provide important insights and models for further research and analysis of rights-based citizenship in South Africa.

The modernist promise of rights is clearly close to the heart of a feminist post-apartheid project at this point, but this commitment does not have to translate into an unexamined incantation of rights as primary solution to social inequalities and gender-based discriminations. There are important arenas of struggles for social and gender justice framed within a language of rights which need to be closely charted. These include the politically creative interpretations and implementations of the universalist discourse of rights by women and men in local community struggles (see e.g. Wilson 2001) and the ways in which the Constitutional Court is fashioning (through its debated interpretations) a 'tradition' of rights-based citizenship (Van Huyssteen, 2000). Of significance for a feminist rethinking of rights and citizenship is the way in which the subject of rights is being constructed in the Court. Is there an interpretation of *ubuntu*, for example, as personal dignity and justice which might best capture the ethos of citizenship that is being propagated in popular women's organizations in Africa and Latin America, for instance, as well as in feminist attempts to reconceptualize personhood in non-masculinist ways (Narayan, 1997), that proffers a more transformative, less identity-bound and more culturally-located notion of egalitarian citizenship for all South Africans?

South Africa: Gendered Mediations of Belonging

The authors of the *Women's Charter* declared themselves categorically as 'citizens of South Africa', members of the nation-state. They affirmed their right to belong fully to the national political community, and claimed a status that transcended sub-national and particularized sites of allegiance such as racially-categorized groups, or ethnically- or territorially-defined collectivities. This appeal to a sovereign nation-state as the site of their belonging was expressing a layered political claim for the establishment of a sovereign, democratic, unified nation-state. However, considerations of the constitution of 'women' as citizens and reconceptualizations of gender and citizenship in South Africa more generally cannot be confined to the conceptual horizons of the nation-state nor its territorialized boundaries. As intimated above, various transnational processes – the shifting sovereignty of the state, the growing prominence of supranational governance, the growth of transnational civil society and the de-linking of national identity and citizenship status that has accompanied mass migrations and growth of diasporas – have contributed to the process of reconfiguring citizenship and necessitated an overhaul of analytic frameworks. These processes have been particularly consequential, I argue, in the making of gendered political subjects in post-apartheid.

Because of the rhetorical and institutional openings provided by the political process of transition, struggles for rights and recognition of women in South Africa have been directed toward the state. The discourse, juridical formulations and strategies deployed in these struggles, however, have been strongly imprinted by transnational state-oriented feminist trends. Over the period of transition, these flows of knowledge and experience were densely mediated by travelling feminist academics and consultants, conferences debating the most appropriate institutions and propitious measures for ensuring gender equality, circulating documents and theory, and importantly, the set of international UN meetings that took place in the early part of the 1990s decade, most notably the World Conference on Women in Beijing in 1995. The practices, language and debates of South African citizenship thus reflect the influences of the transnational women's movement comprising of the more popular, community-based organizations and more elite, professional women's NGOs, state feminisms around the globe as well as of the official, UN-orchestrated institutions and conventions. In policy documents that address gender equality and regulate citizenship, the South African government assiduously acknowledges the conventions it is party to, such as the Beijing Plan of Action and the Convention for the Elimination of All Forms of Discrimination Against Women (CEDAW).[9] In stressing the 'honouring of international commitments', the state is invoking the authority of the international bodies to legitimate its national policy on gender, while simultaneously legitimating its own authority as a sovereign state. International policy and global governance is thus mediated by national states, who variously take on (or fail to take on) the implementation of agreements. This understanding validates the South African state as being a necessary, if not only, locus of struggles for democratic citizenship.

From the perspective of a feminist politics of citizenship, the question to be posed is whether and how the global women's rights regime (that is, the set of discourses, institutions and legal instruments) have positively or negatively affected the citizenship (here understood as the political space and agency) of women in South Africa. Clearly, this regime has provided powerful rhetorical tools armed with which women activists within and without the state can exert pressure on the government to effect changes. At the same time, this regime of global governance must also be understood as configuring and constraining the particular forms of gendered political subjectivity (Manicom, 2001).

As noted earlier, attempts to capture, analytically, the reconfigurations of state sovereignty, emergent sites of governance and cross-national citizen allegiances have advanced notions of global civil society, transnational-, postnational- and cosmopolitan citizenship. Like the concept of citizenship more generally, these notions both express a rhetorical appeal (in this case for new kinds of political identities and for transnational collaborations in opposition to market-based globalization) and attempt to specify new relations between loci of governance and political subjects. South African women (nationally-identified) and women in South Africa (territorially-identified) are clearly located in this framework of transnational citizenship, but in ways that exacerbate the differences in opportunity and the hierarchies between women.

Critiques of global human rights feminism, for example, have argued, firstly, that this particular form of 'transnational citizenship' must be understood within the context of global geo-politics and in particular, the hegemony of the United States (Grewal, 1999). It is noted, too, how 'global feminism' is reliant on a construction of a universal woman subject, where that universality is based on the projection of a shared victim status and a common sense of family or community responsibility (Sum, 2000). Within the prevailing liberal modernist paradigm that privileges certain kinds of rights and a perception of their acquisition as being evolutionary (as in first, second and third, etc. generations of rights), elite women in the powerful and less powerful Third World countries can then distinguish themselves from the abject women in the world who are, in these terms, ostensibly lacking in rights, more oppressed and subordinated within familial and cultural relations. Under the guise of a universal feminist solidarity, some women are thus constituted as objects of rescue, of rights campaigns and women's empowerment programmes while others are, relationally, constituted as agentic, 'global feminist subjects' (Kaplan, 2001). Mindry's (2001) work on international and intra-national relationships between women's NGOs and 'grassroots' women in South Africa, has demonstrated what might be called this 'matronizing' effect. The language of many of the official gender policy documents in South Africa positions rural African women in this victimist, 'othering' way, as the 'most oppressed', the 'poorest of the poor', thus linking them to these global constructions of 'Third World women'.

It is also the case that the claims and opportunities of postnational or transnational citizenship are very unevenly distributed across the population of South Africa. Access to transnational movement is mediated by race, class, heterosexual family forms and racist immigration policy. While some South African citizens can move with facility across national borders, can claim citizen rights in other nation-states, can emigrate and retain sentimental allegiances without obligations, can become part of South Africa's large diasporas with officially encouraged and beneficial economic ties, the majority of citizens are bound to the national territory and relate singularly as citizens, nationals and subjects of the

South African state. The filters of immigration and citizenship on South Africa's own geographical and political borders are inscribed by a different pattern of race, class and gender exclusion (Dodson, 2001). Transnational migration is located mostly in the Southern African region; it involves a high proportion of women refugees and interestingly evidences a 'feminization' of immigration to South Africa, phenomena which must be factored into critical reinterpretations of gendered national citizenship.

A central theme in the discussions of transnational citizenship concerns questions of membership, allegiance and identities of belonging as well as the sites of that membership. Lister (1997) and Yuval-Davis (1997) have been arguing that citizenship must be considered as a 'multi-tiered' or 'multi-layered' concept in acknowledgement of the contemporary situation in which 'states are not the only polities in which people are citizens, although they are the most powerful' (Yuval-Davis, 2002, p.45). As Yuval-Davis (1997b) interprets it, people are formally and informally citizens within various national, sub-, trans- and supra-national collectivities. They exist in a 'variety of co-operative and conflicting relationships which would differentially determine the positions and the access to resources of different people at different times' (Yuval-Davis, 1997b, p.22). While this definition captures the complexity of contemporary forms of citizenship, it also raises the question of how capacious a definition of citizenship can be while still retaining its distinctiveness and usefulness. How significant is a dimension of national belonging to the practice of citizenship, and what basis for national identity is most likely to promote active democratic citizenship? The more pertinent question here is how the centring of gender equality might reshuffle ways of understanding of these issues.

In the face of South Africa's history of deep social divisions and the ethno-nationalist mobilizations around the time of the political transition, the post-apartheid state has been actively engaged in the promotion of a national identity based on allegiance to the constitutional principles and adherence to a culture of rights. Specifically addressing the historic antagonisms and injury, this conception of identity includes an ethical principle of reconciliation and the ambiguous tenet of 'unity in diversity'. This is the official conception to which Enslin (2003) was referring. But also prominent as a discourse of national identity and bearing official government endorsement is that which draws on the notion of *ubuntu* (mentioned earlier) and African Renaissance. *Ubuntu* captures the idea of responsibility to community, claiming a legacy of African communal tradition while the African Renaissance refers to the political project of regeneration of African pride and prospects. These two conceptions of national identity, one emphasizing affinities based on shared political orientations and principles, the other emphasizing membership based on shared cultural understandings, resonate with the familiar normative dichotomy in citizenship theory of political versus cultural, civic versus ethnic forms.[10]

South African feminist activists have come down firmly in support of the former normative concept of citizenship for reasons which are apparent: political citizenship affirms gender equality where cultural citizenship posits women as subordinate to the interest of the nation. This position came out very clearly in the struggle to give primacy to gender equality over the cultural rights (specifically 'customary law') of patriarchally-governed African communities.

Yet, while the distinction between political and cultural citizenship provides a useful orientation for feminist political strategizing, the picture is not as clear-cut as these neat oppositions suggest. Firstly, the notion of a 'pure', civic citizenship based on abstract principles of rights and what Habermas has called 'constitutional patriotism' is a mythical one (Yack, 1999). Political citizenship is inevitably imbued with some sense of shared political culture and a common historical narrative. This is the case even where there is no major initiative underway to construct a national identity, as in contemporary South Africa and in other post-conflict or post-transition states. The official South African citizenship project very clearly and self-consciously incorporates elements that draw on and promote a sense of national-cultural belonging and shared history, those elements of sentiment, in other words, which are normally associated with cultural conceptions of citizenship. A central example here is the principle of national unity and reconciliation which supplied the ethos for the Truth and Reconciliation Commission. Retrieving an earlier argument about 'women' and gender as being integral to the symbolic and practical boundary-making of all imaginaries of political community, it is clear that 'women' and gender relations are more visible and symbolically significant than cultural or ethno-national conceptions of citizenship. However, constructions of 'women' and 'gender' are culturally significant in so-called political citizenship, too. As argued earlier, as categories and constructs they are equally invoked and implicated in the definitions of the parameters of membership in the civic nation – through population policy and immigration policy and in the assumptions embedded within social and 'gender' policy. Gender is thus arguably more insidiously interwoven with constitutionally-based notions of citizenship. However it emerges more legibly in state-sponsored projects of nation-building where these promote exclusive notions of belonging, of claims and obligations as well as normative concepts of citizenly virtue. An important example here is the way in the Truth and Reconciliation principles and process marginalized women even while drawing on cultural conceptions of the moral authority of 'mothers' for its legitimation just as it constituted an exclusionary definition of human rights violations, one which denied the gendered forms of women's experiences of apartheid's rule.

In the article cited previously, Enslin (2003) maintains that while the official South African conception of citizenship is a response to apartheid in many ways, it does not draw on a long tradition of citizenship, and is an emergent and as yet unsettled conception. An analytical focus on the making of gendered political subjects suggests another interpretation, one that detects a deeper continuity with the colonial and apartheid past in the debates about citizenship that are circulating today. One cannot necessarily assume that, even with the active promotion of citizenship education, a stable normative idea of citizenship will be established.

Rather, when the relationship of 'women' and gender to the bounding of national political community is taken into account one sees more potential volatility and contestation within conceptions of citizenship.

Marx (2002) sees an ominous cultural nationalism as being powerfully articulated in the discourse of *ubuntu*. As argued above, there is a popular conception of 'women' within discourses of gendered citizenship that resonates with the *ubuntu* idea of community responsibility. My argument is that there is an equivocality and ambiguity residing in the construct of 'women's citizenship', one that evinces an overlapping or slippage between women-as-citizens within the state and women-as-mothers or carers within the nation. It mirrors the conflation in everyday political discourse (and often in analytical literature too) of the two meanings of nation – as designating the political community organized through the state and as the cultural community of origin (Yack, 1999).

An important contemporary challenge therefore, for a feminist politics of citizenship in South Africa, is to discern how and when feminist discourses of citizenship, even as they invoke the language of rights, gender equality, women's empowerment, etc. are being implicated in state-formation and nation-building in ways that support the self-advancement projects of emergent ruling elites, and in ways that compromise the emancipatory possibilities of citizenship for the majority of women.

Conclusion: Beyond a Politics of Inclusion?

In the article cited at the beginning of this chapter, Yeatman (2001) notes that, although the idea of modern citizenship based on self-government has in some ways been undermined by contemporary transnational developments, in contexts where nation-building is still salient – as in post-apartheid South Africa – feminists should rightly pursue a politics of inclusion. In doing so, they seek to register women's bodies, ideas and demands in the process of transitional state formation and in public deliberations over what it might mean to be a citizen-subject in the new nation. In other words, Yeatman sees the classic-modern citizenship project in these circumstances as proffering a necessary and effective framing of citizenship politics for South African women and feminists.

There can be no question that an aggressive politics of inclusion on the part of feminist activists was extraordinarily effective in achieving not only the political presence of women and gender in the transition process and post-apartheid state, but also in informing emergent normative conceptions of citizenship, even if somewhat *post hoc*. Women's empowerment and gender equality have been entrenched as fundamental principles of government policy and the rather obscure ethic of 'non-sexism' has been constitutionally confirmed. The much-vaunted 'success story' of South African women in the transition can be accounted for in terms of this political strategy of inclusion, one that was based on a deliberately constructed unitary and undifferentiated identity category of 'women'. The question that is posed now, however, is whether that politics of inclusion and its modernist presumptions remain the most strategically viable and analytically valid from a democratic feminist perspective. Do transnational changes and challenges to the institution of citizenship call for a refinement of national feminist approaches? Is there more mileage to be had in 'the classical modern project of citizenship' or has the past decade of post-apartheid consolidation shifted the political terrain for feminist citizenship struggles in South Africa significantly beyond the constructive nation-building moment to which Yeatman was referring?

Several authors in this and other volumes have put forth cogent arguments for pushing for the substantiation of gender equality rights in the various sectors, proposing how that might be achieved and offering sober assessments of the obstacles and prospects for realization (e.g. Samuel, 2001; Friedman et al., 1999). In this chapter I have explored some more abstract conceptual ambiguities and paradoxes in conceptions of contemporary feminist citizenship, tracing the resonances of transnational feminist debates with old and new tensions in post-apartheid citizenship. Here I want merely to signal some of the more relevant shifts in the political context of citizenship in South Africa for these must inform responses to these questions.

The first is South Africa's adoption of a neo-liberal economic development strategy which has inevitably undermined the state's capacity to address social needs and deliver on gender equitable social programmes. Feminists have long been arguing that the provision of social rights is essential to the realization of citizenship for women in need. Secondly, the establishment of a culture of rights and the active promotion of new or reclaimed notions of personhood or dignity have been, at best uneven. More significantly these attempts have not positively transformed the daily quality of life for most South African women. Moreover, as discussed above, rights politics can increasingly be seen to be linked, in complex ways, to privilege and class formation, a recognition that in some parts of the world has fuelled arguments for eschewing rights claims in popular social-movements and propagating a discourse of social justice.

Finally, the achievements of the transitional politics of inclusion have had the effect of remapping the institutional and discursive 'playing field' of current struggles for 'women's citizenship'. 'Gender' categories are now inscribed in policy, entrenching constructs of 'women' and gender equality that are in some ways exclusionary; 'gender structures' have been put in place, ensuring that an elite of women and men are invested in their continuity.

What do such reconfigurations tell us about the limits and possibilities of a modernist conception of citizenship? One answer is provided by Ram (2000) in her discussion of the 'instabilities of rights discourses' in India. After revealing the ways in which Indian feminists' deployment of the politics of rights has been complicit in confirming, rather than challenging, class and caste privilege and in intensifying inter-communal struggles, Ram (2000) interestingly concludes that the best way to reveal the fault-lines of modernity, specifically its ultimate inability to address inequality and power hierarchies, is by pushing for the full realization of the promises of modernity, namely, citizenship, equality and rights. The contradictions will become more apparent, she argues, as those promises are pushed to their limits, through, as in South Africa for example, 'women, claiming their rights, as citizens'. It is difficult, however, to imagine today not only the mobilization of the same coherent constituency of 'women' that energized the *Women's Charter* Campaign but also the equivalent of that clear project of women's inclusion.

There are other scenarios and possibilities to be considered. Along with the formation of new elites in South Africa are increasing poverty levels and growing material disparities between the rich and poor. Disappointment in the unfulfilled promises of citizenship and disaffection with the ruling party and state for the failure to deliver on the perceived entitlements of that status could potentially make other less democratic forms of gendered political agency – those that can draw on 'tradition' or on the maternal authority accorded by many nationalist discourses – more attractive to certain women. This has certainly been the case in many other parts of the world where the more impoverished sectors – and in South Africa, these are largely female – have absorbed the effects of globalized market economies. Inhering in this situation are political possibilities too, but they involve moving away from a discourse that reproduces an undifferentiated and fixed category of 'women' as subject of the politics of citizenship. They suggest more fluidity in political identities, where some women might ally with other constituencies, not 'as women' but contingently identified as marginal, poor, homeless, regionally-based etc. in a differently gendered politics of citizenship, one that is transnational in its scope. I am suggesting, tentatively, that the zenith of the analytics and politics of 'women's citizenship' has been passed.

The implication of my discussion about the imbrication of gender and 'women' within imaginaries of national political community suggests a contrary reading from Yeatman's above. Moments of nation-building might constitute necessary and propitious spaces for feminist political involvement, but they are also times of caution, maybe even danger for a feminist project of citizenship. This is so, I argue, for a couple of reasons. Firstly, the category of 'women-as-citizen' that is mobilized in such moments is, as has been discussed, necessarily unitary but at the same time, erases – or at least is unable to address – difference that is internal to the very category. Secondly, in post-colonial contexts, the articulation of national identity is prone to the influence of nationalist discourses. As Werbner and Yuval-Davis (1999) point out: 'Both as a political imaginary and as a set of practices citizenship is caught, as we have seen, between the normalizing forces of modernity and the essentializing forces of nationalism and exclusion' (p.28). I have been arguing that the ambiguities in conceptions of 'women', of citizenship, subjects or rights and subjects of nations allow a play of meaning and political implications that are not adequately read or monitored for their potentially divergent political rationalities. As I have argued elsewhere (Manicom, 2001) even explicitly feminist projects, like that of interring 'gender equality' within practices and discourses of governance can be, and are mobilized for the self-representation of post-colonial nation-states as they display their progressive credentials for strategic and economic gains in the global arena. The language of women's rights, gender equality and women's empowerment – the language of democratic feminist citizenship, in other words – is today amenable to a range of political projects. The onus is therefore on feminists relentlessly to render visible and contestable the different makings of gendered political subjects, and the ways these inform and are integrated within policy, rights and political practices.

Notes

1. The *Women's Charter* is a manifesto of South African women's demands compiled from the results of a national campaign organized by the Women's National Coalition during the period of negotiations towards the transition. Its intention was both to mobilize women and to influence the first democratic elections and constitution-making process to take into account the specific issues and perspectives of women.

2. Amongst the feminist scholars propagating this view are Yuval-Davis (1997; 2002), Werbner and Yuval-Davis (1999); Pettman (1999); Yeatman (2001) and Sassen (2002; 2003).

3. I am using the singular to refer to feminism as a broad political project, embracing the differences within that project that cannot be reduced to different ideological positions or different feminist identities.

4. The close collaboration of feminist academics, activists and state agents in framing the gender politics of the transition period, is reflected in a certain congruency in the way in which 'women' and 'citizenship' are shaped as objects of theoretical discourse and in political debate. It could be argued, however, that this overlap is diminishing as the term 'gender', a core concept in feminist analytics, has been taken up discursively and institutionalized within a transnational discourse of governance, re-posed as administrative strategy (gender mainstreaming) and policy objective (gender programmes) (see Gouws, this volume; Manicom, 2001).

5. It should be noted here that this view differs from, but does not necessarily contradict Mamdani's (1996) influential distinction between citizens (as those bearing modernist political rights) and the ethnicized subjects of state-endorsed chieftaincies, a distinction that characterizes contemporary post-colonial African ruling systems. Mamdani's formulation is, of course, complicated when gender is taken into account for women have been arguably more and differently 'subject' than men within both modern citizenship and chiefly patriarchies in ways that are not commensurable nor can be measured in progressivist terms. (Gender cannot be understood in this context as separable, particularly from age.)

6. It is interesting to note (without knowing whether this was a considered political choice or not) how the name of the coalition – *Women's* National Coalition – discursively consolidates the primacy or defining place of 'women' in this politics. That the name of the coalition is a bit counter-intuitive to many observers, both from South Africa and beyond, is evident in the several unpublished and published mis-quoted references that I have encountered to a *National* Women's Coalition (e.g. Rosenthal 2001; Steyn 1998). Presumably such authors assume the more transnationally familiar form of a coalition of women that has national jurisdiction.

7. This notion of participation was a central theme in the *Reconstruction and Development*

Programme issued by the ANC and adopted by the Government of National Unity in 1995.

8. A consultative process of reform to bring elements of customary law into alignment with prevailing constitutional principles has been underway even since apartheid days, with more emphasis now being laid on a clearer notion of gender equality, on women's juridical status, rights to land and protection within family law.

9. See, for example, the *National Policy Framework for Women's Empowerment and Gender Equality*, issued by the Office on the Status of Women, Republic of South Africa.

10. Comaroff (2001) traces the persisting tension between these two conceptions in South Africa as an insidious legacy of the colonial project, conducted in the languages of rights and legality, to convert '"natives", simultaneously and contradictorily, into both right-bearing citizens and culture-bearing ethnic subjects' (p.62). Anti-apartheid opposition, both liberal democratic and nationalist, has equally been couched in the language of rights claims.

References

Ahmed, S. (1995), 'Deconstruction and the Law's Other: Toward a Feminist Theory of Embodied Legal Rights', *Social and Legal Studies*, 4, pp.55-73.

Alarcon, N., Kaplan, C. and Moallem, M. (1999), 'Introduction: Between Woman and Nation', in C. Kaplan, N. Alarcon and M. Moallem (eds.), *Between Woman and Nation: Nationalisms, Transnational Feminisms, and the State*, Duke University Press, Durham and London, pp.1-16.

Alexander, M.J. (1994), 'Not just (Any)Body Can be a Citizen: The Politics of Law, Sexuality and Postcoloniality in Trinidad and Tobago and the Bahamas', *Feminist Review*, pp.5-23.

Alexander, M.J. (1997), 'Erotic Autonomy as a Politics of Decolonization: An Anatomy of Feminist State Practice in the Bahamas Tourist Economy', in M.J. Alexander and C.T. Mohanty (eds.), *Feminist Genealogies, Colonial Legacies, Democratic Futures*, Routledge, New York, pp.63-100.

Brooks, A. (2000), 'Citizenship, identity and social justice: The intersection of feminist and post-colonial discourses', in M. Arnot and J-A. Dillabough (eds.), *Challenging Democracy: International Perspectives on Gender, Education and Citizenship*, Routledge, London and New York, pp.41-57.

Brown, W. (1995), *States of Injury: Power and Freedom in Late Modernity*, Princeton University Press, Princeton, New Jersey.

Brown, W. (2002), 'Suffering the Paradoxes of Rights', in W. Brown and J. Halley (eds.), *Left Legalism/Left Critique*, Duke University Press, Durham, pp.420-434.

Carver, T. (1998), 'Sexual Citizenship: Gendered and de-gendered narratives', in T. Carver and V. Mottier (eds.), *Politics of Sexuality: Identity, Gender and Citizenship*, Routledge, New York and London, pp.13-24.

Cock, J. and Bernstein, A. (2002), *Melting Pots and Rainbow Nations: Conversations about Difference in the United States and South Africa*, University of Illinois Press, Urbana and Chicago.

Comaroff, J. (1995), 'The Discourse of Rights in Colonial South Africa: Subjectivity, Sovereignty, Modernity', in A. Sarat and T.R. Kearns (eds.), *Identities, Politics, Rights*, University of Michigan Press, Ann Arbor, pp.193-236.

Comaroff, J.L. (2001), 'Reflections on the colonial state, in South Africa and elsewhere: fragments, fact and fictions', in A. Zegeye (ed.), *Social Identities in a New South Africa: After Apartheid, Volume One*, Kwela Books, Cape Town, pp.37-80.

Comaroff, J. and Comaroff, J.L. (2000), 'Millenial Capitalism: First Thoughts on a Second Coming', *Public Culture*, 12(2), pp.291-343.

Comaroff, J. and Comaroff, J.L. (2001), 'Naturing the Nation: aliens, Apocalypse and the Postcolonial State', *Journal of Southern African Studies*, 27(3) pp.627-651.

Cruikshank, B. (1999), *The Will to Empower: democratic citizens and other subjects*, Cornell University Press, Ithaca.

Deveaux, M. (2003), 'Liberal Constitutions and Traditional Cultures: The South African Customary Law Debate', *Citizenship Studies*, 7, pp.161-180.

Dhaliwal, A.K. (1996), 'Can the Subaltern Vote? Radical Democracy, Discourses of Representation and Rights, and Questions of Race', in D. Trend (ed.), *Radical Democracy: Identity, Citizenship, and the State*, Routledge, New York and London, pp.42-61.

Dillabough, J-A., and Arnot, M. (2000), 'Feminist political frameworks: New approaches to the study of gender, citizenship and education', in M. Arnot and J-A. Dillabough (eds.), *Challenging Democracy: International Perspectives on Gender, Education and Citizenship*, London and New York: Routledge, pp.21-40.

Dodson, B. (2001), 'Discrimination by Default? Gender Concerns in South African Migration Policy', *Africa Today*, 48, pp.73-89.

Enslin, P. (2000), 'Defining a civic agenda: Citizenship and gender equality in post-apartheid education', in M. Arnot and J-A. Dillabough (eds.), *Challenging Democracy: International Perspectives on Gender, Education and Citizenship*, Routledge, London and New York, pp.297-311.

Enslin, P. (2003), 'Citizenship Education in South Africa', *Cambridge Journal of Education*, 33, pp.73-83.

Fernandes, L. (1997), *Producing Workers: The Politics of Gender, Class and Culture in the Calcutta Jute Mills*, University of Pennsylvania Press, Philadelphia.

Friedman, M. et al. (1999), *Translating Commitments into Policy and Practice*, Agenda and Africa Gender Institute Monograph.

Gedalof, I. (1999), *Against Purity: Rethinking identity in Indian and Western Feminisms*, Routledge, London and New York.

Grewal, I. (1999), '"Women's Rights as Human Rights": Feminist Practices, Global Feminism, and Human Rights Regimes in Transnationality', *Citizenship Studies*, 3, pp.337-354.

Gouws, A. (1999), 'Beyond equality and difference: the politics of women's citizenship', *Agenda*, No.40, pp.54-58.

Hassim, S. (1999), 'From presence to power: women's citizenship in a new democracy', *Agenda*, No.40, pp.6-17.

Hindess, B. (2002), 'Neo-liberal Citizenship', *Citizenship Studies*, 6, pp.127-143.

Isin, E.F. and Turner, B.S. (2002), 'Citizenship Studies: An Introduction', in E.F. Isin and B.S. Turner (eds.), *Handbook of Citizenship Studies*, Sage Publications, London, pp.1-10.

Kaplan, C. (2001), 'Hillary Rodham Clinton's Orient: Cosmopolitan Travel and Global Feminist Subjects', *Meridians: feminism, race, transnationalism*, 2, pp.219-240.

Klaaren, J. (2000), 'Post-Apartheid Citizenship in South Africa', in T.A. Aleinikoff and D. Klusmeyer (eds.), *From Migrants to Citizens: Membership in a Changing World*, Carnegie Endowment for International Peace, Washington, pp.221-252.

Lewis, D. (1999), 'Gender myths and citizenship in two autobiographies by South African women', *Agenda*, No.40, pp.38-44.

Lister, R. (1997), *Citizenship: Feminist Perspectives*, New York University Press, New York.

McClure, K. (1992), 'On the Subject of Rights: Pluralism, Plurality and Political Identity', in C. Mouffe (ed.), *Dimensions of Radical Democracy*, Verso, London and New York, pp.108-127.

McClure, K. (1995), 'Taking Liberties in Foucault's Triangle: Sovereignty, Discipline, Governmentality, and the Subject of Rights', in A. Sarat and T.R. Kearns (eds.), *Identities, Politics and Rights*, University of Michigan Press, Ann Arbor, pp.149-192.

Mamdani, M. (1996), *Citizen and Subject: Contemporary Africa and the Legacy of Late Colonialism*, Princeton University Press, Princeton, New Jersey.

Manicom, L. (2001), 'Globalising "gender" in – or as – governance? Questioning the terms of local translations', *Agenda*, No.48, pp.6-21.

Marx, C. (2002), 'Ubu and Ubuntu: on the dialectics of apartheid and nation building', *Politikon*, 29, pp.49-69.

Mayoux, L. (1998), 'Gender Accountability and the NGOs: Avoiding the Black Hole', in C. Miller and S. Razavi (eds.), *Missionaries and Mandarins: Feminist Engagements with Development Institutions*, IT Publishers, London, pp.172-193.

Meintjes, S. (1998), 'Gender, nationalism and transformation', in R. Wildford and R.L. Miller (eds.), *Women, Ethnicity and Nationalism*, Routledge, London and New York, pp.62-86.

Mindry, D. (2001), 'Nongovernmental Organization, "Grassroots", and the Politics of Virtue', *Signs: Journal of Women in Culture and Society*, 26, pp.1187-1211.

Narayan, U. (1997), 'Towards a Feminist Vision of Citizenship: Rethinking the Implications of Dignity, Political Participation and Nationality', in M. Shanley and U. Narayan (eds.), *Reconstructing Political Theory: Feminist Perspectives*, Polity Press, Cambridge, pp.48-67.

Peberdy, S. (2001), 'Imagining Immigration: Inclusive Identities and Exclusive Policies in Post-1994 South Africa', *Africa Today*, 48, pp.15-32.

Perry, R.W. and Obiora, L. Amede (2002), 'Bridging False Divides: Towards a Transnational Politics of Gender', in B.E. Hernandez-Truyol (ed.), *Moral Imperialism: A Critical Anthology*, New York University Press, New York and London, pp.255-268.

Pettman, J.J. (1999), 'Globalisation and the Gendered Politics of Citizenship', in N. Yuval-Davis and P. Werbner (eds.), *Women, Citizenship and Difference*, Zed Books, London, pp.207-220.

Radcliffe, S. and Westwood, S. (1996), *Remaking the Nation: Place, Identity and Politics in Latin America*, Routledge, London and New York.

Ram, K. (2000), 'The state and the women's movement: Instabilities in the discourse of "rights" in India', in A. Hilsdon et al. (eds.), *Human Rights and Gender Politics: Asia Pacific perspectives*, Routledge, New York, pp. 60-82.

Ranchod-Nilsson, S. and Tetreault, M.A. (2000), 'Gender and Nationalism: moving beyond fragmented conversations', in S. Ranchod-Nilsson and M.A. Tetreault (eds.), *Women, States and Nationalism: At home in the nation?* Routledge, London and New York, pp.1-17.

Rosenthal, M. (2001), 'Danger Talk: Race and Feminist Empowerment in the New South Africa', in F.W. Twine and K.M. Blee (eds.), *Feminism and Antiracism: International Struggles for Justice*, New York University Press, New York, pp.97-124.

Ross, F.C. (2003), *Bearing Witness: Women and the Truth and Reconciliation Commission in South Africa*, Pluto Press, London.

Samuel, S. (2001), 'Achieving Equality – how far have women come?' *Agenda*, No.47, pp.21-33.

Sassen, S. (2002), 'Toward Post-National and Denationalized Citizenship', in E.F. Isin and B.S. Turner (eds.), *Handbook of Citizenship Studies*, Sage Publications, London, Thousand Oaks, pp.277-291.

Sassen, S. (2003), 'The Participation of States and Citizens in Global Governance', *Indiana Journal of Global Legal Studies*, 10, pp.5-28.

Schild, V. (1998), 'New Subjects of Rights? Women's Movements and the Construction of Citizenship in the "New Democracies"', in S.E. Alvarez, E. Dagnino and A. Escobar (eds.), *Cultures of Politics, Politics of Cultures: Re-visioning Latin American Social Movements*, Boulder, Westview Press, pp.93-117.

Scott, J.W. (1999), 'Some Reflections on Gender and Politics', in M.M. Feree, J. Lorber and B.B. Hess (eds.), *Revisioning Gender*, Sage Publications, London, pp.70-96.

Scott, J.W. (2002), 'Feminist Reverberations', *Differences: A Journal of Feminist Cultural Studies*, 13, pp.1-23.

Seidman, G.W. (1999), 'Gendered Citizenship: South Africa's Democratic Transition and the Construction of a Gendered State', *Gender and Society*, 13, pp.287-307.

Seidman, G.W. (2000), 'Gendered Politics in Transition: South Africa's Democratic Transitions in the Context of Global Feminism', in J. Jenson and B.D.S. Santos (eds.), *Globalizing Institutions: Case studies in regulation and innovation*, Ashgate, Aldershot, Burlington, pp.121-144.

Siim, B. (2000), *Gender and Citizenship: Politics and Agency in France, Britain and Denmark*, Cambridge University Press, Cambridge.

Stevens, J. (1999), *Reproducing the State*, Princeton University Press, Princeton.

Steyn, M. (1998), 'A New Agenda: Restructuring Feminism in South Africa', *Women's Studies International Forum*, 21, pp.41-52.

Stivens, M. (2000), 'Introduction: Gender politics and the reimagining of human rights in the Asia-Pacific', in A-M. Hilsdon, M. Macintyre, V. Mackie and M. Stivens (eds.), *Human Rights and Gender Politics: Asia-Pacific perspectives*, Routledge, New York, pp.1-36.

Sum, N-L. (2000), 'From politics of identity to politics of complexity: A possible research agenda for feminist politics/movements across time and space', in S. Ahmed, J. Kilby, C. Lury, M. McNeil and B. Skaggs (eds.), *Transformations: Thinking Through Feminism*, Routledge, London and New York, pp.131-144.

Van Huyssteen, E. (2000), 'The Constitutional Court and the Redistribution of Power in South Africa: Towards Transformative Constitutionalism', *African Studies*, 59, pp.245-265.

Walker, R.B.J. (1999), 'Citizenship after the Modern Subject', in K. Hutchings and R. Dannreuther (eds.), *Cosmopolitan Citizenship*, MacMillan Press, Houndsmills, London, pp.171-200.

Werbner, P. and Yuval-Davis, N. (1999), 'Introduction: Women and the New Discourse of Citizenship', in N. Yuval-Davis and P. Werbner (eds.), *Women, Citizenship and Difference*, Zed Books, London, pp.1-38.

Wilson, R.A. (2001), *The Politics of Truth and Reconciliation in South Africa: Legitimizing the Post-Apartheid State*, Cambridge University Press, Cambridge.

Yack, B. (1999), 'The Myth of the Civic Nation', in R. Beiner (ed.), *Theorizing Nationalism*, State University of New York, Albany, pp.103-118.

Yeatman, A. (2001), 'Feminism and Citizenship', in N. Stevenson (ed.), *Culture and Citizenship*, Sage, London, pp.138-152.

Yuval-Davis, N. (1997a), *Gender and Nation*, Sage Publications, London, Thousand Oaks and New Delhi.

Yuval-Davis, N. (1997b), 'Women, Citizenship and Difference', *Feminist Review*, 57, pp.4-27.

Yuval-Davis, N. (2002), 'Some reflections on the questions of citizenship and anti-racism', in F. Anthias and C. Lloyd (eds.), *Rethinking Anti-racism: from theory to practice*, Routledge, London and New York, pp.44-59.

PART II
DECONSTRUCTING THE
DISCOURSE OF CITIZENSHIP

Chapter 2

Nationalism Displaced: Citizenship Discourses in the Transition

Shireen Hassim

Introduction

Between 1990 and 1994 South Africa underwent a significant political transition
from apartheid to democracy. In the course of this transition, the women's
movement also underwent a significant shift, moving from the margins of formal
politics to the centre and impacting on the debate about and the formation of the
new institutions of democracy. In this chapter I address one aspect of this shift,
focusing on the change in the arena of political discourse. I argue that the transition
facilitated a shift away from nationalism as the overarching framework within and
against which women's political identities were conceived and strategies
articulated, to a discourse of citizenship that has implicitly shaped subsequent
women's movement strategies. The *nature* of that transition – that is, the creation
of a liberal democratic state in which citizenship rights were accorded irrespective
of race, gender or ethnicity – unexpectedly allowed feminists to articulate an
agenda of equality that unseated nationalist formulations of women's political
roles. Demands for equality, representation and inclusion in decision-making of
women that had previously been expressed primarily within the ANC were
expanded to the political system as a whole on the grounds of democracy.

Political discourse is important for women's movements. It denotes the
ideological space available to women's organizations to articulate aims and goals
that are distinct from those of the dominant resistance movements (Molyneux,
1998; Jenson, 1987). Molyneux argues that the authority to define goals, priorities
and actions may not always come from within the women's movement but may
derive from external sources, even when there is a separate women's movement
(Molyneux, 1998, p.226). That external authority, in South Africa, derived from
the national liberation movement which to a large extent had the legitimate power
to determine the goals, strategies and tactics of progressive women's organizations.
Jane Jenson has also pointed to the importance of the issue of discursive authority
in her study of the French women's movement. She has argued that the prospects
of women's movements are affected not only by the context of institutions and
alliances in the external political environment but also by the 'universe of political
discourse' within which the movement acts. She defines the universe of political

discourse as comprising 'beliefs about the ways politics should be conducted, and the kinds of conflicts resolvable through political processes' (Jenson, 1987, p.65). The universe of political discourse delineates what is considered to be 'political' as opposed to private, religious or economic. This universe functions at any single point in time by setting boundaries to political action and by limiting the range of actors that are accorded the status of legitimate participants, the range of issues considered to be included in the realm of meaningful political debate, the policy alternatives feasible for implementation, and the alliance strategies available for achieving change. She points out that the universe of political discourse is a political construct that is determined by ideological struggle and changes in response to 'social change, to political action, and to struggles by organizations and individuals seeking to modify the restrictive boundaries of the political imagination' (Jenson, 1987, p.67). Women's organizations' demands are shaped only in part by internal debates about what is desirable; they are also and sometimes more influentially determined by what can be achieved within the prevailing discourse. Jenson argues that women's claims are likely to remain marginalized within a private realm of maternal and familial roles unless there is a change in elite consciousness such that dominant political elites come to see women as citizens rather than as representatives of children or the family.

Taken together, the arguments of Molyneux and Jenson suggest that in the South African context the discursive shifts in the broad political environment have the power to shape the ways in which interests and identities are articulated within the women's movement, although this impact might be subtle. In this chapter I explore the implications of the shift away from the authoritative discourse of national liberation to one of citizenship. Nationalism, as many feminist authors have recognized, has had a dual-edged impact on post-colonial women's movements. On the one hand, women activists were able to leverage greater power for women within the nationalist framework through the privileging of motherhood as the central political identity for women – i.e. by mobilizing women in ways that were consistent with the gendered role definition on which nationalism is predicated. On the other hand, the emphasis on nationalism marginalized alternative discourses, in particular those of feminism. The opening up of fundamental questions about the nature of the new political order in South Africa offered the opportunity for women to insert their claims for women's rights into the institutional fabric of the new democracy on grounds other than nationalism. The key questions of the transition – suffrage and the organization of party political competition, the institutional form of the new democracy, and the key values of the Constitution – all opened avenues for women's organizations to consider the ways in which the nature of women's citizenship might be conceived of as distinct from that of men.

As Jenson (1995) has argued, citizenship discourses can offer an enabling environment for women as they allow women's claims to be disentangled from those of 'the people'. In disentangling women's citizenship from that of 'the nation', women's organizations articulated concerns about both the formal and transformative aspects of citizenship. On the one hand, the relative absence of women in positions of decision-making in the state and political parties propelled women's organizations into an intense focus on how formal representation would be structured. On the other hand, the notion of substantive citizenship that underpinned the demands of women in the African National Congress (ANC), the dominant organization within the new Women's National Coalition (WNC), went beyond a call for simple inclusion in the formal political institutions of democracy. The Women's Charter for Effective Equality, a framing document developed by the WNC, argued for the recognition of the diversity of women's needs as well as the specificity of women's as opposed to men's needs (WNC, 1994). The WNC played an important role in supporting the insertion of the socio-economic rights clause in the Constitution that placed the burden of providing fairly expanded social security provisions (e.g. according citizens the right to housing and health care) on the state (Liebenberg, 1999). More importantly, the shift to discourses of citizenship dislodged the historical subordination of women's rights within those of the nation as a whole, allowing women's organizations to articulate specific needs of different constituencies of women. For example, the emphasis on citizenship allowed women to argue for the right to equality to be specified in the Bill of Rights, and for affirmative action mechanisms to include attention to gender equity.

The emphasis on citizenship also opened up new ways about thinking about women's political participation. On the one hand, citizenship highlights the importance of women's participation in the institutions of democracy – that is, in the formal avenues through which citizens' participation is structured – and, through the exercise of affirmative action, to ensure women's access to decision-making forums. On the other hand, while democracy confers on citizens the right to participate, the conditions for the effective exercise of those rights are set not only by formal institutions but also by the nature of the linkages between state and civil society. Citizenship can often be exercised at least as effectively, if not more so, through participation in social movements outside the state that seek to articulate interests of different groups of citizens autonomously from political parties. This kind of citizenship participation, outside of the formal constraints of party political loyalties and ideological constraints, can challenge the ruling party's definition of policy priorities, offer alternatives and exert pressure for accountability of governments to citizens.

The freeing of the conventional political bounds of organizations – the shift away from old alliances and enmities to new possibilities of alliance in relation to the negotiations process – also created new strategies for women's organizations. As in other transitional situations, the transition to democracy in South Africa propelled women's organizations into alliances across class and party lines that would have been politically unthinkable before political liberalization. A strategic and independent alliance of women, the Women's National Coalition, acted as a pressure group to lobby for extended political rights for women – not just the right to vote, but the right to participate at the highest levels of decision-making. Affirmative action for women was successfully mooted as a mechanism to overcome social and cultural obstacles to women's participation, at least within the dominant political party, and gender representation became a measure of the inclusiveness of the new democracy. In addition, a new set of institutions was created to mediate the implementation of formal commitments of government to gender equality. Women's political and social rights as citizens were firmly placed on the table of the new political order.

The Demand for Inclusion and Representation

In April 1992 the Women's National Coalition (WNC) was launched as a broad front of seventy organizations and eight regional coalitions. The initial mandate of the WNC was to carry out a programme for a period of twelve months, from April 1992 to April 1993, although the mandate was later extended until June 1994. The WNC constitution provided for three categories of participation: national women's organizations, national organizations that included women members and regional coalitions of women's organizations. The organizations that affiliated differed in size, ideology and organizational culture and few could be characterized as feminist in the sense of actively foregrounding issues of gender equality. The WNC had the single purpose of drafting a Women's Charter of Equality, gathering together the demands of individual women as well as women's organizations.

The strategic impetus for an alliance between diverse women's organizations was presented by the political parties' apparent disdain for their women's structures' demands for representation in the multi-party negotiations. In the first round of negotiations (the Congress for a Democratic South Africa, CODESA) in 1992, all political parties negotiating South Africa's transition to democracy selected all-male teams. The omission of women lit a spark that had until then been flickering only faintly. In an unprecedented action, leading members of the ANC Women's League wrote to the press demanding that the ANC address its failure to include women, while simultaneously exerting pressure at internal meetings of the party. By March 1992, the issue had become more widespread, with Helen Suzman, matriarch of the Democratic Party and for thirty years one of a handful of women in the apartheid parliament, castigating both her party and CODESA. An advertisement demanding greater participation of women was placed in the newspapers by a wide range of groups and individuals, from the principals of several universities to senior women in political parties. There could be little doubt that women's marginalization from politics was being challenged as never before. This groundswell of anger fed into the meetings across party-political lines to discuss the formation of a coalition and the common interest it highlighted, while minimal in itself, made the new political formation come alive.

The WNC was a significant step towards the formation of a political movement that was driven by women rather than by the exigencies of men in leadership and its existence contributed to the sense of women as a political force in their own right. For all the differences among women, not least those of political ideology, the initial exclusion of women from decision-making about the shape of the new democracy highlighted an obvious collective interest for all politically active women. More clearly than ever before, exclusion served to distinguish women as a group and to sharpen the awareness of disparities in opportunities for representation in decision-making of women and men. In demanding inclusion the

WNC was using the political opportunity offered by the debate among negotiators on the Bill of Rights, and in particular the promise that these debates would, as they had in Latin America, provide an 'opening for new issues and new ways of doing politics' (Jacquette and Wolchik, 1998; see also Albertyn, 1994; Schneider, 1991).

An inclusive strategy was indeed highly rational in the context of the political transition underway in the country. As various studies of transition have shown, the degree of inclusion – who gets a place at the table – shapes both the nature and scope of institutions under negotiation as well as their long-term legitimacy. Formal processes of negotiation tend to favour political and social groupings that are already organized at national level, or have access to national actors. Poorly organized and resourced organized groupings, such as women and rural poor, tend to be absent from institutional decision-making processes (Waylen, 1994). In the multi-party negotiations in South Africa, the ANC was seen to represent poor and working class people as its main constituency. Its alliance with the South African Communist Party (SACP) and Congress of South African Trade Unions (COSATU) appeared to ensure that constitutional and institutional mechanisms that would facilitate the eradication of both racial and class inequalities would be central to the negotiations. However, women were less obviously represented as a constituency by the major political actors, despite the ANC's well-developed history of recognizing women's demands. Worryingly for feminists, there were powerful forces aligned to the ANC that were actively hostile to the notion of gender equality. The Congress of Traditional Leaders of South Africa, for example, sought to protect their traditional powers to allocate land and resources in areas under their control and viewed women's claims for equality as undermining this agenda. Organizations such as the Rural Women's Movement, on the other hand, wanted to democratize these decision-making procedures and, in particular, give women control over the land which they worked. As this chapter will show, women's participation in the constitutional negotiations tempered, if not completely undermined, the formal power of conservative forces such as Congress of Traditional Leaders of South Africa.

The issue of inclusion, however, went beyond the simple demand of one interest group for special consideration and protections. I would argue that it constituted an implicit questioning of the extent to which non-elite groups could expect that democracy per se would increase their access to power. Some analysts of democratic politics have regarded demands for inclusion as full and equal citizens as symbolic of a fundamental challenge to the legitimacy of democracy (Young, 2000, p.6). The equal right to participate was the basis from which to launch a broader questioning of the extent to which suffrage on its own would reduce deeply embedded gender inequalities. There was a very early recognition among many activists schooled in socialist politics of the trade union movement and the SACP that formal representation at the multi-party negotiations would not guarantee effective representation, and that inclusion might indeed become a form of co-optation into the existing rules and parameters of the political system. Nevertheless representation, imperfect though it may be for ensuring full citizenship, was recognized as an essential precondition for deeper inclusion in debates about the nature of the new democracy.

The WNC did not see inclusion in terms of 'becoming equal to men'. That is, there was no assumption on the part of the WNC's leadership (although there may have been on the part of some constituents) that the men's 'political world' was unproblematic or even coherent in itself. The strategy of inclusion aimed to create the political space for women to articulate a broader notion of citizenship, and to define the content of citizenship in ways that recognized the plurality of interests in society. It was meant to broaden the substantive content of citizenship beyond the class and race interests initially represented at the multi-party negotiations.

From the outset, the WNC worked with a sophisticated organizational notion of the nature of a women's movement. Apartheid highlighted graphically the distinctions between women; the racial structuring of all social relations meant that the illusion of sisterhood never seriously took hold in South Africa. The white women's suffrage movement, for example, was successful in 1930 precisely because it allowed the Hertzog government to reduce the importance of the few remaining black voters in the Cape Province (Walker, 1991). By their complicity in this political manoeuvre, white women placed their racial and class concerns above any solidarity between women. For decades afterwards, there was little political trust between white and black women except in organizations where black leadership was established and accepted. Given this fractured history of women's politics in South Africa, and above all the powerful sense in women's organizations associated with the ANC and the Pan Africanist Congress that women's struggles could not be separated from other political struggles, the WNC never assumed the existence of a 'sisterhood' (Meintjes, 1996). Indeed, right at the beginning, the WNC argued that it was an organization based on solidarity in pursuit of a narrow agenda. Political differences were acute: there was no common language in which to speak of women's needs, particularly as the potentially 'common' discourse of feminism was itself highly contested. As a result, while the mandate of the WNC slowly widened to include issues of violence against women, it was always understood that the terrain of common purpose was very narrow.

Perhaps surprisingly, in this context, the differences within the WNC that threatened to completely undermine the coalition were not expressed in racial but in ideological terms. Indeed, the concerns with racial difference and with the politics of representation within the women's movement that dominated gender debates during 1991 and 1992 – so completely that one commentator suggests that for feminism it was 'a point of no return' (Bonnin, 1996, p.384) – were overshadowed by questions relating to the extent of the demand for equality. As the following discussion on the Charter Campaign will show, the different positions on this demand cannot be categorized along racial lines – participants of all races are to be found on all sides of the debate – but are rather a reflection of broader ideological differences. Nor, indeed, can the Charter be read as the product of white women's interests despite the fact that the drafting team was predominantly white. While racial (and other) differences may certainly shape the ways in which political interests are defined, the relationship between racial identity and political interest is by no means axiomatic.

Equality Debates in the Charter Campaign

In its broadest conception, the Coalition was to be unified through the Charter Campaign, intended both to be a mobilizing and educating (consciousness-raising) tool, as well as a concrete set of demands to be used at the level of national politics. Some argued that it should be attached as an appendix to the new Constitution, as a form of Bill of Rights for women. The idea of a Charter had enormous symbolic and ideological currency that placed women's contemporary demands into an organizational and historical context of the Freedom Charter and the Women's Charter of the 1950s. Indeed, the charterist orientation of the WNC made some affiliates uneasy as it gave pre-eminence to the ANC tradition within the WNC. During the 1980s, the term 'Charterist' signalled broad affiliation to the goals of the ANC, and polarized activists on the left into different ideological factions ('workerist', 'black consciousness', etc.) (Hudson, 1986). It was therefore by no means an inclusive label, even for progressive women activists. The ANC Women's League (ANCWL) was at pains to emphasize that a 'women's charter' was envisaged, not an 'ANC charter'. This was also an important distinction for Inkatha Freedom Party members, who were uneasy about the Women's Brigade of the Party joining a coalition in which the ANC was dominant. Initially the DP and the NP also rejected the idea of a Women's Charter for its organizational associations, while the Afrikaner organization Kontak and the Women's Bureau rejected the 'political' nature of the term (Interview with Sheila Meintjes, 10 March 2000). Nevertheless, the liberal political party, the DP, endorsed the idea of a Women's Charter as part of a rights-based approach to the transition (Democratic Party, 1991).

The Charter Campaign – dubbed 'Operation Big Ears' – was an ambitious proposal. It was envisaged that one hundred fieldworkers would begin focus group discussions with women across the country over a period of three months. This process would identify both issues that women had in common as well as their divergent interests. It would provide the information for the WNC's strategic mobilization, as well as politicize women about their oppression, and would link grassroots-level politics to national processes. Most significantly, the Charter would be the basis of the demands of the WNC in the constitutional negotiations, lending the organization unquestionable political credibility in a context where women's demands for representation were constantly denigrated.

In practice, however, the two levels of politics were not easily brought together. Conceived, at least by some within the Coalition, as a participatory process, the drafting of the Charter represented a form of politics that had a longer term vision, that required some degree of organizational patience, flexibility and responsiveness to the sensitivities and constraints of including unorganized women who may be resistant to political discussions. On the other hand, interventions in national level negotiations required a different form of flexibility – the ability to identify opportunities for lobbying and to respond at short notice, without extensive consultation and education building and often drawing on the technical expertise of academics and professionals rather than 'knowledge from below'. Indeed, very shortly after the formation of the WNC, the day-to-day work of the Coalition was devolved from the National Interim Committee to a small Working Committee in the head office.

Ironically, while Democratic Party and National Party women were persuaded that the Charter would be an important statement of intent and addendum to the Constitution, despite its ANC associations, it was harder to convince feminist activists within the ANC alliance that a focus on formal and constitutional politics was appropriate. Certainly, for the women from white political parties and women's groups, staying within the WNC, even despite its problems, reflected a political pragmatism. It was clear that there was little future in a women's movement without the ANC. To a significant degree, the alliance with ANC women activists allowed them a space and voice in national politics which they lacked given the serious inattention to gender issues and to women's political capabilities in their own parties.

For internal activists, tutored in the participatory politics of the trade union movement and women's organizations of the 1980s, the emphasis on the constitutional negotiations was problematic. Their unease stemmed from the perceived narrowness of a rights-based approach to politics, particularly one which emphasized the achievement of formal equality as the central ambition. There were competing discourses and repertoires of struggle during the 1980s, even within the United Democratic Front-affiliated women's organizations. Discourses of human rights – the assertion of the demands of civic and women's organizations in terms of rights to citizenship and equality (Seekings, 2000) – coexisted with liberatory discourses that emphasized radical transformations in social and economic relations. Although many internal United Democratic Front-aligned activists had been part of the Charterist tradition, with its emphasis on inalienable rights, there had always been contestation about the ability of rights discourses to provide a vehicle for altering power relations. Activists honed in the struggles of the United Women's Congress in the Western Cape, for example, placed a great emphasis on the value of organizational depth, participatory decision-making and grassroots democracy. By contrast rights discourses, with their emphases on the state and on the individual, appeared to ignore the problems of the extent to which women would be able to *exercise* their rights in the context of economic marginalization and cultural subordination. For some women members of the ANC, the very idea of a coalition undermined the radical content of the liberation movement's demands. These concerns were also shared by feminist activists based in the trade unions who had stayed out of alliance politics in the 1980s, seeing in these struggles only the possibility for limited liberal democratic ideals.

For these feminists, an equality clause in the constitution was not so much an achievement as a weapon to be used in the struggle against women's subordination and, as such, strategic energies should not be exhausted by the process of engaging the constitutional negotiators. Their primary emphasis was on the mobilization of women through a process of political education and empowerment. The transition offered a political context for heightened mobilization and an opportunity to raise the level of political consciousness among women. Pregs Govender, the Project Manager for the WNC, says that in her view, the WNC 'started out as more than about the Constitution. I was told to conceptualize (the Charter) campaign in my office. But that is not how I worked. I wanted to go out and meet women, to hear their views, to build the regions' (Interview, 19 January 2001).

The differences between, on the one hand, a rights-based struggle focused on impacting on the constitutional process and, on the other, the opportunities presented by the transition for the creation of a strong social movement of women with the long-term aim of transforming the gender relations of power threatened to destroy the coalition. Debbie Budlender, research coordinator of the WNC, argues that 'I didn't recognize the importance of the Constitution. I didn't think that writing a whole lot of things on paper necessarily meant change ... I didn't see the constitutional thing as the goal, I [was focused on] letting people be heard' (quoted in Abrams, 2000, p.11). In part, this comment signified a crucial tension within the WNC – not between ideologically opposed affiliates and certainly not between black and white women but within the democratic tradition and, in some cases, even more narrowly within the ANC, over the key objectives of the Coalition, over organizational style and over the ways in which citizenship was to be understood.

The conflicts over direction, content and style of the Charter Campaign threatened to derail Operation Big Ears completely, leading to resignations and public disagreements. In attempting to define a strategy to collect women's demands for the Charter, feminists allied with the transformative agenda sought to develop a participatory strategy that would reach the most marginalized women. Eventually these differences were resolved by the formation of a Research Supervisory group that was mandated to oversee the Charter Campaign. At a National Strategy Workshop in June 1993, to which each region sent two delegates, five key themes were identified as the core around which to build a national campaign: women's legal status; women's access to land, resources and water; violence against women; health; and work.

The draft Charter, based on individual submissions, focus group reports and demands made at mass meetings, was finally put together by a small team during 'forty-eight sleepless hours', fine-tuned at a Steering Committee meeting and presented before the final WNC Congress in February 1994. The Charter was finally adopted in June 1994. While recognizing a plurality of interests, the Women's Charter did not assume that all interests were equal. There was a strong emphasis on the historical processes of exclusion and exploitation which produced differences among women, and this historical understanding formed the basis for placing the needs of poor, especially rural, women as a priority. It demanded a consideration of the socio-economic needs of women – access to safe water, access to land, housing, and the like. In so doing, it put on the table the need to deal with issues of substantive equality in the initial framing of the constitution.

The most bitter differences over the Charter within the WNC were those between the Democratic Party and the ANC. These differences centred on the understanding of equality, the value of state intervention in the struggle for gender equality, and the extent to which the Charter should address inequalities in the private sphere – in effect, how the public sphere was to be delineated. The Democratic Party offered a vision in which political rights to equality and participation were to be guaranteed and the extent of state intervention in the structural bases of women's disadvantages were to be minimized. The ANC, on the other hand, argued that social rights should underpin the achievement of political equality. This approach was underscored by the parallel demand by the ANC for a constitutional clause protecting citizens' socio-economic rights. The DP argued against proposals that sought to address the economic basis of women's subordination and was in favour of limiting the Charter to 'what a government can do' and 'leave out' the private sphere altogether (WNC, 1994). The inclusion of Articles 8 ('Family Life and Partnerships') and 9 ('Custom, culture and religion') was opposed on the grounds that the state should not legislate these areas. The Democratic Party also disagreed in principle with the demand for affirmative action, and specifically the idea of 'equal representation' of women in the public sphere, preferring instead to call for equal *access* to representation. The party was concerned that a wide-ranging Charter would lose focus if it 'simply takes on board problems and policy areas that do not specifically spring from the subordinate status of women ... We are then reduced simply to a special interest lobby pushing for various things in the gratuitous name of women. Either we are serious and consistent about equality or we are not. If we aren't, the Coalition will not hold together' (WNC, 1994).

The ANC's comments on the draft reflected an understanding of gender inequality as linked to broader political, economic and social inequalities. The bulk of the movement's comments centred on Article 3 (Economy). The ANC expressed concern that three items that were present in earlier drafts had been dropped, and called for these to be reinstated. These were the demand for full participation in economic decision-making, the recognition of unpaid labour and its inclusion in national accounts, and gender stereotyping of jobs. These demands stemmed from parallel discussions on a Bill of Rights that were taking place within the ANC, and by women activists in response to the ANC's constitutional guidelines. For women activists in the ANC alliance, the notion of equality as sameness between men and women was rejected. The emphasis was rather on how to ensure that women and men experienced both the benefits and the constraints of society equally. Discussions revolved around what kinds of special mechanisms – such as affirmative action – could be put into place to ensure equality of outcomes for women and men. The ANC's draft Bill of Rights issued in 1990 presupposed a state that would proactively implement rights, and envisaged an array of interventionist mechanisms – including affirmative action and redistributive welfare programmes – that could be used. The ANC women's comments on the Charter were premised on the existence of such a state.

These differences between the key political affiliates on the Coalition were not easily resolved. The final Charter attempted to temper and modify language so that all affiliates could feel comfortable ratifying the document. Thus the difference over affirmative action was accommodated in Article 1 (Equality) in the following way:

> The principle of equality shall be embodied at all levels in legislation and government policy. Specific legislation shall be introduced to ensure the practical realization of

equality. Programmes of affirmative action could be a means of achieving equality (WNC, 1994, p.3).

In Article 3 on the economy, on the other hand, the Charter states that 'the full participation of women in economic decision-making should be facilitated' (WNC, 1994, p.4). Nevertheless, not all demands could be reduced to the lowest common denominator in this way, and the differences at the National Convention threatened to split the organization. The compromise finally agreed to was that the Charter would be prefaced by a statement that it was a collection of all demands submitted to the Coalition, and that member organizations did not necessarily support the Charter in its entirety. Through this mechanism, the WNC was able to acknowledge internal differences while at the same time producing a broadly legitimate document that could be put before parties negotiating the Bill of Rights. Specific policy interpretations of women's demands were in effect deferred to parliamentary and legislative debates in the new government.

The interim constitution was completed before the Charter was finalized in 1994. The original multiple strategic intentions of the Charter were of necessity tempered, the broader political landscape having altered significantly with the agreements on electoral arrangements and a Government of National Unity. Nevertheless, it represented the possibility of a national consensus among women about the minimal demands of the women's movement. As Murray and O'Regan (1991) suggested, it 'could become a powerful political document, providing a standard against which to judge legislation and public action politically, if not legally' (p.50). Despite its limitations, the Charter retained many of the demands for substantive equality described above and thereby set an 'aspirational' objective that went beyond limited conceptions of formal equality. In making demands for greater female representation in the legislature, the assumption of ANC women activists was that these demands would form the political touchstone for legislative and policy interventions by women representatives in the democratic state.

A Mixed Legacy

In South Africa, the choice of a negotiated transition, involving consensus among the major political parties and liberation movements, produced a rights-based discourse that opened a space for women activists to extend feminist conceptions of democracy. There was an inherent tension in constitutional debates about democracy. On the one hand, the liberal notion of equality had considerable attraction as a framework within which to supersede apartheid's race-based mechanisms for organizing political representation. Democratic mechanisms needed to be found to ensure that ethnic mobilization was not carried over (and re-institutionalized) into democratic South Africa. On the other hand, the ANC was an organization with a strong socialist component; for large elements of its supporters it was synonymous with an anti-capitalist, anti-liberal struggle. Indeed, the process of transition itself was seen by some members as a 'sellout' of the revolutionary ideals of the movement (Webster and Adler, 1999). Through its alliance with the trade union movement (and in its role as the political arm of the workers' struggle) the movement was acutely aware of the class conflicts that shattered racial – and gender – unity. The use of a liberal discourse – and particularly the stress on *rights*, was therefore by no means an easy one. The approach of feminist lawyers associated with the WNC was important in building a bridge across the two discourses of transformation and rights. For them, as Kaganas and Murray (1994) have pointed out, it was important to look 'beyond law and behind formal equality to identify problems and solutions' (p.15). Indeed the transition was neither a revolutionary victory nor an unqualified triumph for liberalism, but a carefully worked-out compromise in which the ANC in particular had to balance the need for 'peace' with its commitment to social justice. Within this debate, 'women' came to occupy a peculiar status as the proving ground for the extent to which the new order would be inclusive, participatory and permeable to socially excluded groupings. The fact that many of the demands of women – political inclusion, strong national machinery, an equality clause, etc. – could be *relatively* easily accommodated within the crafting of democratic institutions facilitated this political process.

Citizenship, broadly conceived, displaced nationalism as the new political ideal and the political language through which the aspirations of subordinate groups were expressed. The shift away from discourses of nationalism was highly enabling for feminist activists. Feminist activists and scholars had long been concerned about the constraints of nationalism on women's political agency, even within the liberation movement. Within the ANC women's struggles were treated as subordinate to and defined by the larger national struggle, women's roles were confined to a narrow spectrum of movement activities based on stereotypical assumptions about women's interests and capabilities, and for many years feminism was delegitimized as a model of liberation. Women's political subjectivity was understood in terms of the status of motherhood, an identity that was limiting even though it was articulated in terms of a revolutionary imperative to mobilize women. As Dietz (1985) has argued, democratic citizenship must be constituted on more general grounds than the particularistic identity of motherhood (p.20). Rather, 'feminist political consciousness must draw upon … the potentiality of *women-as-citizens* and their historical reality as a collective and democratic power, not upon the "robust" demands of motherhood' (Dietz, 1985, p.34).

Within the framework of citizenship, women were able to articulate claims for strong equality. Citizenship offered a more enabling framework because the rights-based discourses that accompanied it allowed for the use of feminist mobilizing language of women's power and autonomy. Unlike nationalism, citizenship as articulated by feminists during the transition placed emphasis on the individual-in-community rather than primarily on the community. While some political parties wanted to limit citizenship to formal equality and political rights, the strong ANC tradition of social justice was hard to override. As even women within the National Party and Democratic Party eventually conceded, a strong emphasis on the individual would not allow for the creation of programmes and strategies to overcome the historical imbalances of gender relations and of apartheid: the predominance of women among the dispossessed rural populations, the legacies of inequalities in access to education, employment and control over land. On the other hand, the notion of 'community' had long been criticized in South Africa for its tendency to elevate the concerns of the elite within the community over those of the politically weak. From a feminist perspective, as Yuval-Davis (1997) has shown, an emphasis on community (or 'nation') hides inequalities *within* the nation, particularly those of gender. 'Nation', as she points out, is often used in liberation discourse in ways that keep women's role subordinate and private.

Because the ANC itself conceived of citizenship in substantial rather than formalistic terms, the new discourse allowed for women to place themselves at centre as the marker of whether the elite-driven negotiated transition would be inclusive of poor and excluded people. By the time the constitutional negotiations began, women's organizations had already debated the nature of mechanisms in the state and processes in civil society that would be conducive to advancing gender equality. Gender activists pushed hard for socio-economic rights and reproductive rights, establishing a constitutional basis for affirmative action and for a widened notion of social citizenship.

In engaging the opportunities offered by the transition, women's organizations reflected diverse views on the meaning of citizenship and in particular took different positions on the issue of equality. According to Meintjes (1998), the Women's National Coalition Charter for Effective Equality 'redefined the notion of equality in terms of women's differentiated needs' (p.81). The Charter reflected the diversity of needs among women as well as the specificity of women's needs as opposed to men. The Charter pinpointed race, class and regional inequalities among women, raising the need to account for difference in our understanding of the notion of citizenship. Meintjes (1998) points out that the Charter played an important role in 'influencing the shape of the new Constitution, law and public policy' (p.82). The Constitution establishes equality as 'a foundational value and organizing principle of the new democracy' (Albertyn and Goldblatt, 1998).

Yet how the principle of equality will be interpreted and acted upon remains contentious. The spirit of transformation which animates the Constitution may lead to interpretations by the Constitutional Court that favour substantive equality but it is by no means certain that governments will act in this way. Indeed, as Gouws's chapter in this volume shows, despite the ANC's historical support for transformative notions of citizenship, in government it has articulated the principle of equality in formalistic and narrow terms. The contestation between inclusive and narrow conceptions of citizenship and equality will not only take place in the Constitutional Court, but will have to be actively engaged by women's organizations. In this vein, Lister (1997) has argued that the central contribution of feminism to the debate on citizenship is to focus on the issue of human agency. She links the rights tradition and the participatory tradition of citizenship theory through the notion of agency. Lister (1997) makes the important argument that civil and political rights are a necessary, if not sufficient, precondition of full and equal citizenship (p.33). They need to be buttressed by social rights, which serve to weaken the effect of inequalities of power in the private sphere. Lister's reformulation of citizenship as involving *both* status (rights) and practice, as well as recognizing differences of identity, bound together through the participation of citizens in the public life of society, offers a valuable starting point from which to consider dilemmas of citizenship in South Africa. At least in the first ten years of democracy, it would seem that while women have made many gains in the achievement of *rights*, their conditions of life have not significantly improved. Thus far, inclusion and representation in the formal institutions of democracy has not translated into power to expand social rights (Hassim, 2003).

But even this broader conception of citizenship has limitations. A central concern for feminists must be the extent to which citizenship, conceived as public status and participation, can provide a framework within which to address inequalities that derive from the private sphere. Women delegates to the negotiations process, bolstered from outside by the Women's National Coalition and the Rural Women's Movement, were successful in ensuring that the constitutional clause on the status of customary law was subject to the clause on gender equality. However, the nature and extent to which rights to culture would be subject to rights to equality was not clearly spelt out (Goldblatt and Mbatha, 1999, p.102). How will the constitutional commitment to recognizing and protecting culture impact on rural women's ability to argue against the power of traditional leaders or male patriarchs? To what extent will citizenship enable women to recast inequalities in power within the domestic realm? As Catherine Albertyn and I have argued elsewhere (Albertyn and Hassim, 2003), neither formal *nor* substantive equality offers an adequate model in which to situate struggles for women's sexual and reproductive autonomy – the absence of which may be seen as lying at the heart of women's vulnerability to the HIV/AIDS epidemic. It is not yet clear how culture and 'the private' will be engaged by the women's movement. Engaging the public realm alone will not be sufficient; rather, what is needed is a conception of citizenship that draws on a vision of a different set of relationships in the private sphere.

References

Abrams, S. Kristine (2000), 'Fighting for women's liberation during the liberation of South Africa: the Women's National Coalition', MPhil, Wadham College, Oxford.

Albertyn, Catherine (1994), 'Women and the transition to democracy in South Africa', in Felicity Kaganas and Christina Murray (eds.), *Gender and the New South African Legal Order*, Juta, Cape Town, pp.39-63.

Albertyn, C. and Goldblatt. B. (1998), 'Facing the challenge of transformation: Difficulties in the development of an indigenous jurisprudence of equality', *South African Journal of Human Rights*, 14(2), pp.248-276.

Albertyn, Catherine and Hassim, Shireen (2003), 'The Boundaries of Democracy: Gender, Culture and HIV/AIDS', in D. Everatt and V. Maphai (eds.), *The Real State of the Nation*, Interfund, Johannesburg, pp.137-164.

Bonnin, Debby (1996), 'Women's Studies in South Africa', *Women's Studies Quarterly*, 1 & 2, pp.378-399.

Dietz, M. (1985), 'Citizenship with a feminist face: the problem with maternal thinking', *Political Theory*, 13(1), pp.19-37.

Goldblatt, Beth and Mbatha, Likhapha (1999), 'Gender, culture and equality: reforming customary law', in Catherine Albertyn (ed.), *Engendering the State: A South African Case Study*, CALS, Johannesburg, pp.83-110.

Hassim, Shireen (2003), 'The gender pact and democratic consolidation: Institutionalizing gender equality in the South African state', *Feminist Studies*, Vol.29, No.3, pp. 505-528.

Hudson, Peter (1986), 'The Freedom Charter and the theory of national democratic revolution', *Transformation*, 1, pp.6-38.

Jacquette, Jane S. and Wolchik, Sharon L. (eds.), (1998), *Women and democracy: Latin America and central and eastern Europe*, Johns Hopkins University Press, Baltimore.

Jenson, Jane (1995), 'Extending the boundaries of citizenship: Women's movements of Western Europe', in Amrita Basu (ed.), *The Challenge of Local Feminisms*, Westview Press, Boulder, pp.405-434.

Jenson, Jane (1987), 'Changing discourse, changing agendas: Political rights and reproductive policies in France', in Mary Fainsod Katzenstein and Carol McClurg Mueller (eds.), *The Women's Movements of the United States and Western Europe: Consciousness, Political Opportunity, and Public Policy*, Temple University Press, Philadelphia, pp.64-88.

Kaganas, Felicity and Murray, Christina (eds.), (1994), *Gender and the New South African Legal Order*, Juta, Cape Town.

Liebenberg, Sandra (1999), 'Social citizenship – a precondition for meaningful democracy', *Agenda*, No.40, pp.59-65.

Lister, Ruth (1997), *Citizenship: Feminist Perspectives*, New York University Press, New York.

Meintjes, Sheila (1996), 'The women's struggle for equality during South Africa's transition to democracy', *Transformation*, 30, pp.47-65.

Meintjes, Sheila (1998), 'Gender, nationalism and transformation: Difference and commonality in South Africa's past and present', in R. Wilford and R.L. Miller (eds.), *Women, Ethnicity and Nationalism: The Politics of Transition*, Routledge, London, pp.60-82.

Molyneux, Maxine (1998), 'Analysing women's movements', in C. Jackson and R. Pearson (eds.), *Feminist Visions of Development: Gender, Analysis and Policy*, Routledge, London, pp.65-88.

Murray, Catherine and O'Regan, Catherine (1991), 'Putting Women into the Constitution', in Susan Bazilli (ed.), *Putting Women on the Agenda*, Ravan Press, Johannesburg, pp.33-56.

Schneider, Elizabeth (1991), 'The dialectic of rights and politics: perspectives from the women's movement', in K.T. Bartlett and R. Kennedy (eds.), *Feminist Legal Theory*, Westview Press, Boulder, pp.318-332.

Seekings, Jeremy (2000), *The UDF: A History of the United Democratic Front in South Africa, 1983-1991*, David Philip, Cape Town.

Walker, Cherryl (1991), *Women and Resistance in South Africa* (2nd edn.), David Philip, Cape Town.

Waylen, Georgina (1994), 'Women and democratization: Conceptualizing gender relations in transition politics', *World Politics*, 46(3), pp.327-54.

Webster, Edward and Adler, Glenn (1999), 'Towards a class compromise in South Africa's "double transition": Bargained liberalization and the consolidation of democracy', *Politics and Society*, 27(3), pp.347-385.

Women's National Coalition (1994), *Women's Charter for Effective Equality*, Johannesburg.

Young, Iris Marion (2000), *Inclusion and Democracy*, Oxford University Press, Oxford.

Yuval-Davis, Nira (1997), *Gender and Nation*, Sage, London.

Chapter 3

Shaping Women's Citizenship: Contesting the Boundaries of State and Discourse[1]

Amanda Gouws

Introduction

Writing about women's citizenship in South Africa is exciting as well as challenging. Having one of the most revered constitutions in the world that guarantees civil and political rights as well as access to socio-economic rights easily creates the impression that gender equality is strongly enforced and that it remains on the political agenda.

The transition to democracy in South Africa created an opportunity structure[2] for women to move their interests onto the political agenda where previously it was subordinated to the national liberation struggle. It also afforded women the opportunity to organize themselves into a single issue movement around the Women's Charter for Effective Equality through the Women's National Coalition. This process and its political implications have been well documented and is the subject of Hassim's chapter in this book.[3] My concern here will be with the post-1994 socio-political conditions for women's equality in South Africa.

Since 1994 women have been relatively well represented in government. Due to the proportional list system and a one third quota accepted on its list by the ANC there is nearly 30% of women in government, just below the critical mass. Women are also represented as ministers and deputy ministers in significant numbers. Enabling conditions to monitor gender equality have been created through state structures, in the form of the National Machinery for Women and the statutory body of the Commission on Gender Equality. The South African government is a signatory to the Convention for the Elimination of Discrimination Against Women (CEDAW) and is developing initiatives to implement the Beijing Platform of Action. The government is also committed to the South African Development Community's (SADC) Declaration on Gender and Development. These documents bind the government to the implementation of rights-based citizenship for women.

At the same time South Africa has one of the highest statistics for gender based violence as well as one of the highest HIV infection rates in the world, both of which have detrimental effects for women. In the absence of a high economic growth rate and the creation of a social security net the reduction of poverty remains a problem since a high percentage of women in South Africa either live in poverty or are in danger of being classified as poor. This reflects serious shortcomings with the implementation of socio-economic rights.

At first glance then it may seem that women have been included in the body politic and that gender justice is being pursued. Yet, the liberal project of including individuals through rights stands in tension with the claims made by collective identities, such as women. On closer analysis this chapter will show that there are serious shortcomings in women's inclusion into citizenship both on the levels of rights and participation as well as with the opportunity structure created through the state. In the absence of a clearer understanding of the role of the state in the construction of the discourse around citizenship it is difficult to understand the tension between structure (the state) and the agency it leaves for individuals as well as for the women's movement (see Waylen, 1998, p.1). The relationship between the state and the women's movement is not a static one but is dynamic and constantly changing. What opportunities the state affords the women's movement and how the discourse of citizenship is constructed within the state need to be theorized. The aim of this chapter is to initiate this theorization process.

The discourses of gender mainstreaming and rights in the state are important to understand since discourse constructs the dimensions of citizenship that are singled out for policy formation, or determines how citizenship is entrenched in rights, or whether the boundaries between the public and private are shifted. The rights of citizenship that are entrenched in the constitution are only affected in reality through state action such as policy formation and implementation, otherwise they remain on an abstract level where they are universal and ungendered. State action is embedded in discourses that frame rights and gender in very specific ways.

This analysis could, however, not be seen in the absence of the impact of globalization on local political conditions. What happens in Third World states are also a consequence of transnational practices such as the creation of supra-national bodies, the adherence to (or lack thereof) to international treaties and documents and the demands of first world aid organizations that are binding on national states. The reconfiguration of the state (or the reallocation of state authority) is very often directly related to the acceptance of neo-liberal economic policies dictated by the broader international economic climate, very often with far-reaching (frequently negative) consequences for the populations of Third World countries. South Africa may not entirely be a Third World state, but it is not exempt from these conditions as some of my arguments will show.

In the following section I will trace the feminist contours of citizenship. Women's inclusion in citizenship through the extension of rights embodies the liberal ideal of citizenship. Rights claims, however, are dealt with through the political process and the judiciary but also, in the case of South Africa, through the structures that were created in the state. These structures were supposed to open spaces for the women's movement to negotiate their claims and to create platforms for policy intervention. This dual goal of state feminism (the commitment of women who work in the state to women's equality) is aimed at realizing citizenship for women in South Africa. Very often the state fails women because it is inaccessible or the policy processes are impenetrable. When state structures exist the women's movement can engage the state and extract certain gains which is not possible merely through participation in voting or civil society politics. These gains are, however, dependent on how the discourse in the state shapes women's citizenship.

The State

Feminist scholars have studied the state by looking at the unintended effects of state action. The state therefore has not been theorized in a very sophisticated manner and women have been viewed in these analyses as the objects of policy (Waylen, 1996, p.16). As Jacquette (2003) argues, feminists have criticized the state for not being liberal or democratic in its failure to recognize the citizenship of women (p.338). Few feminists have supported the state because of their focus on civil society politics. Neither has their experience with women's machineries been good because of the reversal of gains, the intransigence of bureaucracies and the co-optation of women in these structures.[4]

Post-structuralist feminists have provided more sophisticated analyses of the state and have argued, as Pringle and Watson (1992) do, that the state is a series of arenas or locales where interests are constituted and not merely represented (p.63). In this regard the state needs to be viewed as the historical product of a collection of practices and discourses. What intentionality there is comes from the success various groups have in the articulation and hegemonization of their claims. As Brown (1992) argues the state can be masculinist without intentionally or overtly pursuing the interests of men (p.14). Power is vested in the intentionality of control – in which different forms of masculinist power appear in different sites of the state, regulating through discourse how women's interests will be represented and what type of solutions will be found for women's lack of equality.

Policy outcomes therefore will depend on the interests constituted within the state. For groups to share in policy outcomes their interests need to be articulated, constructed and maintained within the state. The dominant discourses take place through discursive struggles within different locales of the state preventing it from acting as an entity (Pringle and Watson, 1992, p.65). In this regard the state is a construction of sites in which power is vested and which does not act coherently as the agent of any particular group. Inherent in the state is the organization of power relations that determine how women are constituted as subjects and as citizens. The practices of the state construct and legitimate gender divisions and identities through the law and public discourses that emanate from the state. Discursive struggles play an important role in the organization of power relations (Pringle and Watson, 1992, p.70).

The debate on the state has now shifted to an analysis of the 'reconfigured state', mainly applied to the post-industrial western states. The reconfiguration refers to structural changes within the state, to the changing relationship between the state and civil society, as well as a changing discourse on the role of the state due to the construction of supra-national bodies. Reconfiguration therefore is a shift in the allocation of state authority (Banaszak et al., 2003, p.4). What is important about the reconfiguration of the state is the extent to which the relocation of state authority reduces the influence of social movements (Banaszak et al., 2003, p.6). When policy arenas are related to women's issues or concerns, women have a high saliency for the state. This enables the women's movement to shape the debate but also to influence the location of policy implementation (Banaszak et al., 2003, p.25). State structures that create spaces for women's movements in the state are likely to be used to also introduce new issues onto the policy agenda.

While women in South Africa have accepted that the state will be the node through which change toward equality will take place the state has not always been viewed as a women friendly space. In Africa, in general, the state is a contested terrain where it has become the means through which global capitalism exercises local power through structural adjustment programmes (Taylor, 2000, p.30). But as Taylor (2000) argues, the state is viewed as an arbiter of democracy and therefore its role in public policy cannot be ignored (p.13). In post-transitional societies the reconfiguration of the state occurs due to globalization influences but also due to new economic and nation-building policies. In South Africa a part of the state's reconfiguration was due to the creation of structures in the state to represent women's interests. Why the National Machinery for Women can be viewed as part of state reconfiguration is related to its integrated nature and its supposed policy reach aimed at shifting state authority to these structures.

In South Africa the transition afforded women the opportunity to create state structures and institutionalize the women's movement. The successes can not be traced back to individual structures but have to be viewed against the background of the dynamic relationship between civil society organizations, international influences, women's activism and the national machinery.

The Politics of State Feminism

Entrance of women into state structures is another form of interest representation that is aimed at creating enabling conditions for gendered policy-making. Whether state feminism really exists is contested because women in these structures often have to choose between their party interests and their gender interests. Women in civil society, however, often rely on these spaces in the state to promote their interests in policy-making that would enhance their citizenship.

National machineries for women are structures created in the state to promote state feminism. State feminism has two dimensions – one being the influence exercised in policy-making through the femocracy (women in the state) and the other is the access it provides to the women's movement (Stetson and Mazur, 1995). What happens on the one dimension constitutes change in the other.

National machineries are often accused of being co-opted by the state or of being insensitive to women's demands or completely inaccessible. In a comparative study by Stetson and Mazur (1995) of fourteen countries outside Africa the results showed uneven rates of success in promoting women's equality. National machineries that provide a great deal of policy access provide it directly or indirectly to women's groups through which they become powerful actors.

Those machineries that were low on access subordinated feminist interests to official versions of feminist politics or that did not allow feminist interests access at all (Stetson and Mazur, 1995, p.276). They also point out that machineries established by social-democratic governments were more committed to women's equality and more successful in making gains. Integrated structures were more successful than isolated structures.

While national machineries for women exist in Africa their success has also been uneven. As Mama (2000) notes the preliminary evidence of the machineries is that they have achieved the modest, liberal goal of giving women more space in the state but have done little to alleviate the plight of ordinary women (p.15). It has not been on the cutting edge but has merely implemented mainstream policies (Mama, 2000, p.23). Access of women's groups to the state has been limited or they became co-opted in the official rhetoric of the state or captured by First Ladies (wives of rulers) (Mama, 2000, p.6; Mensah-Kutin et al., 2000, p.45). The fragility of national machineries is enhanced when governments accept their inceptions merely to use them as vehicles for donor funding.

The establishment of the National Machinery for Women in South Africa was part of the negotiated settlement of the transition process toward democracy. The process that led to the institutionalization of gender included long discussions among women activists, non-governmental organizations and institutions linked to universities that could apply different types of expertise such as legal expertise. The Centre for Applied Legal Studies (CALS) at the University of the Witwatersrand and key individuals in CALS played an important role as a proposal drafted by the Gender Research Project at CALS guided government decision-makers (Gender Research Project, 2000, p.179). Numerous submissions were made to the Constituent Assembly prior to acceptance of the final constitution in 1996 but a consensus existed in the women's movement that structures should be created on different levels of government (national, provincial and local), in the state departments and an independent statutory body in civil society.

The National Machinery for Women in South Africa is far more advanced and integrated than in other African countries and even in some countries in industrialized societies. A set of structures was created to ensure women's participation in decision-making and accountability to women (Hassim, 2003, p.508).

In South Africa the Office of the Status of Women (OSW) forms the apex with the mandate to draw up a National Gender Policy. In parliament there is a multi-party women's caucus, responsible for monitoring gender equality and a women's empowerment unit, charged with training and supporting women parliamentarians. There are gender focal points in the different state departments with the dual aim of ensuring gender representation and engendering and monitoring policy; and an independent statutory body that has to monitor progress in women's equality in government and the private sector, the Commission on Gender Equality. Gender focal points are also found in the state departments on provincial level, although not all of them are functional yet. A very important committee was formed in 1996 as the Ad Hoc Joint Committee on the Improvement of the Quality of Life and the Status of Women (JCQLSW). In 1997 it became a joint standing committee that has higher status and more permanence than an ad hoc committee. The mandate of this committee is the overseeing of the implementation of CEDAW and the Beijing Platform for Action.

When assessing the machinery on three levels: that of representation, accountability and delivery such as the Gender Research Project (2000) has done, the greatest success is on the level of representation and liaison with constituencies of women. In this regard the Commission on Gender Equality and the Joint Standing Committee on the Quality of Life and the Status of Women[5] were quite successful. Accountability to women is more difficult to measure than accountability to parties. The structures are the weakest on delivery and some such as the CGE are plagued by internal politics (see Seidman, 2003).

On the dimension of creating access for the women's movement the urban bias of the parliamentary process where access is created through participation in public hearings and presentations at parliament makes it very difficult for women who are not organized or who live in the rural areas to engage the process. Where the JSQLW has fast-tracked legislation or has canvassed rural women through women members of parliament and the Rural Women's Movement more gains have been made (Gouws, 2004).

The greatest success has been in policy areas that are directly related to women's concerns such as reproductive rights (abortion), violence, and the regulation of customary marriages. In this regard the groups that were well organized with high levels of skill and grassroots affiliations had the greatest success in participation (Gender Research Project, 2000, p.192; see also Hassim, 2002b, pp.42-43). Attempts at engendering more mainstream laws have also been made through the Women's Budget Initiative (Hassim, 2002b, p.49).

Institutionalizing state feminism created discursive spaces where gender became the operative term for dealing with women's issues. Because of women's reliance on state feminism, citizenship becomes focused on state action and the discursive spaces that it creates for interest representation.

Gender Mainstreaming as Discourse

The discursive framework within which women's interests are constituted within the state is 'gender mainstreaming'. This calls for the integration of gender equality concerns into the analyses and formulation of all policies, programmes and projects.[6] As True (2003) puts it:

> ...mainstreaming initiatives balance the goal of gender equality with the need to recognize gender difference to bring about transformation of masculine-as-norm institutional practices in state and global governance. Furthermore, the process of mainstreaming a gender perspective involves actors working in multiple locations, inside governance institutions, within epistemic and activist communities in local and global civil society (p.369).

According to the South Africa's National Policy Framework gender mainstreaming is a process that is goal oriented.

It recognises that most institutions consciously and unconsciously serve the interests of men and encourages institutions to adopt a gender perspective in transforming themselves. It promotes the full participation of women in decision-making so that women's needs move from the margins to the centre of development planning and resource allocation (p.xviii).

Gender mainstreaming as a policy attempts to integrate gender concerns in the everyday work of government procedures, policy-making and service delivery in order to create a women-friendly state (Hassim, 2003, p.509). In this regard the National Policy Framework goes a long way towards creating a set of strategies to achieve gender mainstreaming. But as True (2003) argues, much more critical attention needs to be paid to initiatives that claim to be mainstreaming a gender perspective (p.386). As she points out, assessing the theoretical and practical implications of gender mainstreaming provides the context for activists and scholars to engage with each other.

True (2003) furthermore argues that three enabling factors have put gender mainstreaming on policy agendas: (1) the language of promoting women's rights and gender equality; (2) the proliferation of women's networks and transnational linkages; and (3) a growing number of gender sensitive women and men in foreign policy and global governance leadership positions (p.374). Governments on nation state level in democracies have increasingly accepted a discourse of rights and equality for women. It is, however, the practical implementation of gender mainstreaming policies that needs to flow from the discourse that requires close scrutiny.

True (2003) argues that gender mainstreaming is a 'potentially transformative project that depends on what feminist scholars, activists and policy makers collectively make of it' (p.368). Her view is that feminists cannot afford not to engage with powerful institutions because they have serious policy implications. For her, engaging with the institutions is more important than worrying about co-optation by these institutions. My concern is with the depoliticization of the feminist project as a consequence of buying into the gender mainstreaming project when the necessary resources are not available to make mainstreaming a reality.

The gender mainstreaming discourse forms part of the institutionalization of gender machinery, setting up of institutional and discursive frameworks, new technologies of governance and regulation of subjects that have meanings for the constitution of gender interests (Manicom, 2001, p.15). Because interests are discursively constructed in the intersection with state arenas political subjectivities are also constructed in an attempt to fix or change identities (Pringle and Watson, 1996, p.74).

While mainstreaming is now the hegemonic state discourse it entered the local context through international conferences and the development literature that is often applied to women in Third World countries. This concept was first used in reference to the national machineries during the United Nations Third World Conference on Women in Nairobi 1985 and later used by the United Nations Development Fund for Women (UNIFEM). Gender mainstreaming became the definitive discursive framework during the United Nations Fourth World

Conference in Beijing in 1995 (Adams, 2001, p.10). Gender as discourse is global, disseminated in international spaces through conferences, in conditions of donor agencies, interpreted by experts across contexts, proliferated by researchers, policy-makers and bureaucrats and dispersed in sites of governance around the world (Manicom, 2001, p.7).

As Manicom (2001) has argued the discourse of gender has now become integrated into most areas of governance dealing with women in social development (p.6). In the governance discourse gender becomes constructed as a space that needs administrative intervention. As she points out gender 'formulaic' solutions lose the substance of gender redress and could even support anti-feminist and undemocratic agendas.

Gender becomes constructed in a way that represents women as lacking agency, as clients of social programmes or victims of political processes (Manicom, 2001, p.9). The 'gender problem' is therefore in need of administrative intervention through which an already defined gender solution exists. Gender is seen as something already out there, not as constructed, and always contested. Gender is consequently taken up in a governance discourse in an unquestioning way.[7]

The concept of gender mainstreaming (the practice of gender work) is embedded in the official national gender policy written by the Office of the Status of Women and titled 'South Africa's National Framework for Women's Empowerment and Gender Equality'. The plan proposes an integrated coordination framework and process for gender mainstreaming. As is stated in the framework – this will be a communication, service delivery and accountability framework through the Management Information System (MIS) which will be 'a network of existing structures, mechanisms and processes effecting gender mainstreaming'. The coordination framework and gender mainstreaming process is expected to guide and mobilize ministries, provinces and local government toward an integrated programme delivery (chapter 5).[8]

Some of the main objectives of the policy with regard to mainstreaming are:

- To establish policies, programmes, structures and mechanisms to empower women and to transform gender relations in all aspects of work, at all levels of government as well as within the broader society.
- To ensure that gender considerations are effectively integrated into all aspects of government policies, activities and programmes.
- To establish an institutional framework for the advancement of the status of women as well as the achievement of gender equality.

The aim of gender mainstreaming is to institutionalize women's equality but through the depoliticization of gender. Women's subjectivity and the activism around women's issues become suppressed. Where the driving force around gender activism used to be women's experience, mainstreaming turns it into a technocratic category for redress that also suppresses the differences between women. The essentialist use of the category gender reflects the same lack of sensitivity toward the accommodation of difference that was exercised with the essentialist use of the category women (that also often reflected only the experience of white Western women). The question is whether gender has replaced the category women but still means women or whether it refers to the relationships between women and men.

Relying on the discourse of gender mainstreaming also closes the political opportunity structure which discursive spaces created in the state for women to pursue their interests. A reliance on a depoliticized type of state feminism forecloses opportunities to engage the state. At the same time that a gender discourse was supposed to expand space in the state for gender concerns it contracts those spaces. And because mainstreaming (especially as conceptualized in South Africa's National Policy Framework) expects all state officials, including ministers, to take responsibility for gender, the chances are good that nobody will, as responsibility will be shifted between officials.

The discourse of gender mainstreaming then becomes the rhetoric of gender mainstreaming; easy to use but weak on implementation. The assumption is that the discourse satisfies the international community – the donor agencies, the international NGOs, but that it will also change institutional cultures by putting women's concerns centre stage. As True observes, there are too few links between gender advocates inside institutions and feminist activists and scholars outside (2003, p.387). And as she aptly comments one of the constraining factors of gender mainstreaming is the conflict between feminist values and the broader ideological framework of neo-liberal economics.

Gender mainstreaming therefore is a blunt instrument that has lost the nuances of the struggle for gender equality, the demands of radical feminism and even the well-intended critiques of development discourse. As an instrument of organizational change its reach beyond institutions still needs to be assessed, especially in communities where the lack of gender equality determines women's everyday existence (dealing with gender based violence, living with HIV/AIDS, living with single parenthood).

If the focus of gender mainstreaming is to change the spaces in the state, it manages to reinscribe the public/private divide into citizenship since the focus is on the state and not on the private sphere. Within these discursive spaces in the state where gender mainstreaming has become the hegemonic discourse the discourse of rights take on a particular shape, as will be discussed below.

Rights as a Discourse

In the liberal rights-based democracy of South Africa it is common for people to talk about their rights and how the constitution enables them to claim rights. But when the implementation of rights or the effectiveness of claiming rights is explored one becomes increasingly aware of the limits of rights.

Pringle and Watson (1996) have argued that the discourse of rights is problematic from a feminist perspective because it constructs universal subjects that are devoid of difference (p.67). Rights discourse uses a universalizing language of rights that obscures conditions of inequality. On a discursive level the language of rights creates the impression that rights have some intrinsic value. It is argued that a rights claim can make a statement of entitlement that is universal and categorical. The entitlement can be negative since it protects against intrusion from the state or positive because it allows the individual to do something (Schneider, 1991, p.319). Rights are linked to possessive individualism because they belong to individuals. In other words individuals own rights and this notion puts boundaries between state and individual and between self and other (Schneider, 1991, p.319). One consequence of this view of rights is that it obscures the connection with community and reliance on others. When rights are viewed in this way it becomes difficult to solve conflicts and to transform social relations of inequality.

Schneider (1991) makes the important point that reliance on rights can keep people passive and dependent upon the state because it is the state that grants them their rights (p.319). This dependency weakens the power of popular movements by allowing the state to define their goals.

With regard to the construction of the subject there is a debate whether rights, interests or needs should be used as part of the discourse about gender equality. Pringle and Watson (1996) argue that interests should replace rights. Interests surpass the use of needs (p.72). Needs are subjective and are also constructed in relation to a universal subject. Interests are constructed within different sites of the state and based on women's subject positions. Interests would avoid essentialist identities and can even accommodate women's contradictory subject positions.

While the concept of women's interests is used by many feminist scholars, I want to show how, in the discourse used by the state, a discursive shift takes place from rights to needs and to entitlement as a negative intervention by the state. Needs imply a specific way of constructing a subject, most often as victims or as deviants. As Pringle and Watson (1996) observe:

> Needs are defined in terms of specific subjects: the single parent, the delinquent, and so on. These new subjects become the focus of a whole range of practices and it is in these practices that the modern forms of domination and repression are found ... The focus is on the way in which these subjects are discursively constructed with particular attributes and defects requiring certain kinds of intervention or surveillance. The social practices which are then directed at these constituted subjects stem directly from the discourses which have created the subjects in the first place (p.71).

How subject positions in terms of rights, interests or needs are constructed can be viewed in social policy. As Pringle and Watson (1996) have argued social policy is a highly normative endeavour that constructs ideal models of society that often hide how power relations construct gender relations (p.70). Needs are at the mercy of those who construct them. They do not have the constitutional protection that rights have nor the subject positions of interests.

As others and I have illustrated elsewhere in an analysis of the South African White Paper on Social Welfare, the familialist understanding of social welfare provision constructs contradictory subject positions for women – on the one hand constructing them as independent self-reliant agents (according to the male model of self-reliance) who should enter the labour force in order to improve their socio-economic conditions, and on the other hand restricting them to the private sphere where they have to continue their care-giving work (see Sevenhuijsen et al., 2003).

In this regard women, children and the disabled are constructed as belonging to the category of people with 'special needs'. By making this shift from rights to needs women become constructed as in need of administrative intervention. Children are constructed as victims of abuse, degradation and neglect. Despite serious neglect of families and domestic abuse, the subject positions of men are not constructed as deviant, rather they are constructed as independent breadwinners.

The discourse of needs is also closely linked to the notion of 'vulnerable groups'. Women, children, the youth and the disabled are 'vulnerable groups' in need of protection, for example, from violence. While the constitution constructs 'bodily integrity' as a right which includes health rights as well as control over reproduction and the right to security and control over your body, the discourse of 'vulnerable groups' does not construct these rights as claim rights but rather as entitlements to negative intervention by the state. For example, when women have no control over sexual and reproductive choices or gender-based violence, HIV/AIDS becomes a prime factor undermining bodily integrity. In the absence of a clear policy on HIV/AIDS by the government the public discourse constructs treatment not as a right but as a medical entitlement.

The Department of Social Development presents the following strategic objectives as central to their framework in dealing with HIV/AIDS [www.welfare.gov.za/documents/htm]:

- To offer comprehensive social development services to *vulnerable groups* (children, youth, women, older persons and people with disability), paying special attention to the HIV/AIDS infected and affected.
- To ensure that comprehensive social development services are rendered to *vulnerable groups* in a coordinated, integrative manner that observes national, regional and international protocols and recognize contribution of all stakeholder groups ... (author's emphasis).

The following concrete activities should be achieved:

> Care and support services by rolling out HIV/AIDS home community based care and support programme; protection measures and services for orphans and *vulnerable* children; appropriate social assistance and social welfare services to people who are affected and infected by HIV/AIDS; promotion and protection of rights to deal with access to services, stigma and discrimination; addressing the *vulnerability* of youth, women, older persons and people with disabilities ... (author's emphasis).

By including women in 'vulnerable groups' (this discourse of 'vulnerability' was constructed in international development literature) women are positioned as victims who are in need of intervention. If the issue of HIV/AIDS had been included in the debate around reproductive rights of which sexual rights (or body rights) form one dimension, the focus could be shifted to positive entitlements and not only negative interventions (such as is also the case with domestic violence).

Medical entitlement with regards to HIV/AIDS is mediated by the market (those who can afford antiretrovirals can get them and those who can't have to live without them). In this regard medicine is not even truly an entitlement because the provision through the market reproduces social stratification which excludes the poor from benefits. As O'Connor, Orloff and Shaver (1999) argue: 'Identifying freedom with the market rather than the state, the ideology of possessive individualism divorces the issue of rights in law from the effective right in actuality' (p.180).

Reproductive rights are body rights. As soon as body rights are viewed as medical entitlements (such as is often the case with abortion) medical authority mediates women's claims. The primary importance of social rights is its underpinnings of women's personhood and autonomy that ensures her participation in social and economic life (O'Connor, Orloff and Shaver, 1999, p.160). Body rights often stand in stark contradiction to cultural practices that also undermine women's autonomy, especially with regard to the transmission of HIV.[9]

The strategies of the most successful NGO mobilizing to pressurize the government into distributing antiretrovirals to people living with HIV/AIDS, the Treatment Action Campaign (TAC), conform to demands for medical entitlement. These demands were supported by the judiciary. Women and feminist activists who campaign for viable government policies on HIV/AIDS have a more gendered approach to the epidemic such as the need to change power relations and cultural practices. This is portrayed in the 'Statement of Concern on Women and HIV/AIDS' distributed at the HIV/AIDS conference held in Durban, South Africa 2000, which states:

> Our vulnerability arises out of a combination of poverty, unequal access to basic needs and resources, oppressive cultures and traditions, the denial of sexual and reproductive choices and the absence of adequate health care and information.

The statement call for a combination of medical entitlement and rights claiming (but not as body rights) such as 'ensuring that the many laws put in place by government to strengthen and expand women's democratic rights are fully implemented to raise their status in reality and not just on paper'.

Petchesky (2000) argues that rights cannot be claimed in the absence of ethical principles and enabling conditions that would allow women to claim sexual rights as a positive right in the form of control over their bodies. Rights are then framed as positive sexuality and not merely as a negative form of control of sexual violence and abuse that characterizes women as victims. Petchesky aims to highlight the lack of agency that is conferred upon women when sexual rights are merely dealt with in the form of prevention and not as a positive right to control over your body. In this regard the discourse of international conferences on population control and sexual rights have played an important role to frame the discourse as one of intervention. Only at the Cairo Conference on population in 1994 did body rights as a positive claim enter the discourse for the first time (Petchesky, 2000, p.81).

In Third World states where the presence of cultural beliefs and practices limit women's autonomy and conditions of underdevelopment mitigate against choice, negative interventions by the state may alleviate the plight of women. Social policies, however, need to move beyond negative interventions to create conditions that would make it possible for women to claim body rights as a positive right and not as a luxury, as it is often perceived in these conditions. These types of social policies need to be championed by the women's movement.

Rights or the construction of interests need to be understood as part of the dialectical relationship between the state and the women's movement. Schneider (1991) argues that rights are formed in the conversation/struggle between the women's movement and the state as a political process from which new visions and understanding of rights is continually negotiated. Rights and interest construction can never be disconnected from the women's movement.[10]

Citizenship as Participation

By now it should be clear that citizenship as a status (having rights) is highly contested in South Africa because the discourse that constructs women's citizenship in the state limits women's realization thereof. If we shift the focus to citizenship as participation we find greater potential for the realization of rights. While Lister equates agency with participation, agency is more than participation. As Hobson (2000) argues: 'Agency is the linchpin concept in gender inequalities because it connects processes and outcomes and provides a meeting place between subject identities and institutions' (p.239). Agency is about having choices.

Korpi (2000) refers to *agency inequality* and *agency poverty* (p.128). This he defines as the scope of an individual's action alternatives and control over resources that would enable choices. When put on a continuum *agency poverty* will be the material inequality at the bottom end, and *agency inequality* will be inequality at elite levels at the top end. Agency inequality can be related to three important arenas – that of democratic politics, the educational system and the labour force, but is not limited to those.

In the political sphere, agency inequality at the top refers to the ability to take part in decision-making on a governmental level and agency poverty refers to the ability to vote. In the education level it refers to access to tertiary education at the top level and access to primary education at the bottom and in the arena of the labour force, which is the central arena where distributive processes take place, it is access to labour force decision-making at the top level and participation in the labour force at the bottom level. Here the question needs to be asked: 'what is the distribution between paid and unpaid work and if policies support women's labour force participation or if it encourages their unpaid word at home' (Korpi, 2000, pp.142-143). Furthermore, do governments leave the formation of gendered agency inequality to markets and families or to the development of public policies granting claim rights as citizens?

In the political sphere in South Africa NGOs providing gender advocacy have shifted their reliance on state feminism to direct representation. The Gender Advocacy Programme's (GAP) 50/50 campaign by 2005 is a call for the mobilization of the women's vote in order to ensure 50% representation by women in government on a national level by the year 2005. It is argued that a 50%

representation will ensure a government that is democratic and that it reflects parity.[11]

In the context of the United Kingdom the research of Chaney and Fevre (2002) has shown that there is a demand for descriptive participation in democracies because democracy is about the self-interest of participants and problems arise when participants represent the interest of groups that are very different from themselves. Although there is always the danger of essentialism the importance of political presence is the way in which the political agenda is transformed and women's issues are placed on the agenda. If women are not part of the decision-making their views and interests are overlooked. Descriptive representation is an issue of parity with men that also gives women greater access to resource utilization. (See also Voet, 1998, p.104; Albertyn, Hassim and Meintjes, 2002, pp.383-389; and Goetz and Hassim, 2003.)

The necessity of the 50/50 campaign reflects agency inequality at the top level.[12] Agency poverty at the bottom level is due to structural conditions that prevent women from voting (such as long distances from the polling booths in rural areas and lack of childcare – even though 1 million more women registered to vote in the 1999 election than men). No gender gap was observed in the first two democratic elections because no party really created a gender platform for women or canvassed visibly for women's issues (see Gouws, 2002a).

In the area of education agency inequality exists on the top level and agency poverty at the bottom. Lack of sufficient education in rural areas and an education crisis due to a lack of enough competent teachers, sufficient resources and gender based violence in schools are big problems (see Gouws, 2003). Since daughters do the care work the increasing care burden due to the prevalence of HIV/AIDS falls on girls, further depriving them of education. Much smaller numbers of women attend post-graduate education than men. African women are the most under-represented. For those women who manage to enter tertiary education they very often end up in fields of study that are traditionally related to women such as the care professions, social science, languages and education (Hassim and Gouws, 1999, p.95; MacLean, 2001). There is a lack of curriculum transformation although women and gender studies have become institutionalized in the last few years but programmes are still in their infancy.

With an unemployment rate of nearly 40% in some areas agency poverty abounds – women are more likely than men to be unemployed or to be employed in the informal sector and first to lose their jobs if conditions worsen. At the top level only around 30% of women are in managerial positions in the private sector and even less than that in the tertiary education sector (see *Mail and Guardian*, 16-22 August 2002, pp.12-13). The glass ceiling for women is a common phenomenon.

With increasing globalization the fear is that governments will leave solutions to gendered agency inequality to markets or families. As research on the social welfare state has shown this can lead to reproduction of the public/private divide if policy support strengthens the nuclear family through support for a male breadwinner. Support of a dual earner family model is preferable since it leads to women's labour force participation and a redistribution of social care work (Korpi,

2000, p.143). The weak social security net in South Africa in the context of high levels of poverty and family disintegration makes a market or family solution problematic. One suggestion of providing social security for greater numbers of people is a basic income grant through which each South African citizen (from cradle to grave) will be entitled to R100 per month. This solution of cash transfers is already criticized for the so-called dependency it will create and for the lack of a means test. Critics of the basic income grant want to make it available to people who work, something that will once more have a disproportionately negative effect on women.[13] A basic income grant can define citizenship away from a focus on the labour market and construct more gender neutral citizenship rights (McKay and Vanevery, 2000).

Conclusion

This chapter demonstrates the tension between structure and agency of the women's movement and the importance of how the discourse around gender mainstreaming and rights limits the realization of rights for women in South Africa. The gender mainstreaming discourse has taken gender into the state in such a way that everybody working in the state should take responsibility for gender. At the same time it has limited the organic construction of interests and depoliticized gender.

The chapter has also shown that political opportunities are structurally gendered. Unless the women's movement takes advantage of the political changes and organizations adapt their strategies, they may not make the gains they anticipate. The women's movement needs to employ discursive shifts to shape their political opportunities and their successes (Beckwith, 2000, p.454).

This chapter has emphasized the importance of the relationship between the state and the women's movement and the dynamic relationship between them. Much more research is needed to understand the present shape and policy agenda of the women's movement in South Africa. Previous arguments by Hassim and Gouws (1999) indicated that the women's movement had become demobilized or fragmented because of a reliance on state structures and women in the state. Nearly ten years after the first democratic election in South Africa the women's movement has had its own disillusionment with state structures and new strategies seem to involve closer relationships with *individuals* in the state, or closer working relationships with gender NGOs. What is needed however is a collective or more focused policy agenda where women target specific government policies as well as their implementation.

Karen Beckwith (2000) has argued that women's movement activism is sustained under the following conditions (p.452):

- fluidity of electoral politics
- alliances with progressive or left political parties
- feminist or women-centred discourse as part of party discourse
- a unified women's movement with multiple political venues for participation

- willingness or ability to persist in party politics in a post-transition period
- capacity to negotiate women's policy concerns as a condition of movement support for a party or state
- regime changes.

While all these conditions presently exist in South Africa women are not engaging them, except for the engagement with the electoral system through the 50/50 campaign. The fluidity in the electoral system due to the floor-crossing legislation[14] that enable members of parliament to start new parties and still retain their seats have opened possibilities for women. In the cross over period of March 2003 seven new parties have been formed (albeit with limited possibilities of mobilizing large number of voters) but these parties could benefit if they were prepared to mobilize the women's vote. Up till now voting in South Africa has been largely ideological (and some would argue based on race)[15] due to the apartheid history and the shift to interest-based voting has not yet occurred. It is only then that women would be able to make their support for parties conditional.

The construction of citizenship through the liberal rights-based project in South Africa since 1994 has homogenized the category of women and constructed a universal subject. The articulation of difference between women very often only becomes understood at the point of policy implementation. The discourse of gender mainstreaming and of needs (instead of rights) has limited the agency of women and has put boundaries on the political opportunity structure through which the women's movement can engage the state. Citizenship as status, as agency and as an engagement with the state as a site of struggle is fraught with problems for women. While gains have been made to include women's interests on the political agenda political activism is needed to shift the discursive shape of present politics.

Globalization is also eroding women's citizenship through the limits it places on the implementation of socio-economic rights. The shift by government from the Reconstruction and Development Programme (RDP) to the macro economic policy of Growth, Employment and Redistribution (GEAR) which as a pro-growth policy has embodied neo-liberal mechanisms such as faster deficit reduction and budget discipline, labour market regulation, relaxation of exchange controls and privatization. GEAR was a response to South Africa's sensitivity to greater globalization and its impact on South Africa's markets. It was also an attempt to generate growth to enable redistribution. These type of neo-liberal policies have detrimental effects for people living in poverty or who are facing poverty. As Dickenson (2002) points out, those facing poverty rely on extended families who still have formal sector employment, also dragging them into poverty (p.14). About 50% of the South African population is poor with a 72% rural poverty rate (May, 2001, p.303). The poor in South Africa are largely African, rural and women (May, 2001, p.306).

Globalization is changing labour markets and the nature of work so that job creation takes place in the informal sector, creating casual, temporary or home-based work. But it is also creating an army of unemployed, underemployed and rural poor. The consequences are growing poverty and inequality, job insecurity, crime and a disintegration of the social fabric (Taylor, 2002, p.7).

The impact on women is far-reaching, trapping them in poverty. Elson (2002) points to three types of biases of neo-liberal policies that are detrimental to women (p.85): (1) a deflationary bias: governments are prevented from dealing effectively with recession and women in the informal sector lose their jobs faster than men, (2) a breadwinner bias: policies reward labour in the market economy of commodities around a norm of full-time, life-long participation and do not reward care work of the unpaid care economy, (3) a privatization bias: the poor cannot afford to pay for services.

In the absence of a social security net the government is trying to develop policies to help people deal with poverty. One such suggested policy is 'comprehensive social protection' that 'incorporates developmental strategies and programmes designed to ensure, collectively, at least a minimum acceptable living standard for all citizens. It embraces the traditional measures of social insurance, social assistance and social services, but goes beyond that to focus on causality through an integrated policy approach including many of the developmental initiatives undertaken by the state' (Taylor, 2002, p.30). Whatever the distribution processes that will be put in place, women's reproductive and care roles need to be considered.

Citizenship therefore cannot be limited to rights (or status) only. The relationship between rights, participation and struggles in the locale of the state determines the shape of women's citizenship. How rights and gender are constructed in discourse and implemented in reality makes the difference between having citizenship and living it.

Notes

1. The author wants to thank Shireen Hassim, Linzi Manicom and Mikki van Zyl for helpful comments on an earlier draft of this chapter.
2. It was an important time as the broader political system structured opportunities for collective action, and the capacity for social movements to reshape the broader political landscape was at a peak. See McAdam, 1996, p.20.
3. See for example Hassim (2002a; 2002b) as well as Cock and Bernstein (2002).
4. But for a perspective on analysing the state see Goetz and Hassim (2003).
5. My own research on the Recognition of the Customary Marriages Act of 1998 has shown that the JCQLSW was the pivotal structure to get this legislation passed and to make the voices of rural women heard.
6. See training package developed for the Cape Provincial Administration.
7. Just how unquestioning gender has become in the South African context is revealed by the training material developed for the Provincial Administration of the Western Cape. This material refers to 'mainstreaming human rights for women, youth and the disabled'. The very same material is used for all three identity categories on the assumption that their needs/interests around equality are the same.
8. For a more detailed analysis see Gouws, A. (2002b).
9. See e.g. Albertyn and Hassim (2003).
10. See Du Plesssis and Gouws (1992) for reference to the South African context.
11. See GAP Conference Report (2002).

12. See for example Henson (2002) on women's participation in the rural water committees in South Africa.
13. See Seekings (2003) and the Basic Income Grant Fact Sheet.
14. Floor crossing legislation allow candidates who represent a specific party to cross the floor to join another party during specified periods of the year and still keep their seats. The undemocratic aspects of this practice have been widely discussed.
15. This is a highly contentious issue – see Mattes and Gouws (1998).

References

Adams, Ubanesia (2001), 'Promoting Gender Equality in the Provincial Administration of the Western Cape: An Appraisal Based on Perceptions of Gender Focal Persons and the Head of the Western Cape Office of the Status of Women for Gender Equality', Unpublished MPhil Thesis, University of Stellenbosch.
Albertyn, Catherine and Shireen Hassim, (2003), 'The Boundaries of Democracy: Gender, HIV/AIDS and Culture' in David Everatt and Vincent Maphai (eds.), *The Real State of the Nation – South Africa After 1990*, Johannesburg, Interfund, pp.137-164.
Albertyn, Catherine, Hassim, Shireen and Meintjes, Sheila (2002), 'Making a Difference? Women's Struggle for Participation and Representation', in Glenda Fick, Sheila Meintjes and Mary Simons (eds.), *One Woman, One Vote*, Electoral Institute of Southern Africa, Johannesburg, pp.24-52.
Banaszak, Lee Ann, Beckwith, Karen and Ruch, Dieter (2003), *Women's Movements Facing the Reconfigured State*, Cambridge University Press, New York.
Basic Income Grant Coalition, Fact Sheet 2003.
Beckwith, Karen (2000), 'Beyond Compare? Women's Movements in Comparative Perspective', *European Journal of Political Research*, 37, pp.431-468.
Brown, Wendy (1992), 'Finding the Man in the State', *Feminist Studies*, 18:1, pp.7-34.
Chaney, Paul and Fevre, Ralph (2002), 'Is there a Demand for Descriptive Representation? Evidence from the UK's Devolution Programme', *Political Studies*, 30:5, pp.897-915.
Cock, Jacklyn and Bernstein, Alison (2002), *Melting Pots and Rainbow Nations*, University of Illinois Press, Urbana.
Dickenson, David (2002), 'Confronting Reality: Change and Transformation in the New South Africa', *Political Science Quarterly*, 73:1, pp.10-20.
Du Plessis, Lourens and Gouws, Amanda (1992), ''n Dialektiese Perspektief op die Statutêre en Grondwetlike Verwesenliking van Vroueregte in Suid-Afrika', *Stellenbosch Law Review*, 4:2, pp.240-260.
Elson, Diane (2002), 'For an Emancipatory Socio-Economics', *New Agenda*, 5, pp.83-95.
GAP Conference Report (2002), 'Women's Representation in Government, Unfinished Business … 50/50 by 2005', 7-8 March 2002.
Gender Research Project of the Centre for Applied Legal Studies, University of the Witwatersrand (2000), 'Engendering the Political Agenda: The Role of the State, Women's Organizations and the International Community', United Nations International Research and Training Institute for the Advancement of Women (INSTRAW), Dominican Republic.
Goetz, Ann Marie and Hassim, Shireen (2003), *No Shortcuts to Power*, Zed Press, London.
Gouws, Amanda (2002a), 'Women as Political Participants: The Gender Gap in Voting Behavior' in Glenda Fick, Sheila Meintjes and Mary Simons (eds.), *One Woman, One Vote*, Electoral Institute of Southern Africa, Johannesburg, pp.116-135.

Gouws, Amanda (2002b) 'Back to the Drawing Board?' *Network News*, April (GETNET Newsletter).

Gouws, Amanda (2003), 'Democracy and Gendered Citizenship: Educational Institutions as Sites of Struggle', Unpublished Manuscript.

Gouws, Amanda (2004), 'The Politics of State Structures: Citizenship and the National Machinery for Women in South Africa', *Feminist Africa*, Vol.2:1 (forthcoming).

Hassim, Shireen (1999), 'From Presence to Power – Women's Citizenship in A New Democracy', *Agenda*, No.40, pp.6-17.

Hassim, Shireen (2002a), 'Identities, Interests and Constituencies: The Politics of the Women's Movement in South Africa, 1980-1999', Unpublished PhD Dissertation, York University.

Hassim, Shireen (2002b), 'The Dual Politics of Representation: Women and Electoral Politics in South Africa', in Glenda Fick, Sheila Meintjes and Mary Simons (eds.), *One Woman, One Vote*, Electoral Institute of Southern Africa, Johannesburg, pp.102-115.

Hassim, Shireen (2002c), '"A Conspiracy of Women": The Women's Movement in South Africa's Transition To Democracy', *Social Research*, 69:3, pp.693-732.

Hassim, Shireen (2003), 'The Gender Pact and Democratic Consolidation: Institutionalizing Gender Equality in the South African State', *Feminist Studies*, 29:3, pp.505-528.

Hassim, Shireen and Gouws, Amanda (1999), 'Gender, Citizenship and Diversity', in M. Cross, E. Beckham, A. Harper, J. Indiresan and C. Musil (eds.), *Diversity and Unity – The Role of Higher Education in Building Democracy*, Maskew Miller Longman, Cape Town, pp.80-106.

Henson, David (2002), '"Women are Weak When They are Amongst Men": Women's Participation in Rural Water Committees in South Africa', *Agenda*, No.52, pp.24-32.

Hobson, Barbara (2000), 'Agency, Identities and Institutions', *Social Politics*, 7:2, pp.238-243.

Jacquette, Jane S. (2003), 'Feminism and the Challenge of the "Post-Cold War" World', *International Feminist Journal of Politics*, 5:2, November, pp. 331-354.

Jones, Kathleen B. (1994), 'Identity, Action, and Locale: Thinking about Citizenship, Civic Action, and Feminism', *Social Politics*, Fall, pp.256-270.

Korpi, Walter (2000), 'Faces of Inequality: Gender, Class, and Patterns of Inequalities in Different Types of Welfare States', *Social Politics*, 7:2, Summer, pp.127-191.

Lister, Ruth (1997), *Citizenship: Feminist Perspectives*, New York University Press, New York.

McAdam, Doug, McCarthy, John and Zald, Mayer (1996), 'Introduction: Opportunities, Mobilizing Structures, and Framing Processes – Toward a Synthetic, Comparative Perspective on Social Movements', in D. McAdam, J. McCarthy and M. Zald (eds.), *Comparative Perspectives on Social Movements*, Cambridge University Press, Cambridge, pp.1-20.

McKay, Ailsa and Vanevery, Jo (2000), 'Gender, Family, and Income Maintenance: A Feminist Case for Citizens' Basic Income', *Social Politics*, 7:2, pp.266-284.

MacLean, Emilou (2001), 'Basic Education for All: Realities in the South African Education System', *Rights Now*, 10, December, pp.14-17.

Mama, Amina (2000), 'National Machinery for Women in Africa', Third World Network – Africa, Ghana.

Manicom, Linzi (2001), 'Globalising "gender" in – or as – governance? Questioning the Terms of Local Translation', *Agenda*, No.48, pp.6-21.

Marshall, T.H. (1950), *Citizenship and Social Class*, Cambridge University Press, Cambridge.

Mattes, Robert and Gouws, Amanda (1998), 'Race, Ethnicity, and Voting Behavior: Lessons from South Africa' in Timothy Sisk and Andrew Reynolds (eds.), *Elections and Conflict Management in Africa*, Unites States Institute of Peace Press, Washington, DC, pp.119-142.

May, Julian (2001), 'Meeting the Challenge? The Emerging Agenda for Poverty Reduction in Post-Apartheid South Africa', in F. Wilson, N. Kanji and E. Braathen (eds.), *Poverty Reduction – What Role for the State in Today's Globalized Economy?* Zed Books, London, pp.302-326.

Mensah-Kutin, R. Mahama, A. Ocran, S. Ofei-Aboagye, E. Okine, V. and Tsikata, D. (2000*)*, *The National Machinery for Women in Ghana: An NGO Evaluation*, Third World Network – Africa, Ghana.

O'Connor, Julia, Orloff, Ann and Shaver, Sheila (1999), *States, Market, Families, Gender, Liberalism and Social Policy in Australia, Canada, Great Britain and the United States*, Cambridge University Press, Cambridge and New York.

Petchesky, Rosalind (2000), 'Sexual Rights: Inventing a Concept, Mapping an International Practice', in R. Parker, R.M. Barbosa and P. Aggleton (eds.), *Framing the Sexual Subject: The Politics of Gender, Sexuality, and Power*, University of California Press, Berkeley, pp.81-103.

Phillips, Anne (1992), 'Must Feminists Give Up on Liberal Democracy?' *Political Studies*, 40, pp.68-82.

Pringle, Rosemary and Watson, Sophie (1992), '"Women's interests" and the post-structuralist state' in M. Barrett and A. Phillips (eds.), *Destabilising Theory*, Polity Press, London.

Pringle, Rosemary and Watson, Sophie (1996), 'Feminist Theory and the State: Needs, Rights and Interests', in B. Sullivan and G. Whitehouse (eds.), *Gender, Politics and Citizenship in the 1990s*, University of New South Wales Press, Sydney, pp.64-78.

Schneider, Elizabeth, M. (1991), 'The Dialectic of Rights and Politics: *Perspectives* from the Women's Movement [1986]' in K.T. Bartlett and R. Kennedy (eds.), *Feminist Legal Theory*, Westview Press, Boulder, pp.318-332.

Seekings, Jeremy (2003), 'Providing for the Poor: Welfare and Redistribution in South Africa', Inaugural Lecture, University of Cape Town, 23 May.

Seidman, Gay W. (2003) 'Institutional Dilemmas: Representation Versus Mobilization in the South African Gender Commission', *Feminist Studies*, 29:3, pp.541-563.

Sevenhuijsen, Selma (1998), *Citizenship and the Ethics of Care*, Routledge, London.

Sevenhuijsen, S., Bozalek, V., Gouws, A. and Minnaar-McDonald, M. (2003), 'South African Social Welfare Policy: An Analysis of the Ethic of Care', *Critical Social Policy*, 23:3, pp.299-321.

Siim, Birte (2000), *Gender and Citizenship*, Cambridge University Press, New York.

Stetson, Dorothy McBride and Mazur, Amy G. (eds.), (1995), *Comparative State Feminism*, Sage, London.

Taylor, Vivien (2000), *Marketisation of Governance*, SADEP, Cape Town.

Taylor, Vivien (2002), 'What Kind of Social Security', *New Agenda*, 5, pp.6-47.

True, Jacqui (2003), 'Mainstreaming Gender in Global Public Policy', *International Feminist Journal of Politics*, 5:3, pp.368-396.

Voet, Rian (1998), *Feminism and Citizenship*, Sage, London.

Waylen, Georgina (1996), *Gender in Third World Politics*, Open University Press, Buckingham.

Waylen, Georgina (1998), 'Gender, Feminism and the State: An Overview' in Vicky Randall, and Georgina Waylen, (eds.), *Gender, Politics and the State*, Routledge, London, pp.1-17.

Chapter 4

Masculinity, Citizenship and Political Objection to Military Service in Apartheid South Africa[1]

Daniel Conway

Do you and your family sleep safely at night? Who do you have to thank for that? Are you aware of the Communist threat to your and my country? Can you deny that if you love your country you fight for it? Please do South Africa a favour and leave and take your fellow cowards with you. Why should anyone fight for your kind? Please go.

Letter addressed to Ms. Kirsten, National Secretary of the End Conscription Campaign, from N. Harding, 19/1/1986.

Introduction

Military conscription, being called upon to defend the state, is a key moment in defining personal as well as political identity. In certain contexts participation in military service becomes a minimal requirement for belonging to the nation. The act of objecting to compulsory military service challenges some of the most fundamental tenets of political and social organization. It disputes a society's conception of national interest and good citizenship. Furthermore, men who object to military service challenge what it means to be a 'real man' in society and will be open to charges that they are not 'true men', that they have not only defied the conventions of accepted political agency but that their personal identity is 'deviant'. As Helman (1999a) notes in her study of conscientious objection in Israel:

> The refusal of individuals to fulfil their prime duty towards the state struck at the heart of the institutional body (military service and the army), the practices (soldiering), and the meanings (participation in the defence of the political community) through which citizenship has been socially constructed for Israeli-Jewish males (p.46).

Conscientious objection involves an alternative discourse of citizenship to the hegemonic one constructed by the state. There are many definitions of citizenship but as Lister (1997) notes: 'At its lowest common denominator, we are talking about membership of a community ... and about the relationship between individuals and the state and between individual citizens within that community' (p.3). Citizenship defines who is included and excluded from the political community and who is a legitimate and illegitimate political actor. 'Struggles over citizenship are thus struggles over the very meaning of politics and membership in a community' (Werbner, 1999, p.221). Werbner (1999) also contends that it is those who are marginalized or excluded who are most likely to challenge hegemonic definitions of citizenship. The link between citizenship and modes of personal identity, such as gender, are forged because citizenship and gender are both 'group markers', they both assign roles to individuals and also define who is included and excluded from the group (Isin and Wood, 1999, p.20). Concepts of citizenship and gender are also hierarchical, defining who holds greater and lesser power in society.

Objection to military service within the South African Defence Force (SADF) by white males for political or moral reasons represented an extraordinary challenge to the apartheid regime from within the ranks of the ruling white oligarchy and was interpreted as dangerous by the regime. The investigation of this political act from an individual and group level is therefore necessary. The analysis of the nexus between personal and political identity has been a long-term feminist project. The reciprocal interaction between citizenship and gender and the inscription of political identity on individual attributes and normative gender roles was a primary method of political mobilization and control in apartheid South Africa. Compelling men to undertake military conscription requires that the personal become, quite literally, the political. Personal qualities, attitudes and even activities such as sport became the foundation of a militarized system. Exhibiting alternative qualities (or articulating alternative interpretations of what it was to be courageous, patriotic and orderly) therefore challenged the building blocks of the state's authoritarian system.

Masculinity

The interplay between constructions of gender and militarization has been examined in the South African context (Cock 1993; Cock and Nathan, 1989). However, the precise role of compulsory military service for all white males and the implications this had for the construction of personal and political identity has not been extensively studied. Furthermore, little research has been done on the theoretical significance of objection to conscription from a gendered perspective. Feminist scholarship has always sought to interrogate the iniquitous operation of power, but as Scott-Swart (1998) notes, '[g]ender history is too often conflated with the history of women' (p.5). Widening the scope of gender studies to include men as a separate category (rather than as a trope to highlight the oppression of women), has been a key development in gender studies over the past two decades. The study of masculinity reveals that although men and masculinity possess the cultural and political capital to subordinate women and femininity, men themselves can be subordinated by other men and that there is not one, but multiple masculinities.

The advance of critical men's studies has been to ... show that not all men have the same amount of power or benefit equally from it, and that power is exercised differently depending on the location and the specific arrangement of relations which are in place (Morrell, 2001, p.9).

Kimmel (1994) defines masculinity as, 'a constantly changing collection of meanings that we construct through our relationships with ourselves, with each other, and with the world. Manhood is neither static nor timeless, it is historical' (p.120). Kimmel's contention that masculinity is socially constructed is the central assumption in the new men's studies. Masculinity as a construct is unstable and is formed in a shifting process that involves conflicting definitions, indeed there is not one but multiple masculinities in any given society. Connell's (1987; 1995) groundbreaking work classifies these masculinities into hegemonic, complicit (conservative) and marginalized (subordinate) groups. At the centre of this classification is the Gramscian concept of hegemony. Hegemony, 'refers to the cultural dynamic by which a group claims and sustains a leading position in social life', in terms of gender, 'one form of masculinity rather than others is culturally exalted' and it is this hegemonic construct of masculinity which forms the gender 'norm' of any given society (Connell, 1995, p.77). The majority of men are unlikely to display hegemonic masculinity, but hegemonic masculinity is what they will be encouraged to embody and admire.

Butler's (1999) concept of gender as an ongoing performance that can encompass any gender characteristic regardless of sex also pertains to men's masculine identity. Men have the agency to choose the gender identity they perform and their masculine identity varies across time and culture. 'Masculinity is never fully possessed, but must perpetually be achieved, asserted and negotiated' (Roper and Tosh, 1991, p.18). Men engage in a constant performance of masculinity and never truly achieve or own hegemonic status. Masculinity 'must be proved, and no sooner is it proved than it is again questioned and must be proved again – constant, relentless, unachievable' (Kimmel, 1994, p.122). This competition to 'prove' masculinity makes it an unstable and often violent process. The majority of men embody complicit masculinity. This means they will not embody true hegemonic forms of masculinity but that they acquiesce to hegemonic forms and draw the dividends of power over women as a result. Although hegemonic forms of masculinity are historically and culturally specific, a common theme is that 'heterosexuality and homophobia are the bedrock of hegemonic masculinity' (Donaldson, 1993, p.645). The rejection of femininity within hegemonic masculinity is a central mechanism for men to ensure that their individual position in the hierarchy of masculinity be maintained. 'Any kind of powerlessness, or refusal to compete among men readily becomes involved with images of homosexuality' (Carrigan, Connell and Lee, 1987, p.86). Men who display, or are perceived to display, 'effeminate' traits will be relegated to the bottom of the masculinity hierarchy, their masculinity subordinated and marginalized. Men from marginalized groups can contest and challenge hegemonic masculinity (as has happened with the gay rights movement). The yoking of masculinity with violence and specifically military service, as a method for achieving hegemonic masculinity, was a central tenet of apartheid society. It was this gendered power structure that the conscientious objectors had to operate in and challenge.

Military

The military is a primary institution for the construction of hegemonic masculinity. The existence of conscription and the primacy the SADF had in the South African state meant that the imagery associated with the South African soldier and the values needed to become a soldier resonated throughout white society. 'In military affairs the state apparatus is visibly constructing forms of masculinity and regulating relations between them, not as an incidental effect of its operation, but as an actual precondition of them' (Connell, 1990, p.529). The constructions of military identities also makes direct links between masculinity and the state and are fundamental in forming gender and civic identities (Sasson-Levy, 2002, p.359). Violence, racism, dominance and control were all tied into the construct of hegemonic masculinity for white men as a result. Morrell (2001) and Du Pisani (2001) identify South African hegemonic masculinity as tied with Afrikaner identity. Afrikaner masculinity was authoritarian and intolerant of criticism: 'Hegemonic Afrikaner masculinity was intrinsically bound up with the social and political power of Afrikaner society and hence with Afrikaner nationalism' (Du Pisani, 2001, p.157). Du Pisani characterizes Afrikaner masculinity as essentially puritan; liberalism and homosexuality were marginalized and subordinated. A pervading sense of guilt and respect for authority coerced and enticed men into obediently accepting the value of military service.

Violence

Violence became a primary factor in masculine identity as the state increasingly struggled, by military means, to control the country and region. 'One of the central themes of militarist discourse is the centrality of war in the constitution of individual identity, the cultural attributes of society, and the underpinning of the state' (Jabri, 1996, p.99). The militarization of South Africa had a profound impact on modes of interpersonal relations and upon individuals' identities and expectations; a higher incidence of violence was an inevitable result. Marks and Andersson (1990) interpreted apartheid as a form of structural violence, of which military service was just one aspect: 'In South Africa the culture of violence exists at every level; and overt political violence must be located in this wider social context as but one of many forms and varieties of endemic violence' (p.30). High levels of suicide (particularly amongst young white men), alcoholism, road accidents and interpersonal violence were all unusually high in the white population; a reflection of the extent of South Africa's advanced state of militarization.[2] Objectors and the End Conscription Campaign (ECC) worked within an extremely difficult and hostile environment and had to compete with and challenge a dominant and deeply entrenched militarism if they were to gain any influence within the white population. However, as Morgan (1994) notes,

The nexus linking masculinity, violence and the military, although providing some of the most gendered images in many cultures, is far from being a straightforward one. Indeed, the apparent simple linkages represent a major cultural achievement rather than the natural order of things (p.179).

The ECC could and did uncover and attack the artificial constructions and assumptions upon which South African militarized identity depended.

Republican Citizenship

The concept of citizenship, particularly republican citizenship, can, like gender identity, be interpreted as a performance and one that is inherently bound with particular gender norms that are tied to military service:

> Dating all the way back to ancient Greece, the civic republican tradition directly addresses the interconnections between gender, military service, and citizenship through its central ideal of the manly Citizen-Soldier. Standing at the very centre of civic republican tradition, this figure embodies the twin practices of civic republican citizenship: military service and civic participation (Snyder, 1999, p.1).

The focal point and moment when man becomes a true republican citizen is, therefore, the performance of military service in the name of the state. It is at this moment when the individual can claim to be a 'true man' and a 'good citizen'.

Citizenship is a 'status' within the republican model, 'a status to be sought and, once achieved, to be maintained'. Civic republicanism constitutes,

> full membership of the political community … Within civic republicanism, citizenship is an activity or a practice, and not simply a status, and that not to engage in the practice is, in an important sense, not to be a citizen. Secondly, civic republicanism recognizes that, unsupported, individuals cannot be expected to engage in the practice (Oldfield, 1990, p.159).

Civic republicanism diverges from the concept of citizenship in liberal individualism, 'in that it believes the ultimate expression of selfhood is in the service of the public good, which is greater than individual good (Lister, 1997, p.23). Service in the army is an ideal method for creating republican citizens; men as soldiers move beyond individual self-interest: 'The soldiers, as soldiers give up their individual identities to assimilate themselves in a single collective identity' (Norton, 1993, p.156). Republican citizens claim their right to political agency by embracing common, collective goods over private, individual need. Military service, risking one's life for the nation, is an incomparable means of achieving this. The ultimate expression of this service for the common good is the act of sacrifice. Elshtain (1995) interprets republican citizenship as a construct that is not based on killing but on men *dying*, 'dying for others, to protect them, sacrificing himself so that others might live' (p.206). Elshtain (1992) also explains how civic republicanism implodes the divisions between state and individual:

It is in war that the state is tested, and only through that test can it be shown whether individuals can overcome selfishness and are prepared to work for the whole and to sacrifice in service to the more inclusive good. The man becomes what in some senses he is meant to be by being absorbed by the larger stream of life: war and the state. To preserve the larger civic body, which must be 'as one', particular bodies must be sacrificed (p.143).

In apartheid South Africa (as in other comparable republican societies, such as contemporary Israel) military service served as the bridge that links the achievement of republican citizenship and hegemonic masculinity. A man must serve in the army to embody a citizen, a patriotic South African and a 'real' man.[3]

The Masculine Political Actor

Feminist scholars have critiqued republican citizenship for its exclusionary and martial construction of political identity at the expense of women. Furthermore, 'political man' as presented in republican theories (as in political philosophy generally), both genders political actors as masculine and de-genders the construct. Qualities such as rationality, autonomy and courage are conflated with masculinity and posited on political man but their political exercise is presented as gender neutral; qualities to be attained by all political actors in the public sphere (Carver, 1996). Women and 'femininity' are thereby devalued and excluded, relegated to the private sphere. Indeed, Pateman (1988) views the very creation of political society, when we enter the 'social contract' as an inherently masculine act. The public sphere is thus gendered masculine and femininity must be excluded and controlled in the private sphere. Furthermore, with the conflation of war, masculinity and citizenship that is present in republican theory, men who question military service will be feminized themselves and their right to political agency revoked. The masculine, heterosexual body will come to define the body politic, 'The image of the warrior will come to personify the society, and individual soldiers will be called on to identify their occupation with the core values of the nation' (Morgan, 1994, p.170). Threats to the body politic will therefore be presented in gendered terms and individuals who do not conform to the hegemonic ideal of masculinity (i.e. those who embody subordinate masculinities such as gay men or women) will be potential threats (Pettman, 1996, p.50; Phelan, 1999). The state and nation, therefore, come to embody the identity of the hegemonic construct of individual identity. To embody feminine qualities, therefore, jeopardizes one's ability to be a political agent and citizen. South Africa offers a striking example of this; the state (and its agents) often branded men who were members of the End Conscription Campaign as gay and traitors to the nation. Essentially, republican citizenship relies on a particular conception of hegemonic masculinity in order to structure society according to its gender vision. A soldier will have proved that he can overcome self-interest for the common good, that he has entered the public realm and rejected the feminine concerns and pursuits of the private realm and achieved hegemonic, heterosexual masculinity.

The State

The state was the primary agent for articulating hegemonic forms of citizenship and masculinity, the vehicles for this articulation were the legal system, education system, the media and, of course, the military. Tilly (1995) contends that citizenship ranges from 'thin' to 'thick', with thin requiring few obligations of service to the state and thick requiring many obligations (p.8). South African citizenship for white men could be classed as thick and becoming thicker as military service obligations and the discourse justifying it intensified from the late 1970s onwards until democratization. However, this classification can only be applied to the white population; the black population experienced 'thin' citizenship, or none at all. The state's articulation of hegemonic forms of masculinity and citizenship were not always uniform and evolved over time as the apartheid system adapted and changed. For example, the requirement of national service, although framed in military terms in state discourse, eventually encompassed non-military forms, for example, recognizing religious objectors while the SADF increasingly tried to incorporate those who did not wish to see active service into military institutions (Seegers, 1993). This was a reflection of the depths to which ECC discourse had penetrated the South African public sphere and also the fact that the Nationalist regime was losing its sense of unity and purpose. P.W. Botha's 'neo-apartheid' philosophy of reform and concomitant military control meant that the SADF represented an upholder of peace and a valuable asset and cooperator with the communities of South Africa; some of the SADF's projects strikingly resembled those advocated by the ECC.

Apartheid South Africa

The South African state's discourse about the necessity of military service can be grouped into a number of main themes:

1. South Africa faced a 'Total Onslaught' from world communism, manifested in the border war in Namibia, insurgency within the Republic and an insidious attempt to undermine the white population's 'morale';
2. the Republic's 'survival' was at stake;
3. in response, from 1967[4] all white males had to undertake two years of compulsory military service and a subsequent period of reserve service;
4. service in the SADF developed the physical and mental potential of the men that undertook it;
5. the SADF provided a 'shield' behind which the government could undertake 'evolutionary reform' at its own pace;
6. the SADF was apolitical and served the public good of all racial groups, and that;
7. those within the white community who opposed conscription were part of the Total Onslaught.

Conscientious objectors and the End Conscription Campaign articulated a message that challenged and competed with the hegemonic discourse of the state. Their broad themes can be arranged as follows:

1. the SADF was engaged in an unjust, racial civil war;
2. Namibia was being illegally occupied by South Africa;
3. as a result of the 'Just War' interpretation, white men had a right to object to service in the SADF on grounds of conscience;
4. South Africa was a dangerously militarized society, leading to excessive violence;
5. conscription was a primary mechanism for the militarization of South Africa;
6. alternative, non-military, forms of national service in the form of community work would serve the needs of the South African nation;
7. these themes were an expression of true patriotism and meaningful civic participation.

Pro- and anti-conscription arguments varied from the crude to the sophisticated and from implacable opposition to contestation over shared ideological terrain (for example, as was the case in the claims to actively serve 'common interest' and 'public good' through some form of civic participation). The key variable when analysing these debates is the recognition that at the heart of these contestations lay an attempt to define the political and personal characteristics of 'good' white South Africans: notions of courage, dignity, manhood, service, community, security and personal development were all contested terrains within pro and anti-conscription discourse. The claim to true South African citizenship was the political focus of these oppositional stances, with the state claiming the exclusive right to define normative citizenship and conscientious objectors and their supporters radically challenging this and seeking to reconstitute citizenship from a non-racial, demilitarized and inclusive basis.

The Total Onslaught

South Africa faced a 'Total Onslaught' concluded Prime Minister (and later President) P.W. Botha shortly after assuming office in 1978 (Cawthra, 1986, p.60). This onslaught was directed by world communism and threatened to overthrow the South African state and everything it stood for. As the Minister of Defence explained, this onslaught, 'involves so many different fronts, unknown to the South African experience, that it has gained the telling but horrifying name of total war' (Malan, cited in Cock and Nathan, 1989, p.xiii). This assumption created an interpretive paradigm from which all aspects of South African politics and society were to be framed by the state and was 'one of the most potent tools in the state's armoury of political mobilization' (Frankel, 1984, p.69). A significant aspect of this counter-revolutionary governing strategy was that the onslaught was not only military, but also psychological and aimed at undermining the morale of the white population. 'In this physical and psychological battle', wrote General Malan, 'the enemy seeks to overthrow the established order and to destroy the fabric of our society. It is imperative in this situation that every citizen is fully trained and motivated to assume his share of the burden' (Malan, 28/1/1985). This served as a licence for the state to manipulate the education system and media to support its militarized aims and also framed the rhetoric the state used against the End Conscription Campaign and conscientious objectors.

The SADF

The SADF was the central tenet of South Africa's response and defence against this perceived onslaught. The SADF was primarily represented as a 'shield' against outside aggression. It was a shield that would not only protect the state, but also allow the state to enable 'reforms' of the apartheid system to take place at a pace suited to the government; 'it is the shield behind which change can be and is being brought about' stated *The Citizen* newspaper (12/4/1987). Writing about Namibia, Willem Steenkamp accepted that negotiations would eventually have to take place, but until then, 'the SADF has managed to dominate the essential military phase that precedes negotiations' (1983, p.66). The SADF was presented as a defensive force and this contention was a primary focus for the End Conscription Campaign. Even opposition politicians uneasy with conscription and critical of the role of the SADF accepted the need for this shield and warned of the danger of abolishing conscription (*The Star*, 6/2/1985). Secondly, South Africa was presented as fighting 'for its very survival', the SADF was enabling the state to exist and undermining conscription could lead to the nation's destruction. If the ECC had its way, wrote Steenkamp, there would be 'disaster for all South Africans ... I am talking about survival – survival not of the whites but of South Africa itself' (Steenkamp, *Cape Times*, 24/10/1984). When the business community raised concerns about the impact of two years' service and subsequent reserve service on the economy, General Webster responded: 'Businessmen must realise we're fighting for our survival. I don't think there should be any doubt about that. So their commitment must increase' (*Financial Mail*, 1/6/1979). This drew on the historical discourse of the Voortrekkers, a threatened and isolated people, battling for survival and was undoubtedly framed with the intention to foster unity within the white populace and mobilize support for the militarization of the country.

The concept of 'survival' also invokes biologistic associations with the state; it connects the state to the 'body politic' that is under threat of violation or even death. The call to military service, according to the state, was a call to defend the very existence of South Africa: 'You stand at the threshold of service of the highest order', wrote Colonel Viljoen (1984) to each new national serviceman in 1984, service 'to yourself, your nation and your fatherland' (p.8). As the SADF manual for that year explained: 'The defence of that which is your own cannot be left to anybody else. It is the privilege of every citizen of the RSA to help protect *his* (my emphasis) country against onslaught. National service is therefore not so much an obligation as a call and a privilege' (Van der Merwe, 1984, p.29).[5] This discourse clearly sets up a republican paradigm, where men must fulfil their duty to become part of the community which is in dire threat. A state fighting for its very survival against an enemy onslaught can expect the right of its citizens to be prepared to sacrifice themselves in the state's defence and for the wider, common good. The enactment of military service is presented not just as a duty, but as a privilege as well; men can fulfil their true personal and political potential by undertaking it. An article in *Paratus* (the SADF magazine on sale to the public) promoting national service quoted radio presenter, and advocate of republican citizenship, Patricia Kerr as saying, 'most South Africans love their country and I think if you love the country you were born in, you would be prepared to do something for it. If you defend your country, you are defending a way of life'. TV Newsreader Roelf Jacobs put it even more bluntly: 'The defence of this country is a duty, a necessity ... our children must realize that they must be prepared to sacrifice their lives, if necessary, in the struggle for survival' (*Paratus*, September 1980).

Hegemonic Citizenship

The state relied on a number of key themes to advocate national service and to create an environment where resistance to conscription became extremely difficult. A predominant discursive method was to bind the personal growth of a man to the performance of national service and to tie the qualities needed to be an effective soldier to the desired characteristics of a successful citizen in the home, workplace and civic life. President Botha ordered an enquiry in 1986 to investigate 'ways in which South African youth can be equipped and positively motivated for responsible citizenship and active participation and involvement' (President's Council, 1987, p.1). It is therefore apt to begin with the conclusions of the resultant Report as a basis for investigating the state's conception of hegemonic masculinity and citizenship. The President's Council Report (1987) noted that: 'Young people, motivated for loyal citizenship can form one of the pillars of any society and nation' (p.1) and contended that South African youths were being prevented from taking their place in civil society (and also having their 'lives destroyed') because of a decline in authority and discipline, coupled with a rise in permissiveness, promiscuity, drug addiction, suicide[6] and divorce (p.89). The basis for creating good citizens was consequently: a strong family life, discipline, Christian morality, a sense of community and patriotism. One of the primary mechanisms for achieving this, concluded the Council, was through national service in the SADF. The Report (President's Council, 1987) contended that military service, 'fosters discipline and is accompanied by basic guidance and a large degree of community involvement, and can accordingly make a very important contribution to the moulding of many thousands of young people towards responsible and meaningful existence and citizenship' (p.99). Controversially, the Report (President's Council, 1987) advocated the extension of conscription (and the school cadet system) to black people[7] as a means of engendering stability (p.68). As the apartheid state reformed and attempted to extend its boundaries of citizenship, military service is presented as the means by which the state can incorporate citizens into the polity. The Report confirms Helman (1997, p.306) and Sasson-Levy's (2002, p.359) opinions that military service is a mechanism for managing and controlling the populace, extending conscription to blacks would therefore impose discipline on the 'unruly' black population. The metaphor of 'moulding' young people to create 'responsible' and 'meaningful existence and citizenship' is Foucauldian in that the apartheid state was aware that it needed to 'mould' individuals in their personality and physical abilities in order to uphold the wider power of the state.

The proposal for the extension of military service contained in the President's Council Report was attacked from the perspective that there should be a direct link between legal citizenship and military service. *The City Press*, with a largely black readership, commented that: 'National service implies that you have full citizenship and therefore a duty to defend your country. We do not have full citizenship, to say the very least, and it would be cynical for anybody to expect us to join an army which actively helps prop up the system of apartheid' (*City Press*, 21/6/1987). The Labour Party, with its support base in the Coloured population, accepted the proposals so long as political reforms increasing Coloured people's citizenship rights were implemented (*Eastern Province Herald*, 19/6/1987). To be a soldier one had to be a citizen.

Hegemonic Masculinity

In response to a letter advocating alternative, non-military forms of national service, General Malan wrote: 'national service prepares and matures a young man for his future role in the life of the nation. It helps to shape and strengthen the character of each individual, emphasises the importance of teamwork and self-discipline' (Malan, 19/1/1986). Here, Malan states the President's Council's belief in the necessity of military service in creating good citizens and introduces some of the individual characteristics also engendered by service. These qualities form the basis of the state's conception of hegemonic masculinity and their achievement defined a 'true man'. By tying their achievement to military service, men who refused to do military service were excluded from the achievement of true 'manhood'. It is important, therefore, to investigate these qualities in greater depth.[8]

The school system has been identified as a primary site for creating gender expectations and forming hegemonic ideals for individuals. The school cadet system, where white boys took part in military drill exercises and ideological training, was thus a primary mechanism for constructing hegemonic masculinity and binding it to military service. The state identified the cadet system as an arena where young men could be 'moulded'. The Cape Education Department's Cadet's Training Manual outlined the qualities military training and preparation for national service created. The Department concluded, 'national service may be virtually regarded as a modern initiation school ... It is generally considered that the defence force makes a man (*sic*) out of boys' (1986, p.6).

National service was presented in terms of 'personal growth' and 'self-fulfilment'. Personal gains of national service include discipline, self confidence (in a man's own body and his abilities), good judgement, independence, physical readiness, an ability to use a gun and defend himself, love of one's country and, of course, courage. A serviceman also 'cultivates a pride in his country and his uniform, his attitude reflects his inner convictions and self-confidence – also valuable character traits in civilian life' (Cape Education Department, 1986, pp.5-

6). Here, the department states its conception of hegemonic masculinity. The metaphors used are also replicated in the discourse justifying military service and good citizenship. Many of the qualities advocated by the education department are psychological ones, but the physical preparation of men was also a priority (and in a notorious paragraph that was subsequently removed from the Department's manual, National Socialist Germany was praised for physically preparing its citizens). The emphasis on sport and developing physical strength and ability was a primary focus for the government and the SADF. Du Pisani (2001) notes that 'the physical prowess and moral strength of sporting heroes were celebrated and highlighted as examples for the youth of puritan masculinity' (p.166). As the SADF's official newspaper, *Uniform*, explained:

> Sporting activities and the goals they strive for cannot be divorced from the development of the soldier's mind and body ... teamwork, co-ordination and spirit are as essential to the fighting mould of the soldier as they are to the player on the field ... sport provides, namely, the development of a man as a whole for the purpose of equipping him to defend his country ably (Evans, 22/4/1985).

The values of competition, teamwork, physical strength and agility are here being marshalled by the SADF for specific ends, and the values and activities that could otherwise be defined in peaceful ways, are militarized. The article also points out that sport 'moulds' the characters of the men who undertake it, invoking the 'moulding' metaphor as the process by which the state creates good citizens. *Paratus* magazine carried an article in 1980 highlighting the national service of a leading South African tennis player, who had rejected lucrative sports scholarships to the US in favour of doing his national service. Schalk van der Merwe, explained that, 'Military discipline permeates right through to your approach to sport and has, without a shadow of a doubt, benefited my tennis. In short, I regard national service as an essential component of any young man's armoury'. The article commended Van der Merwe 'as a model soldier, and a balanced citizen of South Africa who possesses the right priorities' (*Paratus*, September 1980). Civilian and potentially peaceful qualities are militarized and every day leisure activities, such as sport, are masculinized and linked to national military defence.

The careers adviser at the University of the Witwatersrand noted, 'If the prospective student is immature and unsure of himself, we may advise him to do his national service first. The two years will give him time to get in touch with himself' (*Paratus*, January 1980). Self-development and, in particular, maturity and independence, were also primary mechanisms for legitimizing military service and incorporating its performance into individual identity. *Paratus* even claimed that national servicemen attained higher grades at university after service than those who had deferred and entered university before military service (January 1980). As, the 'National Serviceman of the Month' for January 1981 explained: 'Before I started my national service I did not know what I wanted to do, but the past two years have given me time to mature and make up my mind' (*Paratus*, January, 1981). In terms of state hegemonic discourse, objecting to national service excludes a man from this self-development and he cannot embody 'true' masculinity. By excluding himself from 'true' manhood, the man who has not served in the SADF calls his right to political agency into question. The qualities required of a 'true' man were tightly bound to the qualities of the 'good citizen' by the apartheid state. This has implications for the mechanisms by which the state sought to vilify objectors.

National service was the means by which the government could engender and identify the autonomous, masculine citizens it desired, creating legions of men who embodied hegemonic masculinity and citizenship. 'National service brings self-knowledge', the Cape Education Department (1986) contended. Serving in the army also engendered the ability to overcome 'egocentricity'; creating awareness that one is part of a community, as the Department concludes: 'He learns that he cannot isolate himself from his fellow man' (p.4). This notion of involvement in the wider community is a preoccupation of republican theorists. It is not inevitable that individuals will participate in civic life and assume their responsibilities toward the state; therefore there must be mechanisms (like military service) that create this participation in the wider community and create the bonds of citizenship. The President's Council Report was also concerned that individualism could undermine the bonds of citizenship. Community involvement is a primary tenet of republican citizenship; it is also used as a means of coercing men to undertake military service. The argument that 'everybody does it' normalizes and constructs the community's boundaries around military service (Helman, 1999b, p.296). In a congenial open letter addressing prospective national servicemen's (and their parents') concerns, General Geldenhuys marshalled the concept of 'everybody does it'; 'hundreds of thousands who have gone before you have felt the same', he wrote, 'and thousands after will also have the same apprehensions' (Geldenhuys, *Sunday Times*, 11/1/1987). Whatever the individual may feel about military service, he can know that he is part of a national phenomenon and participating in a common life experience with his fellow men; to exclude himself from this experience risks exclusion from the nation and his contemporaries.

National service also served as a tool for the political homogenization of the otherwise divided white population (Seegers, 1987, p.160). A 1984 law offered citizenship to all white male immigrants between the ages of 15 and 25 after two years' residence in return for military service. The state could therefore legally incorporate white males into the polity through military service. When this legislation was first proposed, the government supporting newspaper, *The Citizen*, concluded that if male immigrants 'are so chicken-hearted that they do not wish to defend their country of adoption, then they may as well go. South Africa has no place for draft dodgers and the likes of them' (*SA Digest*, 3/3/1978, p.27). *Rapport* added that when an immigrant is faced with military service: 'A difficult test is being put to him, but after this we will know where we stand with each other. Once a man has worn the uniform of a South African soldier, we shall be able to depend on him. The others we can do without' (*SA Digest*, 3/3/1978, p.19). The 'others' South Africa did 'do without'; those who refused to take citizenship automatically lost residence rights. In this formulation 'manly' personal qualities, military service and good citizenship are conflated. *Rapport*, in particular, highlights the public nature of this performance: wearing the SADF uniform constructs a political identity and achieves a hegemonic societal identity by which men could be judged (and accepted or rejected) by others. Masculinity, citizenship and military service were presented as natural and an inevitable part of a man's life cycle and duty to the state by the apartheid regime. The artificial constructions of these identities and their linkages came under scrutiny as the state began to lose legitimacy and was questioned by the ECC.

Objection to Military Service

Cock (1989a) found that the majority of white males' response to the call-up was 'compliance'. However, emigration, deferment and suicide were also significant responses. A minority chose to 'challenge' and conscientiously object. Conscientious objection as an anti-apartheid political statement emerged at the 1974 South African Council of Churches Conference. The Conference passed a resolution stating that the SADF was defending a 'fundamentally unjust and discriminatory society' and challenged Christians to conscientiously object to military service (ECC and CIIR, 1989, p.79). The government swiftly responded by making criticism of compulsory service or incitement to object a criminal offence and it was not until the late 1970s that conscientious objection emerged as a political weapon. In 1979 Peter Moll was sentenced for objecting and in 1980 Richard Steele was convicted. Their objection was significant because, although their stance was heavily influenced by their religious convictions, they were not members of the 'peace churches' and they consciously sought to enmesh their religious objection with a political opposition to apartheid and the SADF's role in defending it. Moll and Steele's stance was followed by Neil Mitchell and Billy Paddock in 1982 and Pete Hathorn and Paul Dobson in 1983, all of whom were imprisoned. These public and highly politicized stances reflected a burgeoning trend of conscripts failing to report for duty. Estimates suggested that between 1975 and 1978 an average of 10% of the call-up failed to report; this rose to 50% by 1985 (over 7000 people) (ECC and CIIR, 1989, p.61). The majority of individuals evading were not doing so because of political convictions, although the figures did reflect the increasingly violent role the SADF played in South African society. A significant proportion of draft evaders emigrated or went into voluntary exile, the more politically conscious of this group established the Committee of South African War Resisters (COSAWR) in London and Amsterdam. This group sought to campaign against conscription and highlight the role of the SADF in Southern Africa.

The End Conscription Campaign

This period saw an increase in the activities of the End Conscription Campaign, which, like its predecessor, the Conscientious Objectors Support Group, comprised a broad range of political viewpoints but focused on campaigning against conscription. The ECC had been formed at the 1983 Black Sash conference. The conference passed a resolution that contained the following:

South Africa is illegally occupying Namibia and this is cause for many in conscience to refuse military service. When South Africa withdraws from Namibia there would be no need for a massive military establishment unless there has been a political failure to respond to the desires of the citizens, and that army will be engaged in civil war, which is a good cause for many to refuse military service. In such a civil war, if the state has to rely on conscription to man its army, the war is already lost (Spink, 1991, p.219).

The ECC based its approach on this discourse of an unjust war and the right of every citizen to object to serving in this war. The 1983 Defence Act doubled the sentence for objection to six years and allowed for purely religious objectors to apply for non-combatant military service. By the mid-1980s the ECC was subjected to 'merciless vilification, the thrust of which was we were traitors, cowards, "mommy's boys"' (Nathan quoted in Truth and Reconciliation Commission, 1998, p.229). In August 1987, 23 men publicly announced they would refuse to report for duty. Of this group, Dr. Ivan Toms was sentenced. In 1988, 143 men made the same public declaration; within two weeks the ECC was banned. Despite this, from 1988 to 1990 David Bruce, Saul Batzofin, Charles Bester and Douglas Torr all decided to stand trial for objection. There was no single explanation for conscientious objection. Objectors had different (and sometimes conflicting) perspectives. They represent a small minority of those who avoided military service and are distinct from purely religious objectors because of the political message they wished to convey and their affiliation with the anti-apartheid and UDF affiliated ECC.

The State's Response to Objectors

The state's response to the End Conscription campaign and objectors is revealing. P.W. Botha interpreted the early objectors in the late 1970s as being part of, 'a new phase in the total onslaught ... manifested in the malevolent efforts to question the very essence of military service' (quoted in Cawthra, 1986, p.49). In the foreword of the *1986 SADF Yearbook*, the chief of the army, Lt. General Liebenberg wrote 'the alienation of a nation's people from its security forces is a basic strategy in communist revolutionary warfare', in a clear reference to the ECC he continued, 'the fact that some people not only lend a ready ear to such propaganda rhetoric, but also allow themselves to be used to help undermine their own security, is also no surprising phenomenon'. These people were 'useful dupes' for the communists. Liebenberg (1986) added that the SADF knew perfectly well that these people's ('a small, albeit vociferous minority') aims were obvious: '[T]o destroy a nation's trust in and respect for its armed forces, undermine a people's sense of security and you are three quarters of the way towards making a country helpless against terrorist attacks' (p.1). General Malan charged that the ECC, 'was in the vanguard of those forces that are intent on wrecking the present dispensation and its renewal ... No citizen can decide of his or her free will which laws to respect' (*The Citizen*, 5/8/1988). Wynand Breytenbach, Malan's deputy, stated 'We think the ECC is dangerous for South Africa. These are people who plead excuses but lack the moral fibre to defend the country against Russia and its surrogates' (*Cape Times*,

15/8/1987). Major General Van Loggerenberg believed that the ECC 'have only one aim in mind and that is to break our morale and eventually leave South Africa defenceless' *(Natal Mercury*, 21/10/1985). Even individual objectors were regarded as a dire threat; the magistrate sentencing Phillip Wilkinson pronounced Wilkinson's stand as an attempt to 'disrupt the whole administration of the country' (Desmidt, 15/5/1987). It is clear that a central theme of the state's attack on the ECC was the accusation that they formed a dangerous tenet of the 'communist total onslaught' and would undermine even their own security by disabling the SADF. The second theme in the government's attacks on the ECC focused on the male individuals' personal identities. Here, the government accused ECC members and objectors of being cowards, afraid of serving in the army and articulating political reasons merely to conceal that fear. This attack on objectors' and their supporters' personal identities was part of the state's efforts to subordinate and marginalize the masculinity of objectors, in doing so, the state hoped to marginalize their political views as well and attach personal deviance to their politically deviant stance. Malan branded the men in the ECC as 'mommy's little boys' (Cock, 1993, p.73) and propaganda attacking the ECC frequently adopted a homophobic tone.

Homosexuality

The attachment of a homosexual identity to men who objected to military service deserves some analysis. In the President's Council Report (1987), homosexuality had been identified as a cause of social breakdown and an impediment to good citizenship:

> Homosexuality in men and women is a serious social deviation … a homosexual person experiences the following stages: He becomes isolated from his friends, he regards himself as an outcast, he makes contact with other homosexuals, he accepts his new lifestyle and defends his actions. The fact that homosexuality is increasingly regarded as normal by the community is cause for concern (p.48).

Homosexuality is here presented as the antithesis of republican citizenship, isolated from the group ('outcast'), different from the norm and deviant. The conflation of homosexuality and objection thus aimed at isolating and 'othering' the men who objected, thereby neutralizing their political stance. The 'Veterans for Victory' group, an SADF supported pressure group, conflated gays and objection. A study of 'Vets'' literature and cartoons found that:

> The soldier, the warrior, the redeemer. Find his juxtaposition in the Other, in this case the Other is the ECC member who refuses to answer the call-up and take up arms: the marginalizing of this Other is given added emphasis by the threatening of 'his' sexual identity. In stark contrast to the potency of the warrior the ECC member is stripped of his virility and manhood and made into a member. The ECC member is a Nerd, a moffie, a queer (Graaf et al., 1988, p.49).

The objector refusing to do military service was 'deviant', effeminate, subversive, impotent, untrustworthy, disloyal and a dangerous conduit for communist domination.[9] The analysis of the case of Dr. Ivan Toms reveals the dilemmas of an objector who was actually gay and demonstrates that the End Conscription Campaign was uneasy at binding their political message to a personal one, preferring to engage the state from a heterosexual basis. Toms had served his national service and became aware of the iniquitous role the SADF played in upholding apartheid whilst doing so, he subsequently refused to undertake his legal obligations to serve in army training camps and was the first person to challenge the 1983 Defence Act. Toms (1994) reflects that 'to the South African Defence Force, it seemed obvious to use the fact [that] I was gay to discredit me'; this would build on the general thrust of anti-ECC discourse which conflated homosexuality with cowardice and objection to military service (p.258). Toms was keen to use his sexuality as a central theme of his objection: 'My decision to object and stand trial was most certainly informed by my growing gay consciousness' he explains. Toms's subordinated masculinity gave him a deeper insight into the racial subordination the SADF upheld. Phillips (forthcoming 2005), who went into exile to avoid service, writes how, in this sense, gay identity is empowering:

> It forces me onto a liminal path from which centralized power and the singular absolutism of its 'truth' are inevitably challenged … being queer offers a direct understanding of marginality, a recognition of subordinated truths with a concomitant questioning of authority and a subversion of 'certainties' that might otherwise be taken for granted (p.1).

This ability to challenge hegemonic constructions of identity and, by doing so, to reconstruct values and qualities is apparent in Toms's desire to use his sexuality as a basis for objection. Toms (1994) wished 'to show that gays were just as brave and principled as the many straights who had refused to serve', thereby disrupting the link between gays and cowardice (p.259). The End Conscription Campaign felt deeply uneasy about highlighting Toms's sexuality and persuaded him to remove all references to it from his statement of objection. The question of Toms's sexuality was never fully explored at his trial either. The prosecution did raise the issue, but the magistrate made no mention of it in his summing up and it was not widely reported in the press. The political action of his objection was 'de-sexualized' for fear that the use of sexuality would discredit the individual who used this stance and weaken the ECC's political message. The ECC was willing to engage the state on meanings of good citizenship and also to contest the hegemonic constructions of courage, maturity and service, but they were not prepared to take this further by contesting the conflagration of homosexuality and cowardice or the bind the state made between heterosexual masculinity and military service.

Other Case Studies

David Bruce provides a different insight into the process of objection. Bruce never served in the SADF and was imprisoned for his objection. In a striking resemblance to the discourse that offers 'personal growth' to conscripts through 'becoming a man' or 'seeing the world' by joining the army, Bruce adds his time in prison 'was my experience of seeing the world'. His objection mirrors Toms's to the extent that he expresses it in terms deeply connected with his own identity. Bruce's political consciousness was deeply influenced by his Jewish identity and his objection was premised on an understanding of the links between anti-Semitism in Nazi Germany and the role the SADF played in upholding a racist regime. The experience of his objection, he said, 'enabled me to become another kind of person … I know it was brave' (Bruce, 1997, p.176). Bruce's comments could be interpreted as 'mirroring' state discourse in expressing his objection to military service in terms of fulfilment of identity, he is also redefining those terms by offering a de-militarized definition of bravery, growth and political agency.

Saul Batzofin also linked his Jewish heritage to his objection, but believes that it was his experience in the army that enabled and inspired him to object. 'It was really the SADF experience that changed me from a totally normal, apolitical white South African male to a political activist prepared to go to jail … I think the SADF created the space for me to actually work toward ending apartheid' (Jaster and Jaster, 1993, p.49). This account seems to concur with Helman's (1997) belief that service in the army gives men agency and the ability to oppose military service in the future (p.322). However, unlike the conscripts in Helman's study, Batzofin rejected the notion that his military service was ever worthwhile and that he believed the military service he undertook in Namibia was politically and morally wrong. Batzofin claims that 'the most important' variable in his decision to object was knowing that the End Conscription Campaign existed and was there to support him and that 'I wouldn't be acting in isolation' (Jaster and Jaster, 1993, p.42). The ECC provided a community from which objectors could gain a sense of agency and ability politically to challenge apartheid, it was also an alternative community to that offered by the state. Certainly, Rauch (1989) found that the objectors in her study felt a sense of empowerment and agency, not a sense of alienation or exclusion that state discourse aimed at engendering.

The ECC was much more comfortable in engaging the state in terms of citizenship. In particular, the ECC aimed at deconstructing the state's conception of national service and aimed to reconstruct it in peaceful, non-military terms. A long-running campaign of the group was the 'Working for a Just Peace Campaign' (also dubbed the 'Construction not Conscription Campaign'), whereby members of the ECC would take part in community development projects. The ECC formally requested that the SADF restructure national service to copy this system. This approach had some success, the *Sunday Star* noted in an editorial focusing on alternative service 'there are many patriotic young men who – far from being cowards – display immense courage and strong will, but who reject township duty' (7/8/1988). Indeed, the magistrate when sentencing Ivan Toms (who had worked as a Doctor in Crossroads) said, 'you are not a criminal … you are not a menace to society. In fact you are just the opposite' (Toms, 1994, p.262).[10]

The ECC was engaging the state on its own terms, in terms of republican citizenship. The ECC accepted the need for some kind of national service and the creation of citizens through participation and community involvement, it sought to reformulate the nature of that participation and demilitarize South Africa's conception of good citizenship. Rauch (1989) found in a study of the 143 men who objected in 1988 that most of their statements were framed in terms of patriotism, civic duty and community involvement. The engagement with some of the basic tenets of republican citizenship did allow the ECC to present a credible message to wider South African society and was able to gain influence. The SADF even sought to engage the ECC on its terms – a reflection of the growing influence of the group – the SADF emphasized its own role in community development.[11]

Conclusion

The legacy of the apartheid state's construction of masculinity is still pervasive and is evident in the high levels of rape, violence and HIV infection in contemporary South Africa (Morrell, 2001, pp.19-20). However, the state's discourse has been transformed; the ANC pledged to abolish conscription during its negotiations with the National Party in the early 1990s and gender rights (particular rights for sexual minorities) have been inscribed into the constitution. The activists and objectors of the End Conscription Campaign undoubtedly had a considerable influence in these positive developments. Enloe (1993) reflects that: 'If a state's military begins to lose its legitimacy, the tension between masculinity and military service can become acute' (p.54). These tensions did become acute in 1980s South Africa as the SADF's role in racial oppression and violence became increasingly difficult to legitimize. The state's republican discourse, framed in the ideological imperatives of the 'Total Strategy', was nonetheless a powerful mechanism for engendering obedience within the white population. As a leading ECC organizer conceded, the majority of whites considered the ECC 'irrelevant and subversive' (Nathan, 1989, p.306). Whilst this may have been the case, the ECC's challenge to the supposedly 'natural' bonds between masculinity, military service and citizenship posed a serious threat to the state's ideological foundations. The strength of this threat was demonstrated by the banning of the ECC in 1988 and the vitriolic attacks to which the ECC was subjected by government ministers and pro-government groups.

The ECC found it consistently easier to challenge the state in terms of proposing alternative modes of citizenship, albeit ones that accepted the need for civic participation. Jabri (1996) contends that, 'A transformative discourse seeking peace ... must seek to uncover processes which generate dominant identity formations of the self' (p.185). The inscription of a militarized masculinity into personal identity was challenged in so far as meanings attached to courage, bravery and duty were used by objectors and their supporters to describe their own actions, challenging the hegemonic masculine construction of those values, which equated them to the performance of military service. The ECC did not, however, engage directly with the state's attacks on their individual masculinity. The conflation of homosexuality, cowardice and ECC membership was aimed at 'othering' the ECC and its political message. The opportunity to expose and reformulate the 'construction of the self' offered by the Ivan Toms case was not taken. Greater research needs to be completed before making definite conclusions about the implications this had on the ECC's political message and effectiveness, but one could suggest that the failure fully to engage with this aspect of the state's construct of hegemonic masculinity and not to deconstruct the conflation of homosexuality with cowardice, undermined the ECC's potential of reformulating the nexus of hegemonic masculinity, military service and republican citizenship.

Notes

1. I am grateful to Lee Jones, Louise Vincent and Amanda Gouws for their comments on this chapter.
2. See Van Zyl et al. (1999) for discussions about increasing 'deviance' – drugs, alcoholism, suicide etc. – from conscripts over the 1970s to 1980s.
3. Cock (1989b) discusses the ideological positioning of women in the SADF.
4. In 1967 'the SADF moved over to full conscription for white men in response to the launching of armed struggles in Namibia, Zimbabwe, Angola and Mozambique' (Cawthra, 1986, p.63).
5. The most striking aspect of all the government and associated literature I reviewed was the absence of women. This is despite the fact much of the literature refers in neutral terms to citizenship, community involvement, national service and personal self-fulfilment. Political involvement in the South African state was defined in male terms and within a specific masculine framework designed to complement the military needs of the state. Where women are referred to, they are merely to admire, support and sustain men in the sacred duty of militarily defending the state.
6. Ironically, suicide rates in the SADF were escalating. In May 1981 suicide became a 'notifiable disease' in the SADF, and records show about 14 military personnel committed suicide in a year. In March 1986 the official figures for 1985 were 35. By 1986 the figure had risen to 429 (cited in Van Zyl et al., 1999, p.64).
7. 'The selling of the tricameral parliament to whites included promises to conscript coloured and Indian people (obligations for getting voting rights), but it was never enforced' (Van Zyl et al., 1999, p.36).
8. Cock (1989b) and Enloe (1988) discuss the complexities and complications arising with the inclusion of women in defence forces. Cock makes specific reference to the SADF.
9. For a detailed analysis of the SADF attitudes and treatment of homosexuals as 'other', see Van Zyl et al. (1999).
10. Toms was sentenced to 18 months imprisonment nonetheless!
11. In one *Paratus* article focusing on the SADF's community activities in Natal, Colonel Harwood said, 'the local population recognizes the fact that when they are in trouble, the men of the SADF ('Amasoja' – our soldiers) are often the first people outside the local hospital staff to arrive and assist them'. The SADF had an annual Sword of Peace award, given to the regiment that most furthered the state's 'winning hearts and minds' objectives. *Paratus* commented that Harwood's unit demonstrated the 'dedication, unselfishness and caring humanitarian attitudes', which were, 'perhaps, the epitome of man's humanity to man' (Aarons, 1984).

References

Aarons, J. (1984), 'SADF also a Friend of the Common People: Natal Medical Command's Fight Against Cholera Rewarded with the Sword of Peace', *Paratus*, June.

Bruce, D. interviewed by Gordon, J. (1997), in Suttner, I. (ed.), *Cutting Through the Mountain: Interviews with South African Jewish Activists*, Penguin, London and Sandton.

Butler, J. (1999), *Gender Trouble: Feminism and the Subversion of Identity*, Routledge, New York and London.

Cape Education Department (1986), *Cadet Training Programme: Manual 1986*, Government Printer, Cape Town.

Carrigan, T., Connell, B. and Lee, J. (1987), 'Toward a New Sociology of Masculinity', in H. Brod, (ed.), *The Making of Masculinities: The New Men's Studies*, Allen & Unwin, Boston, pp.63-102.

Carver, T. (1996), '"Public Man" and the Critique of Masculinities', *Political Theory*, Vol.24, no.4, pp.673-686.

Cawthra, G. (1986), *Brutal Force: The Apartheid War Machine*, International Defence Aid Fund, London.

The Citizen, (3/3/1978), '"Settling a Problem" Editorial'.

The Citizen, (12/4/1987), '"Salute to the SADF" The Citizen Comment'.

The Citizen, (5/8/1988), '"The ECC" The Citizen Comment'.

City Press, (21/6/1987), '"Army Service is for Citizens" City Press Comment'.

Cock, J. (1989a), 'Conscription in South Africa: A Study in the Politics of Coercion', *South African Sociological Review*, Vol.2, No.1, pp.1-22.

Cock, J. (1989b), 'Manpower and militarisation: women and the SADF', in Jacklyn Cock and Laurie Nathan (eds.), *War and Society: The Militarisation of South Africa*, David Philip, Cape Town, pp.51-66.

Cock, J. (1993), *Women and War In South Africa* (2nd edn.), Pilgrim Press, Cleveland.

Cock, Jacklyn and Nathan, Laurie (1989), 'Preface' in Cock, J. and Nathan, L. (eds.), *War and Society: The militarisation of South Africa*, David Philip, Cape Town, pp.xiii-xiv.

Connell, R. (1987), *Gender and Power*, Polity Press, Cambridge.

Connell, R. (1990), 'The State, Gender, and Sexual Politics: Theory and Appraisal', *Theory and Society*, Vol.19, No.4, pp.507-544.

Connell, R. (1995), *Masculinities*, University of California Press, Berkeley and Los Angeles.

Desmidt, M. (15/5/1987), 'Wilkinson Fined for Failing to Report for Camp', *Eastern Province Herald*.

Donaldson, M. (1993), 'What is hegemonic masculinity?', *Theory & Society*, 22, pp.593-621.

Du Pisani, K. (2001), 'Puritanism Transformed: Afrikaner Masculinities in the Apartheid and Post-Apartheid Period', in Morrell, R. (ed.), *Changing Men in Southern Africa*, Zed Books and University of Natal Press, London and Scottsville, pp.157-176.

Eastern Province Herald, (19/6/1987), 'Army Service Acceptable if there is also Reform, say Labour Party'.

Elshtain, J. (1992), 'Sovereignty, Identity, Sacrifice' in V. Spike Peterson (ed.), *Gendered States: Feminist (Re) Visions of International Relations Theory*, Lynne Rienner, Boulder, pp.141-154.

Elshtain, J. (1995), *Women and War* (2nd edn.), University of Chicago Press, Chicago and London.

End Conscription Campaign (ECC) and Catholic Institute for International Affairs (CIIR) (1989), *Out of Step: War Resistance in South Africa*, CIIR, London.

Enloe, C. (1988), *Does Khaki become you? The militarization of women's lives*, Pandora Press, London.

Enloe, C. (1993), *The Morning After: Sexual Politics at the End of the Cold War*, University of California Press, Berkeley and London.

Evans, B. (14/1/1985), 'SADF Sport: An Integral Role in the Soldiers Preparedness', *Uniform: Newspaper of the South African Army.*

Financial Mail, (1/6/1979), 'Defence: The Fight for Survival'.

Frankel, P. (1984), Pretoria's Praetorians: Civil-Military Relations in South Africa, Cambridge University Press, Cambridge.

Geldenhuys, J. (11/1/1987), '"Have You Been Called Up?": Open Letter from General Jannie Geldenhuys, Chief of the South African Defence Force', Advertisement in *Sunday Times*, Johannesburg.

Graaf, M. (ed.), Louw, P., Joosten, A., Murray, A., Pestana, A., Savage, J., Sutherland, C., Tomaselli, K., Tomaselli, R. and Urbasch, M. (1988), *Hawks and Doves: The Pro- and Anti-Conscription Press in South Africa*, Contemporary Cultural Studies Unit, University of Natal, Durban.

Helman, S. (1997), 'Militarism and the Construction of Community', *Journal of Political and Military Sociology*, 25 (Winter), pp.305-332.

Helman, S. (1999a), 'Negotiating Obligations, Creating Rights: Conscientious Objection and the Redefinition of Citizenship in Israel', *Citizenship Studies*, Vol.3, No.1, pp.45-70.

Helman, S. (1999b), 'From soldiering and motherhood to citizenship: a study of four Israeli peace protest movements', *Social Politics*, 6(3), pp.292-313.

Isin, E. and Wood, P. (1999), *Citizenship and Identity*, Sage, London.

Jabri, V. (1996), *Discourses on Violence: Conflict Analysis Reconsidered*, Manchester University Press, Manchester.

Jaster, R. and Jaster, S. (1993), *South Africa's Other Whites: Voices for Change*, Macmillan, London.

Kimmel, M. (1994), 'Masculinity as Homophobia: Fear, Shame, and Silence in the Construction of Gender Identity', in H. Brod, and M. Kaufman (eds.), *Theorizing Masculinities*, Sage, Thousand Oaks and London.

Liebenberg, A. (1986), 'Message by the Chief of the Army, Lt. General A.J. Liebenberg, SSAS, SD. P.', in South African Defence Force, *The SADF Yearbook*, Walker Ramus, Durban.

Lister, R. (1997), *Citizenship: Feminist Perspectives*, Macmillan, London.

Malan, M. (28/1/1985), Letter from the Minister of Defence, General M. de M. Malan to Mr. P.M. Graham, General Secretary, Christian Education and Youth Department in the ECC Archive, William Cullen Library, Johannesburg.

Marks, S. and Andersson, N. (1990), 'The Epidemiology and Culture of Violence', in N. Manganyi, and A. du Toit (eds.), *Political Violence and The Struggle in South Africa*, Macmillan, London, pp. 29-69.

Morgan, D. (1994), 'Theatre of War: Combat, the Military, and Masculinities', in H. Brod and M. Kaufman (eds.), *Theorizing Masculinities*, Sage, Thousand Oaks, CA and London.

Morrell, R. (2001), 'Times of Change: Men and Masculinity in South Africa', in R. Morrell (ed.), *Changing Men in Southern Africa*, Zed Books and University of Natal Press, London and Scottsville, pp.3-37.

Natal Mercury, (21/10/1985), 'ECC is Aiming to Leave SA Defenceless'.

Nathan, L. (1989), '"Marching to a Different Beat": The History of the End Conscription Campaign' in Jacklyn Cock and Laurie Nathan (eds.), *War and Society: The Militarisation of South Africa*, David Philip, Cape Town, pp.308-323.

Norton, A. (1993), *Reflections on Political Identity*, Johns Hopkins University Press, Baltimore and London.

Oldfield, A. (1990), *Citizenship and Community: Civic Republicanism and the Modern World*, Routledge, London and New York.

Paratus (January 1980), 'Higher Pass rate after National Service'.

Paratus (September 1980), 'National Serviceman of the Month: Schalk van der Merwe "My Country Came First"'.

Paratus (September 1980), 'SABC Personalities Speak Out on ... Why Every South African Should Serve His Country'.

Paratus (January 1981), 'National Serviceman of the Month: L.S. Rouncivell, "Responsibility was a Challenge"'.

Pateman, C. (1988), *The Sexual Contract*, Polity Press, Cambridge.

Pettman, J. (1996), *Worlding Women: A Feminist International Politics*, Routledge, London and New York.

Phelan, S. (1999), 'Bodies, Passions and Citizenship' in S. Heckman (ed.), *Feminism, Identity and Difference*, Frank Cass, Ilford and Portland.

Phillips, Oliver (forthcoming 2005), 'Ten White Men Thirteen Years Later: The Changing Constitution of Masculinities in South Africa, 1987-2000' in Melissa Steyn and Mikki van Zyl (eds.), *Shaping Sexualities: A Reader* (provisional title), Kwela, Cape Town.

President's Council: Republic of South Africa (1987), *Report of the Committee for Social Affairs on the Youth of South Africa*, Cape Town, Government Printer.

Rapport, (3/3/1978), '"Fight Together": Editorial', in *SA Digest*, Pretoria, Government Printer.

Rauch, J. (1989), 'Stepping Out of Line: Conscientious Objectors in Contemporary South Africa', unpublished MPhil. in Criminology, University of Cambridge.

Roper, M. and Tosh, J. (1991), 'Introduction: Historians and the Politics of Masculinity', in M. Roper and J. Tosh (eds.), *Manful assertions: Masculinity in Britain Since 1800*, Routledge, London, pp.1-24.

Sasson-Levy, O. (2002), 'Constructing Identities at the Margins: Masculinities and Citizenship in the Israeli Army', *The Sociological Quarterly*, vol.43, no.3, pp.357-383.

Scott-Swart, S. (1998), 'Letter to the Editor', *Agenda*, No.37, pp.4-6.

Seegers, A. (1987), 'Apartheid's Military: Its Origins and Development', in W. James (ed.), *The State of Apartheid*, Lynne Rienner, Boulder.

Seegers, A. (1993), 'South Africa: From Laager to Anti-Apartheid', in C. Moskos and J. Whiteclay Chambers II (eds.), *The New Conscientious Objection: From Sacred to Secular Resistance*, Oxford University Press, New York and Oxford, pp.127-134.

Snyder, R. (1999), *Citizen Soldiers and Manly Warriors: Military Service and Gender in the Civic Republican Tradition*, Rowman and Littlefield, London and Boulder.

Spink, K. (1991), *Black Sash: The Beginning of a Bridge in South Africa*, Methuen, London.

The Star, (6/2/1985), 'ECC Drive on Call-Up Very Naïve – Slabbert'.

Steenkamp, W. (1983), 'The South African Defence Force: Rogue Elephant, Slave of Circumstance or Cyclops in the Land of the Blind', *Leadership SA*, vol.2, no.1, pp.52-71.

Steenkamp, W. (24/10/1984), 'On Parade: Vacuum after Conscription', *Cape Times*.

Sunday Star, (7/8/1988), 'Alternative Service to Build Our Nation', Editorial.

Tilly, C. (1995), 'Citizenship, Identity and Social History', *International Review of Social History*, Vol.40, No.3, pp.1-7.

Toms, I. (1994), 'Ivan Toms is a Fairy? The South African Defence Force, the End Conscription Campaign, and Me', in M. Gevisser and E. Cameron (eds.), *Defiant Desire*, Ravan Press, Johannesburg.

Truth and Reconciliation Commission (1998), *Volume 2: Truth and Reconciliation Commission of South Africa Report*, Juta & Co., Cape Town.

Van der Merwe, G. (ed.), (1984), *National Service '84*, Gordon Publishing, Sandton.

Van Zyl, Mikki et al. (1999), *The aVersion Project: Human rights abuses of gays and lesbians in the South African Defence Force by health workers during the apartheid era*, Simply Said and Done, Cape Town.

Viljoen, C. (1984), 'Foreword: General C.L. Viljoen, SSA, SM, Chief of the South African Defence Force', in G. van der Merwe (ed.), *National Service '84*, Gordon Publishing, Sandton.

Werbner, P. (1999), 'Political Motherhood and the Feminisation of Citizenship: Women's Activism and the Transformation of the Public Space', in P. Werbner, and N. Yuval-Davis (eds.), *Women, Citizenship and Difference*, Zed Books, London and New York, pp.221-245.

PART III
EXTENDING THE
BOUNDARIES OF THE LAW

Chapter 5

Citizenship and the Right to Child Care[1]

Beth Goldblatt

Introduction

In this chapter it will be argued that the right to citizenship in the Bill of Rights should entail state assistance for parents including, in particular, the provision of childcare. This argument draws a distinction between the broad concept of citizenship in our Constitution and the more specific right to citizenship within the Bill of Rights that may be one of the vehicles for giving effect to the concept. Citizenship is generally understood narrowly by lawyers to involve questions of nationality. It will be argued that the concept has a much wider reach and concerns the entitlements of citizens as well as questions of democratic participation in the civic and political life of the country. The chapter draws on the important insights of feminist political theory to support an expansive and transformative interpretation of citizenship in our Constitution.

This body of feminist theory highlights the gendered obstacles to citizenship. A significant constraint on women's economic, political and social participation relates to gender divisions in society that result in most of the responsibility for the care of children being taken by women. In South Africa, the vast majority of women lead exhausting lives and face terrible poverty. They spend their days caring for children and engaged in basic tasks (such as the collection of water and firewood, farming and hawking) to ensure their own and their family's survival. Caring for their children means that their ability to look for employment or engage in wage labour or other subsistence or economic activity is severely constrained. They also lack the time and energy to participate as actively as they would wish in community structures, representative politics and other forms of civic participation. Without some childcare assistance (as well as other improvements to their position) most South African women will continue to be denied full citizenship of South Africa. It will be argued that state provision of childcare is one of the important measures needed to make the promise of citizenship in our Constitution a reality for South African women. If we understand the Constitution to require transformation of our society, then the right to citizenship needs to be given substantive meaning.

This chapter first discusses women's position with regard to childcare in the South African context. Then it looks at the political theory, feminist and legal theory debates about the meaning of citizenship. It also examines the relationship between citizenship and childcare. It then considers the concept and the right to citizenship within our Constitution and discusses how the issue of childcare may be able to be framed within the right to citizenship. Finally, it considers some of the strategic issues involved in making a rights claim to childcare.

The Need for Childcare in South Africa

South African women have to take the primary responsibility for child rearing, household reproduction, childcare arrangements and often financial support for the household, without significant assistance from the state, the workplace or men. As a result, their ability to participate fully in the economy and the society outside the home is severely restricted. This situation is the result of the sexual division of labour (unequal gender roles and responsibilities) in our society that places the responsibility for children on women. This division is supported ideologically through the notion of the public/private dichotomy. Women's unpaid work in the household is seen as part of the private realm which provides the state with its justification for failing to intervene to improve their position. The situation is made worse by the disproportionate burden of poverty carried by most South African women.

There is very little formal childcare available in South Africa. The number of children with access to some form of non-family childcare in South Africa is somewhere between 6% and 21% (Padayachie et al., 1994, pp.1-2; Kruger and Motala, 1997, p.100; Department of Education, 2001, pp.11-12) with rural Africans having the least access to such facilities. The analogy of access to water is apposite here. Every South African has access to water – if they did not they would die. But what type of access do they have, what is the quality of the water they have access to, and what is the cost to themselves in accessing water? Similarly with childcare, particularly for infants and toddlers, someone is looking after these children because without some care they would not survive. But what type of care are they receiving and at what cost to their carers whose opportunities for economic survival are in all likelihood being severely constrained?

A large number of South African heads of household are women (as much as 41% of African households) (Budlender, 1996, p.45). Women-headed households are generally poorer than male-headed ones (CEDAW Report, 1998, pp.1-4). The majority of African women do not live with the fathers of their children and bear primary responsibility for childcare and support of children. Often, because of high rates of teenage pregnancy, the actual carers of these children are grandmothers or other female relatives of the children. Often, older sisters care for younger children, which has an adverse effect on their educational and other life chances. It is assumed that HIV/AIDS will also have a significant negative impact on families with the increasing deaths of income producers and the number of orphans. Older girls and the elderly will assume greater responsibility for childcare adding to their burden and that of their communities.

Most women in South Africa do not earn any income (only 46% of South African women over the age of 15 are economically active, as opposed to 63% of men). Women in rural areas are even more unlikely to earn anything (only 38% of these women are economically active) (CEDAW Report, 1998, p.11). Of the economically active women, a high proportion have no formal employment (38% overall, and 47% of all economically active African women). Most self-employed African women are engaged in 'elementary occupations such as street vending, domestic work and scavenging' (Budlender, 1997, p.26).

The vast majority of employed women tend to be engaged in low earning, insecure forms of employment without benefits. While some of these jobs (such as street vending) allow women to take their children with them to work, many jobs (such as domestic work) require women to leave their children elsewhere.

Unemployed women have to look for work opportunities while caring for children or have to give up these opportunities when they cannot make satisfactory childcare arrangements. The lack of employment for women in rural areas means that mothers are available to look after children during the day. But, the lack of water, fuel and other resources means that these women have to spend many hours away from the home in accessing these resources and thus cannot provide proper care to children. At the same time, their responsibilities for childcare impact on their ability to engage in these subsistence activities. In rural areas, most African households (55%) use wood for cooking fuel. Over half of these households have to travel more than one kilometre to gather this wood (Budlender, 1997, p.26). Between 12 and 14 million South Africans do not have immediate access to clean water. It is mostly women in rural households who spend more than four hours a day collecting water and wood (Liebenberg, 1998, p.3). Small children cannot walk or be carried over these distances. Their mothers have to make arrangements to leave them in the care of others, where such care is available.

Women engaged in economic activity away from the home use a number of mechanisms for the care of their children. These include (the relatively few) state, private and charitable crèches; home care by paid child minders; care by other household members; care by relatives and neighbours; dispersing of children to other families; leaving children in the care of older siblings; and leaving children at home without care. The breakdown of kinship networks and extended families has seen many of these forms of assistance diminish in recent years (see Niehaus, 1988, p.12; Cock, Emdon and Klugman, 1984).

Because of very limited subsidized childcare provision, parents (generally women) have to bear the costs of childcare. Mothers have physically to ensure that children get out of home care. They have to worry about leaving work on time to fetch children and worry about their work performance when problems with childcare arrangements encroach on their work time and performance.

A particular South African phenomenon that should be mentioned here is the large number of Black domestic workers who care for the children of White parents. Many of the difficulties that would face White working women regarding childcare are displaced onto Black women who suffer tremendous exploitation and abuse. These women often care for other people's children at the expense of their own.

Poverty and lack of state support make many of the universal difficulties with childcare particularly onerous for (mainly Black) South African women. These are not problems facing most fathers in this country because there are women taking responsibility for their children. At the same time, the nature of gender roles in our society means that men fail to benefit from more active involvement with their children. Improved childcare provision should not only address women's disadvantaged position but should also attempt to redefine the way in which men and women in society approach the care of children. This would mean that not only would women receive practical assistance but that a broader transformation of gender relations may begin to occur.

There are many reasons, economic, moral and developmental, why increased and improved provision of childcare would benefit South Africa. These are some of the most common motivations: firstly, it would prepare children to benefit from their schooling. Currently, a quarter of South African pupils drop out of school in their first year.[2] This contributes towards the skills shortage, gangsterism and crime (Lund, 1998, p.1). Secondly, it would assist in dealing preventatively with the health and nutritional needs of South African children, thus averting later burdens on the state's health care system. And thirdly, a comprehensive childcare system would create thousands of new jobs.

This chapter provides a less frequently articulated motivation for improved childcare. It argues that childcare is a human rights issue with important implications for gender equality and the transformation of gender relations in society. Proper provision of childcare would enable South African women to participate more effectively in the economy and the civic life of our country. It would go some way towards addressing the disadvantages faced by most South African women and might assist in creating a society based on equality, dignity and freedom.

It is clear from the experience of countries where childcare is almost universally provided, that it alone cannot transform gender relations. Childcare is nevertheless an important aspect of any systematic attempt to address gender inequality and transform gender relations in society. The government needs to play a central role in regulating and coordinating improved childcare provision, even if not funding it entirely.[3]

The Right to Childcare

South Africa's adoption of a new Constitution[4] and Bill of Rights has mandated the development of a new legal culture. Demands for social and political change can now be voiced in terms of constitutional rights that go beyond rhetoric and have a justiciable form (see Mureinik, 1994, p.31; and Klare, 1998, p.146). This chapter argues that provision of adequate, universal childcare is a fundamental human right. Childcare here refers to the provision of facilities, whether home-based or outside of the home that accommodate the care and educational needs of pre-school children (under the age of 6).[5] Since childcare is not referred to explicitly in the Bill of Rights, it is argued that the right is contained within the meaning of a number of express rights within the Bill of Rights. The Preamble to the Constitution states that the Constitution aims to, inter alia, 'improve the quality of life of all citizens and free the potential of each person' and the interpretation clause (Act 108 of 1996, s 39) requires the Bill of Rights to be interpreted by promoting the 'values that underlie an open and democratic society based on human dignity, equality and freedom'. Based on these prescriptions, it is argued that the provision of childcare as a right is necessary to improve the quality of life and free the potential of all South Africans, particularly women, and is a requirement for a society based on the values of equality, dignity and freedom.

To date, the courts have not directly considered the issue of childcare as a right in any case. Practically, such a case could reach the courts in a number of ways. A piece of legislation or government policy dealing with existing childcare facilities could be challenged, a taxpayer might choose to argue that childcare is a deductible business expense (as in the Canadian case of *Symes v. The Queen* [1993]), or an employee might challenge the lack of childcare assistance from the employer. In such cases, the applicant would be able to frame the argument for the right to childcare within a number of possible constitutional rights:

Firstly, the children's rights clause (Act 108 of 1996, s 28) of the Constitution might be used to argue that children are promised 'social services' and therefore must be provided with childcare. The right also states that children cannot be required to perform work that places the child's development at risk. This aspect of the right could be interpreted to mean that older children who currently have to care for younger children while their parents work should not be losing out on education or other aspects of their development, and therefore, that childcare must be provided. Secondly, the right to education (Act 108 of 1996, s 29) could be used to argue that the right to a 'basic education' includes early childhood development prior to the school age. Thirdly, the right to health care, food, water and social security (Act 108 of 1996, s 27) might be interpreted to include childcare where reference is made in the right to 'social security, including, if they are unable to support themselves and their dependants, appropriate social assistance'. Arguably, families whose members need to work or search for work and who cannot look after their children at the same time, require such assistance in the form of childcare. The family's survival may depend on the income of the person who is currently looking after the children but who cannot acquire such income without childcare assistance. Fourthly, the labour relations clause (Act 108 of 1996, s 23) could be understood to entail provision of childcare benefits by employers as contained within the meaning of 'fair labour practices'.

The second and third of the above rights are part of the set of 'socio-economic' rights contained in our Bill of Rights. They are seen as rights that will enable our courts to require substantive delivery of services to South Africans. The citizenship right is generally regarded as a first generation or civil and political right, with less ability than the socio-economic rights to result in material changes for people. This chapter argues that all rights need to be understood substantively if we are to achieve the constitutional aim of transforming our society. This means that rights must be expanded and their traditional meanings developed so as to effect deep-rooted and material changes to the law and society. This chapter argues that the substantive right to childcare is entailed within the right to citizenship based on the correct interpretation of the Constitution and its values. Before developing this legal argument, the chapter will discuss the meaning of citizenship within political and legal theory.

The Meaning of Citizenship

Theories of Citizenship

There is a burgeoning literature among political theorists about the meaning of citizenship (Kymlicka and Norman, 1994, p.352; and Mouffe, 1992). Certain feminist writers have recently begun to engage with this literature so as to give gender content to the meaning of citizenship (Pateman, 1992, p.17; Yuval-Davis, 1993, p.621; Walby, 1994, p.379; Dietz, 1992; and the various writings by Ruth Lister, 1990, p.445; 1991, p.65; 1995, p.1) including a number of South African feminists.[6] Feminist legal theorists are beginning to draw on these theories in examining issues of constitutionalism (Higgins, 1997, p.1657) and the role of law (Stellings, 1993, pp.215-21 Oliver, 1994, pp.442-444), in noting the diverse meanings of citizenship, sets out four major notions of citizenship that have developed historically. First, the classical Graeco-Roman idea of citizenship entailing individual political participation for the community's benefit as well as for the individual's own; second, the Roman notion of civic republicanism involving 'loyalty to the State' and 'responsibility and respect' for the political process; third, liberalism's emphasis on the rights of the individual to participate in the political process; and fourth, the ideas associated with the theories of T.H. Marshall, of the citizen's entitlements to social benefits as well as political and civil rights. Marshall's notion moved away from liberalism's negative protection of individual autonomy to a 'citizenship of entitlement' where civil rights were complemented by an entitlement to participate politically. Crucially, this participation was based on the prerequisite of state provision of a 'decent standard of living' (Jowell and Oliver, 1994, p.448).

Marshall's ideas were based on the concern that class inequalities were a threat to stability and nationhood in post-war Britain. The state had to take responsibility for market failures and a liberal democratic welfare state was needed (Kymlicka and Norman, 1994, p.354). The premise of such a state had to be universal provision of civil and political, but most importantly, social rights. The South African situation is in some ways similar – economic disparities threaten democracy and social cohesion. The drafters of our Constitution, in considering the type of democracy we need, chose to include socio-economic rights in addition to civil and political rights. This reflects a substantive conception of citizenship and democracy based on the need to transform South African society (Klare, 1998).

Contemporary political theorists takes Marshall's conception of citizenship as a starting point and develop two major critical responses (Kymlicka and Norman, 1994, p.355). Firstly, it challenges the passive role of the citizen within this conception and argues for a more 'active exercise of citizenship responsibilities and virtues'. This idea is reflected in our Constitution which speaks of 'duties and responsibilities of citizenship' (Act 108 of 1996, s 3(2)(b)). The second response involves a call to accommodate cultural and social plurality within the notion of citizenship. This raises questions about whether citizenship can be experienced in the same way by all members of society and whether special measures are needed where equal inclusion of historically excluded groups has proved to be inadequate.

Feminist Theories of Citizenship

Feminist theorists have contributed to debates on both of these arguments. A number of feminists have taken issue with the call for active citizenship. While the idea of participatory citizenship is seen as important for the full inclusion of women in society, they challenge some of the patriarchal assumptions underlying discussion of active citizenship. These 'materialist' feminists focus on the practical constraints and material conditions in society which limit women's citizenship. They point out that women have less time, opportunity and resources to participate politically or civically (Lister, 1990, pp.455-458). This is due to the sexual division of labour in society, the double shift and the disproportionate burden of poverty on women. The way in which active citizenship is understood is also gendered. The historical and traditional location of citizenship is within the public sphere of society. Since women have been confined in many ways to the private sphere, their citizenship is of necessity attenuated (Walby, 1994, p.385). Women are generally under-represented in formal political structures but this does not mean they show no interest in electoral[7] or grassroots politics. Women, despite time constraints, are frequently engaged in community work and politics with a small 'p' (Lister, 1995, p.8). Thus, in many respects women are active citizens but the whole notion of citizenship needs to be reframed to take into account these social divisions.

Another important group of feminist thinkers on citizenship is what Dietz labels the 'maternalists' (1992, p.71). This group emphasizes motherhood as the basis for respect of women as citizens. It locates citizenship within the private sphere and urges that the values of caring, love and respect be used to inform political processes (Dietz, 1992, p.72).[8]

Feminist critiques of the notion of active citizenship lead to arguments for the extension of additional rights and benefits to women to enable them to fulfil their responsibilities as citizens. For example, the critique of the inability of the concept of citizenship to accommodate all groups equally is addressed in the idea put forward by Young (cited in Kymlicka and Norman, 1994, pp.369-371) of a 'differentiated citizenship' which extends procedural and substantive inclusive measures to marginal groups. The notion of citizenship has been challenged for its 'modernist universalism' and for being formulated on the basis of a male life experience (Kymlicka and Norman, 1994, pp.369-371). As a result of this, Pateman (1992) argues that men and women may require different forms of citizenship (because of women's role in motherhood), but that this difference should not entail the subordination of women. Pateman's approach to citizenship is inextricably linked to the concept of substantive equality. She says 'for citizenship to be of equal worth, the substance of equality must differ according to the diverse circumstances and capacities of citizens, men and women' (Pateman, 1992, p.29).

Stellings (1993) also looks at gender and citizenship from a rights perspective (pp.208-209). She argues that one's capacity to participate publicly must be supported by ensuring that civil rights extend to the private sphere. She says that 'citizenship shows us that public self-governance begins with private self-governance. That is, if people have both a right and a responsibility to participate in the project of governing themselves politically, then the kinds of private constraints under which people live become matters of public concern' (Stellings, 1993, pp.215-216).

An important contribution from feminist theory is the work of Sevenhuijsen (1998) who argues (along with others such as Nedelsky) for a conception of the rights-bearing individual within a network of interdependent relationships. She argues for a feminist understanding of care that does not try to emancipate women from caring functions but recognizes and integrates care into democratic citizenship and justice.

Drawing on the above approaches, the content of the right to citizenship is opened up to a range of new and exciting possible interpretations. If we look at citizenship relationally, we are required to look at how the right protects the interests of some people in society at the expense of others. Because women assume the major household and childcare burdens, men are freed to participate publicly. If the right is to be 'reconceived' (Nedelsky, 1993) so as to foster full citizenship for all society's members, it must include measures which address (and ultimately transform) the unequal social relations between women and men. With this as the broad framework, we now need to understand how the provision of childcare might contribute towards the actualization of the reconceived right to citizenship.

Citizenship and Childcare

Almost all of the feminist theorists dealing with citizenship referred to above note, as a key concern, the importance of childcare to citizenship. The 'maternalist' feminist framework sees women's role in childcare as the basis for their citizenship. Just as male citizens go to war, women citizens engage in the care of children (Pateman, 1992, p.21). This framework is valuable in challenging the inferior social value attached to motherhood but is also constraining in that it keeps women tied to traditional gender roles and fails to challenge the fundamental social divisions that allocate different roles to women and men because of their biological role in relation to child bearing. The materialist feminist thinking on this issue is more useful. Writers such as Lister and some of the Scandinavian feminists focus on the practical issues which tie women to childcare and the policy implications of these.

Women's practical inability to participate as citizens is directly linked to their childcare responsibilities. The unequal distribution of childcare is reinforced by the unwillingness of governments to recognize the huge amount of unpaid caring work that women do. Because of increasing longevity, caring work by many women involves care of the elderly as well as care of children and the sick. This burden is even greater for the increasing number of single mothers (Lister, 1990, pp.455-448). Lister cites time-use studies which show how women in paid employment spend far more time than their male partners on domestic work, even when the men are unemployed. This position limits women's ability to participate in public life as do other factors such as lack of transport and fear of violence. While Lister's description is based on English data, much of what she describes is true of South Africa, only more so (Cock et al., 1984). In a South African study looking at the position of Black working class women, there was not a single instance where a woman's husband helped with the preparation of food. The long hours and dual shift led one informant to describe herself as 'exhausted to the point of death'. This situation severely hampered women's participation in trade union and community organisation (Cock et al., 1984, p.6).

Leira (as discussed in Lister, 1990, p.460), writing in the Scandinavian context, develops the idea of a dual concept of citizenship involving 'citizen the wage-earner' and 'citizen the carer'. These citizens are treated differently and unequally and there is a failure to incorporate the role of care-giving into a unified notion of citizenship. The state has a responsibility to alter this division by providing childcare to enable women to access paid employment and by paying women a wage for the caring work they do. Of course, these suggestions are made in the context of wealthy countries with a history of welfarism. Nevertheless, the arguments have a universal value. The idea of large-scale childcare provision or a care-giving wage may seem unrealistic in a poor country such as ours but these arguments force us to reconsider the way in which society is structured and the role of the state in contributing to or challenging the status quo.

Support for women's workplace or caring work must be accompanied by changes in the sexual division of labour. The Scandinavian countries have tried, largely unsuccessfully, to encourage men to share domestic work and parenting. Part of the problem with parental benefits for fathers is that men still 'command, on average, higher rewards from the labour market than women ... (so it makes) economic sense for women to make greater use of parental leave provisions than men' (Lister, 1995, p.19). Men also often work extremely long hours which reflects society's attitude to the male worker as being unencumbered by domestic responsibilities. Lister (1995) argues for the synthesis of an 'ethic of care and of justice or rights'. This would address a key dilemma regarding women's social citizenship: 'how to value the caring work that still falls mainly to women without trapping women into a privatized caring role that is in danger of reinforcing their exclusion from citizenship's public face' (Lister, 1995, p.33). Adequate provision of childcare is a central dimension of this endeavour.

In South Africa, the ending of apartheid brought with it the promise of equality of opportunity and the belief that all South Africans were valued citizens of a society undergoing transformation. Without serious efforts to address the sexual division of labour and assist women with childcare responsibilities, full citizenship for all South Africans will remain elusive (Liebenberg, 1999, p.59).

Citizenship in the Constitution

There are two important sections of the Constitution dealing with citizenship. The first is section 3 entitled 'Citizenship' in Chapter 1 of the Constitution, the Founding Provisions. The section reads as follows:

(1)   There is a common South African citizenship.

(2)   All citizens are –

   (a) equally entitled to the rights, privileges and benefits of citizenship; and

   (b) equally subject to the duties and responsibilities of citizenship.

(3)   National legislation must provide for the acquisition, loss and restoration of citizenship.

The other important reference to citizenship in the Constitution is section 20 of the Bill of Rights also entitled 'Citizenship'. This section simply states that 'no citizen may be deprived of citizenship'. 'Citizenship' is not defined in the Constitution. The corresponding section in the Interim Constitution (Act 200 of 1996) entitled 'citizen's rights' (s 20) was more detailed and has been replaced by the more pared down phrasing. The earlier section provided that 'Every citizen shall have the right to enter, remain in and leave the Republic, and no citizen shall without justification be deprived of his or her citizenship'. The references to entering, remaining in and leaving the Republic have been moved to section 21 dealing with 'Freedom of movement and residence' which seems to indicate that the drafters reconsidered the earlier conflation of those concepts with the right to citizenship. The removal of the words 'without justification' result in a more categorical right and seem to indicate the greater importance attached by the drafters to this right.

By reading section 3 and section 20 together it becomes clear that there are two dimensions to citizenship in our Constitution. The first relates to the issue of what qualifies a person as a citizen of South Africa and matters related thereto.[9] Section 3(3) refers to national legislation that deals with this. The second dimension follows from the first i.e. having been defined as a citizen, the Constitution entitles one to 'rights, privileges and benefits' and creates 'duties and responsibilities' of citizenship. This more substantive notion of citizenship entails active participation in all aspects of society and promises that the preconditions for such participation will be provided equally to all citizens.[10]

Does the right to citizenship in section 20 deal with this second, more substantive notion of citizenship, or does it only mean that one's nationality cannot be taken away? Is section 20 a right at all, or is it simply a protection as indicated by its negative phrasing? Why is there reference to nationality elsewhere in the Bill of Rights and is the concept interchangeable with the concept of citizenship? What is the relationship between section 20 and section 3 of the Constitution? These are very important questions that have been given scant attention by either the courts or by academic writers since the enactment of the new Constitution. In order to answer these questions, judicial and academic references to citizenship in the Constitution will be examined. The proposed proper interpretation of citizenship in the Constitution will be advanced.

Citizenship v Nationality

Some of the leading South African constitutional law textbooks have given only passing attention to the right to citizenship.[11] Others (Rautenbach and Malherbe, 1997, pp.43-44; Devenish, 1998, pp.37, 63) give greater attention to the right to citizenship but collapse its meaning with that of nationality. South African politicians and lawyers use the terms interchangeably as does our legislation (Dugard, 1994, pp.173-174), for example, the *South African Citizenship Act 44 of 1949* and the new *South African Citizenship Act 88 of 1995* (Keightley, 1998, pp.411, 412-413). John Dugard offers definitions of the two terms: Nationality is an international law term dealing with 'the legal connection between the individual and the state for external purposes' (Keightley, 1998, p.173). It concerns matters such as travelling on a South African passport. Citizenship is a constitutional law term describing the 'status of individuals internally, particularly the aggregate of civil and political rights to which they are entitled' (Keightley, 1998, p.173). This is based on Appellate Division authority in the judgment by Nestadt JA in *Tshwete v Minister of Home Affairs* 1988.[12] The distinction is particularly important in South Africa's recent past where black South Africans who had nationality were denied citizenship (for example, people who were forced to become 'citizens' of non-independent Bantustans but were able to travel on South African passports) (Keightley, 1998, p.413). It therefore seems correct to view the citizenship section in the Bill of Rights as entailing something other than a protection of nationality since the two concepts have quite distinct meanings.

Nationality in the Children's Rights Clause

The above distinction is supported by the use of the term nationality elsewhere in the Bill of Rights. Section 28 of the Constitution dealing with children's rights refers to the right of a child to 'a name and a nationality from birth'. The word 'nationality', like every word in the Constitution, was chosen deliberately to entail a particular meaning. Keightley (1998, pp.414-415) seems correct in suggesting that 'nationality' here entails the child's relationship with the state in international law rather than the domestic relationship with the state involved in citizenship. Section 28 thus covers children who are not South African citizens and who are entitled to a nationality which may not be South African so as to protect them against statelessness. It is submitted that the use of the word 'nationality' indicates a clear distinction within the Constitution between the terms 'nationality' and 'citizenship' with nationality involving international law issues and citizenship entailing the relationship between the state and its subjects.

Citizenship as a Constitutional Right?

Before discussing the meaning of citizenship in the Bill of Rights, a prior debate needs to be resolved i.e. does section 20 create a right to citizenship? The section is phrased negatively – 'no citizen may be deprived of citizenship'. It has been suggested (Keightley, 1998, p.414) that as a result of this phrasing people are not provided with a right to citizenship. Instead, they need to have a pre-existing claim to citizenship extended to them by legislation (the *South African Citizenship Act*) which is then protected by section 20. While the section may not guarantee a right to the acquisition of citizenship, it is submitted that once citizenship has been acquired, section 20 guarantees the full content of the right of citizenship to citizens. The fact that it is negatively phrased does not detract from the argument that *all* the elements of citizenship attach to citizens by right and they cannot be deprived of these. This is supported by the location of section 20 within the Bill of Rights (Chapter 2 of the Constitution). Section 7(1), the introductory section of the chapter, states that:

> This Bill of Rights is a cornerstone of democracy in South Africa. It enshrines the rights of all people in our country and affirms the democratic values of human dignity, equality and freedom.

This seems to indicate that the entire contents of the chapter are regarded as rights. Section 7(2) says that the rights in the Bill of Rights must be respected, protected, promoted and fulfilled by the state. It seems unlikely that this requirement applies only to those sections of the Bill of Rights which specifically mention the word 'right'. Similarly, section 7(3) that makes the rights subject to the limitations 'in section 36, or elsewhere in the Bill' must apply to all sections in the Bill. It seems highly unlikely that certain sections of the Bill would be exempt from a limitations analysis simply because the word 'right' does not appear within them.

The Meaning of Citizenship in the Constitution: the Concept and the Right

It is important to draw a distinction between citizenship as a concept and a right in our Constitution. Section 3 sets out the concept of citizenship. It is located within the Founding Provisions which means that citizenship is a foundational concept for the entire Constitution.

The concept emerges from South Africa's specific history and has been formulated in line with the values[13] that inform the 1996 Constitution. South Africa's history has involved the denial of human rights to the majority of its people. Apartheid confiscated Black people's citizenship (in the narrow sense) through the imposition of the Bantustan system. It withheld citizenship (in the broader sense) from all non-whites through the Group Areas Act, the denial of the franchise, designating separate amenities and numerous other laws and policies which violated people's fundamental rights.

The new Constitution recognizes that citizenship entitles citizens to rights. These rights (found in the Bill of Rights) include a full set of civil, political and social rights. But citizenship offers more than rights. It also entitles people to privileges and benefits. Thus, the Constitution envisages a state that attempts to provide for its citizens to alleviate poverty and to improve people's lives. The concept of citizenship also makes citizens subject to duties and responsibilities. This is an important assertion of the need for active participation by all citizens in the building of a new society. Both elements of citizenship (rights, privileges, benefits and duties, responsibilities) challenge the classical liberal notion of citizens as separate individuals owing nothing to others but non-interference and the notion of the state as protector of individual rights not being required to provide anything more to its citizens. Section 3 also includes the word 'equally' in reference to the entitlement of citizens and the duties and responsibilities of citizenship. This ties the value of equality directly to the concept of citizenship.

The concept of citizenship also has a special relationship to democracy since active participation in society is central to a vibrant democracy, and true democracy requires that citizens be provided with the means and opportunities to make a proper contribution to the democratic process. Our Constitution is littered with references to democracy which point to its centrality – in the preamble, founding provisions, the introductory section to the Bill of Rights as well as in the limitations and interpretation section of the Bill of Rights.

The foundational concept of citizenship contains a bundle of rights and much more. It infuses the whole Constitution and needs to inform the interpretation of all of the rights in the Bill of Rights. But what is its relationship to the citizenship right in section 20?

Section 20 is capable of being used for the purposes of both the broad and narrow meanings of citizenship. Clearly, a person may not be deprived of his/her status as a citizen of South Africa. But the section may also be used to protect the citizen against deprivations of the full content of citizenship, as described in section 3. Section 20, the right, thus becomes one of the mechanisms for ensuring that the concept is given effect. It is a weapon that allows citizens to go out into the world and claim fulfilment of the promise of section 3.

The question this begs is whether section 20 is necessary to make claims against section 3. Are not the other rights in the Bill of Rights sufficient to realize the full meaning of section 3?

The Bill of Rights protects many of the civil and political rights one would expect to be associated with citizenship i.e. freedom of expression (section 16), freedom of assembly (section 17), freedom of association (section 18) and the right to vote, form and campaign for political parties and stand for public office (section 19). Does the citizenship right entail anything more? Citizenship requires the full involvement of all South Africans in decision-making about their lives and the society of which they are a part. Thus, unlike section 19 dealing with formal political rights within representative structures of government, the right to citizenship covers a wider spectrum of political activity. It includes participation in 'organs of civil society' (a term used elsewhere in the Bill of Rights – section 31(1)(b) and other forms of political participation (such as in participatory fora connected to government). Sachs J (1998, pp.131-133) in the case of *City Council of Pretoria v Walker* has used the term 'citizenship' in this sense. Discussing the behaviour of a formerly white city council in attempting to integrate the neighbouring black townships, he said:

> Its evident purpose, substantially successful in respect of debt-recovery, was to achieve equal, across-the-board enjoyment of rights and assumption of responsibilities. It sought to establish the practices and habits of municipal citizenship ... at the end of the day, the case was not really about money but about the rights and responsibilities of citizenship.

And in describing the actions of the residents he had the following to say:

> The people of Atteridgeville and Mamelodi had in an earlier period used non-payment for services as a weapon to secure full citizenship rights for themselves both at the national and local level. The coming into force of the Constitution after the elections of 27 April 1994 might have ushered in for them a period of palpable enjoyment of citizenship rights at the national level. Yet, at the local level where their day-to-day lives had to be lived, such a sense of inclusion had still to be constructed.

These passages point to a notion of citizenship in which people become involved in matters of importance to them at all levels of society. South Africa's history of excluding people from such involvement makes the right to citizenship particularly crucial in our new democracy. The passages also show that citizenship is about a set of rights and entitlements as well as about participation in democratic processes.

The Relationship between Childcare and Citizenship (The Concept and Right)

The Citizenship right can also be used to give effect to the concept in section 3 on matters of state provision of benefits to citizens. While the various socio-economic rights in the Bill of Rights also concern such issues, the citizenship right can be used where the socio-economic rights are silent on certain important matters. Thus, the provision of childcare is not given any specific mention in the Bill of Rights. Since, it is argued, childcare is a requirement for the full participation of women in society, the right to citizenship should be used to ensure state provision of this benefit. The Constitution requires the eventual transformation of South Africa through the reconstruction of our society (Albertyn and Goldblatt, 1998, p.249). Power imbalances based on gender and entrenched through mechanisms such as the sexual division of labour must be altered. Childcare provision is an important benefit needed to address these imbalances and transform gendered social relations.

The call for adequate state provision of childcare within a citizenship rights framework needs to be taken forward by civil society and women's rights groups. That is the most likely terrain for success. There is, in addition, the possibility of childcare as a citizenship right reaching the court for adjudication. Take the example of a municipally funded nursery school threatened with closure due to a budgetary reallocation by the local authority. It would be possible to approach the court to argue that the removal violates parents' citizenship rights as the facility enables (mainly mothers) to work, run homes and participate in the activities of the society. The claim could be brought under section 20 by arguing that the closure of the facility deprived citizens (in this case, parents) of their citizenship. Citizenship would be defined with reference to the concept in section 3. Thus, the rights, benefits and privileges of citizenship that were being deprived would here be the use of the nursery school. Clearly, section 20 would not be the only possible right that could be used in these circumstances and may not be the most appropriate. The equality right might be used better if it could be shown that the removal of the facility discriminates against parents or mothers of children. Nevertheless, the promise in section 20 that 'no citizen may be deprived of citizenship' should not be limited to a narrow meaning of citizenship. If section 3 informs its use, which it should, then it is one of the rights that can be used to give effect to the concept of citizenship.

There would obviously be limitations arguments raising other priorities for municipal spending such as refuse removal, provision of public parks and libraries etc. The process of weighing up the competing needs and deciding whether the right to citizenship should be limited must entail a gender analysis which highlights the importance of childcare to women's social participation.

There will be practical questions which determine how the issue of childcare reaches the court based on the facts of each case. Strategic decisions will also need to be taken as to which rights to use in a particular case to frame the issue of childcare. Even if childcare is argued for on the basis of equality, children's rights or socio-economic rights, the concept of citizenship should be used to infuse these rights with important content. The right and the concept of citizenship need further and substantive development in academic writing and in our case law so that they become useful mechanisms for social transformation.

Conclusion

The lack of childcare has a significant impact on South African women. This is due to the sexual division of labour in society that results in women taking primary responsibility for the care of children and the maintenance of the home. Men, while benefiting from this position in terms of less responsibility and more leisure time, also lose out since they do not develop themselves through their relationships with their children. On a more general level, men and women are both disadvantaged by gender constructs that constrain their freedom to develop to their full human potential.

In South Africa, high levels of unemployment and poverty have a particular impact on women with childcare responsibilities. They have to look for work, engage in basic subsistence activities such as hawking, and gather meagre resources such as water and firewood, while looking after children. Approximately one third of African households are women-headed which means that millions of South African women support their children financially and in every other way, without assistance from men. Apartheid has contributed significantly towards the breakdown of African families due to the migrant labour system. For those women with children who are in formal employment, South Africa's labour laws provide little support. There is no requirement that employers provide childcare facilities and little job flexibility around the needs of working mothers.

When the African National Congress (ANC) government came to power following the first democratic elections in 1994, it was faced with a wholly inadequate and racially divided childcare situation. It was also faced with very severe budgetary constraints and many competing areas of need. Since then, the government has made certain policy commitments to improving the education and care of children from birth to age nine (Dept. Education 2001). To date, however, little has been done to give practical effect to these commitments. Reasons for this are numerous and include resource and other constraints on government, the difficult legacy it inherited and the lack of pressure from women's organizations and worker representatives to increase childcare provision.

The Right to Citizenship

The right to citizenship has been given very limited consideration by our courts. It is traditionally understood as a right dealing with issues of nationality. This chapter has argued that citizenship has a much wider meaning. It involves the democratic participation by citizens in the civic and political life of the country. This meaning accords with the definition of citizenship found in much of contemporary political theory. Feminist theorists have challenged this notion of citizenship by arguing that the constraints on women's full participation in society prevent them from accessing the full entitlements of citizens. This chapter has argued that we need to reconceive the right to citizenship along feminist lines, i.e. in order to foster full citizenship for all society's members, the unequal relations between men and women must be addressed.

This chapter has argued that citizenship is both a concept and a right in our Constitution. The concept (in s 3) entitles citizens to a full set of rights. It also provides citizens with privileges and benefits while making citizens subject to duties and responsibilities. The right to citizenship (in s 20) is one of the mechanisms that may be used to give effect to the concept to ensure that the promise of citizenship is fulfilled. The chapter has used the concept and the right to citizenship as the basis for a claim for a right to childcare. Lack of childcare is a critical obstacle to women's full and equal citizenship. Therefore, if the right to citizenship is to have meaning, women need to be provided with childcare and other assistance which will enable them to participate properly in society. Even if the right in section 20 is not regarded as the best basis on which to found a claim for childcare, the concept of citizenship in section 3 (as understood in this chapter) should infuse a claim based on any other right.

Resource issues will arise at the stage of the limitations enquiry and much will depend on the way in which a particular case reaches the court.

The Strategic Use of Constitutional Rights

It must be stated clearly that the courts are just one mechanism for bringing about social change, and a relatively limited one at that. Attempts to require the state to coordinate, fundraise and develop policy for the provision of childcare need to take a number of forms. Policy proposals must be developed based on thorough research. Advocacy and lobbying needs to take place. Educational organizations need to come together with trade unions and women's organizations so as to develop an alliance of organizations working for childcare. The private sector needs to be approached for funding and other assistance.

All of these methods need to be pursued to ensure that childcare becomes a government priority and to make maximum use of all the resources (research, existing childcare projects, etc.) already available concerning childcare. The law should be used as an additional weapon to ensure improved childcare provision.

This chapter also proposes that the Constitution should be used to bring a claim for childcare to court in South Africa.

- Strategically, the courts should be used where a policy process is moving too slowly and some urgency needs to be brought to bear on the government. Litigation often forces an issue and may lead to a Constitutional Court judgment which refers a matter to the legislature to remedy.
- Litigation can also be used to create precedent which others are then compelled to follow. For example, where a profitable company is ordered to provide childcare facilities for its employees, other companies in a similar position may have to follow suit. Similarly, if one government office is required to provide childcare facilities, others may feel compelled to do the same.
- Litigation can be used to raise awareness about the issue of childcare. For example, a high profile case dealing with the lack of childcare facilities in Parliament might make the public and policy-makers more aware of the importance of childcare.
- If a childcare claim succeeds, the court would develop a rights framework within which to locate the issue of childcare. This framework would be of great importance in shaping government policy on the issue. Moser (1993) gives the example of a policy decision to locate childcare facilities at the father's workplace. This would assist women with their practical need for childcare. It would also meet a strategic gender need by involving men in responsibility for children and creating the possibility for the transformation of gender relations in society. This example could be followed in a case requiring a municipality to redirect resources used for childcare away from wealthy areas to poorer ones. The applicants could ask the court to make an order which might involve locating childcare facilities near fathers' workplaces.

This chapter shows that childcare is a critical area of need in South Africa which has major implications for women's lives and gender relations in our country. Our Constitution offers the possibility of improving this situation for the benefit of all South Africans – women, children and men.

Notes

1. This chapter is drawn partly from an LLM Thesis 'A Constitutional Framework for Child Care Provision in South Africa from a Gender Perspective' (1999), University of the Witwatersrand, Johannesburg.
2. According to research by various NGOs cited in Lund (1998, p.1).
3. Note that there is a government commitment to do this in Dept. of Education (2001) *White Paper 5: Early Childhood Development*. This policy is however, broad and vague beyond the issue of a reception year for five-year-olds. There is no clear programme or budget allocated to addressing the needs of under-fives.
4. Unless stated otherwise, where reference is made to the Constitution in this chapter it is to the *Constitution of the Republic of South Africa Act 108 of 1996*.
5. The recent policy statements of the Department of Education (2001) in the White paper 5 propose a nationally provided reception year for all five-year-olds by 2010.
6. There is an emerging South African literature in this area (see Hassim, 1999, p.6; and Gouws, 1999, p.54).
7. Lister, 1990, p.458 cites a USA study which showed higher voting turnout by poor women than poor men but lower participation in other electoral activities.
8. Also see Lister (1997, p.150) and Voet (1998, p.14).
9. This issue has been canvassed to some extent by the courts in cases dealing with the rights of permanent residents – *Larbi-Odam and others v Member of the Executive Council for Education (North-West Province) and another* 1997 (12) BCLR 1655 (CC). Also see *Dawood and another v Minister of Home Affairs and others* 2000 (8) BCLR 837 (CC); and aliens – *Certification of the Amended Text of the Constitution of the Republic of South Africa 1997* (1) BCLR 1 (CC) at paras. 17-21. The references in the Bill of Rights reserving certain rights for 'citizens' (ss 19, 20, 21 & 22) refer to citizenship rights in the first sense i.e. they are rights that are only extended to those who possess South African citizenship. Whether non-citizens should be entitled to the right to citizenship in its second and broader sense is debateable but will not be considered here.
10. See John Dugard's (1994, pp.173-174) definition of citizenship as a constitutional law term describing the 'status of individuals internally, particularly the aggregate of civil and political rights to which they are entitled'. Our Constitution seems to go further by providing socio-economic rights as well as offering benefits and privileges. It also requires citizens to fulfil duties and responsibilities.
11. There is a brief section which largely conflates nationality and citizenship in Davis, Cheadle and Haysom (1997). There is no dedicated chapter on citizenship in Chaskalson et al. (1996).
12. 1988 (4) SA 586 (A) referred to in Dugard (1994, pp.173-174); and in Keightley (1998, p.412).
13. These are set out in section 1 of the Constitution and include, inter alia, dignity, equality, human rights, democracy and freedom.

References

Albertyn, C. and Goldblatt, B. (1998), 'Facing the challenge of transformation: Difficulties in the development of an indigenous jurisprudence of equality', in *SAJHR* Vol.14, pp.248-276.
Budlender, D. (ed.), (1996), *The Women's Budget*, Idasa, Cape Town.

Budlender, D. (ed.), (1997), *The Second Women's Budget*, Idasa, Cape Town.

CEDAW Report *see* Government of the Republic of South Africa (1998).

Chaskalson, M., Kentridge, J., Klaaren, J., Marcus, G., Spitz, D. and Woolman, S. (1996), *Constitutional Law of South Africa*, Juta, Kenwyn.

Cock, J. Emdon, E. and Klugman, B. (1984), 'Child care and the working mother: A sociological investigation of a sample of urban African women', Carnegie Conference Paper No.115.

Constitution of the Republic of South Africa Act 108 of 1996.

Interim Constitution – Constitution of the Republic of South Africa Act 200 of 1996.

Davis, D,. Cheadle, H. and Haysom, N. (1997), *Fundamental Rights in the Constitution: Commentary and Cases*, Juta, Kenwyn.

Department of Education (2001), *White paper 5: Early Childhood Development*, Pretoria, Department of Education, pp.11-12.

Devenish, G. (1998), *A Commentary on the South African Constitution*, Butterworths, Durban.

Dietz, M. (1992), 'Context is All: Feminism and Theories of Citizenship', in C. Mouffe (ed.), *Dimensions of Radical Democracy: Pluralism, Citizenship and Community*, Verso, London, pp.63-85.

Dugard, John (1994), *International Law – A South African Perspective*, Juta, Kenwyn.

Gouws, A. (1999), 'Beyond equality and difference: the politics of women's citizenship' in *Agenda*, No.40, pp.54-58.

Government of the Republic of South Africa (1998), *Convention for the Elimination of All Forms of Discrimination Against Women: First South African Report*, Pretoria, referred to as the 'CEDAW Report'.

Hassim, S. (1999), 'From presence to power: women's citizenship in a new democracy' in *Agenda*, No.40, pp.6-17.

Higgins, T. (1997), 'Democracy and Feminism', in *Harvard Law Review*, Vol.110, No.8, pp.1657-1703.

Jowell, J. and Oliver, D. (1994), *The Changing Constitution* (3rd edn.), Clarendon Press, Oxford.

Keightley, R. (1998), 'The Child's Right to a Nationality and the Acquisition of Citizenship in South African Law', in *SAJHR*, Vol.14, Part 3, pp.411-429.

Klare, K.E. (1998), 'Legal Culture and Transformative Constitutionalism', in *SAJHR*, Vol.14, Part 1, pp.146-188.

Kruger, J. and Motala, S. (1997), 'Welfare' in S. Robinson and L. Biersteker (eds.), *First Call: The South African Children's Budget*, Idasa, Cape Town, pp.65-114.

Kymlicka, W. and Norman, W. (1994), 'Return of the Citizen: A Survey of Recent Work on Citizenship Theory', in *Ethics*, Vol.104, pp.352-381.

Liebenberg, S. (1998), 'The National Water Bill: Breathing Life into the Right to Water', in *ESR Review*, Vol.1, No.1, pp.3-6.

Liebenberg, S. (1999), 'Social citizenship – a precondition for meaningful democracy', in *Agenda*, No.40, pp.59-65.

Lister, Ruth, (1990), 'Women, Economic Dependency and Citizenship', in *Journal of Social Policy*, Vol.19, No.4, pp.445-467.

Lister, Ruth, (1991), 'Citizenship Engendered', in *Critical Social Policy*, Vol.11, No.2, pp.65-71.

Lister, Ruth, (1995), 'Dilemmas in Engendering Citizenship', in *Economy and Society*, Vol.24, No.1, pp.1-40.

Lister, Ruth, (1997), *Citizenship: Feminist Perspectives*, Macmillan, London.

Lund, T. (1998), 'Primary Schools Drop-out Crisis', in *The Cape Times*, 2 April 1998, p.1.

Moser, C. (1993), *Gender, Planning and Development: Theory, Practice and Training*, Routledge, London.

Mouffe, C. (ed.), (1992), *Dimensions of Radical Democracy: Pluralism, Citizenship and Community*, Verso, London.

Mureinik, E. (1994), 'A Bridge to Where? Introducing the Interim Bill of Rights', in *SAJHR*, Vol.10, Part 1, pp.31-48.

Nedelsky, J. (1993), 'Reconceiving rights as relationships', in *Review of Constitutional Studies*, Vol.1, pp.1-26.

Niehaus, I.A. (1988), 'Domestic dynamics and wage labour: a case study among urban residents in Qwaqwa', in *African Studies*, Vol.47, No.2, pp.121-143.

Padayachie, R., Atmore E,. Biersteker, L., King, R., Matube, J., Muthayan, S., Naidoo, K., Plaatjies and D. Evans, J. (1994), Report of the South African Study on Early Childhood Development: Recommendations for Action in Support of Young Children, The World Bank, Washington, DC.

Pateman, C. (1992), 'Equality, difference, subordination: the politics of motherhood and women's citizenship' in G. Bock and S. James (eds.), *Beyond Equality and Difference: Citizenship, feminist politics and female subjectivity*, Routledge, London, pp.17-31.

Rautenbach, I. and Malherbe, E. (1997), *Constitutional Law* (2nd edn.), Butterworths, Durban.

Sevenhuijsen, Selma, (1998), *Citizenship and the Ethics of Care: Feminist considerations on justice, morality and politics*, Routledge, London.

Stellings, B. (1993), 'The Public Harm of Private Violence: Rape, Sex Discrimination and Citizenship', in *Harvard Civil Rights—Civil Liberties Law Review*, Vol.28:185, pp.215-216.

Voet, R. (1998), *Feminism and Citizenship*, Sage Publications, London.

Walby, S. (1994), 'Is Citizenship Gendered?', in *Sociology*, Vol.28, No.2, pp.379-395.

Yuval-Davis, N. (1993), 'Gender and nation', in *Ethnic and Racial Studies*, Vol.16, No.4, pp.621-632.

Case References

Certification of the Amended Text of the Constitution of the Republic of South Africa 1997 (1) BCLR 1 (CC) paras. 17-21.

City Council of Pretoria v Walker 1998 (3) BCLR 257 (CC), at 131-133.

Dawood & another v Minister of Home Affairs & others 2000 (8) BCLR 837 (CC).

Larbi-Odam and others v Member of the Executive Council for Education (North-West Province) and another 1997 (12) BCLR 1655 (CC).

Symes v The Queen: Attorney General of Quebec, Charter Committee on Poverty Issues and Canadian Bar Association (Interveners) [1993] 19 C.R.R (2d).

Tshwete v Minister of Home Affairs 1988 (4) SA 586 (A).

Chapter 6

Towards Enhanced Citizenship and Poverty Eradication: A Critique of *Grootboom* from a Gender Perspective

Danwood Mzikenge Chirwa and Sibonile Khoza

Introduction

A major challenge facing South Africa slightly more than a decade after the end of the apartheid era is the eradication of deep poverty among its citizens. The incidence of poverty is a concern that is arguably most widespread and affects the largest numbers of people. Behind the veil of the statistics of poverty lurks the naked revelation that women are the most affected group of people. However, most approaches to the eradication of poverty are insensitive to the gender dimension of poverty (Taylor, 1997). This concern highlights the fear that existing systemic inequalities between men and women may be accentuated.

Poverty imposes severe limitations on the full enjoyment of citizenship by its victims. This article proposes that citizenship should be construed broadly to incorporate the enjoyment of economic, social and cultural rights. Thus, serious denials of economic, social and cultural rights can lead to or aggravate poverty, which in turn can result in a denial of citizenship and vice versa. For this vicious circle to be broken, programmes aimed at poverty eradication must be structured within a human rights framework – especially economic, social and cultural rights. However, little gains would be made in this regard if sight were lost to the fact that women are the worst victims of poverty.

The 1996 South African Constitution features economic, social and cultural rights prominently side by side with civil and political rights. The Constitutional Court has had a few opportunities to elaborate on the value, meaning and enforcement of these rights.[1] However, the case of *Government of the Republic of South Africa and Others v Grootboom and Others (Grootboom)*[2] is widely regarded as a landmark regarding the transformation and reconstruction of the South African society in the post apartheid era. Despite an increasing volume of literature on the case, analyses of it from a gender perspective are remarkably rare (Budlender and Liebenberg, 2002). This article seeks to explore the implications of this case for the eradication of poverty and the enjoyment of citizenship rights from a gender perspective.

A Gendered Outlook on Poverty in South Africa

Poverty statistics in South Africa belong to familiar terrain, but their meaning has not become any less shocking. According to the World Bank, 18 million people (approximately 45% of the entire South African population) live on less than US$2 a day (see World Bank Report, 2000).[3] Further analysis of statistics indicates that poverty is unevenly distributed in many respects.[4] The unequal distribution along gender lines is arguably most stark. For example, by 1995 about 61% of poverty-stricken families in South Africa were female headed compared to 31% which were male headed. In the same year, the unemployment rate for women stood at 45% compared to 31% for men (Report on Poverty and Inequalities in South Africa, 1995).

Poverty constitutes the denial of human dignity for its victims as it leads to poor physical and mental health often resulting in early death;[5] limits access to education, housing, employment, food and other basic necessities of life; and forms the basis of discrimination and exclusion of women from participation in democratic processes (Report prepared for the Office of the Executive Deputy President and the Inter-Ministerial Committee for Poverty and Inequality, 1998). The effects of poverty also tend to have a spill-over effect to those that live affluent lives in such forms as communicable diseases, increased criminal activity, civil strife/wars and kindred problems.

For poor women, in the context of a male dominated society, poverty means double suffering. In addition to experiencing the general effects of poverty like any other individual, women operate as shock absorbers of poverty for others. Owing to gender-based and predetermined roles, women bear the primary responsibility for undertaking alternative means of running poor households including rendering psychological support to their poor husbands, care and maintenance of children and the elderly, and child-bearing. Added to this, they have to survive such other abuses as domestic violence and rape. They are also particularly vulnerable to HIV/AIDS because of their weak position in society as well as their greater physical vulnerability to infection by the virus (Liebenberg and O'Sullivan, 2001, p.73). The foregoing means that poverty affects women in uniquely different ways from men. This realization merits that actions aimed at effectively redressing poverty should have a gender bias towards women.

Towards Poverty Eradication: The Role of Economic, Social and Cultural Rights

The notion of poverty should not easily be conflated with the lack of economic, social and cultural rights.[6] However, the two concepts overlap in important ways, especially if poverty is understood to mean something more than income – or material deprivation. In this sense, poverty connotes a state in which a person is unable to live a long, healthy and creative life, nor to enjoy a decent life worthy of self-respect and the respect of others (UNDP, 2000, p.73). In *The Programme of Action of the World Summit for Social Development* (1995), the meaning of poverty has been captured as follows:

> Poverty has various manifestations, including lack of income and productive resources sufficient to ensure sustainable livelihoods; hunger and malnutrition; ill health; limited or lack of access to education and other basic services; increased morbidity and mortality from illness; homelessness and inadequate housing; unsafe environments; and social discrimination and exclusion. It is also characterised by a lack of participation in decision making and in civil, social and cultural life.

Thus, poverty signifies a lack of basic capabilities essential to a dignified life.[7] Viewed from this standpoint, economic, social and cultural rights can serve as important instrumental values in ending poverty since they are aimed at ensuring that people are free from want (UNDP, 2000, pp.74-75). Through the synergetic enjoyment of rights such as the right to food, education, adequate standards of living, work, health, housing, and a share in scientific progress and social security it is possible that poverty can be stamped out in a given society.[8] Conversely, when economic, social and cultural rights are viewed as intrinsic values or ends in themselves, poverty makes it impossible for poor people to enjoy these rights. The two notions are demonstrably interrelated and interdependent. Therefore, access to economic, social and cultural rights is a key to breaking the downward spiral of entrapment in poverty as much as eradication of the latter can improve the enjoyment of the former.

Understanding the Notion of Citizenship

Citizenship is a fluid term whose scope has been subjected to constant review over a long period. The concept has a wider import than the common narrow perception that it relates to membership of a state. It concerns conferment of individual status, rights and duties, and the ascription and delimitation of state power (Hassim, 1999, p.6). As defined by Marshall, citizenship is:

> ... a *status* bestowed on those who are full members of a community. All who possess the status are equal with respect to the rights and duties with which the status is endowed (quoted in Lister, 1997, p.14, emphasis in original).

Viewed thus, citizenship is a crucible in which rights and obligations are expressed and state/individual relations are defined. It is about both inclusion and exclusion in that it delimits the terms of its attainment and loss. In modern times, certain conditions of citizenship are settled, e.g. birth, naturalization, marriage, and age. However, the definition of the rights that appertain to citizenship and their beneficiaries has been limited in scope and restricted to certain people respectively at various periods in history (Lister, 1997, p.67). Along with others, women as a group have distinguishably been denied formal status and rights of citizens for a long time.[9]

A dominant view in scholarship on citizenship has been that the status of citizenship confers on individuals a range of civil and political rights. This standpoint is traceable to the liberal tradition closely associated with the natural rights theory of the seventeenth and eighteenth century. The natural rights theory was formulated as a justification of the institution of the state in the context of a burgeoning capitalist society (Baker, 1990). This theory considered the state as a natural phenomenon necessary for individuals to realize their potential. Its authority, however, rested on a social contract with individuals who submitted themselves to state authority in return for the promise by the state to protect their natural rights. Central to this theory was the belief that human beings could maximize their potential if the state refrained from interfering in the market and with an individual's freedom in the private sphere. It advocated for the inviolability of the private sphere and allowed limited regulation of the public sphere. Under this theory, therefore, natural rights were defined as negative injunctions summoning the state to refrain from interfering with individual freedom. They covered rights which have conventionally come to be called civil and political rights (Donnelly, 1989; Shivji, 1989; Shestack, 1998).

The conception of citizenship as conferring only civil and political rights on citizens has been criticized for being 'aggressively male' (Lister, 1997). For one thing, the natural rights theory itself was explicitly male chauvinist. Aristotle (quoted in Gaete, 1993), for example, considered it natural for women to be second-class citizens:

> From their very birth some are marked out for subjection and others for rule (...) It is both natural and advantageous for the body to be governed by the soul, and for the emotional to be governed by the mind ... Also the male has a different nature than the female, the one being superior and the ruler, the other being inferior and the ruled. The same condition necessarily applies to all mankind (p.114).

For another thing, although women have since been recognized as autonomous individuals with full rights of citizenship, the definition of rights under the liberal tradition theory rests on the wrong presumption that people are born free, equal and under same circumstances. The liberal theory is intricately associated with the concept of formal equality, which places the state under an obligation to pass laws or implement policies that are blind to personal characteristics of individuals such as race and gender. The state has no obligation to take positive steps to remove systemic disadvantages of groups of people. By treating women and men equally without having regard to extant structural inequalities between them, the liberal conception of citizenship fails to address the historical exclusion of women from citizenship. At a formal level, women are guaranteed the right of recognition as autonomous beings and to participate in public life through the enjoyment of negative freedoms implicit in civil and political rights but in practice this guarantee is meaningless because of their historically disadvantaged position in society. Pateman (1989) has captured this position beautifully:

The political lion skin has a large mane and belonged to a male lion; it is a costume for men. When women finally win the right to don the skin it is exceedingly ill-fitting and therefore unbecoming (p.6).

It is therefore argued that in order for women to enjoy full rights of citizenship, systemic inequalities that inhibit their political participation must be removed. There is an urgent need to move beyond formal equality to achieve substantive equality. For such inequalities to be removed, access to basic necessities of life such as food, clean water, basic education, shelter and health care services is indispensable. Marxists have established that there is an inseparable link between political participation and access by individuals or groups of them to basic needs. As summed up by Engels (quoted in Eddy, 1979):

Marx discovered the simple fact (heretofore hidden beneath ideological overgrowths) that human beings must have food, drink, clothing and shelter first of all, before they can interest themselves in politics, science, art, religion and the like. This implies that the production of the immediately requisite material means of subsistence, and therewith the existing phase upon which the state institutions, the legal outlooks, the artistic and even the religious ideas are built up. It implies that the latter must be explained out of the former, whereas the former have usually been explained as issuing from the latter (p.20).

Thus, the Marxist conception of citizenship places much premium on economic, social and cultural rights as a precondition for securing a more equal society. These rights are important in that they place the state under an obligation to take positive measures to provide access to everyone to basic goods and services. Positive measures are critical to redressing past historical and contextual disadvantages of individuals or groups of them such as women.

The contention that the enjoyment of civil and political rights can secure the enjoyment of economic, social and cultural rights has increasingly been discredited. Most contemporary writers take the view that the two sets of rights are parts of a single whole and non-satisfaction of one set cannot be compensated for by a sanguine expectation of the satisfaction of the other (Liebenberg, 1999a; Vincent, 1986). In this connection, the UN Committee on Economic, Social and Cultural Rights (ESCR) has stated emphatically that:

Full realisation of human rights can never be achieved as mere by-products, or fortuitous consequence of some other developments, no matter how positive. For that reason suggestions that the full realisation of economic, social and cultural rights will be a direct consequence of, or will automatically flow from enjoyment of civil and political rights are misplaced.[10]

It is therefore argued that the liberal conception of citizenship, which limits rights to civil and political rights, is retrogressive from a gender perspective. Substantive equality is critical to meaningful exercise of citizenship rights. In order to achieve this, economic, social and cultural rights must form an indispensable part of the definition of citizenship rights. Citizenship would on this basis then comprise of three elements, namely, civil, political and social rights[11] defined by Marshall (quoted in Lister, 1997) as follows:

The civil element is composed of the rights necessary for individual freedom – liberty of the person, freedom of speech, thought and faith, the right to own property and to conclude valid contracts, and the right to justice. The last is of a different order from the others, because it is the right to defend and assert all one's rights on terms of equality with others and by due process of law ... By the political element I mean the right to participate in the exercise of political power, as a member of a body invested with political authority or as an elector of the members of such a body ... By the social element I mean the whole range from the right to a modicum of economic welfare and security to the right to share to the full in the social heritage and to live the life of a civilised being according to the standards prevailing in the society (pp.16-17).

Although not directly relevant to the central focus of this chapter, it must also be mentioned that the liberal worldview of citizenship is also unsatisfactory in its definition of rights and duties as applicable between individuals and the state only. This state-centric construction of citizenship needs to be dismantled to permit the application of citizenship rights to individual relations as well. Feminist jurisprudence demonstrates that the public/private divide thrives on male/masculine hegemony (Lister, 1997). This dichotomy designates as 'private' all functions and qualities that are inconsistent with the exercise of citizenship rights in the public realm. The fact that it is women who are stereotypically relegated to the private sphere of the family because of the sexual division of labour has meant that they do not possess qualities associated with the exercise of citizenship rights in the public realm. It has also meant that women's admission to citizenship has been on different terms from those applicable to men. However, women suffer much abuse such as domestic violence in the private sphere (MacKinnon, 1989; Engle, 2000; Schneider, 1991). In addition, women's day-to-day life is in great measure affected at the workplace, education institutions, the church and other private associations. The restriction of the reach of citizenship rights to state/individual relations has therefore meant that citizenship rights cannot be claimed against private actors.

The critique of the state-centric outlook of citizenship is particularly relevant in the context of globalization, which has seen private actors amassing enormous power regarding the direction of the global and domestic economic and social policies (Clapham, 1992; Kamminga and Zia-Zarifi, 2000; Chirwa, 2002b). Non-state actors have increasingly taken part in the provision of basic goods and services, which was previously the exclusive preserve of state actors. These developments mean that the enjoyment of citizenship rights cannot be ensured by the state alone. Many other actors can limit or provide access to these rights. For example, access to medicine and housing in South Africa is to a large degree also dependent on the policies of pharmaceutical companies and banks (e.g. through determining criteria and terms of loans) respectively (Liebenberg, 2003). The ongoing privatization of municipal services also means that private actors will play a central role in ensuring access to them.[12] If poverty of women is to be eradicated and full enjoyment of citizenship rights by women is to be ensured, it is imperative that the notion of citizenship be opened up to define the rights and duties in the private realm.

Citizenship under the Constitution: A Snapshot

Citizenship has been given firm constitutional protection in the Constitution. Section 20 states that no citizen shall be deprived of citizenship. This guarantee extends to women and men alike. Regarding the rights that flow from this citizenship, the Constitution breaks with traditional liberal constitutions by giving express recognition in reasonable detail to almost all economic, social and cultural rights known to the international system of human rights alongside civil and political rights.

However, the Constitution articulates economic, social and cultural rights in two different ways. There is a set of these rights that are defined in a manner that suggests that they are capable of immediate implementation. An individual may claim these rights upon demand and enforce them in a court of law. This is the case with the right to choose one's trade, occupation or profession freely; fair labour practices; and the right of employees to form and join trade unions, and of employers to form and join employer's organizations. The rights to property, basic education, use of one's own language and participation in the cultural life of one's choice, and belonging to a cultural, religious or linguistic community are formulated in a similar fashion.

With the exception of the rights to basic education, it can be argued that these rights have attracted lesser controversy regarding their recognition and judicial enforceability. This is so because they, arguably, involve a relatively lesser degree of positive action and expenses from the state to ensure their enjoyment as compared to other economic, social and cultural rights such as the right to adequate housing, health, food, water, and social security. The right to property has in fact been a central right in the liberal conception of citizenship while trade union rights, and the right to use one's language and participate in one's own cultural life uncontroversially found full recognition as justiciable rights under the International Covenant on Civil and Political Rights (ICCPR).[13] Although these rights can contribute to the eradication of inequalities that exist in society, the classical economic, social and cultural rights such as the right to health, food, water, social security, housing, are more significant because they involve more positive action from the state. The Constitution defines these rights with qualifications such as 'progressive realization' and 'available resources' in sections 26[14] and 27.[15] This is also the case with the right of access to land and the right to higher education.[16] The adoption of this language is an imitation of the approach of the International Covenant on Economic, Social and Cultural Rights (ICESCR),[17] which served to underscore the fact that these rights are incapable of immediate implementation and judicial enforcement. Rather, they are only realizable over time depending on the availability of state resources. *Grootboom* provides useful guidelines for understanding the meaning of these rights as defined with those qualifications and sets out the nature of the obligations of the state engendered in them. These principles are vitally important to the eradication of poverty and achievement of substantive equality in South Africa. They are discussed critically below.

The South African Constitution also departs from the narrow conception of citizenship limited to state/individual relations by permitting the horizontal application of human rights.[18] As argued above, gender imbalances cannot be fully eliminated unless women are able to assert their rights in the private realm as well.

Significantly, the Constitution explicitly entrenches the concept of substantive equality. According to section 9(2), 'Equality includes the full enjoyment of all rights and freedoms'. 'In order to promote the achievement of equality', the section proceeds, 'legislative and other measures designed to protect or advance persons, or categories of persons, disadvantaged by unfair discrimination may be taken'. The Constitutional Court has heralded this section as embodying 'restitutionary equality':

> Particularly in a country such as South Africa, persons belonging to certain categories have suffered considerable unfair discrimination in the past. It is insufficient for the Constitution merely to ensure, through its Bill of Rights, that statutory provisions which have caused such unfair discrimination in the past are eliminated. Past unfair discrimination frequently has ongoing negative consequences, the continuing of which is not halted immediately when the initial causes thereof are eliminated, and unless remedied, may continue for a substantial time and even indefinitely. Like justice, equality delayed is equality denied ... One could refer to such equality as remedial or restitutionary equality.[19]

Moreover, in terms of section 1 of the Constitution, the Republic of South Africa is founded on, among other key principles 'the achievement of equality' and 'non-sexism'. The elimination of gender imbalances is therefore a central benchmark against which economic, social and cultural rights must be interpreted. However, it is argued below that the Constitutional Court has given negligible attention to construing economic, social and cultural rights in a manner that is responsive to the bitter gender inequalities in South Africa.

The Implications of *Grootboom* for Poverty Eradication and Citizenship from a Gender Perspective

Factual Background

The applicants, including a number of children, occupied private land which had been earmarked for low cost housing after moving from an informal settlement because of appalling conditions they were living in. They were later forcefully evicted from the private land. The eviction was carried out in a manner that resulted in the destruction of their personal possessions and building materials. Consequently, they were unable to erect adequate shelter on a sports field in the area where they camped following the eviction.

They applied to Cape High Court for an order requiring the government to provide them with adequate housing or basic shelter until they secured permanent accommodation. The High Court held that the relevant organ of government was enjoined by section 28(1)(c) of the Constitution to provide adequate shelter to children. This section provides that 'Every child has the right to basic nutrition, shelter, basic health care services and social services'. The High Court further held that parents were entitled to be accommodated with the children by reason of the principle of the child's best interests. All three spheres of government appealed to the Constitutional Court against the order of the High Court.

The South African Human Rights Commission and the Community Law Centre (University of the Western Cape) intervened jointly as friends of the court (amici curiae)[20] in the appeal. While the parties to the case confined their case to section 28(1)(c), the amici supported the decision of the lower court based on section 26, which recognizes the right of access to adequate housing. They argued in essence that this section entrenched the minimum core obligation on the part of the state to provide the applicants with basic shelter.

The Decision

Economic, social and cultural rights as juridically enforceable values Economic, social and cultural rights are often regarded as being intrinsically different from civil and political rights. Those who hold this view contend that economic, social and cultural rights are political manifestos. They are imprecise involving difficult policy choices and make heavy cost demands on the state for their realization. It is often argued therefore that these rights are incapable of immediate implementation and the judiciary has no competence to adjudicate on them.[21] These arguments are responsible for the rejection of the expansion of the notion of citizenship to encompass economic, social and cultural rights. They also resulted in the bifurcation of the Universal Declaration of Human Rights (UDHR) into the International Covenant on Civil and Political Rights (ICCPR) and the International Covenant on Economic, Social and Cultural Rights (ICESCR) when the decision to enact a binding international bill of rights was taken in the United Nations. It has since become fashionable to define economic, social and cultural rights with the qualifications that they are realizable 'progressively' within the 'maximum' of 'available resources'.

In South Africa, although this formulation has been mimicked in respect of many key economic, social and cultural rights, contestation about their justiciability was laid to rest at a theoretical level in *First certification judgment.*[22] In this case, the Constitutional Court held that these rights were capable of judicial enforcement. At the very minimum, it was held, the state is enjoined to refrain from violating the negative obligation engendered by these rights. The state is also under a constitutional duty to comply with the positive obligations inherent in these rights.

These pronouncements did not gain practical significance until *Grootboom.*[23] Reaffirming its earlier decision in the case mentioned above, the Constitutional Court held that when confronted with an alleged violation of economic, social and cultural rights, the question was not whether these rights were justiciable under the Constitution, 'but how to enforce them in a given case'. This decision cannot be made in the abstract. Rather, it is one that has to be 'carefully explored on a case-by-case basis' (para. 20).

It was held in *Grootboom* that although section 26(1) did not expressly say so, there was, 'at the very least, a negative obligation placed upon the State and all other entities and persons to desist from preventing or impairing the right to adequate housing' (para. 34). Consequently, the state, it was held, had an obligation to ensure, at the very least, that the eviction was executed humanely. The fact that the eviction was carried out a day earlier than the day stipulated in the court order and that the possessions and building materials of the respondents were destroyed and burnt amounted to a breach of the negative obligation embodied in the right of access to adequate housing recognized under section 26(1) of the Constitution. The Court also reaffirmed that positive obligations are also capable of juridical adjudication. This holding is discussed in detail below.

The holding that economic, social and economic rights can be enforced through judicial procedures is a landmark in the quest for attaining social justice in South Africa. In making this decision, the Court explicitly acknowledged that economic, social and cultural rights have the potential to bridge gender inequalities:

> There can be no doubt that human dignity, freedom and equality, the foundational values of our society, are denied those who have no food, clothing or shelter. Affording socio-economic rights to all people therefore enables them to enjoy the other rights enshrined in Chapter 2 [of the Bill of Rights]. *The realisation of these rights is also key to the advancement of race and gender equality and the evolution of a society in which men and women are equally able to achieve their full potential* (para. 23, Per Yacoob J, authors' emphasis).

Judicial remedies are critical for holding policy-makers accountable for the duties imposed upon them by the Constitution. They remove from the realm of political discretion or personal choice those important decisions and actions that bear on the daily lives of people to the field of accountability. The promise of gender equality is therefore made more concrete than if economic, social and cultural rights were left to the vicissitudes of politics. Additionally, the judiciary plays a significant role in developing the content of the rights and obligations entrenched in the human rights framework based on a critical assessment of people's daily experiences. Thus, by holding that the enforcement of these rights falls within the province of the courts, it is possible to develop them in a manner that incorporates gender consciousness. The accomplishment of the mission of gender equality, which is a prerequisite for full enjoyment of citizenship by women, is therefore rendered more possible.

Enforcement of positive obligations   The enforcement of the negative obligation implicit in economic, social and cultural rights is unquestionably important. However, its value remains at the level of maintaining the status quo of the persons concerned. As has been argued earlier in this chapter, substantive equality is critical to the enjoyment of citizenship. However, the achievement of substantive equality is impossible by maintaining the status quo. Deliberate positive action aimed at eradicating systemic inequalities is indispensable. On this basis, it is vitally important that judicial enforcement of positive obligations is recognized.

Grootboom contains important guidelines regarding the discharge of the positive obligations engendered by economic, social and cultural rights by the state. In this case, the Constitutional Court rejected the contention that section

26(1), which recognises the right of access to adequate housing, created a minimum core obligation to provide basic shelter enforceable immediately upon demand. It held that section 26(1) should be read together with subsection 2, which enjoins the state 'to take reasonable legislative and other measures, within its available resources, to achieve the progressive realisation of this right'. Thus, in any challenge based on section 26(1) in which it is alleged that the state has failed to meet the positive obligations imposed upon it by section 26(2), it was held, 'the real question will be whether the legislative and other measures taken by the state are reasonable' (para. 41). It was emphasized that the Court would not enquire into whether other more desirable or favourable measures could have been adopted, or whether public money could have been better spent.

A reasonable programme is one that 'clearly allocates responsibilities and tasks to the different spheres of government and ensures that appropriate financial and human resources are available'. It must be coordinated, comprehensive and coherent (paras. 39-41). Additionally, it must be 'balanced and flexible and make appropriate provision for attention to housing crises and to short-term, medium and long-term needs' (para. 43). Thus, a programme that 'excludes a significant segment of society cannot be said to be reasonable' and those 'whose needs are the most urgent and whose ability to enjoy all rights therefore is most in peril' must not be ignored (paras. 43-44).

Furthermore, the Court held that by requiring the state to realize the right to housing progressively, it was envisaged that this right could not be realized immediately. However, the state was under an obligation to move towards the achievement of this goal:

> The term 'progressive realisation' shows that it was not contemplated that the right could be realised immediately. But the goal of the Constitution is that the basic needs of all in our society be effectively met and the requirement of progressive realisation means that the State must take steps to achieve this goal. It means that accessibility should be progressively facilitated: legal, administrative, operational and financial hurdles should be examined and, where possible, lowered over time. Housing must be made more accessible not only to a large number of people but to a wider range of people as time progresses (para. 45).

Positive obligations entrenched in economic, social and cultural rights do not obligate the state to do more than is permissible by available resources. According to the Constitutional Court, the requirement of 'within available resources' means that:

> ... both the content of the obligation in relation to the rate at which it is achieved as well as the reasonableness of the measures employed to achieve the result are governed by the availability of resources (para. 46).

It was therefore held that a balance has to be struck between the duty to attain the goal of realizing a right expeditiously and effectively and the availability of resources in order for a court to determine whether a measure taken by government is reasonable (para. 46).

In *Grootboom*, the Court found that what had been done in the execution of the programme in issue as 'a major achievement'. 'Considerable thought, energy, resources and expertise' had been devoted to it in order to achieve the progressive realization of the right to housing (para. 53). Nevertheless, the programme was found to be unreasonable on the basis that it was not sufficiently flexible to respond to those in desperate need.

Protection of vulnerable groups   By reason of the *Grootboom* decision, therefore, economic, social and cultural rights under the South African Constitution are not entirely incapable of immediate enforcement. Not only is the negative obligation to respect them judicially enforceable, but positive obligations can be enforced as well. This decision is a groundbreaking decision as far as efforts aimed at securing substantive equality in society are concerned.

What is perhaps worrisome from a gender perspective is that in the definition of what is a reasonable measure is somewhat gender insensitive. By holding that a reasonable programme is one that does not exclude a significant segment of the population who live in desperate circumstances, it is possible to imply that gender is a relevant consideration. However, the Court did not define these phrases. Also, the Court in its determination of whether the relevant programme was reasonable did not consider whether the programme made adequate provision for women.

The Constitutional Court's holding in respect of the rights of children further demonstrates its reluctance to developing jurisprudence on economic, social and cultural rights in the direction of according special protection to vulnerable groups. In this case, an argument was advanced on behalf of the respondents who were children that the government had an obligation to provide them with shelter under section 28(1)(c) of the Constitution. The High Court agreed with this contention and further held that it was in the best interests of the children to be accommodated together with their parents in the shelter so provided by the state to them. However, the Constitutional Court disagreed with this holding. Instead, it held that the primary obligation to provide shelter for children rests with parents. Only failing such care does the state assume that primary duty.

This holding has far-reaching implications for children's (as well as their parents') rights. Children are a vulnerable group of people deserving of special protection (see e.g. Sloth Nielsen, 2003; Viljoen, 2002).

In *TAC* (Treatment Action Campaign), the Constitutional Court appears to have mitigated the sweeping effect of *Grootboom* in this regard by holding that 'the primary obligation to provide basic shelter rests on those *parents who can afford to pay*'.[24] Acknowledging that the provision of a single dose of Nevirapine to a mother and her child to prevent transmission of HIV is essential to a child, it was held that the government was in violation of the right of children to basic health care services recognized under section 28(1)(c) on the ground that the policy prevented poor mothers and their children from accessing the drug. However, the outcome of the decision in *TAC* turned on the fact that the policy infringed on the obligation to respect the general right to health care services recognized under section 27(1). The case fell far short of according children's rights the priority they deserve.[25]

In both *Grootboom* and *TAC*, therefore, the Constitutional Court failed to include a requirement that a reasonable programme must make explicit provision for vulnerable groups in the application of the test of reasonableness. In its current form, this test rests on the wrongly assumed premise that people are affected in the same way by poverty. Without such a requirement, inequalities might not be easily eliminated and vulnerable groups might not be afforded sufficient protection.

Gender and the question of minimum core obligations In adopting the reasonableness test the Constitutional Court rejected the contention that economic, social and cultural rights entail a minimum core of positive obligations on the part of the state. The minimum core obligations concept was developed by the Committee on Economic, Social and Cultural Rights, which monitors the implementation of the ICESCR by state parties. This concept was intended to ensure that every human being has access to basic goods and services essential for a dignified life. The full enjoyment of citizenship rights is, as has been argued earlier, dependent on this.

The importance of the minimum core concept lies in the recognition that requiring a state to satisfy minimum core demands might cripple under-resourced governments. At the same time, it guards against possible evasion by states of their obligations under the disguise of resource constraints by requiring them to prioritize the satisfaction of those minimum obligations. The concept of minimum core enjoins states alleging lack of resources to 'demonstrate that every effort has been made to use all available resources that are at its disposition in an effort to satisfy, as a matter of priority, those minimum obligations'.[26]

The Constitutional Court refused to adopt this concept arguing, among other things, that 'millions of people were living in deplorable conditions and in great poverty' in South Africa.[27] The fear was therefore that the state would be financially overstretched if it were compelled to satisfy the minimum core obligations. However, the larger part of the millions of poor people alluded to by the Court are women. The implication for women of this decision is that, as far as positive obligations of the state are concerned, they are entitled to reasonable policies. A litigant shoulders an onerous burden of showing that a given measure of government is unreasonable. Even if such burden is discharged, it is difficult to foresee that a litigant or group of them can obtain tangible or immediate relief. The bottom line is that the state has no obligation to ensure the satisfaction of minimum essential levels of basic needs as a matter of priority. Given the deep gender imbalances, among other structural disadvantages, an approach to the implementation of economic, social and cultural rights that does not entrench a modicum of priority to satisfy minimum essential levels of subsistence is insufficient to secure the better enjoyment of citizenship by every member of society.

150   *(Un)thinking Citizenship*

Conclusion

The South African Constitution heralds better prospects for women in that it broadens the scope of its citizenship rights by including elaborate provisions of economic, social and cultural rights. These rights play a valuable role in eradicating poverty and systemic inequalities that prejudice women's full enjoyment of citizenship including full, effective and equal participation in public and private institutions. *Grootboom* is a milestone in that it establishes that economic, social and cultural rights are in certain circumstances capable of being immediately enforced. These rights can be enforced judicially to prevent non-interference with their enjoyment and to ensure that the relevant duty holders discharge their positive obligations generated by these rights. In respect of positive obligations the state has an obligation to devise and implement reasonable measures aimed at giving effect to these rights. Through the discharge of this obligation, it is possible to achieve substantive equality among all South Africans, which would ensure that everyone enjoys full rights of citizenship.

However, this chapter has demonstrated that the interpretation of economic, social and cultural rights could be improved to ensure that vulnerable groups are directly and sufficiently protected. One limb of our argument is that the definition of the reasonableness test by which measures taken by government in the realization of economic, social and cultural rights are tested, should include a requirement aimed at affording special protection of vulnerable groups such as women and children. Otherwise, it may not be possible to remedy extant structural imbalances, stereotypes and prejudices such as those that affect women. Meaningful enjoyment of citizenship by those that have been historically disadvantaged is largely dependent on the recognition of their position and positive action aimed at uplifting that position.

Further, or in the alternative, the other limb of our argument is that the Court must entrench the principle priority to the satisfaction of minimum core obligations engendered by these rights. The reasonableness test in its current form does not prioritize poverty alleviation. Given that it is women who are the most and worst affected by poverty, this test does not adequately respond to the urgent need to solve the problem of gender domination. One way of getting round this problem is by adopting the minimum core obligations concept. This concept strikes a reasonable balance between resource constraints and the need to ensure that a state does not abdicate its obligations to fulfil economic, social and cultural rights under the disguise of lack of resources. The other way is by bringing this concept to the centre of the reasonableness test. At the moment, although the Constitutional Court suggested that this concept was possibly relevant to the test, it has not yet elaborated its significance. Neither in *TAC* nor *Grootboom* was it mentioned, nor was there an allusion to how it would be affected by the relevant programmes.

Notes

1. See e.g. *Ex parte Chairperson of the Constitutional Assembly: In re Certification of the Republic of South African Constitution* 1996 (4) SA 744 (CC); 1996 (10) BCLR 1253 (CC), *(First certification judgment)*; *Soobramoney v. Minister of Health, KwaZulu-Natal* 1998 (1) SA 765 (CC), 1997 (12) BCLR 1696 (CC) *(Soobramoney); Minister of Public Works and Others v Kyalami Ridge Environmental Association and Others* 2001 (7) BCLR 652 (CC); *Minister of Health and Others v Treatment Action Campaign and Others* 2002 10 BCLR 1033 (CC) (TAC). For a critical discussion of these cases see Liebenberg, (2003).

2. *Government of the Republic of South Africa and Others v Grootboom and Others (Grootboom)* 2001 (1) SA 46 (CC), 2000 (11) BCLR 1169.

3. However, the above may not represent a true picture of the poverty situation in South Africa. The World Bank has been criticized for defining poverty in terms of a fixed amount of dollars per day in that it fails to capture in full the humiliation, powerlessness and brutal hardship faced by the poor. See M. Chossudovsky, (1999); and Reddy and Pogge, (2002).

4. For example, in terms of racial, provincial, and urban/rural distribution (see generally McDonald, Piesse and Van Zyl, 1999).

5. It was predicted, for example, that 1.7 million children would die in 2000 worldwide because of a failure by the international community to reduce poverty levels (see Oxfam, 2002).

6. The term poverty is complex and does not lend itself to easy definition. It is a condition that is relative and, as a result, the determination of the poor across disparate societies living under different circumstances is extremely difficult. By contrast, the concept of economic, social and cultural rights constitutes a set of entitlements claimable against specific duty holders (see International Human Rights Council on Human Rights Policy, 2002, pp.23-24).

7. In the Taylor Committee Report (2002), poverty is also defined as the 'inability of individuals, households and entire communities to command sufficient resources to satisfy a socially acceptable standard of living'.

8. In this connection the Committee on Economic, Social and Cultural Rights has rightly stressed that these rights must be taken into account if anti-poverty policies are to be effective, sustainable, inclusive, equitable and meaningful to those living in poverty. See Statement adopted by the Committee on Economic, Social and Cultural Rights on 4 May 2001 on 'Substantive issues arising in the implementation of the International Covenant on Economic, Social and Cultural Rights: Poverty and the implementation of the International Covenant on Economic, Social and Cultural Rights', A/ CONF.191/BP/7.

9. Other groups that have historically experienced exclusion from citizenship rights include slaves, natives in the context of colonialism and poor people.

10. Statement to the World Conference on human rights on behalf of the Committee on Economic, Social and Cultural Rights adopted by the Committee on ESCR, 7th Session, Supp. No.2, p.82, 3 UN Doc. E/1993/22E/C.12/1992/2, Annex III, (1993). Vincent (1986) has captured the critical role of economic, social and cultural rights as follows: the right to life has as much to do with providing the wherewithal to keep people alive as with protecting them against violent death. Dismal expectation about either of these aspects would not be compensated for by sanguine expectation about the other.

11. However, the catalogue of rights that the term citizenship may encompass should not be considered closed. Human rights arise historically from struggles of people experiencing instances of domination. It is an ideology, which has expanded exponentially from its narrow early conception. Thus, talk about the recognition of third generation rights comprising the right to development, healthy environment, and sovereignty of natural resources, for example, has intensified in recent times.

12. For some insight into privatization in South Africa, see McDonald and Smith (2002).

13. The ICCPR was adopted by the UN General Assembly on 16 December 1966 and entered into force on 23 May 1976 to translate human rights obligations entrenched in the Universal Declaration of Human Rights (UDHR) into binding norms. Owing to the ideological differences that animated the Cold War, the West rejected economic, social and cultural rights as human rights capable of judicial enforcement. As a result the ICCPR contained only those rights (mainly civil and political rights) which were considered suitable for immediate implementation.

14. Section 26 provides: '(1) Everyone has the right to have access to adequate housing. (2) The state must take reasonable legislative and other measures, within its available resources, to achieve the progressive realization of this right. (3) No one may be evicted from their home, or have their home demolished, without an order of court made after considering all the relevant circumstances. No legislation may permit arbitrary evictions.'

15. Section 27 provides: '(1) Everyone has the right to have access to – (a) health care services, including reproductive health care; (b) sufficient food and water; and (c) social security, including, if they are unable to support themselves and their dependants, appropriate social assistance. (2) The state must take reasonable legislative and other measures, within its available resources, to achieve the progressive realization of this right. (3) No one may be refused emergency medical treatment.'

16. See sections 25(5) and 29(1)(b).

17. The ICESCR was adopted by the UN General Assembly on 16 December 1966 and entered into force on 23 May 1976. Unlike the ICCPR, it codified those rights (mainly economic, social and cultural), which were considered incapable of being implemented immediately and judicially. To underscore this, the ICESCR was enacted without a complaints procedure.

18. See section 8(2) and (3). For a discussion of these provisions see Chirwa (2002a).

19. See *National Coalition for Gay and Lesbian Equality v Minister of Justice* 1999 (1) SA 6 (CC), paras. 60-1.

20. An 'amicus curiae' (literally, 'friend of the court') is a person or organization that is not a party in a case before court, but is allowed to intervene in a case and make legal or factual submissions. For an amicus to be admitted, the submissions made must be relevant to the proceedings and introduce information or arguments that are different to those raised by the parties, and which are useful to the Court. An amicus usually makes written submissions, but can also be allowed by the court to present oral argument to the court.

21. These arguments have since been adequately rebuffed (see Beetham, 1999; De Vos, 1997; Liebenberg, 1999b; 2001; Scott and Macklem, 1992).

22. The African Commission confirmed in *Social and Economic Rights Action Centre and the Centre for Economic and Social Rights v Nigeria* (Communication 155/1996) that economic social and cultural rights can also be enforced at an international level by finding that the Government of Nigeria had violated a range of these rights under the African Charter on Human and People's Rights in relation to oil exploration in

Ogoniland. For a review of the case see Chirwa (2002b).

23. Between *First certification judgment* and *Grootboom, Soobramoney* was decided. This case concerned a claim by a 41-year-old man suffering from terminal renal failure against the state that he is provided with ongoing dialysis treatment pursuant to section 27(3) of the Constitution, which guarantees the right not to be denied emergency medical treatment. The Constitutional Court rejected the claim on the ground that the section relied on did not extend to provision of ongoing treatment of chronic illness for prolonging life. Rather, it has application only in the case of a sudden catastrophe or emergency.

24. Para. 77. For a brief review of the case see Khoza (2002a; 2002b). For a critique of the same case from a children's rights perspective see Proudlock (2002).

25. In making this decision, the Court seems to have engaged in the application of the reasonableness test, which is supposedly applicable in the case of the general socio-economic rights provisions under sections 26 and 27 (see Chirwa, 2003a).

26. See General Comment No. 3, 1990, 'The nature of state parties' obligation', adopted by the ICESCR on 14 December 1990, para. 36.

27. Para. 25. For an insightful critique of *Grootboom* on the rejection of the minimum core concept see Bilchitz (2002).

References

Baker, R. (1990), *Political Legitimacy and the State*, Clarendon Press, Oxford.

Beetham, D. (1999), *Democracy and human rights*, Polity Press, Cambridge.

Bilchitz, D. (2002), 'Giving socio-economic rights teeth: The minimum core and its importance', *South African Law Journal*, Vol.119(3), pp.484-501.

Brodsky, G. and Day, S. (2002), 'Beyond the social and economic rights debate: Substantive equality speaks to poverty', *Canadian Journal of Women and Law*, Vol.14, pp.185-220.

Budlender, D. and Liebenberg, S. (eds.), (2002), 'Rights, Roles and Resources: An analysis of Women's Housing Rights – Implications of the *Grootboom* case', unpublished paper produced by the Women's Budget Project of IDASA.

Chirwa, D.M. (2002a), 'Towards revitalizing economic, social and cultural rights in Africa: Social and Economic Rights Action Centre and the Centre for Economic and Social Rights v Nigeria', *Human Rights Brief*, Vol. 10(1), pp. 14-25.

Chirwa, D.M. (2002b), Obligations of non-state actors in relation to economic, social and cultural rights under the South African Constitution', Community Law Centre, Cape Town. Also published in *Mediterranean Journal of Human Rights*, Vol.7(1) pp.29-68.

Chirwa, D.M. (2003), '*Minister of Health and Others v. Treatment Action Campaign and Others*: Its implications for the combat against HIV/Aids and the protection of economic, social and cultural rights in Africa', *East African Journal of Peace and Human Rights*, (forthcoming).

Chossudovsky, M. (1999), 'Global falsehoods: How the World Bank and the UNDP distort the figures on global poverty', available at www.globalissues.org/TradeRelated/Facts.asp (accessed 31 January 2003).

Clapham, A. (1992), *Human rights in the private sphere*, Clarendon Press, Oxford.

Committee on Economic, Social and Cultural Rights on 4 May 2001 on 'Substantive issues arising in the implementation of the International Covenant on Economic, Social and Cultural Rights: Poverty and the implementation of the International Covenant on Economic, Social and Cultural Rights', A/ CONF.191/BP/7.

De Vos, P. (1997), 'Pious wishes or directly enforceable human rights? Social and economic rights in South Africa's 1996 Constitution', *South African Journal on Human Rights*, Vol.13, pp.67-101.

Donnelly, J. (1989), *Universal human rights in theory and practice*, Cornell University Press, New York.

Eddy, W.H.C. (1979), *Understanding Marxism: An approach through dialogue*, Basil Blackwell, Oxford.

Engle, K. (2000), 'After the collapse of the public/private divide: Strategising women's rights', in H. Steiner and P. Alston (eds.), *International human rights in context: Law, politics and morals*, Oxford University Press, New York, pp.218-220.

Hassim, S. (1999), 'From presence to power: Women's citizenship in a new democracy', *Agenda*, No.40, pp.6-17.

Fick, G. (1999), 'The gender-sensitive check-list for free and fair elections', *Agenda*, No.40, pp.66-74.

Gaete, R. (1993), *Human rights and the limits of critical reason*, Dartmouth, Aldershot.

International Human Rights Council on Human Rights Policy (2002), *Duties sans frontier: Human rights and global social justice*.

Kamminga, M.T. and Zia-Zarifi, S. (eds.), (2000), *Liability of multinational corporations under international law*, Kluwer Law International, The Hague, 2000.

Khoza, S. (2002a), 'HIV, infant nutrition and health care: Implications of the state's obligation in providing formula milk to prevent HIV transmission through breast-feeding', Community Law Centre, Cape Town.

Khoza, S. (2002b), 'Reducing mother to child transmission of HIV: The Nevirapine case', *ESR Review*, Vol.2, pp.2-6.

Liebenberg, S. (1999a), 'Social citizenship – a precondition for meaningful democracy', *Agenda*, No.40, pp.59-65.

Liebenberg, S. (1999b), 'Socio-economic rights', in M. Chaskalson et al. (eds.), *Constitutional Law of South Africa*, Juta, Cape Town, pp.41-1–41-56.

Liebenberg, S. (2001), 'The protection of economic and social rights in domestic legal systems', in A. Eide et al. (eds.), *Economic, social and cultural rights*, Martinus Nijhoff Publishers, Dordrecht, pp.55-84.

Liebenberg, S. (2003), 'South Africa's evolving jurisprudence on socio-economic rights: An effective tool in challenging poverty?', *Law, Democracy and Development*, (forthcoming).

Liebenberg, S. and O'Sullivan, M. (2001), 'South Africa's new Equality legislation: A tool for advancing women's socio-economic equality?', *Acta Juridica*, 73, pp.70-103.

Lister, R. (1997), *Citizenship: Feminist perspectives*, Macmillan, London.

McDonald, D.A. and Smith, L. (2002), *Privatising Cape Town: Service delivery and policy reform since 1996*, Municipal Services Project, Cape Town, Occasional Paper No.7.

McDonald, S., Piesse, J. and Van Zyl, J. (1999), 'Exploring Income Distribution and Poverty in South Africa', Paper prepared for the Biennial Conference of the Economic Society of South Africa, hosted by the University of Pretoria, South Africa in September 1999, available at www.shef.ac.uk/~devecres/research/incdistza.pdf (accessed 31 January 2003).

MacKinnon, C. (1989), *Towards a feminist theory of the state*, Harvard University Press, Cambridge.

Oxfam, *Missing the target: The price of empty promises*, June 2000.

Pateman, C. (1989), *The Disorder of Women*, Polity Press, Cambridge.

Proudlock, P. (2002), 'Children's rights: Do they have a right to special protection?', 2 *ESR Review*, Vol. 2, pp. 6-8.

Reddy S.G. and Pogge, T.W. (2002), 'How not to count the poor', available at www.columbia.edu/~sr793/count.pdf (accessed 31 January 2003).

Report on Poverty and Inequalities in South Africa (1995) http://www.und.ac.za/und/indic/archives/indicator/winter98/Fmay/htm (accessed on 28 January 2003).

Report prepared for the Office of the Executive Deputy President and the Inter-Ministerial Committee for Poverty and Inequality Summary Report, 13 May (1998), available at www.polity.org.za/html/govdocs/reports/poverty.html?rebookmark=1 (accessed 31 January 2003).

Schneider, E. (1991), 'Violence of privacy', *Connecticut Law Review*, 23(4), pp. 973-999.

Scott, C. and Macklem, P. (1992), 'Constitutional ropes of sand or justiciable guarantees? Social rights in a new South African Constitution', *University of Pennsylvania Law Review*, Vol.141(1), pp.1-148.

Shestack, J.J. (1998), 'The philosophic foundations of human rights', *Human Rights Quarterly*, Vol.20, pp.202-234.

Shivji, I.G. (1989), *The concept of human rights in Africa*, CODESRIA Book Series, London.

Sloth-Nielsen, J. (2003), 'Too little? Too late? Too lame? The implications of the *Grootboom* case for State responses to child-headed households', *Law, Democracy and Development*, Vol.7(1), pp.113-136.

Taylor Committee Report (2002) on a 'Comprehensive Social Security System in South Africa', prepared for the Department of Social Development, submitted to the Minister of the Department in May 2002.

Taylor, V. (1997), 'Economic gender injustice: The macro picture', (1997), *Agenda*, No.33 pp.9-25.

UNDP (2000), Human development report.

Viljoen, F. (2002), 'Children's rights: a response from a South African perspective', in D. Brand and S. Russel (eds.), *Exploring the core content of socio-economic rights: South African and international perspectives*, Protea Book House, Pretoria, pp.201-206.

Vincent, R.J. (1986), *Human Rights and International Relations*, Royal Institute of International Affairs, Cambridge.

Case References

Ex parte Chairperson of the Constitutional Assembly: In re Certification of the Republic of South African Constitution 1996 (4) SA 744 (CC), 1996 (10) BCLR 1253 (CC), (First certification judgment).

Government of the Republic of South Africa and Others v Grootboom and Others (Grootboom) 2001 (1) SA 46 (CC), 2000 (11) BCLR 1169 (Grootboom).

Minister of Public Works and Others v Kyalami Ridge Environmental Association and Others 2001 (7) BCLR 652 (CC).

Minister of Health and *Others v Treatment Action Campaign* and *Others* 2002 10 BCLR 1033 (CC) (TAC).

National Coalition for Gay and Lesbian Equality v Minister of Justice 1999 (1) SA 6 (CC), paras. 60-61.

Social and Economic Rights Action Centre and the Centre for Economic and Social Rights v Nigeria (Communication 155/1996).

Soobramoney v. Minister of Health, KwaZulu-Natal 1998 (1) SA 765 (CC), 1997 (12) BCLR 1696 (CC) (Soobramoney).

Chapter 7

The Impact of the HIV/AIDS Epidemic on Women's Citizenship in South Africa

Anneke Meerkotter

Introduction

No doubt HIV/AIDS has had an immense impact on the position of women in society, placing additional burdens on and increasing the vulnerability of women affected and infected by HIV/AIDS.[1] Women with HIV/AIDS need access to health care, information, counselling, social security and protection from various forms of discrimination. Women who are not infected with HIV have similar needs which must be fulfilled if they are to be empowered to leave abusive relationships, negotiate safer sex, make reproductive and other life choices, and to enable them to cope with the effect of HIV/AIDS on them emotionally and physically as partners, mothers and care givers.

In the context of HIV/AIDS, notions of citizenship and participatory democracy have become increasingly abstract and limited for many people. This paper tries to identify how the HIV/AIDS epidemic impacts on a society of 'individual citizens', particularly women, and explores whether there is a need to reassert notions of citizenship and democracy to ensure survival beyond HIV/AIDS.

The paper is written in a context where the South African government's HIV/AIDS policy has often been criticized for being indecisive and not doing enough to assist people living with HIV/AIDS. In short it is noted that the government's policy, specifically on improving access to health care for people living with HIV/AIDS, has necessitated a public response outside formal public participation processes to reassert the right to health care and the urgent need for treatment of people living with HIV/AIDS. For the purpose of this discussion the specific detail of the South African government policy on all aspects of HIV/AIDS will not be discussed as it is well documented elsewhere. What is important to note is that the government's policies on preventing HIV/AIDS have many good aspects to them, and that the major shortfalls are in the areas of health care services that offer HIV testing and counselling, provision of antiretrovirals and treatment for opportunistic infections. For many years the government refused to provide antiretrovirals to prevent mother-to-child HIV transmission or as a post-exposure prophylaxis for rape survivors. Communities rallied behind the calls for the latter two services to be provided. The government was eventually taken to court around its failure to have a rational policy on preventing mother-to-child transmission of HIV. Shortly before this court case, the government announced that it would make antiretrovirals available for rape survivors. The contentious issue remains the provision of antiretrovirals for people living with HIV/AIDS to slow the progression of the disease. For the most part the government has claimed that the main reasons for its refusal to provide these medicines are the costs associated with them, and the potentially toxic effects of the medicines. Many studies have shown that these arguments are not substantiated if compared with the benefits that these medicines would have on the quality of life for people living with HIV/AIDS and their families.[2]

This chapter assumes that the HIV/AIDS epidemic can only be approached from a human rights perspective as opposed to coercive[3] or purely preventative[4] health policy approaches. A human rights approach should be adopted as a means of empowering communities and individuals with knowledge about HIV/AIDS, both to avoid HIV infection, to encourage openness and to enable individuals and communities to cope with the disease. The approach emphasizes the need to include people living with HIV/AIDS in communities and to treat them with respect and dignity. The aim would be to encourage the whole population to realize or acknowledge their own vulnerability to HIV, to encourage voluntary counselling and HIV testing and to provide care, support and treatment for people living with HIV/AIDS and their families.

Equal and Unequal Citizens?

Marshall (quoted in Siim, 2000) defines citizenship as:

> ... the status bestowed on those who are *full* members of a community. All who possess the standards are equal with respect to the rights and duties with which the status is endowed. There is no universal principle that determines what those rights and duties shall be, but societies in which citizenship is a developing institution create an image of an ideal citizenship against which achievement can be measured and towards which aspiration can be directed (pp.26-27, author's emphasis).

Marshall's theory of 'democratic' citizenship, which identified the interrelation of social, civil and political rights, was based on an analysis of British history (Siim, 2000, p.26). As such, and in the context of many of the criticisms raised against it, South African theories of citizenship must take the critical step towards defining citizenship within their own terms and context. Marshall's theory and definition of citizenship are nevertheless useful in understanding how the current South African legal framework and Constitution defines citizenship, which has been derived from a largely Westernized conception of citizenship.

Whilst the process of transformation provides the platform for the development of a new, more relevant, conception of citizenship, South Africa's acceptance of the global economic framework creates the danger of increasingly excluding a vast number of people from the conception of citizenship. In the context of a serious HIV/AIDS epidemic, large unemployment and poverty, we find that people are increasingly struggling to hold on to the limited rights they do have. It is in this context that the impact of HIV/AIDS on women's citizenship should be analysed.

The South African Constitution refers to the existence of a common citizenship, stating that '[a]ll citizens are equally entitled to the rights, privileges and benefits of citizenship, and equally subject to the duties and responsibilities of citizenship' (Act 108 of 1996, section 3).

The Bill of Rights proceeds to define the fundamental rights of citizens, including civil, political and social rights. In this sense, the Constitution is what Marshall refers to as an 'ideal citizenship against which achievement can be measured and towards which aspiration can be directed' (quoted in Siim, 2000, pp.26-27). The Constitution therefore provides people with a tool for struggle, encapsulating those general demands that are deemed 'reasonable'.

Of course the Constitution has its own limitations and the interpretation of the rights in the Bill of Rights will provide a further nuance in such struggles over definition. This has been the case when attempts have been made practically to enforce rights contained in the Constitution, by approaching the Constitutional Court to determine whether the government has met its responsibility to realize those rights.

Even though citizen rights are included in the Constitution, it remains a contested terrain of struggle. The interpretation of these rights will remain inextricably bound to the social and economic context that prevails in South Africa and the rest of the world. Capitalism and patriarchy have entrenched the exclusion of the vast majority of people, creating a political paradigm of rights that limits inclusion and participation. Bustelo (2001, p.5) also criticizes Marshall's notion of citizenship for assuming that social rights will inherently tend towards equity, and ignoring the logic of capitalism that produces deep inequalities and conceptualizes rights as individual rights. Bustelo (2001) concurs with Heuer and Schirmer (1998) when he points out that, to the extent that social rights cannot be ascribed to individual subjects, they are not implementable in a context where civil and political rights are only formal recognitions (p.5). To counteract large-scale marginalization, the rights in the Bill of Rights could form the basis of demands by communities, and any infringements of these rights should consistently be challenged. This is not, however, an easy option where marginalization as a result of social inequality means the absence of social rights and thus unequal citizenship. Dierckxens (2000) explains:

> In subjective terms, citizenship came to mean people's identification with the same market that was slashing their rights along with objective citizenship. This resulted in an alienating commitment to the market and to an abstract society threatening to exclude them (pp.112-113).

Nevertheless, Siim (2000) argues that 'active citizenship' and 'the interaction of institutions and human agency are the key to democratic citizenship' (p.8). 'Active citizenship', for Siim (2000) covers activities in a number of political arenas (neighbourhoods, the workplace, informal organizations, social movements, the state and formal political organizations) (p.8). An essential part of citizenship and claiming citizen rights involves a person or community's ability to engage at various levels to assert their rights. The extent to which 'active citizenship' is possible, nonetheless depends on a person or group's existing level of marginalization within society. Heuer and Schirmer (1998) point to the interrelation of rights and its impact on the possibility for participation as 'active citizens':

> The wretched of today's world – the poor, the starving, the homeless, the children condemned to starvation and disease, the women without rights, the old people left to live out their lives in want, even when in full possession of civil and political rights are not free. Nor are people really free when they are socially secure but politically disempowered (p.10).

Having 'citizenship' of a country promises equal rights, yet in practice, some citizens are invariably more equal than others, having a greater advantage that enables them to seize their rights. This does not mean that the poor and marginalized do not engage in struggle to assert their rights, it simply means that the current, implied notion of citizenship does not automatically grant them these rights. Dierckxens (2000) describes how:

> Deep down the long-time excluded – such as women and 'minorities', among others – have never been a real part of the system, in other words they have never been true citizens. In contrast to the newly excluded, their demands for involvement are not usually developed at the expense of others. Never having been a real part of it before they now demand a society that has room for everyone (p.119).

It is in this context that working class social movements, often formed around the demand for a specific right, have the potential to challenge broader notions of citizenship and social exclusion. It is no coincidence that social exclusion cannot easily be changed through existing political processes. Hassim (1999) suggests that the current situation begs the question whether democracy is 'understood in narrow formalistic terms or in terms which encompass social and economic rights? Is democracy seen as processes of consensus building among elites or driven by broad citizen participation?' (p.7). Hassim's question starts to engage the different notions of democracy and the degrees of social inclusion envisioned by it. Meiksins Wood (1995) describes how the concept of democracy was gradually distorted into a concept of rights which does not, and never intended to, include people in decision-making processes which affect their lives:

> The effect was to shift the focus of 'democracy' away from the active exercise of popular power to the passive enjoyment of constitutional and procedural safeguards and rights, and away from the collective power of subordinate classes to the privacy and isolation of the individual citizen (p.227).

Can the achievement of citizenship be defined as the extent to which people have equal rights and equal opportunities to exercise those rights and participate in decision-making processes that affect their rights? If so, how do we address the lack of citizenship faced by many people whose socio-economic position marginalizes them, gives them unequal rights and limits their opportunities to exercise their rights? Can the systemic exclusion of the majority of people be remedied by short-term legal solutions?

HIV/AIDS and the Perpetuation of Women's Social Exclusion

Marshall recognized that, for equal citizenship to emerge, rights would have to be guaranteed institutionally (Voet, 1998, p.35). Indeed the South African Constitution theoretically provides women with equal rights to men in all respects. In addition, women now have the right to be free from discrimination on the grounds of sex, gender, pregnancy and marital status. Women also have the right to reproductive choice, health care and freedom from violence. Unfortunately these are mere formal rights. It does not ensure women's status as equal citizens. Voet (1998) makes a very important point in this regard: reference to citizenship in general obscures the specific oppression faced by people in reality (pp.54-5).

From the above discussion, it should be clear that people who are socially excluded as a result of their socio-economic position are not equal citizens. Women's citizenship is therefore limited to the extent that they are poor, but women also face a more pervasive burden to the extent that women's second class status could exacerbate their poverty, as could the impact of social conditions, including the HIV/AIDS epidemic. Reference to citizenship in general often ignores the particular pressures faced by women. In this respect, Young (cited in Voet, 1998) identified four aspects that bear consideration when trying to identify this oppression: marginalization, powerlessness, cultural imperialism and violence (p.55). It is precisely these factors that have contributed to women's vulnerability to HIV and the burden HIV/AIDS places on women.

Marginalization

Young defines marginalization as the 'process of expelling a whole category of people from useful participation in socio-economic life, and thus potentially subjecting them to severe material deprivation and even extermination' (cited in Voet, 1998, p.55). Nowhere is this definition so devastatingly true than in the context of HIV/AIDS, where the marginalization of the poor, particularly women,[5] has resulted in many avoidable deaths across the developing world.

Whilst AIDS is a relatively new disease, some of the factors contributing to its alarming prevalence have been around for much longer. The power relations between men and women, rich and poor, developed and developing countries have shaped both the prevalence of HIV/AIDS and the extent to which it is prioritized through prevention and treatment efforts. These power relations have often been institutionalized in international institutions like the World Trade Organization, World Bank and International Monetary Fund, which function to secure a continual increase in trade, often at the expense of poor countries and poor people. One example would be the Agreement on Trade Related Aspects of Intellectual Property Rights, which forces countries to respect and promote patent rights,

TRIPS

including patents of pharmaceutical products, to the detriment of more important public health concerns. Developing countries and their citizens are ignored in the decision-making on the terms of these agreements.

Retrenchments, low wages, long working hours, unemployment, and stressful or unhealthy working conditions, and other features of the unfettered search for profit throughout the world, similarly impact on the health of workers and their families, increasing their risk of HIV infection and developing AIDS, and reducing their ability to care for themselves and for people living with HIV/AIDS in their families. Unemployment also contributes to migration, a significant factor in the prevalence of HIV in South Africa. People often have no choice but to leave their homes and families to look for employment elsewhere, facing new challenges wherever they go. People living with HIV/AIDS are further marginalized, and find it impossible to find work or sustain their current living standards, something that is essential if they want to maintain their health. The emotional and financial effects on people living with or affected by HIV/AIDS are severe.

The socio-economic position of people directly affects their vulnerability to HIV/AIDS and the impact of the disease on them. The increase in poverty, food insecurity and unemployment as a result of national and international economic policies, in effect means that the struggle for daily survival is often a far more pertinent issue in the minds of poor people than their risk of HIV infection[6] (Heywood, 1998, para. 9). Marginalization in this respect relates to the increasing number of people battling for their lives, with little space for social participation or the exercise of their rights. In this context, sex can be one of two things, a comfort at the end of a trying day, or a means of eliciting food, money or shelter in exchange.[7] For men it is often the former, and for women the latter. In both cases, safer sex is not always a key determinant in the decision whether or not to have sex.

HIV/AIDS also reinforces poverty and inequality, perpetuating the vicious circle, as it is described by Heywood (1998), who explains that HIV/AIDS inevitably means that a larger amount of the household income is spent on health care for the ill and eventually burial costs (1998, para. 15). Among other things, the death or illness of a breadwinner means a loss of income for the household,[8] additional burdens on relatives to care for orphans and little money for education (Heywood, 1998, para. 15).

Marginalization is an important factor in assessing a person's status as 'equal citizen'. If the government is, through the Constitution, committed to the idea of citizens being equal, what role should it then play in a situation where socio-economic conditions, often reinforced by the government's macro-economic policies, marginalizes people and contributes to their risk of HIV infection and the detrimental impact HIV/AIDS has on them? In addition, how should the government respond when people are denied the opportunity to live with dignity and earn a living, because they cannot afford the medication which would enable them to do so? Unfortunately South Africa has reached the stage where hundreds of people, mostly in poor communities, are dying on a daily basis from AIDS-related illnesses. In this way, the epidemic is challenging the fundamental myth of 'equal citizenship', exposing deep inequalities in the starkest way.

Powerlessness

Women's position in society increases their risk of infection. The degree of women's risk depends on the extent to which they can make decisions about their lives, bodies and relationships. Women are not always able to decide when, where and how to have sex. That women lack authority in sexual decision-making is exacerbated by the fact that women are, biologically, more prone to HIV infection during unprotected sex than men, making safer sex a far more pertinent issue for women. The risk of infection is further determined by women's lack of control over whether and which barrier methods to use, and are more at risk during forced or dry sex, when the vaginal membranes can easily tear (Vetten and Bhana, 2001, p.10).

Women's lack of access to health services for sexually transmitted infections further increases their risk of HIV infection. In general, women in developing countries access health care services less for their medical conditions, because they either don't have the resources to do so or do not value themselves enough to present their health problems. In the latter case, women are sometimes intimidated by health care workers and fear their reactions, especially where the health concern is of a sexual nature (Tallis, 2001, p.10). Young women who have sex with older men – a frequent occurrence – are particularly at risk of infection because of their inferior status in relation to the men, their sexual immaturity and the potential physiological trauma of sex.

Women's lack of status and low sense of self-esteem, not only affect their ability to insist on safer sex, but impact on the extent to which they face discrimination, abuse and stigma if they disclose their HIV status and their (in)ability to cope with living with HIV/AIDS. Powerlessness is therefore an important determinant for the degree to which women can exercise their rights and become equal citizens. Powerlessness also influences women's participation as 'active citizens' since women are under-represented in most decision-making structures within government and communities.

Cultural Imperialism

Young (cited in Voet, 1998) defines cultural imperialism as the 'universalisation of a dominant group's experience and culture and its establishment as the norm' (p.55). Whilst cultural imperialism can be understood in various ways, for the purpose of this discussion, I refer to the patriarchal values that underlie all cultures in South Africa, whether colonial or indigenous, and which permeate society and entrench stereotypes of women. Cultural imperialism in the context of HIV/AIDS affects women in three different ways:

Firstly, women are required to be monogamous, submissive sexual partners while men are not stigmatized for having multiple sex partners, thus increasing women's risk of HIV infection (Vetten and Bhana, 2001, p.10). Women who insist on safer sex face accusations of 'unfaithfulness' and 'disrespect'.

Secondly, the perception that women with HIV/AIDS are sexually promiscuous, increases the stigma and discrimination they face should they disclose their HIV status. Women's activism in South Africa is slowly trying to inculcate the notion of sexual and reproductive rights, arguing that women have the right to decide when, where, how and with whom to have sex. Women who want to claim autonomy over their bodies are often tainted with allusions to promiscuity, and moralizing against women (rarely men) frequently with religious undertones, making it extremely difficult for women to disclose their status in an overtly religious community.

Thirdly, the stereotype that society demands from women is that they fulfil the role of caring and nurturing for their partners, children, the sick and the elderly. This means that women end up carrying the burden of care for the sick and dying.[9] In the context of such high HIV prevalence and inadequate health care services, this fate awaits many women. Already a quarter of public hospital admissions are for AIDS-related illnesses. Health care workers, mostly women, take care of these patients. As health care services become more overstretched, this burden will increasingly be pushed onto females as mothers, wives, partners, grandmothers, sisters, girl-children and home-based carers.

Women's status as second-class citizens cannot be ignored when trying to assess and address the devastating impact of HIV/AIDS on society.

Violence

Violence against women is rife, both inside and outside their homes. It is difficult for women to discuss safer sex practices, such as condom use, especially in the context of abusive relationships, as this could be construed as disrespect, infidelity or lack of commitment to the relationship. Women who decide to go for an HIV test often face violence or the threat of violence from their partners and women's fear of their partner's reaction affects their choice to go for HIV testing and to disclose their results (Maman et al., 2001). Women's experience of violence also limits their ability to take preventive health action, thereby placing them at risk of HIV infection and limiting their access to care and support services.

Among younger women aged between 15 and 19 years, rape is most common, and it is simultaneously the group with a higher risk of HIV infection, especially where genital injury and bleeding was present (Kim, 2000, p.3; Vetten and Bhana, 2001, p.5). In the context of an HIV epidemic, young women are often singled out for sex by men who believe that young women will not have HIV (Kim, 2000, p.3). Rape by more than one perpetrator is on the increase, placing women at higher risk of HIV infection due to repeated exposure and increased injuries (Kim, 2000, p.4).

Violence against women contributes to their marginalization and powerlessness and detracts from their ability to exercise their rights.

It should be clear that rights are not a panacea for citizenship. Women's equal rights does not mean that men share their burden to care for the sick, or that women are less vulnerable to HIV infection. Voet (1998) argues that key to becoming an equal citizen is the ability to exercise one's rights, to be an 'active citizen' (p.67). Thus for women to become equal citizens, two prerequisites are essential: social participation and socio-economic equality (Voet, 1998, p.77).

Essentially, the oppression faced by women hampers their social participation in all spheres of society. Women's oppression also indicates that they have particular concerns and needs that should be met but which are, precisely because of their oppression, ignored. The link between a lack of socio-economic equality and social participation and unequal citizenship is clear in a context where decisions that impact on citizens are often made at a governmental or international level where affected groups are continuously excluded from decision-making processes on a formal and informal level.

Nevertheless, people living with HIV/AIDS, including women, have used various strategies to exercise their rights. Thus whilst practising safer sex, getting tested for HIV and looking after the needs of people living with HIV/AIDS is important, the prevalence and impact of HIV/AIDS is such that it cannot be addressed adequately on an individual or person-to-person level. What we need is a community-based response to HIV/AIDS addressing the stigma that surrounds the disease but we also need to fight on a broader level against policies and practices that hamper prevention and treatment, and those which stretch beyond pure health policies and entrench poverty and social exclusion.

Affirming Rights through the Courts

Over the past five years there have been active campaigns in South Africa against the absence of a government plan to treat people living with HIV/AIDS, and against the high cost charged by international pharmaceutical companies for medicines used to treat people living with HIV/AIDS. Activist organizations like the Treatment Action Campaign sought to achieve their demands through both mass mobilization and legal action.[10] In both methods, activists relied heavily on the rights enshrined in the South African Constitution as support for their demands, including the rights to dignity and access to health care.

Activist organizations that sought to use the law to improve access to health care for people living with HIV/AIDS, found themselves with a sympathetic Constitutional Court that had already ruled in favour of a prospective employee who had been refused a position as a cabin attendant of an airline on the basis of his HIV status.[11] This case was significant because the Constitutional Court took judicial notice of the link between HIV and AIDS. At the time, controversy and government inaction prevailed on this issue after the president of South Africa, Thabo Mbeki, had refused to acknowledge the link between HIV and AIDS. The Court defined people living with HIV/AIDS as 'one of the most vulnerable groups in our society' – people who 'have been subjected to systemic disadvantage and discrimination' and 'have been stigmatized and marginalized' (para. 28). The Court explicitly stated that 'prejudice can never justify unfair discrimination' and '[p]eople who are living with HIV must be treated with compassion and understanding' (paras. 37, 28). The case centered on the interrelated rights to dignity and the protection from unfair discrimination.

In contrast, the Pharmaceutical Manufacturers Association and many international pharmaceutical companies tried to affirm their rights to patent protection and profits, by challenging the South African government's Medicines and Related Substances Control Amendment Act 90 of 1997, which was aimed at broadening access to medication through generic substitution of off-patent medicines and parallel importation of patented medicines. The case gained prominence when trade union and community activists focusing on access to treatment for people living with HIV/AIDS joined the litigation, and organized national and international protests to highlight the prioritization by pharmaceutical companies of their patent rights, as opposed to the rights of people living with HIV/AIDS to access affordable medication to improve their health and prolong their lives.[12] The huge public outcry against the case forced pharmaceutical companies to withdraw their action. The case took four years, in the process delaying the implementation of the Act, and potentially, access to more affordable medication for people. In practice, after the case was withdrawn, the government further delayed promulgating the Regulations to the legislation and refused to make use of similar legal mechanisms like compulsory licensing to access cheaper medication for people living with HIV/AIDS.

Although this case did not end in a judgment, it is important in many respects. Heywood (2001) describes how national and international law becomes the subject of contestation when 'access to resources is dependent on the cooperation of non-state actors, such as multinational companies, that are not governed by traditional human rights legislation' (p.135). The Treatment Action Campaign argued that the Amendment Act which introduced generic substitution and parallel importation of medicines formed part of the government's positive duty to 'protect and promote life and dignity, and to improve access to health care services' (Heywood, 2001, p.154). For Heywood (2001), the case is an example of 'one of the major strategies of human rights violators in the "new world order" – dressing rights-incursions in the language of rights-protection and using unlimited economic power to pursue legal strategies to consolidate this' (p.135). Unfortunately issues around access to medicines are often pre-determined by the extent that multinational companies lobby their government allies. In this case the South African government had to endure immense pressure from the United States, spurred on by the pharmaceutical companies to withdraw this legislation, despite the beneficial impact the legislation would have on the health of the people in South Africa (Heywood, 2001, p.135). The government found an ally in the Treatment Action Campaign and federation of trade unions, COSATU, whose intervention in the case managed to draw out the pertinent real life issues facing people living with HIV/AIDS, and for which the pharmaceutical companies had no valid answer. The national and international protests and media coverage surrounding this intervention ensured a moral victory against the pharmaceutical companies, even though their withdrawal from the case prevented a legal judgment with a more binding, albeit jurisdictionally limited, force.

Litigation had often been used as a tool in the fight for civil rights – for example against the Apartheid state, and this strategy was also used by the civil rights movement in the United States. Some circles in the United States expressed caution with regard to this approach because of the gradual shifts in the American courts from sympathetic 'victim'-based perspectives on civil rights, to a 'perpetrator' perspective which led to negative or limited results in court (Crenshaw, 2000, p.67). Critics argued that such cases abstracted rights, demobilized people and did not focus on the more urgent issues. For Crenshaw (2000) however:

> the very articulation of a civil right by a community which has for generations been denied such rights was transformative, and therefore real at an existential level, notwithstanding the success or failure of the right to bring about material change (p.67).

Crenshaw (2000) makes an important statement on the strategy of the civil rights movement.

> In the context of the civil rights movement, the articulation and subsequent enforcement of rights was not automatic but was the product of efforts to politicise a contradiction between dominant ideology and certain material realities. Sometimes such contradictions force elites to close the gap or to render the conditions somehow consistent with dominant ideologies. Thus barriers might be lifted or formal rights might be granted, yet the scope of the reform is probably limited by the dynamic that gave rise to the contradiction-closing gesture in the first place. Circumstances may be adjusted only to the extent necessary to close the contradiction. As argued earlier, 'although it is the need to maintain legitimacy that presents powerless groups with the opportunity to wrest concessions from the dominant order, it is the very accomplishment of legitimacy that forces greater possibilities' (p.70).

To a certain extent Crenshaw's analysis holds sway if one looks at the Constitutional Court case on the need for a mother-to-child HIV transmission prevention programme.[13] Campaigns on this issue were initiated long before the actual court case and sparked a wide range of civil society actions, instilling in people the confidence to demand access to a right regardless of the existing stigma and discrimination against people living with HIV/AIDS.[14]

Despite the fact that the purpose of and conditions created by capitalism lead to a narrow definition of citizenship and citizen rights, the Constitution provides the opportunity for an assertion of civil, political and social rights by the poor. The destructive impact of the HIV/AIDS epidemic has made such attempts necessary and urgent to prevent the deaths and destitution faced by the many people living with or affected by HIV/AIDS.

In the mother-to-child transmission case, the Constitutional Court, whilst confirming its ability to adjudicate social rights,[15] firmly declined the opportunity to define the core minimum that a government would be required to provide to avoid violating a social right, as argued by one of the amici curiae in the case.[16] Although this is a complex issue, and most courts steer away from deciding on matters best decided on by the government, it does point to the limited ability of citizens to approach the courts to enforce their social rights.

Nonetheless, the Constitutional Court judgment, in deciding against the government, raised important issues around the government's responsibility to prevent mother-to-child transmission outside its originally conceived pilot or research sites.[17] The Constitutional Court raises the key question in this regard: 'What is to happen to those mothers and their babies who cannot afford access to private health care and do not have access to research and training sites?' (para. 17). In addition, the Constitutional Court emphasized that, not only could it evaluate the constitutionality of government policies, but it also had to provide appropriate relief, which could include the issuing of a mandamus and the 'exercise [of] some form of supervisory jurisdiction to ensure that the order is implemented' (para. 104).

In a more recent case on the constitutionality of legislation that criminalized the act of sex work and brothel-keeping, the Constitutional Court's judgment indicated a tendency towards conservatism when enforcing rights, even civil rights.[18] The judgment upheld the constitutionality of the legislation and argued that '[i]f the public sees the recipient of reward as being "more to blame" than the "client" ... that is a social attitude and not the result of the law' (para. 16). The minority judgment in this case, in this author's view correctly, challenged this argument on the basis that:

> [I]t is no answer then to a constitutional complaint to say that the constitutional problem lies not in the law but in social values, when the law serves to foster those values. The law must be conscientiously developed to foster values consistent with our Constitution (para. 72).

In this case, the State argued that one of the factors which necessitates criminalization of sex work is HIV/AIDS. The Court was unsympathetic to counter-arguments raised about how criminalization marginalizes sex workers and increases their risk of HIV/AIDS. Even the minority judgment sought to curtail a sex worker's claim to dignity and privacy, arguing that any limitation on those rights follows from the choice to engage in sex work (para. 74) and is 'not severe' (para. 94). Whatever one's opinion about the rationality of criminalization might be, the moral views which underlie the judgment indicate that one cannot rely on the Court's sympathy in all cases, a fact underscored in Crenshaw's analysis above. In addition, the level of mobilization by groups outside of the court case itself, and its moral high ground within communities affect whether 'the very articulation of a civil right ... was transformative' despite its failure at Court (Crenshaw, 2000, p.67).

The mother-to-child transmission case is an example of a demand that has great public support regardless of the outcome of the judgment. The case on sex work has however, met with the opposite result. The absence of visible public discussion or campaign against criminalization impacted on the view adopted by the Court and left activists who oppose criminalization in a worse position than before, having the task now, not only of convincing people of their argument, but also of persuading people why this is correct in the light of a Constitutional Court judgment that found the opposite. The mother-to-child HIV transmission case succeeded in this respect because the demand already had wide support from communities and was propagated by communities themselves who experienced the need for this health service and saw the effect of its absence. The participation of people living with HIV/AIDS, especially women, in this campaign to assert their rights, notwithstanding the many obstacles to participation as 'active citizens', is instructive.

Struggles to 'Reclaim' Citizenship

The struggle for access to health care for people living with HIV/AIDS has not been easy. The right has not been realized by the government of its own accord, despite numerous demands for this. In the mother-to-child HIV transmission case activists approached the courts to facilitate speedy access to a prevention programme for mother-to-child HIV transmission, in the absence of concrete government policy and lack of certainty on its commitment to providing this service. It should be noted that, in spite of the Constitutional Court judgment, some provinces remained reluctant to implement mother-to-child HIV transmission prevention programmes.

The campaign for treatment of opportunistic infections and antiretroviral medication for people living with HIV/AIDS has however not moved the South African government towards speedy action. This begs the question by Hassim (1999), raised earlier, on the extent to which 'democracy [is] seen as processes of consensus building among elites or driven by broad citizen participation' (p.7). The articulation of demands by citizens has not persuaded the government to act, even if only through progressive realization as required by the Constitution. Instead, many citizens feel that there is a brick wall separating them from government, mooting civil disobedience as a final strategy to convince the government of the urgency of its demands. In this case, instead of individualizing citizen demands, the struggle to be treated with dignity and respect and to have access to health care services have seen many joint actions as 'active citizens'.

It should be appreciated that the process that leads to the participation of people living with HIV/AIDS in such actions is not easy or uncomplicated. In a society where stigma still prevails against HIV/AIDS, the realization of one's HIV status precipitates individual struggles for self-acceptance, acceptance within one's family and the development of a lifestyle which enables one to cope with that status in addition to other issues in life. In the absence of hope, this internal struggle can easily lead to a decline in the level of health and quality of life of that person. Participation in struggles which can facilitate access to treatment that would provide more life security can be empowering. It provides hope, fosters an awareness of solidarity with others who are engaged in similar life struggles and encourages openness and understanding.

The extent of one's participation as an 'active citizen' could be influenced by various factors. HIV/AIDS is a complex disease and many myths prevail around it. The possibility for mobilization on issues around HIV/AIDS has, to a large extent, depended on sustained efforts to create awareness about the disease, how it works, and the possibility of medication that can affect its progression. Women's ability to participate in this struggle is affected by the extent to which their other responsibilities and position within society allows them. Nevertheless, it is precisely these responsibilities that have made women acutely aware, in the absence of adequate treatment, of the impact of HIV/AIDS on their communities – they are the ones who must care for the sick, and ensure the survival of their families. It is therefore not surprising that women form the backbone of campaigns to alleviate the impact of HIV/AIDS, whether it be on an individual basis as home-based carers or as part of group struggles to assert rights and challenge unfair practices, both within their own communities and in broader society.

Meiksins Wood's (1995) description of the gradual move 'away from the collective power of subordinate classes to the privacy and isolation of the individual citizen' nevertheless prevails (p.227). There are many people living with or affected by HIV/AIDS who are starting to assert their rights, yet many more operate outside this discourse, caught in denial, blame, hopelessness and self-hate. The burden of HIV/AIDS therefore perpetuates existing levels of social exclusion from contemporary notions of citizenship.

Conclusion

Campaigns that use the Constitution as a platform to reassert rights is one way of achieving results in the absence of concrete government support. Similar campaigns are developing around the right to services, housing, land, food and social security. In the absence of such emerging social movements, the 'individual citizen' must rely on formal government mechanisms that allow for public participation in decision-making. These avenues are however, not widely accessed and have historically tended to curtail women's participation.

Women's subordinate position in society not only increases their vulnerability to HIV infection but creates a climate where HIV/AIDS will have a devastating, cruel impact on every infected and affected person's ability to participate in formal decision-making processes. In this context the need to broaden notions of citizenship and challenge the exclusiveness of decision-making and the unequal distribution of resources is overwhelming. Such a challenge will only be effective if collectively organized by communities. Communities have had to overcome many obstacles to achieve a more just dispensation, with women at the forefront of struggles for an improvement in living conditions and an eradication of poverty. Campaigns for treatment and health services are often lead by women who through their experiences of bearing the responsibility of health care, either formally as nurses and social workers, or informally as care givers, mothers, sisters, grandmothers and partners within the family and broader community, have a better understanding of the limitations of present reforms and the challenges that lie ahead. Campaigns unfortunately seldom address the broader issue of unequal citizenship, which underpins many social ills including HIV/AIDS.

Notes

1. Statistics released in 2002 revealed that 12.8% of South African women and 9.5% of men are living with HIV/AIDS (Shisana et al., 2002, p.46). For young women between the age of 15 and 24 years, the HIV prevalence is 12%, compared to 6.1% of young men

in this age category (Shisana et al., 2002, p.48). In three of South Africa's nine provinces, Free State, Gauteng and Mpumalanga, roughly one in five adults aged 15 to 49 years are living with HIV/AIDS, with the majority living in informal urban areas (Shisana et al., 2002, pp. 50-51). A study by the Medical Research Council has estimated that 40% of all deaths in 2000 of persons aged 15 to 49 years was AIDS related (Kenyon et al., 2001).

2. Campaigners have tried to sweeten the pill for government, arguing that additional costs would be saved if the government made use of legal mechanisms like compulsory licences and parallel importation to procure cheaper medication. These measures are allowed in terms of the Medicines and Related Substances Control Amendment Act and the Patents Act. However, pharmaceutical companies and developed countries often try to persuade governments not to use these mechanisms, as reflected in many of the negotiations in the World Trade Centre and around its agreement in Trade Related Intellectual Property Rights. The South African government finally agreed to provide antiretroviral treatment in November 2003. Unfortunately there have been unnecessary delays in the actual availability of antiretrovirals at hospitals and clinics.

3. According to Kenyon et al. (2001) a coercive approach would include measures such as forced testing and making the disease a notifiable condition. These measures are likely to add to discrimination and stigma and will force the disease underground. Despite concerns about the overall impact of mandatory testing on public health, few objected when mandatory testing was mooted for prisoners, sex workers and persons arrested in sexual offence cases. Measures that are driven by prejudice discriminate against groups of people despite concrete evidence of the effectiveness of mandatory testing and violate a whole range of civil rights.

4. Kenyon et al. (2001) equate the preventive approach to a war or moral crusade against an external threat – HIV/AIDS is externalized and viewed as someone else's problem, whilst people living with HIV/AIDS would be isolated, blamed and excluded. A preventive approach should be one aspect of a comprehensive strategy to address HIV/AIDS and should include the promotion of non-discrimination. In the absence of a comprehensive strategy, people living with HIV/AIDS would be allowed to get ill and eventually die, without adequate state intervention to protect their rights to dignity and access to health care.

5. Vicci Tallis (2001) refers to statistics on the 'feminization of poverty' and the trend that women are 'more likely to be poor and malnourished and are less likely to have access to services (health, sanitation, clean water, education) and formal sector employment (pp.6-7).

6. A national food consumption survey by the Department of Health in 1999 found that 52% of South African households experienced hunger – 62% of these lived in rural areas and 42% in urban areas (Kane-Berman et al., 2001, p.312). These figures are likely to be much worse as a result of high food inflation and increased poverty over the past few years. UNAIDS explains how, 'bereft of food, people are compelled to adopt survival strategies that might further endanger their lives. Some migrate, often to urban slums where they are likely to live in marginalized circumstances and lack access to education and health facilities (including HIV prevention and care services). Women and children are being forced, as a last resort, to barter sex for jobs, food and other basic essentials. Large numbers of children are leaving school to find work or forage for food. Communities and social networks are breaking down. HIV/AIDS thrives amid such social displacement and disintegration' (UNAIDS/WHO, 2002, p.33).

7. UNAIDS tries to explain the particular vulnerability of young women as follows: 'Women and girls are commonly discriminated against in terms of access to education, employment, credit, health care, land and inheritance. With the downward trend of many African economies increasing the ranks of people in poverty, relationships with men (casual or formalized through marriage) can serve as vital opportunities for financial and social security, or for satisfying material aspirations. Generally, older men are more likely to offer such security ... The combination of dependence and subordination can make it very difficult for girls and women to demand safer sex (even from their husbands) or to end relationships that can carry the threat of infection' (UNAIDS/WHO, 2002, p.19).
8. A recent UNICEF report confirms that desperation fuels the HIV epidemic, stating that 'an HIV-infected family can see its income drop by up to 80% and its food intake by up to 30%' (Peta, 2003).
9. Tallis (2001) refers to an additional factor in women's marginalization – women's time spent on work, formally, informally and at home, tends by far to exceed that of men, leaving them with less time for other activities, including participating in politics and accessing health care for their own health (p.7).
10. The latest case is a complaint by civil society organizations at the Competition Commission against excessive pricing of antiretrovirals by the pharmaceutical companies GlaxoSmith Kline and Boehringer Ingelheim. The Treatment Action Campaign has also launched an application to enforce the Constitutional Court Order to provide Nevirapine to prevent mother-to-child HIV transmission, in one of the provinces refusing to implement the initial Order. For more information on these cases, visit the Treatment Action Campaign website: http://www.tac.org.za.
11. *Hoffmann v South African Airways* 2000 (11) BCLR 1211 (CC), judgment 28 September 2000.
12. See Heywood (2001, p.133-162) on the history of the case and the campaigns behind it.
13. *Minister of Health and others v Treatment Action Campaign and others* 2002 (10) BCLR 1033 (CC), judgment 5 July 2002, <http://www.concourt.gov.za>. The case centred on two issues: 1) whether the government is entitled to refuse to make a registered drug, Nevirapine, available to pregnant women who have HIV and who give birth in the public health sector, in order to reduce the risk of transmission of HIV to their infants and 2) whether the government is obliged to implement and set out clear time-frames for a national mother-to-child transmission prevention programme, including voluntary counselling and testing, antiretroviral therapy and the option of using formula milk for feeding.
14. The campaigns in this regard were extensively documented in newspaper articles in all the major newspapers. The Treatment Action Campaign website also has more information: <http://www.tac.org.za>. It must be noted that whilst public marches, press conferences and national meetings received most media coverage, the campaign spawned awareness and activism on a whole range of levels, within homes, schools, religious organizations and communities.
15. 'The question in the present case, therefore, is not whether socio-economic rights are justiciable. Clearly they are. The question is whether the applicants have shown that the measures adopted by the government to provide access to health care services for HIV-positive mothers and their newborn babies fall short of its obligations under the Constitution' (para. 25).
16. The Community Law Centre and Institute for Democracy in South Africa argued that, whilst certain aspects of socio-economic rights can only be realized progressively and

within budgetary constraints, all individuals should have an immediate claim to a minimum core level of services, as opposed to the claim for an abstract policy. Their arguments can be accessed on the Community Law Centre website: http://www.communitylawcentre.org.za.

    The Constitutional Court responded that '[I]t is impossible to give everyone access even to a "core" service immediately. All that is possible, and all that can be expected of the State, is that it act reasonably to provide access to the socio-economic rights identified in sections 26 [housing] and 27 [health] on a progressive basis' (para. 35).

17. The government had selected certain health centres for pilot studies where anti-retroviral drugs were available.
18. *Ellen Jordan and others v The State* 2002 (11) BCLR 1117 (CC), available from <http://www.concourt.org.za>. The majority in this case held that the Sexual Offences Act's prohibition of sex work does not unfairly discriminate against women.

References

Adar, J. and Stevens, M. (2000), 'Women's Health' in *South African Health Review 2000*, Health Systems Trust, available from <http://www/hst.org.za/sahr>.

Adede, A. (2001), *Streamlining Africa's responses to the impact of the review and implementation of the TRIPS Agreement*, IPR & Sustainable Development No.2, International Centre for Trade and Sustainable Development.

Bond, P. (ed.), (2002), *Fanon's Warning: A Civil Society Reader on the New Partnership for Africa's Development*, Alternative Information Development Centre, Cape Town.

Bustelo, E. (2001), 'Expansion of Citizenship and Democratic Construction', in W. van Genugten, and C. Perez-Bustillo (eds.), *The Poverty of Rights: Human Rights and the Eradication of Poverty*, Zed Books, London, pp.3-28.

Crenshaw, K. (2000), 'Were the Critics Right About Rights? Reassessing the American Debate About Rights in the Post-Reform Era', in M. Mamdani (ed.), *Beyond Rights Talk and Culture Talk: Comparative Essays on the Politics of Rights and Culture*, David Philip, Cape Town, pp.61-74.

Dierckxsens, W. (2000), *The Limits of Capitalism: An Approach to Globalisation without Neoliberalism*, Zed Books, London.

Hassim, S. (1999), 'From Presence to Power: Women's Citizenship in a New Democracy', *Agenda*, No.40, pp.6-17.

Heuer, U. and Schirmer, G. (1998), 'Human Rights Imperialism', *Monthly Review*, Vol.49 No.10, March 1998, pp.5-16.

Heywood, M. (1998) 'How the Poor Die: HIV/AIDS and Poverty in South Africa' Memorandum by AIDS Law Project submitted to South African Human Rights Commission, Commission of Gender Equality and National NGO Coalition Hearings on Poverty, available from http://www.hri.ca/partners/alp/resource/poor.shtml.

Heywood, M. (2001), 'Debunking "Conglomo-Talk": A Case Study of the Amicus Curiae as an Instrument for Advocacy, Investigation and Mobilisation', *Law Democracy and Development Journal*, 2001(2), pp.133-162.

Isaacs, S. (1997), *South Africa in the Global Economy*, Trade Union Research Project, Durban.

Kane-Berman, J. et al. (2001) *South Africa Survey 2001/2002*, South African Institute of Race Relations, Johannesburg.

Kenyon, C, Heywood, M. and Conway, S. (2001), 'Mainstreaming HIV/AIDS: Progress and Challenges in South Africa's HIV/AIDS Campaign' in *South African Health Review 2001*, Health Systems Trust, available from http://hst.org.za/sahr/2001/chapter9.htm.

Kim, J.C. (2000), 'Rape and HIV Post-Exposure Prophylaxis: The Relevance and the Reality in South Africa', Discussion Paper prepared for WHO Meeting on Violence Against Women and HIV/AIDS: Setting the Research Agenda, Geneva, 23-25 October 2000.

Kwa, A. (2002), *Power Politics in the WTO*, Focus on the Global South.

Lal Das, B. (1998), *An Introduction to the WTO Agreements*, Third World Network.

Lal Das, B. (1998), *The WTO Agreements: Deficiencies, Imbalances, and Required Changes*, Zed Books and Third World Network.

Lister, R. (1997), *Citizenship: Feminist Perspectives*, Macmillan, Basingstoke.

Maman, S. et al. (2001), 'HIV and Partner Violence: Implications for HIV Voluntary Counselling and Testing Programs in Dar es Salaam, Tanzania', Horizons publication, Population Council, available from
http://www.popcouncil.org/pdfs/horizons/vctviolence.pdf.

Meiksins Wood, E. (1995), *Democracy against Capitalism: Renewing Historical Materialism*, Cambridge University Press, United Kingdom.

Meiksins Wood, E. (2003), *The Empire of Capital*, Leftword Books, India.

Peta, B. (2003), 'AIDS and Hunger Claim One Life Every Minute', *Cape Argus*, 5 March 2003, available from http://www.iol.co.za.

Shisana, O. and Simbay, L. (2002), *HSRC/Nelson Mandela Foundation Study of HIV/AIDS: South African National HIV Prevalence, Behavioural Risks and Mass Media*, A Household Survey, Human Science Research Council, Johannesburg.

Siim, B. (2000), *Gender and Citizenship: Politics and Agency in France, Britain and Denmark*, Cambridge University Press, United Kingdom.

Tallis, V. (2001) 'Treatment Issues for Women', Discussion Document produced for the Treatment Action Campaign.

Townsend, J. et al. (1999), *Women & Power*, Zed Books, London.

UNAIDS/WHO (2002), *AIDS Epidemic Update: December 2002*, available from http://www.unaids.org/worldaidsday/2002/press/update/epiupdate2002_en.doc.

Vetten, L. and Bhana, K. (2001), *Violence, Vengeance and Gender: A Preliminary Investigation into the Links Between Violence Against Women and HIV/AIDS in South Africa*, Centre for the Study of Violence and Reconciliation, Johannesburg.

Voet, R. (1998), *Feminism and Citizenship*, SAGE Publications, London.

Case References

Ellen Jordan and others v The State 2002 (11) BCLR 1117 (CC).

Hoffmann v South African Airways 2000 (11) BCLR 1211 (CC), judgment 28 September 2000.

Minister of Health and others v Treatment Action Campaign and others 2002 (10) BCLR 1033 (CC), judgment 5 July 2002.

PART IV
CITIZENSHIP AS AGENCY

Chapter 8

Gendered Citizenship in South Africa: Rights and Beyond

Cheryl McEwan

Introduction

The aim of this chapter is to theorize what citizenship means in the context of post-apartheid South Africa and, specifically, what it means to those most often marginalized, namely black[1] women. Citizenship in South Africa has always been a politically charged and contested notion. Today it serves as a unifying symbol within the broader political project of nation building. However, the meanings of citizenship at a variety of spatial scales (international, national and local) are by no means clear or uncontested. For most South Africans, the term is inextricably bound up with the struggle for liberation and democracy. It is clear, however, that the transition to democracy does not mark the endpoint of political struggle, of contestations over the meanings of citizenship, or the eradication of social and economic inequalities, including those of gender (Hassim, 1999). As with other post-independent states, the struggle for women lies in the (im)possibilities of translating *de jure* equality into de facto equality, and of translating state level commitment to gender equality (at least discursively) into tangible outcomes at the local and individual levels.

International feminist debates have revealed that citizenship must encompass more than formal political rights. It must acknowledge that universal inclusion does not exist, because in reality citizenship is based on power, which is exercised through social, economic and political structures that perpetuate the exclusion of certain social groups (such as women and working class people). Lister (1997) argues that civil and political rights are a necessary, if not sufficient, precondition for full and equal citizenship for women, but these need to be buttressed by social rights, which serve to weaken the effect of inequalities of power in the private sphere. Similarly, Jones (1994) argues that definitions of citizenship need to be broadened beyond formal participation in voting to include the idea of citizenship being an action practised by people of a certain identity in particular locales. In other words, individuals have agency in the construction and contestation of their citizenship, rather than being passive recipients of a pre-determined concept. These reformulations of citizenship as involving both status and practice, as well as recognizing differences of identity bound together through the participation of citizens in the public life of society, offer a valuable starting point from which to consider citizenship in South Africa.

Activists in South Africa recognized that the process of democratic transformation had the potential to create radically different relationships between the state and its citizens than those that had evolved in other post-independence/post-revolutionary countries (Seidman, 1999). Converting this potential into actuality is essential in constructing a gender equitable democracy. The tendency of abstract theories of democracy to overlook gender dynamics might have been exacerbated in South Africa, where racial inequality is obviously paramount. Therefore, the success that activists have had in inserting gender issues into the processes of constructing new institutions, a new democracy and citizenship is noteworthy. Questions remain, however, concerning the effectiveness of this mainstreaming of gender (Manicom, 2001), of how concepts of citizenship are being deployed and how people at grassroots level understand and experience citizenship. In this chapter, I attempt to posit answers to some of these questions by exploring the interconnections and disjunctures between national/state level definitions of gendered citizenship and local level understandings, experiences and contestations.

In what follows, I discuss the concept of gendered citizenship against the backdrop of the continuing democratic transformation in South Africa and broader feminist theorizing. The centrality of rights and rights discourse in nation building and the problem of 'difference' in constructions of citizenship based on a notion of universal rights are examined. Specifically, the chapter discusses the ways in which citizenship in South Africa continues to be mediated by relationships of power between different groups of people and the constraints on socio-economic citizenship for black women. It then examines how the national picture of rights and gendered citizenship translates at the local level, exploring concepts of active and participative citizenship. This is discussed in relation to the restructuring of local governance and its implications for women's citizenship, since the Constitution and the national government define local government as the most effective sphere through which to deepen democracy and construct participative and meaningful citizenship. The chapter concludes with a brief discussion of the significance of the South African context for theorizing gendered citizenship internationally, thus problematizing the dominance of Western feminist theory within international citizenship debates.

Citizenship as Rights: Gender and Nation-Building

Citizenship purports to be a gender-neutral concept but is in fact deeply gendered, being historically constructed in masculine terms and predicated on the exclusion of women (citizens being propertied men) (Pateman, 1988a; 1988b). Social-liberal notions of citizenship, which predominate in the West and which to some extent have influenced South African notions of citizenship, are founded upon, and in turn construct, separate public and private spheres. The public sphere is the sphere of justice, where everyone is treated equally. In the private sphere – the sphere of the family – citizens may act upon personal ideas and notions of morality. In the former the basic rules are to be tolerant, not to impose claims on others and to intervene as little as possible in each other's lives; in the latter, there is scope for the exercise of strong limitations based upon private patriarchies.

This construction of citizenship has been the focus of feminist criticism since, despite claims to justice and fairness, women still appear to be second-class citizens (Voet, 1998). In the light of this, the notion of a single model of citizenship applying equally to women and men has been brought into question (James, 1992; Lister, 1997; Pateman, 1992; Walby, 1997). The different experiences and structural position of women is seen to militate against their full access to the rights of citizenship. Feminist critiques draw on the notions of different levels of citizenship (civil, political, social) articulated by Marshall (1965), focusing particularly on the notion of social citizenship (which Marshall argued was the product of civil and political citizenship). One of the problems identified is that social citizenship usually depends upon being a paid worker for full access to these rights;[2] it is therefore profoundly gendered, although rarely recognized as such. Against this theoretical background, it is significant that the South African state is including women in the national imaginary, not as vulnerable citizens to be protected, but as proactive stakeholders with a part to play in the future development of the nation-state.

State Building

The transition to democracy involved a mass exercise in participation and was based around such concepts as civil society and citizenship, universality and equality, and the pluralization of politics at all levels. Activists endeavoured to ensure that the model of citizenship being constructed contained not only the fairness and justice of social-liberalism, but also guarantees that would protect all minorities on the basis of sex, gender, race, ethnicity, culture, class and so on. Notions of communitarianism and participatory democracy have helped produce a potentially radical notion of citizenship. Civil society is conceived of much in the same way as it was in Eastern European democratic movements, as a medium through which individuals become citizens, members of the political community and participants in public life (Marais, 1998; Einhorn et al., 1996a). In South Africa there is a strong sense, particularly among women activists, that civil society can exert some democratic control over the state, and is indispensable to the maintenance of a democratic pluralistic political culture.

Through negotiations with civil society groups, the South African state crafted an inclusive notion of citizenship as defined in the Constitution and the Bill of Rights. The Constitution does not merely limit the encroaching powers of the state, but it defines the obligations of the state (e.g. equality of work opportunities). It also recognizes certain socio-economic rights, including land rights, housing rights, employment and education rights, rights relating to health-care services (S. Liebenberg, 1999). The Bill of Rights guarantees social and economic rights, but is extremely broad ranging and goes beyond traditional notions of citizenship. Constitutional guarantees are potentially of profound significance, but questions remain over their likely impacts on the lives of the majority, especially women. In particular, there are questions about if and how guarantees to equal rights can be translated into everyday life, and whether attempts to account for difference in the construction of equal and substantive citizenship will be effective.

Questions of how and where citizenship is articulated and how and where women's political activities take place are of significance. The state has certainly been important in creating formal structures with the aim of transforming gender relations. However, as other contexts have illustrated, state restructuring alone cannot transform entrenched gender relations. As Watson (1990) argues, in countries such as Australia where feminists have gained some footholds in government,[3] the possibilities and limitations associated with access to institutionalized forms of power have posed serious questions to feminists within and outside institutional structures. These questions revolve around the relations between the 'femocracy' (Watson, 1990, p.ix) to grassroots feminisms, the compromises that women in government have had to make, the dilution of demands and the real gains of feminist intervention. By the same token, feminist activities are not necessarily confined to organized women's movements, or the state and the constitution. As Butler (1990) argues, it is the everyday social and cultural practices that transform and recreate gender relations. It is widely recognized in South Africa that private patriarchies (residing beyond formal law in households, in particular) might prove a hindrance to women's citizenship and an analysis of state level attempts to mitigate these hindrances is therefore important. However, as feminists elsewhere have demonstrated,[4] homes and communities are also the places where contestations over citizenship might be more effective than state policies in transforming patriarchies.

Domestic Citizenship

Women activists in South Africa sought a democracy in which domestic relations, in addition to relations in the public arena, could come under state scrutiny (Albertyn, 1994a; 1994b). One of the major achievements of the women's movements during the negotiations of the new Constitution was an agreement that rights to culture/tradition and customary law apply only insofar as they are consistent with the provisions in the Bill of Rights and the Constitution generally.

In 'modernizing' states there is often conflict between private and public patriarchies, and this is likely to remain the case in South Africa for several generations. The major battles take place over the control of women's bodies (fertility) and their minds (education), between the bureaucrat and the male head-of-household. By also recognizing customary law or ethnic 'tradition' within the Constitution, the South African government created a potential area of conflict between ethnic constructions of gender and 'modern' ones. Legislation has also been passed to enable women living under customary law to exercise their rights as citizens, recognizing the fact that women in customary marriages, especially African women, have not enjoyed the rights extended to other citizens. The Recognition of Customary Marriages Act (1998) aims to reconcile the preservation of culture and tradition with the competing claims posed by the Constitution to establish equal treatment and non-discrimination (Samuel, 1999). The aim of the legislation is to lift the extreme limitations placed on women in customary marriages, giving them the capacity to sign documents, raise credit, own land and enter into transactions. The extent to which these legal rights translate into tangible outcomes remains to be seen.

Debates over women's citizenship and customary law are likely to be viewed as a contest between feminism and tradition in South Africa. As Walker (1994) argues, rural patriarchy becomes legitimized as tradition; so that, for example, attempts by the state to redistribute land to women is often depicted as a threat to tradition by imperialist feminism. This results in constructing a binary opposition between traditional/customary law and state law. Walker argues that the key institutions of rural society need to be transformed, as well as the legitimizing discourses of 'tradition', 'custom' and 'African culture'. She assumes that the state, through its structures and law, can be used to counter rural patriarchy, but this is potentially problematic. It requires major investments of resources in education as well as monitoring and resources on the ground. Furthermore, as Stewart (1996) argues, a model of state-generated rights which rural women must be educated to claim, has been found wanting in other African contexts. Instead, African women are trying, as they have always done, to strengthen their position within existing contexts, developing their own legal scholarship to break down constructed dichotomies and actively seeking to understand the ways in which the power of tradition and custom can strengthen their position. There are clearly practical hurdles to citizenship and full inclusion for certain groups of women, and there is a need to understand different regulatory regimes, women's position within them, and the nature and locations of women's political action. The latter is not located only in electoral and formal politics, but also in homes, communities and neighbourhoods.

Despite struggles by women to define and assert their position as citizens, their traditionally assigned roles in communities and households continue to constrain their participation as political actors. In South Africa, popularized definitions of 'belonging' in the nation as it defines citizenship are deeply gendered and in ways different to those in the West. Lewis (1999) discusses how the legacy of the anti-apartheid struggle of defining women in relation to the community and nation has reinforced traditions in which women's citizenship is mediated by their subordination to men and their symbolic roles. Motherhood is particularly important. Masculine 'dignity' (as power and control) is still predicated on women's indignity and silence, and some would argue that this continues to be a disturbing element of South African gender politics. The implications this has for a covert and unacknowledged asymmetry in citizenship are profound. Lewis suggests that there are emotional and social pressures for women to collude in their own humiliation and oppression. One example of this is the scarcity of discussion in the Truth and Reconciliation Commission about the rape and sexual torture of women (Goldblatt and Meintjes, 1996; Seroke, 1999). However, there is a much more positive story to be told about the agency of African women in transforming private patriarchies and challenging the more public masculinities that are responsible for rape, violence and conflicts in their neighbourhoods. Diverse groups of women are challenging aspects of the social and political order in which they live, empowering themselves by organizing around community and youth issues, through peace organizations, campaigns against rape,[5] and everyday resistances that are actively transforming patriarchies.

Clearly, citizenship in South Africa is inextricably connected to naturalized social roles, which legal rights and policy-making cannot easily dislodge. As Lewis (1999) argues, these roles are particularly resilient since they buttressed a liberation struggle. The legal rights and state restructuring that women in their diversity have fought for are of real significance, but cultural barriers and localized patriarchies remain largely untouched by sweeping political changes. Mangaliso (1997) argues that, 'the home, where gender inequality begins and is reinforced, can remain mostly untouched by outside institutional forces, including government policy' (pp.140-141). Thus, she argues, the benefits of democracy have not been extended to the majority of women who are black, poor, subjected to private patriarchies and vulnerable to violence. It is perhaps not to the state, government policy or institutional change, therefore, that one should look for future possibilities of transforming private patriarchies and constructing substantive citizenship, but to those localized resistances in homes, communities and neighbourhoods. However, it is also recognized that political participation, in its broadest sense, is central to citizenship, overcoming historically entrenched inequalities and ensuring that constitutional guarantees to equality are realized. The state is trying to create spaces for citizen participation through legislation in ways that might also have significance for women's citizenship.

Citizenship as Rights: The Problem of 'Difference'

One of the greatest concerns for gender activists in South Africa is whether the framing of citizenship as rights will be conducive of substantive citizenship for women. Central to these concerns are debates within feminist theory about whether citizenship *should* be gendered. There are great differences on this issue. For example, Mouffe (1993) pleads for gender-neutral citizenship, whereas Pateman (1992) and Young (1989) strongly propose a citizenship that incorporates 'women as women', though they differ on what this might mean. A third position linking these arguments, suggests that the only way citizenship can become gender-neutral is by incorporating 'women as women' in citizenship theories and practices (Lister, 1989; Phillips, 1991). Gender-neutrality would be attained not through gender-blindness, but through the gendering of citizenship for both women and men. This intersects with debates over whether or not universal or equal citizenship can be combined with plurality (a topic neglected by classical theorists and of considerable significance in South Africa).

Walby (1997) questions whether the concept of citizenship can ever be successfully universal, or whether it is always affected by deeply rooted social divisions of gender, class and ethnicity (p.166). Fundamental tensions exist between acknowledging difference and conceiving universality as both generality and equal treatment (Young, 1989; Fraser, 1997). Young's position is that feminists should aspire to the idea of universal citizenship as the inclusion and participation of everyone in decision-making, but that this should be based on a 'differentiated citizenship' in the sense of emphasizing women's difference and differences among women. Poststructuralist feminists are suspicious of notions of universality but also recognize the dangers of differentiated citizenship that might stigmatize or further isolate already marginalized groups, in addition to the risk of fragmenting the category of 'woman' so much that it makes feminist politics impossible. An alternative is a more moderate deconstructionism that accepts the category of 'women' as constructed, combined with a willingness to use this political subjectivity if and when it appears sensible (Voet, 1998).

Understanding citizenship in South Africa and the obstacles to participation faced by certain groups connects to these broader debates about the notion of 'difference'. Research on citizenship has exploded the assumption that once suffrage was achieved for women, 'blacks' and other groups, all citizens automatically become equal subjects of the political community (Yuval-Davis and Werbner, 1999). A central question in present debates is the extent to which the diversities between people and the socio-economic positions they occupy discriminates between citizens. In South Africa, the theoretical notion of extending rights to all citizens equally is fraught with practical problems because of the difficulty of incorporating difference into the definition of liberal democracy. There is a clear tension between the notion of universal and equal citizenship and the fact that in reality citizenship is based on power which is exercised through social, economic and political structures that perpetuate the exclusion of members of certain social groups (Staeheli and Cope, 1994). The government has attempted to take account of this in some of its social policies and in order to achieve equality some groups receive differential treatment (e.g. affirmative action in public sector employment). Despite this, nation building has not seriously engaged identity construction constituted through difference and related power imbalances (Gouws, 1999); this explains the failure of rights discourse to construct equal political, social and economic citizenship for women.

In theoretical terms, feminists have called for debates to move beyond questions of equality and difference to integrate the ethics of gender justice and caring and to develop a conception of citizenship that embodies neither maternalism (the idea that women's citizenship is separate from men's on the basis of their prescribed social roles) nor abstract universalism, but a 'differentiated universalism' (Phillips, 1993, p.86). The South African context demonstrates that if equality means sameness and the annihilation of difference, little is achieved in eradicating dominant and entrenched power relations (Gouws, 1999). The mediation of equal citizenship by other collective, historically determined identities is still of importance and extending equality to all citizens does not necessarily deal with difference. Indeed, in liberal democratic societies equal treatment often results in unequal outcomes. In South Africa, the construction of a liberal democratic society was seen as the solution to the legacies of apartheid and inequality. However, as Gouws suggests, it is the interpretation of these concepts and the construction of policies to give substance to these concepts that are of significance. Thus, although the Constitution guarantees against discrimination the Equality

Clause makes provision for differential treatment to deal with disadvantage (affirmative action) and the Constitutional Court is interpreting equality in substantive rather than formal terms.

Social and Economic Citizenship

Concepts of social and economic citizenship have some currency in South Africa in understanding how citizenship is mediated by difference. It is recognized that substantive equality is required to take account of social and economic status. However, Gouws (1999) argues that this leads to citizenship based on rights claims, which oversimplify complex power relations. Rights discourses are not likely to be abandoned in South Africa because the political culture prioritizes and emphasizes political and civil rights, even though power relations often stem from poverty and entrenched structural inequalities. For Gouws, rights discourses are often blind to social and economic disparities between groups and, therefore, access to social and economic rights also needs to be recognized. In South Africa rights discourses have failed to transform gender relations and construct equal political, social and economic citizenship for women. As Sandra Liebenberg (1999) argues, '[t]o the extent that poor, black women are excluded from effective access to social services, economic resources and opportunities we have failed to achieve full citizenship for all in South Africa' (p.64).

The harsh economic reality could be considered a diminution of women's citizenship rights and anti-democratic, with some groups unable to participate beyond the ballot box. It could also be argued that unless these structural problems are addressed democracy in South Africa will have little meaning. As Budlender (1999) argues, 'when we talk about the unemployment problem in our country, it is African people who are suffering badly, and African women who are suffering most of all'. The situation is now worse than it was in 1994. Unemployment clearly does not affect all people in the same way (age and location are also significant), and this needs to be acknowledged. Although jobs were a priority of all political parties in the run-up to the 1999 election, there was little, if any, attention to the special circumstances and needs of women. Affirmative action policies indicate the willingness of the state to intervene to ensure equality, but these are not themselves sufficient. Although quotas exist in the public sector, gender is still a low priority for the private sector, despite the Constitution and statutory requirements obligating this sector to address issues of inequality between women and men (Madonsela, 1995; CGE press release, 22.4.99). Some are also critical of the South African government's embracing of the global economy, neo-liberal economic policies associated with this and the polarizing effects these might have (Maharaj, 1999).

Against this backdrop, Sandra Liebenberg (1999) argues that political and civil rights have limited meaning for most women unless socio-economic rights are accorded centrality and interpreted in gendered terms. Social and economic models of citizenship, developed within a Western welfare state context and placing emphasis on the need for the state to achieve redistributive effects, have some limitations in a lower-middle income country such as South Africa with enormous racialized inequalities. However, they are clearly of significance. The government is committed to redistributive policies and a broader understanding of citizenship, as displayed in the Constitution and the commitment to participation. Other government policies, such as its embracing of neo-liberalism, might perhaps be interpreted less cynically as an attempt to engage with the real dilemmas of economic governance in circumstances of impoverishment and globalization. Feminists in government are unlikely to be able to avoid these trade-offs at present. It might also be appropriate to consider what it means to suggest that without equalization women in South Africa have no hope of achieving full citizenship. One way of thinking through these questions is to explore the meanings, negotiations and contestations of citizenship in the daily lives of South African women in their diversity. The question remains as to whether government measures will begin to have an impact on the economic divides in South Africa and whether democracy and marketization will facilitate a meaningful citizenship for marginalized women. A consideration of more localized interpretations of citizenship might provide an important alternative perspective.

Beyond Rights: Citizenship at the Local Level

If we accept that rights alone are not sufficient to bring about substantive citizenship, the question that is raised is how substantive citizenship can be created and how this would be conceptualized and defined. The South African Constitution, structures of governance at all levels and legislation place great emphasis on citizen participation. For example, Chapter 7 of the Constitution, which sets out the policy directive with regard to local government, clearly assigns it a development role and emphasizes the participation of communities and community organizations (152(1)). These principles were also central to the Reconstruction and Development Programme (RDP), conceived to meet the socio-economic needs of previously disadvantaged communities and are reflected in the 1998 White Paper on Local Government. The definition and meaning of participation is, however, open to interpretation, and the potential for substantive citizenship depends upon that interpretation. For example, it might be interpreted as 'a process through which stakeholders influence and share control over development initiatives and the decisions and resources which affect them' (World Bank, in Otzen et al., 1999, p.6); as 'the act of allowing individual citizens within a community to take part in the formulation of policies and proposals on issues that affect the whole community' (Onibokun and Faniran, 1995, p.9). More radical definitions of participation, however, not only emphasize community involvement in the processes of local development, but also demand that social development leads to the empowerment of community members. This involves social change to bring about improved living standards within the community and is especially significant to women, empowering them to liberate themselves from oppressive social structures and to create development structures that work for everyone.

For some feminist theorists (e.g. Jones, 1994), participation in community politics can be a locus for women's empowerment. Indeed, involvement in community politics in some Latin American countries led to women's engagement with more formal political activity (Alvarez, 1990; Jacquette, 1989; Jelin, 1990). However, confining women's political activity to community politics can also be disempowering if this lacks involvement with the state. Given the emphasis on participation as citizenship in South African discourses, it is important to explore the nature of women's involvement and the potential for their empowerment as citizens within communities. Significantly, there is no word for 'citizen' or 'citizenship' in most African languages, but whilst the abstract concept of citizenship might lack meaning for many South Africans, even the most marginalized of people are aware that they have rights under the new dispensation – rights to vote, to housing, to land and the right to participate in matters that affect their communities. Political activities are often organized around claiming these rights.

Many communities in South Africa are replete with community-based organizations (CBOs) and area and street committees and the proportion of women involved in these organizations is generally very high. However, there is presently a lack in many places of strong civil society structures that can connect such forms of organization with other non-governmental organizations and formal arenas of governance which represent the interests of the majority. There is also an apparent lack of capacity amongst citizens to respond meaningfully to complex matters of governance (L. Liebenberg, 1999). Therefore, emphasis on participation is crucial to social development and substantive citizenship. In this sense, participation is an end in itself and control over and access to resources by women and poor people is central. In reality, however, the notion of participation creates a fundamental anomaly. Citizens' interests are cared for by elected representatives and the policies they determine are implemented by bureaucrats acting in organizational structures that are the antithesis of democracy. Thus democratic expectations are imposed on governmental structures that were never designed to function democratically (Brynard, 1996). Balancing the conflict between structures of governance and citizen participation is a major challenge in South Africa's political transformation.

Evidence from Local Studies

Local level studies of poor women's experiences of 'participatory citizenship' are revealing,[6] particularly of the extent and quality of community participation within local development planning processes. Levels of education in urban and peri-urban areas are often relatively high. A majority of residents have at least basic literacy skills and the capacity to participate in community matters if no other constraints exist. In addition, because of the high rates of unemployment, poor housing and poor living conditions, women in 'townships' and informal settlements have every incentive to be active in local governance and development projects:

> We can't wait for the council to give us the things that they decide we need. We have to
> get involved and tell them what we need and how things should progress. Then we will

improve our communities and create jobs ... They need to listen to us about what needs to be done (LB, Harare, 8.2.01).

This desire to be involved in community development projects and local governance is common amongst women in marginalized communities, as is the frustration of not knowing how to participate. Throughout South Africa, many women are members of street or area committees, which operate almost like village structures in peri-urban areas, but very few are involved with civic organizations. Indeed, in the Western Cape few women express any knowledge of civic organizations within their areas. A few are members of housing savings schemes, and have acquired formal housing through these schemes. These women tend to be more satisfied with their own involvement in their communities, but still express dissatisfaction with their levels of involvement with local governance.

With regard to community participation, there seems to be a lack of knowledge about development projects, indicating black women's marginalization in community development. The minority of women who are aware of community projects identify women as among the major participants:

Yes, women are very much involved in projects here. Women are involved in most things taking place. We can't afford to just wait for things to happen. We are the most in need (AX, Harare, 8.2.01).

Participation is seemingly more difficult in more recently formed settlements and informal settlements. A large majority of women in the Western Cape either do not know if local government tried to involve women in their activities or suggest that there have been no attempts to do so. This suggests a failure on the part of local government to inform or educate communities about the possibilities of participation and of its importance for the successful transformation towards developmental local governance.

Evidence suggests that most women in poorer communities believe that their communities should be involved in local governance structures and have the ability to do so. When asked about how participation could be improved they mention the need for training workshops, which should be run at times when women are able to attend:

We need more training, but this is no good if the workshops are at times when women cannot attend because they are working or caring for children (LB, Harare, 8.2.01).

Other women also refer to the need for education and empowerment of communities, as well as the need for local government to give people the opportunity to participate. Most articulate the importance of community involvement in all stages of development projects, from needs assessment to project planning, budgeting, implementation, monitoring and evaluation. However, they also express disillusionment at not being approached to get involved:

We are never asked for our opinion on what should be done. If anything happens it comes from the council and we are not asked for the things that we think are important ... No, our community is not consulted about what we need (XM, Khayelitsha, 9.2.01).

Lack of information is seen by most to be critical. Perhaps not surprisingly, the majority of women interviewed have not attended local government meetings recently nor met their councillor since the elections in 2000, highlighting the non-participatory nature of community–council relationships. However, this does not reflect a lack of interest in communities because many women do attend community meetings on a regular basis. They are involved in matters that concern them and projects that are initiated and based in their communities and are less involved in projects launched without consultation and failing adequately to address their needs.

The level of socio-economic development within communities clearly has a direct bearing upon access to information and, therefore, opportunities for community participation:

> Every day I get up at 5am to prepare breakfast for my grandchildren and walk to the train station. When I get home from work in the evenings I have to feed my daughter and her children and take care of the house. I just moved into my first house from a shack. I don't have to carry water now, but there is still a lot of work to be done, plastering and so on … My daughter is ill. I don't have time to attend meetings during the week, even in the evenings (LT, Khayelitsha, 19.3.01).

There is a persistent lack of understanding within communities and local government about the multiple tasks that women perform in homes, communities and economies and how time-consuming they are. Women tend to have less flexibility than men. This also means that they have less time for public participation, particularly if they are heads of households as many women are in poorer communities. Cultural norms surrounding gender roles also exacerbate problems of non-participation:

> I don't say anything at the meetings. The men do all the talking. Even though I might have opinions about things I don't raise them at the meetings (AM, Khayelitsha, 9.2.01).

> We are expected to keep quiet in meetings (XM, Harare, 8.2.01).

It seems that if women do attend meetings, they tend only to participate as observers and do not contribute beyond this. Despite the respect accorded older women in many communities they are largely passive observers. On occasions when women meet independently of men to try to press their claims, they often face intimidation and threats. Indeed, several recent meetings of rural women in KwaZulu-Natal were disrupted by men brandishing spears and other weapons. As a consequence, few women-related issues are raised and included in community programmes.

Very often in poorer communities, there is disparity between community needs, as defined by women, and local government. This is reflected in growing disappointment and dissatisfaction with non-delivery of services and the non-involvement of communities. Participation in specified activities (i.e. budget process, housing, water and electrification projects) – a requirement of local government legislation – is extremely low. It is difficult to find women in poorer communities who have ever been involved in a local government budget process:

> They think women don't understand budgets and so they don't bother to explain. Listen, every woman in this community knows about budgets because we deal with them every day (PN, Khayelitsha, 6.2.01).

Many women feel that there is a need for local government to involve them more directly and to come to the communities to develop an understanding of what is needed in their areas. These problems are more pronounced in rural areas where communities are often remote from centres of governance and lacking in resources. Very few women are aware of the requirements within local government legislation for community participation in local socio-economic development and governance. If the concept of participatory citizenship is not being communicated to communities its effectiveness in social development has to be questioned.

Surveys (e.g. Kehler, 2000; McEwan, 2003) have demonstrated that women can only participate in decision-making processes if they have appropriate information upon which to make informed decisions. However, poor women are often ill-informed about issues that affect their lives directly. Furthermore, they do not simply need information to participate in decision-making; they also require time to attend meetings and the confidence to speak up as equal participants in discussions. As a consequence of prevailing patriarchies, these conditions are often absent in many communities. Not only does local government have a role to play in devising creative strategies to ensure that these conditions are met, it has a constitutional responsibility to promote gender equity. If it does so it *can* become an important agent for social change and the construction of substantive and participatory citizenship for women, where they are able to engage with state structures and to participate in decision-making and resource distribution within households and communities. The potential for enabling active and participative citizenship within communities also demands a re-theorizing of the supposed dichotomy between formal and informal political activity, especially as it relates to citizenship. As Seidman (1999) argues, if 'women's interests' are defined, in part, by the spaces through which political participation is channelled, the democracy that is being constructed in South Africa may offer a new vision of gendered citizenship. Institutional mechanisms requiring officials to consider the impact of their policies on gendered citizens may be the closest any democracy has come to incorporating gender into the definition of citizenship.

Rethinking Participation?

Active and participative notions of citizenship, such as those being conceptualized in South Africa, point towards a re-theorizing of political participation long demanded by feminist theorists. As Squires (1999) argues, to concentrate on formal political participation alone as evidence of active citizenship is to reproduce masculine assumptions that have worked to erase the significance of women's informal political participation. Women *are* political actors if 'political' is held to include all power-structured relations from the interpersonal to the international. If this broader notion of the political is adopted, it becomes evident that women have long been political actors and as such are critical in the construction and maintenance of participatory democracy and meaningful citizenship in South Africa. The nature of democracy here, and the ways in which citizenship is being defined, constructed and contested, certainly informs a broader theoretical feminist context that currently places emphasis on extending the boundaries of the political beyond institutions of the state and civil association. A key concern of current feminist writing about women's political participation is focused on ways of 'reconfiguring representation such that it is more responsive to, and integrated with, women's informal political activities' (Squires, 1999, p.197).

Narayan (1997), for example, stresses the connection between formal and informal political activities, arguing that negotiations with a partner over domestic chores allows for a development of a political awareness that can then be carried into the realms of public political activity. Lister stresses the importance of distinguishing between women's political representation and their political activity. If the two are simply conflated, the conventional wisdom that women are less interested than men in fulfilling their potential as political citizens, is reinforced (Lister, 1997). Like Narayan, Lister affirms the centrality of informal as well as formal politics, claiming that the former is a central feature of women's political citizenship. However, informal politics should not be theorized as a different politics, since this runs the risk of being marginalized; rather it should always be conceptualized as part of the full citizenship equation. Lister recognizes that political empowerment through informal politics is not the same as gaining power in the wider society; both are required. Any citizenship that promotes women's equality, as well as their difference, needs to engage the formal as well as the informal political system.

The current problem for poorer women in South Africa is that while they are active in community-based structures, they still appear largely divorced from structures of governance at the local level. This is partly because of the patriarchal nature of both structures of governance and community politics. Women are participants within their communities but are still not able to access power over resources and decision-making that would make their citizenship substantive and meaningful. As a consequence, they are still largely marginalized. However, this does not mean this is uncontested or that women are not active as citizens in other ways. Indeed, as suggested, women continue to mobilize in opposition to patriarchal power relations at both national and local levels, articulating their demands and empowering themselves around community and youth issues, most notably in anti-crime and peace organizations.

Recent debates in feminist theory suggest that it is not clear whether informal participatory politics alone can address the complex questions of individual liberty and social justice. The apparent dichotomy between formal and informal political activity, between representative and participatory conceptions of the political, has been displaced in favour of a reconsideration of the inter-relationship between the two. This attempt at synthesis echoes the move to go beyond equality and difference and reflects the moderate deconstructionism outlined previously. As Squires (1999) argues, formal political equality within the representative structures of the polity is recognized as a necessary, though not sufficient, precondition for a more substantive political equality. The importance, frequently overlooked in the more informal understandings of politics, of formal, constitutional frameworks within which participatory democracy must be located, is recognized. These theoretical debates have practical resonance in South Africa, particularly given continuing efforts to deepen democracy and create conditions for citizen participation through the restructuring of local governance. This continuing transformation of the local sphere of governance is potentially critical to the creation of substantive citizenship for women, despite the obvious barriers that still remain to their social and economic citizenship.

Exploring citizenship at the local level allows for the reconceptualizing of informal and formal political activity as a continuum. It is at this level that black women in South Africa, because of their central role in communities and their historical exclusion from more formal politics, are likely to be more active and potentially more effective as citizens (Robinson, 1995; Cole and Parnell, 2000). The ways in which women can access power and resources at the local level and their lived experiences of citizenship are still poorly understood, especially with regard to the majority of women who remain marginalized by the legacies of apartheid.[7] There is clearly a need, therefore, for a sustained and critical analysis of the relationship between local governance, women's lived experiences of citizenship and constitutional guarantees to gender equality. This is given greater expediency by the fact that the transitional period of local government ended with the local government elections in 2000, and the constitutional, legal and policy mechanisms are now mostly in place. Unless black women's voices are heard in local government processes their political and economic marginalization will continue and local government will fail to fulfil its developmental role (GAP/FCR, 1998, p.11).

Conclusions

Much of the literature on democratic transitions utilizes a narrow definition of democracy and citizenship, identifying a top-down approach to democratization and the construction of citizenship (Stenning, 1999). Democracy is defined as a formal process involving free and fair elections, freedom of expression and association and inclusive citizenship based upon rights (in other words, liberal democracy). According to Stenning, 'there is an emphasis on rights rather than abilities and a focus on central state institutions rather than local level representation and participation' (1999, p.592).

This chapter has argued that while the importance of rights cannot be underestimated, the South African context suggests that the exploration of alternative notions of democracy and, in particular, alternative definitions and experiences of citizenship are required. These alternative notions point towards locally rooted and participatory democracy, which in turn relates to ideas of radical (Mouffe, 1992) and substantive (Einhorn et al., 1996a; 1996b) citizenship. Further democratization in South Africa requires the creation of spaces for participation of even the most marginalized of citizens, where emphasis is placed on the abilities of people to mould the policies that shape their everyday lives (Staeheli, 1994) and to have access to and control over resources. It is precisely these spaces that African women in their diversity are struggling to create. In addition, resistances to the social and cultural practices of everyday life should not be overlooked, since it is these resistances that hold out the possibility of transforming entrenched gender inequalities and creating space for women's active and participative citizenship.

Despite persistent and racialized inequalities in South Africa, it is possible to be optimistic about the state of democracy and long-term citizenship prospects for African women. Activists have exposed the false universalism of citizenship and continue to mobilize to ensure that their rights as 'women' are guaranteed by the Constitution. They are attempting to create a policy framework that is able to incorporate difference into citizenship in ways that do not undermine progress towards gender equality. This requires a public policy acknowledging that women's citizenship derives as much from the private sphere as it does from the public sphere.

In the political sphere, the future development of women's citizenship depends on women in their diversity being actively involved, through formal and informal political systems, in the development of public policies (Lister, 1997). This requires making formal political systems accessible to informal political groupings. Current activism by South African women is targeted on domestic divisions of labour, violence, and the protection of bodily and reproductive rights. It is essential, therefore, that women activists maintain a strong, highly organized, visible, civil society movement. Women are beginning to organize in new ways and are creating new social movements through which their interests can be articulated. The nationally based Rural Women's Movement and the Western Cape based, left-wing New Women's Movement are examples of these new forms of organization in which even the most marginalized of poor women are contesting their rights as citizens. In addition, there is a productive relationship between women's movements and academic feminism, rooted in a long history of shared non-racial political commitments, and together they provide important links to policy-makers and government officials on the one hand and communities on the other.

The gendering of democracy and citizenship also relates to broader questions about the relationship between women and the state in South Africa (McEwan, 2000). It seems strategically important at present to target 'women' for policy attention, and to have 'women's' machinery in the state. However, as Manicom (1996; 2001) suggests, from the perspective of democratization, it is critical to deconstruct and politically challenge the rigidities, limitations, exclusions and suppressions of official discourses of gender, and the ways in which they are interred within policy and state regulatory practices. There needs to be a more flexible approach, with emphasis at times being on questions of redistribution and the recognition of difference, which will inevitably disrupt gender relations without entrenching a category of 'women'. The South African context also raises the need to reconceptualize the practices of citizenship as a constant process of contestation at different scales. Citizenship might in some instances embrace a transnational reach (Lister, 1997), at other times be focused on actions directed at the state, but it might also take account of the multiple spaces of women's political engagement (neighbourhoods, workplaces, homes and 'official' or 'formal' politics).

The South African context illustrates the fundamental importance of social citizenship. As Walby (1997) argues, social citizenship for women is incompatible with, and unobtainable under, women's confinement to the household and dependency on a private patriarch:

> When half the population might be denied effective citizenship because of gender, then gender matters to citizenship. The question of the relationship of the public and private is not incidental (p.178).

In the West, political citizenship for women has destabilized private patriarchies. In South Africa, political citizenship in conjunction with everyday resistance in communities and households has the potential to do the same. What can be concluded is that citizenship is not merely about Western notions of democracy filtering around the world. International cultural flows certainly informed the nature of the debates about gender and citizenship in South Africa in the 1990s, but the nature of citizenship being constructed is moulded to the needs and complexities of South African society. In the long-term it might inform the establishment of gender equality, which accommodates difference, on national political agendas and in policies to effect real change.

The apparent success of South African activists in changing the terms of democracy demands rethinking democracy less as an end-point or a definable moment in the 'democratic transition', but as a process around which activists can mobilize and participate to shape democratic aspirations. Citizenship is a site of contest in which women in South Africa from across political, racial, ethnic, cultural, religious, class and geographical differences have been effective and from which they have been successful in negotiating a gendered notion of citizenship. The fundamental transformations in South Africa (political, economic, social) have created opportunities for rethinking notions of citizenship, particularly as they relate to women and other marginalized groups, the relationship between national and local policies and to citizenship debates within international feminism. The ways in which women might use their legal status to challenge practical barriers to full inclusion, empowering their citizenship and using citizenship for empowerment (Staeheli and Cope, 1994) will be of significance in the immediate future.

Notes

1. I use the term 'black' as inclusive of all women of colour, whilst being mindful of the sensitivities associated with such terminology.
2. The term 'worker' here is used in a restricted sense of being employed outside the home. Marxist feminists in particular have argued that women are unpaid workers, and in places where many people are active in informal sector economies, it is arguable that they also do not have social citizenship.

3. For this reason, Australia perhaps provides a more relevant set of theoretical debates for South African feminism than Europe or North America, where women's participation in formal political structures has been much lower.
4. South American feminist experiences are especially relevant (see, for example, Alvarez, 1990; Jacquette, 1989; Jelin, 1990).
5. For example, in 1999, gender activists mobilized to pressure the government to call a National Emergency to deal with violence against women (womensnet.org.za). Women are also forming locally based organizations. One example is the Manenberg Peace Organisation in the Cape Flats, which was set up by women to combat gangsterism and crime.
6. Information in the following section is based on case study research (in-depth interviews) conducted between January and September 2001 with women community members in Western Cape and KwaZulu-Natal (funded by ESRC, R000223286). As a consequence of the specific demographics and politics in both areas these findings are not likely to be representative of women's experiences of local governance in other provinces. However, they do raise issues that might also be of significance for women throughout South Africa.
7. Gender planning, local government restructuring, housing and the informal sector appear to have been the main areas of enquiry in the early 1990s (see Todes, 1995). Since the local government elections of 1995, what analysis there has been has had a clear focus on influencing local government policy and budgeting (Budlender, 1999; Skinner, 1999; Van Donk, 1998a; 1998b; 1999).

References

Albertyn, C. (1994a), 'Two steps forward', *Work in Progress*, 95, pp.22-23.
Albertyn, C. (1994b), 'Women and the transition to democracy in South Africa' in C. Murray (ed.), *Gender and the New South African Legal Order*, Juta, Cape Town, pp.39-63.
Alvarez, S. (1990), *Engendering Democracy in Brazil*, Princeton University Press, Princeton.
Brynard, P. (1996), 'Realities of citizen participation', in K. Bekker (ed.), *Citizen Participation in Local Government*, J.L. van Schaik, Pretoria, pp.39-50.
Budlender, D. (1999), 'Rising unemployment hits women hardest', *The Election Bulletin*, 1, 3, http://womensnet.org.za/election/eb3-jobs.htm.
Butler, J. (1990), *Gender Trouble: Feminism and the Subversion of Identity*, Routledge, London.
Commission on Gender Equality (1999), 'Gender still a low priority for the private sector', CGE Press Release, http://cge.org.za/press/22.4.99.0.htm.
Cole, J. and Parnell, S. (2000), *A Report on Poverty, Gender and Integrated Development Planning in South African Municipal Practice*, Department of Provincial Local Government, Cape Town.
Einhorn, B. (1993), *Cinderella Goes to Market. Citizenship, Gender and Women's Movements in East Central Europe*, Elgar, Cheltenham.
Einhorn, B., Kaldor, M. and Kavan, Z. (1996a), 'Introduction', *Citizenship and Democratic Control in Contemporary Europe*, Elgar, Cheltenham.
Einhorn, B., Kaldor, M. and Kavan, Z. (eds.), (1996b), *Citizenship and Democratic Control in Contemporary Europe*, Verso, London.

Fraser, N. (1997), 'Equality, difference and democracy: recent feminist debates in the United States', in J. Dean (ed.), *Feminism and the New Democracy*, Sage, London, pp.98-109.

Gender Advocacy Programme and the Foundation for Contemporary Research (1998), *Local Government and Gender: A Reality Check. Survey of Selected Municipalities in the Western Cape*, GAP/FCR, Cape Town.

Goldblatt, B. and Meintjes, S. (1996), *Gender and the Truth and Reconciliation Commission*, submission to the TRC, http://www.truth.org.za/submit/gender.htm.

Gouws, A. (1999), 'Beyond equality and difference: the politics of women's citizenship', *Agenda*, No.40, pp.54-58.

Hassim, S. (1999), 'From presence to power: women's citizenship in a new democracy', *Agenda*, No.40, pp.6-17.

James, S. (1992), 'The good-enough citizen: female citizenship and independence', in G. Bock and S. James (eds.), *Beyond Equality and Difference: Citizenship, Feminist Politics and Subjectivity*, Routledge, London, pp.48-65.

Jacquette, J. (1989), *The Women's Movement in Latin America*, Unwin Hyman, London.

Jelin, E. (1990), Women and Social Change in Latin America, Zed, London.

Jones, K.B. (1994), 'Identity, Action, and Locale: Thinking about Citizenship, Civic Action, and Feminism', *Social Politics*, 1,1, pp. 4-29.

Kehler, J. (2000), 'Community participation in the process of Integrated Planning Development (IDP). Evaluating realities and community perceptions in areas on the Western and Eastern Cape', Nadel Research Report No.15, Nadel/Austrian Development Cooperation, Cape Town.

Lewis, D. (1999), 'Gender myths and citizenship in two autobiographies by South African women', *Agenda*, No.40, pp.38-44.

Liebenberg, L. (1999), *The IDP Experience: An Analysis of Two Western Cape Processes*, Foundation for Contemporary Research, Cape Town.

Liebenberg, S. (1999), 'Social citizenship – a precondition for meaningful democracy', *Agenda*, No.40, pp.59-65.

Lister, R. (1989), *The Female Citizen*, Liverpool University Press, Liverpool.

Lister, R. (1997), *Citizenship: Feminist Perspectives*, Macmillan, London.

McEwan, C. (2000), '"Walking the walk"? The state and gender transformations in the "new" South Africa', *South African Geographical Journal*, 82, 1, pp.75-84.

McEwan, C. (2003), 'Bringing government to the people: Gender, local governance and community participation in South Africa', *Geoforum*, 34, 4, pp.469-482.

Madonsela, T. (1995), 'Beyond putting women on the agenda', *Agenda*, No.24, pp.27-36.

Maharaj, Z. (1999), 'Globalisation's dark side overshadows women's rights', *Business Report* 11.5.99.
http://www.busrep.co.za/cgi-bin-br/main/article.chi?ID=5520&issue=19990511.

Mangaliso, Z.A. (1997), 'Gender and Nation-Building in South Africa', in L. West (ed.), *Feminist Nationalism*, Routledge, London, pp.130-144.

Manicom, L. (1996), 'Citizens, mothers, women: reflections on gender, democracy and nation-building in South Africa', Unpublished paper.

Manicom, L. (2001), 'Globalising "gender" in – or as – governance? Questioning the terms of local translations', *Agenda*, No.48, pp.6-21.

Marais, H. (1998), *South Africa. Limits to Change: The Political Economy of Transformation*, Zed, London.

Marshall, T.H. (1965), *Class, Citizenship and Social Development*, Anchor, New York.

Meintjes, S. and Goldblatt, B. (1997), 'Dealing with the aftermath: sexual violence and the Truth and Reconciliation Commission', *Agenda*, No.36, pp.7-18.

Mouffe, C. (1992), 'Feminism, citizenship and radical democratic politics' in J. Butler and J. Scott (eds.), *Feminists Theorize the Political*, Routledge, London, pp.369-384.

Mouffe, C. (1993), *The Return of the Political*, Verso, London.

Narayan, U. (1997), 'Towards a feminist vision of citizenship: rethinking the implications of dignity, political participation, and nationality' in M.L. Shanley and U. Narayan (eds.), *Reconstructing Political Theory*, Polity, Cambridge, pp.48-67.

Onibokun, A.G. and Faniran, A. (1995), 'Community based organisations in Nigerian urban cities', Centre for African Settlement Studies and Development, Nigeria.

Otzen, U. et al. (1999), 'Integrated Development Planning. A new task for local government in South Africa. Participatory planning for socio-economic development in two municipalities in Mpumalanga', GTZ, Braamfontein.

Pateman, C. (1988a), 'The fraternal social contract', in J. Keane (ed.), *Civil Society and the State*, Verso, London, pp.231-60.

Pateman, C. (1988b), *The Sexual Contract*, Polity, Cambridge.

Pateman, C. (1992), 'Equality, difference and subordination: the politics of motherhood and women's citizenship', in G. Bock and S. James (eds.), *Beyond Equality and Difference: Citizenship, Feminist Politics and Subjectivity*, Routledge, London. pp.17-31.

Phillips, A. (1991), *Engendering Democracy*, Polity, Cambridge.

Phillips, A. (1993), *Democracy and Difference*, Polity, Cambridge.

Pringle, R. and Watson, S. (1992), 'Women's interests and the poststructuralist state' in M. Barrett and A. Phillips (eds.), *Destabilising Theory*, Polity, Cambridge.

Robinson, J. (1995), 'Act of omission: gender and local government in the transition', *Agenda*, No.26, pp.7-18.

Samuel, S. (1999), 'Women married in customary law: no longer permanent minors', *Agenda*, No.40, pp.23-31.

Seidman, G.W. (1999), 'Gendered Citizenship. South Africa's democratic transition and the construction of a gendered state', *Gender and Society*, 13(3), pp.287-307.

Seroke, P. (1999), 'Welcoming statement. The Aftermath: Women in Post War Reconstruction Conference', 20 July 1999, Johannesburg.

Skinner, C. (1999), 'Local Government in Transition – A gendered analysis of trends in urban policy and practice regarding street trading in five South African cities', CSDS Research Report 18, School of Development Studies, University of Natal, Durban.

Squires, J. (1999), *Gender in Political Theory*, Polity, Cambridge.

Staeheli, L. (1994), 'Restructuring citizenship in Pueblo, Colorado', *Environment and Planning A*, 26, pp. 849-871.

Staeheli, L. and Cope, M. (1994), 'Empowering women's citizenship', *Political Geography*, 13(5), pp.443-460.

Stenning, A. (1999), 'Marketisation and democratisation in the Russian Federation: the case of Novosibirsk', *Political Geography*, 18, pp.591-617.

Stewart, A. (1996), 'Should women give up on the state? – The African experience', in S. Rai and G. Lievesley (eds.), *Women and the State: International Perspectives*, Taylor and Francis, London, pp.23-44.

Todes, A. (1995), 'Gender in metropolitan development strategies', *Cities*, 12(5), pp.327-336.

Van Donk, M. (ed.), (1998a), *Local Government and Gender: A Reality Check. Survey of Selected Municipalities in the Western Cape*, GAP/FCR, Cape Town.

Van Donk, M. (1998b), *Women in Local Government in South Africa: From Marginalisation to Empowerment*, GAP, Cape Town.

Van Donk, M. (1999), *Women in Local Government as Change Agents*, GAP, Cape Town.

Voet, R. (1998), *Feminism and Citizenship*, Sage, London.

Walby, S. (1997), *Gender Transformations*, Routledge, London.

Walker, C. (1994), 'Women, "tradition" and reconstruction', *Review of African Political Economy*, 61, pp.347-358.

Watson, S. (1990), *Playing the State: Australian Feminist Interventions*, Verso, London.

Young, I.M. (1989), 'Polity and group difference. A critique of the ideal of universal citizenship', *Ethics*, 99, pp.250-274.

Yuval-Davis, N. (1997), *Gender and Nation*, Sage, London.

Yuval-Davis, N. and Werbner, P. (eds.), (1999), *Women, Citizenship and Difference*, Zed, London.

Chapter 9

Merely Mothers Perpetuating Patriarchy? Women's Grassroots Organizations in the Western Cape 1980 to 1990[1]

Gertrude Fester

Introduction

> We women have the greatest force in the world in our hands; it is the courage and
> determination of mothers to fight for the rights of the children … (they) had borne in
> pain and suffering. There is no power on earth that can prevent the mothers of SA, and
> of the world, from achieving justice for their children, if women organize and go
> forward, together with their men, on the march to freedom (quoted in Wells, 1998,
> p.256).

Women as mothers represent the epitome of difference from men, for only women
as mothers can reproduce the next generation of citizens. Women's roles as
mothers link them directly to the sphere of the family. This very close connection
with the private sphere has been seriously criticized in Western feminism as
reinscribing the private sphere that prevents women's political agency, into the
concept of citizenship.

Yet, in African contexts motherhood has been viewed as a platform of action
around which women often become mobilized to improve their material conditions
(see Fester, 1997). Activism and mobilization linked to motherhood deserves
greater analysis and interpretation, especially in the South African context where
historically women have mobilized and organized as mothers.

Two of the main feminist proponents for motherhood are Elshtain (1981;
1982a; 1982b; 1983), and Ruddick (1983a; 1983b; 1989). Elshtain (1983) aims to
rid feminism of its 'anti-family bias' and its 'matriphobia'. According to her,
mothering is 'rich, complicated, ambivalent, vexing, joyous activity which is
biological, natural, social and emotional' (p.243). Elshtain celebrates mothering as
'the purpose of the private familial sphere in the context of an ethical polity,
imbued with values' (Lister, 1997, p.150). She wants to promote the idea of
maternalist thinking through which women could become politically conscious.
This she calls 'social feminism' and argues that through it democracy can be
attained.

Motherism, Female and Feminist Consciousness

Ruddick (1983; 1989) sees maternalist thinking as an antidote to a male-dominated culture. She also sees females as nurturers who, through their potential experiences of motherhood and caring are inherently peaceful and anti-war. She emphasizes the qualities women as mothers can bring to politics and specifically peace politics. For her maternalism develops out of the nurturing perspectives of mothers. But she also makes it clear that maternal thinking is an ideal against which mothers can measure themselves, rather than their reality (Lister, 1997, p.151).

Women's collective action spurred on by their roles as mothers has been characterized as motherism. This term was coined by Kaplan (1982; 1992; 1997). It refers to a phenomenon that has emerged from many women's political movements globally at various historical junctures. What is common is that this type of women's activism has been inspired repeatedly and effectively by the women in their roles as mothers, their care for and defence of their children. Wells (1991) maintains that even though most Western feminists call for women to be defined in terms other than mothers only, it must be acknowledged that throughout the world, many effective political gains have been made by women mobilizing as mothers, e.g. in India, Chile, El Salvador and South Africa (pp.1, 2). Argosin (1987) has written extensively about motherist movements, especially with reference to women in Latin America.

According to Kaplan, motherist movements may evolve in consciousness. To elaborate on this, Kaplan uses the terms 'female consciousness' and 'feminist consciousness'. Kaplan introduces the concept of 'female consciousness' as an important dimension of women's collective mobilization. This consciousness stems from women's nurturing role in society as defined by the gendered division of labour. Women have an awareness or consciousness of themselves as producers and nurturers of life. Female consciousness can manifest itself collectively when there is a danger or some outside threat to the children or the community. Women will then use their traditional networks and/or collective action in the name of motherhood to fight this danger.

Interestingly, these activities are initially only seen in terms of defending their children (who are usually involved in political struggles), i.e. mobilizing on the basis only of being mothers, but simultaneously being involved in life sustaining activities. The protests of mothers/women of Plaza De Mayo in Argentina, are an example of this (Lister, 1997, p.149). They protested against the disappearance of so many of their children and demanded to know where they were. During these activities, spurred on by female consciousness, women undergo a radical change in consciousness through which they become politicized. The mothers are then confronted with greater threats either to their children and/or later to themselves personally. These conditions make them aware of the greater context of related struggles paralleling those of their children. This awareness results in actions whereby the mothers/women sometimes confront the legitimacy of the government and/or participate in more blatant political actions.

Thus, under specific conditions female consciousness may be potentially transformative to the extent that it values human life more generally. It is related to quality of life protests and ideologies of emancipation. When women as mothers realize that not only are conditions threatening their children, but their own roles as women and mothers are endangered, transformation takes place in their consciousness and in their commitment to political struggles. When this happens the female consciousness becomes transformed into a feminist consciousness, whereby they make demands that are radical and challenge the status quo. Female consciousness, however, could be used to mobilize women for both progressive and reactionary aims.

Dietz (1985) rightly criticizes Elshtain's vision of the separation between the public and private realms. Elshtain posits no link between what happens in private or public or that they can affect each other. This private/public dichotomy, in which the family and motherhood are seen as private, is especially inappropriate in the case of pre-1994 South Africa where state legislation caused the fragmentation of African families. Not only were African families subjected to an abundance of laws restricting their movements,[2] but persons from different race groups were not allowed to marry or have intimate relationships. Almost universally families (private realm) are dictated to by legislation (public).

Other weaknesses of Ruddick's and Elshtain's theories are that they generalize women's characteristics as democratic, anti-war and peace-loving. Dietz (1985) questions how all mothers can be inherently democratic. According to Elshtain, women become democratic because of their nurturing tasks. But when we look at a mother/child relationship, it is not an equal democratic relationship initially. It is one of unequal power, with a powerful mother and a weak dependent and vulnerable child. Feminists cannot rely on maternalism to transform society into democracies, as there is no basis for assuming that females will act democratically. Elshtain provides no link or theoretical connection to how maternalist thinking can bring about democracy Dietz argues that the important lessons from Plaza de Mayo is that the moral power of mothers did not translate into political power in democratic structures.

Furthermore, this type of thinking essentializes pacifist tendencies (Lister, 1997, p.153). The differences between women and men are exaggerated and the differences between women ignored. One would be able to argue that this type of thinking is too narrowly biologically deterministic and that it confirms gender stereotypes (see Lewis, 2001, p.6).

Ruddick and Elshtain present us with a one-dimensional view of women. They adopt a position which assumes that all females have a maternalist consciousness arising out of the female body's potential to bear children. They do not consider the consciousness of women who are not maternalistic, e.g. those who do not want to be, or cannot be, biological mothers. Kaplan differs from Elshtain and Ruddick because she is less essentialist and proposes that a female consciousness need not be present in all women all the time. Kaplan explores examples of women's collective behaviour empirically and uses her theory of female consciousness as an explanation for their actions. Kaplan (1997) has outlined a detailed description of how a women's committee mobilized and fought to make their informal settlement, Crossroads, outside Cape Town a legal one. She uses this and many other

examples to substantiate her theory that a female consciousness, under certain
conditions, can be transformed into a feminist one.

The value of analysing motherist movements is recognizing how, when female
consciousness transforms into feminist consciousness, women challenge their
limited private roles and involve themselves as political activists in the public
sphere.[3] Other women may develop a feminist consciousness in ways other than
through motherism. We can also argue that women through organizing themselves
and taking pride in their primary identity as mothers are not necessarily
perpetuating their roles in the 'private sphere' as 'mothers' only. Mothers are not
only individual mothers, but also symbolic mothers of the community. These
arguments contradict Wells's argument that motherist actions cannot be seen as an
indication of political maturity nor as feminist. In this chapter I will revisit Wells's
argument that motherist actions cannot be seen as an indication of political
maturity or feminism.

Women Mobilizing for Their Rights as Citizens

The rest of this chapter explores how women in the Western Cape in South Africa
organized, often on the basis of motherhood. Motherhood was at various times a
public and community-based position of influence. In doing so, I want to contest
Wells's assertion that motherist movements cannot be seen as politically mature
movements, by applying Kaplan's female/feminist consciousness theory with
specific reference to women's activism in the Western Cape in the 1980 to 1990
period.

Because of the centrality of motherhood in South African women's struggles,
much has been written about it.[4] References to motherhood in writings in
developing countries, including South Africa, have centred on the mobilizing and
political agencies motherhood has brought about (See Drew, 1995; Fester, 1997;
2000; Kaplan, 1997; Soiri, 1996; Walker, 1995; Wells 1991). Other voices have
been more critical by arguing that the implications of mothering for black South
African women are ambiguous – for some it has confined them to supportive roles
but for others it was potentially liberating by giving them a platform from which to
challenge their oppression (Hendricks and Lewis, 1994, p.67).

Walker states that motherhood in South Africa is under-theorized (1995) and
Meintjes (1996) emphasized the awe in which black women are held because of
their organizing ability to mobilize as women and as mothers. My aim is to
examine the motherist appeal through these struggles of women in the Western
Cape during the 1980s. I will question to what extent they fought for citizenship
and to what extent they have achieved it ten years after the first democratic election
in South Africa. I will concentrate on examples that have been particularly
motherist[5] in origin. I will trace its development and examine to what extent there
has, over the years, been a broadening out to more women-centred issues, as
opposed to mother/children-centredness, and to what extent these struggles of
women were for full citizenship.

Compared to the debates on motherism that have taken place in the West which focus mostly on the individuality and private domain of mothers, much has been written about the power and strength of African women as 'Mothers of the Nation'. There is a large gap in signification between speaking about mothers as individualized actual mothers, and Mothers, a (powerful) symbol of femininity which derives its origins on a pro-natal continent where motherhood per se is arguably more valued than in the West. In this context, there may be an assumption that an adult woman is a mother, and hence a conflation frequently occurs between the terms mother and woman. Some people perceive black women's mobilization as quite limited: 'Black women have tended to unify only under direct political pressure, such as the pass laws' (Clayton, 1989, p.1).

Whereas African women are admired because of their ability to mobilize (Meintjes, 1996), Brink (1990) refers to the ideologically manipulated position of Afrikaner women as the Volksmoeder.[6] Lewis (1993) adds that even though women have, through their participation in the liberation movement, been seen in terms of their patriarchal roles of sisters, mothers and wives, many women have found an authority and strength in these positions, which is different from the conventional conceptions of privatized mothers and wives in Western middle class ideology. Though these ascriptions may be limited and ambiguous, they represent more agency than the passivity and silence of Western models. However, Besha (1994) outlines the potential powerlessness or trap that motherhood may be for women, and Lewis (2001) issues a warning:

> Celebrating purely symbolic roles for women, or affirming gendered roles of service and nurturing, ... ultimately reinforces standard gender stereotypes. ... The assumption that identities and life strategies that are historically determined, profoundly oppressive and coercively policed can provide the only basis for an alternative to western feminism is disturbing (Lewis, 2001, p.6).

Grassroots Women's Movements in the Western Cape

It was in the absence of mass mobilization at grassroots level since the banning of oppositional political organizations in the 1960s, and in the aftermath of the 'children's revolution of 1976' that various women's organizations re-emerged or formed.[7] For example, *Women for Peace* was a multi-racial women's organization which did not directly challenge the status quo. *Women for Peace* was sincere in its attempts to bring peace to South African communities, however limited. Their analysis did not call for transformation and hence they were trying to promote and work for peace within apartheid with its injustices and inequality.

> In 1981 the United Women's Organisation (UWO) was officially launched as 'a response to the cries of South African children in 1976' and for the liberation of all South Africans. The organisation was initiated by 8 women in 1979. Some of them were members of the African National Congress Women's League (ANCWL) from the 1950s while the rest emerged out of the 1976 uprisings. Dorothy Zihlangu, chairperson of UWO (1982) and later president of FSAW (1987) explains why they organised: 'We

saw we had no voice to speak for us and for our children' (quoted in Barrett et al., 1985, p.242).

An analysis of the invitation to the first conference (1, 2 April 1981) indicates that women's rights and liberation were concerns. It is interesting that although women organized as 'mothers' this did not feature in the invitation. The first aim on the pamphlet states unequivocally:

The United Women's Organisation was formed to unite all women to work for the removal of all political, legal, economic and social disabilities (UWO, 1981).

Does the aim of removing women's 'disabilities' equate to women's liberation and therefore full citizenship? This was not discussed. But what was quite clear for women in UWO was that women's lives would not improve without national liberation. Four out of eight issues listed by UWO in this pamphlet dealt directly with women's inequality.

We strive for all women to obtain:
- the right for women to vote;
- the right for full opportunities for work, with equal pay for equal work;
- equal rights with men in relation to property, marriage and children;
- the removal of all laws that discriminate against women.

However, in attempting to achieve those aims, it was clear to UWO that black men did not have those rights either. From their own reality they knew that their black husbands and comrades did not have these rights but this was only added to their literature at a later stage. It was clear from this list that they perceived neither women (black and white) nor black men as citizens of South Africa. It was therefore imperative for UWO to work for national liberation. All UWO documents emphasize that the liberation of women cannot be achieved in isolation – the entire exploitative, racist and sexist hierarchy needed to be radically transformed. It is interesting to note that even though all speeches and introductions use the phrase 'we as mothers' as a starting point, it does not feature in the introductory pamphlet.

One needs to bear in mind that membership was not homogeneous. There were different ranges of political understanding: there were branches in white middle-class suburbs like Gardens that consisted of mainly middle-class white feminist graduates, as well as branches in the townships, such as Guguletu which consisted mostly of domestic workers. The content of pamphlets often depended on who wrote them. At most times pamphlets were jointly drawn up to reflect organizational positions.

The majority of the membership agreed that women's issues were numerous and complex and included apartheid, housing, poverty, violence in general and violence against women etc., but what was most important was that the majority considered themselves united by their common motherhood. Full citizenship entails having access to resources and having decision-making powers – this was not the case for all women and black men. The distinction between women's issues as second generation rights (i.e. a two-stage revolution where national liberation must precede women's liberation) or as integrated in national issues was a question which was raised intermittently in middle-class branches and at public meetings in middle-class areas. This debate also led to deeper insights around the intersectionality between race, gender and class: because white women could vote, did this mean that they had full citizenship? The fact that women were discussing issues around race, class and differentiated oppression was an indication of female consciousness being transformed into feminist consciousness.

Initially, there was also an acceptance and understanding that being mothers was a natural and normal role for all women. At this stage of organizing, patriarchy had not yet been clearly identified and articulated as an obstacle to women's liberation. Gradually 'patriarchy' became part of the discourse, though many may not have used the word 'patriarchy' as there is no equivalent in Xhosa. The way people spoke about it was as 'the triple oppression of women: race, class and gender'. These debates often led to tensions – some thought that there should be national liberation first and then women's liberation. What also occurred in this multi-class and multi-race organization was that this tension between 'women's liberation after national liberation' and 'women's liberation as part of national liberation' sometimes reflected class and race membership. It was African working class women who insisted that both should take place simultaneously. The tension within the women's and national liberation position was sometimes equated with race and gender loyalty. The fact that the discourse and debates focused on emancipatory tactics is evidence of this movement of 'mothers' becoming a more feminist one – even though the word feminist was not generally used.

Campaigns

Most of the UWO campaigns were 'motherist' in origin. They also illustrate how women's consciousnesses were radicalized over time and how issues were broadened. These will be interrogated in order to understand whether it was a case of female consciousness that was being transformed to feminist or political consciousness.

One of the mobilizing principles of UWO was to start with issues which were most relevant to specific women, whether they be church women or factory workers. During political education it was recommended to 'start where the women are at'. When the prices of bus fares (1984) and bread (1985) increased, UWO initiated the bread and bus boycotts. These increases were seen as directly challenging to mothers – as there were no increases in wages these increases meant mothers would not always be able to feed and send their children to school. Central to this campaign was political education. With the bread boycott, analyses were made of how the apartheid government allocated its budgets. The bread subsidy was decreased but at the same time white farmers were heavily subsidized. Increased militarization meant more repression for communities in townships and an increase in the defence budget. Here is a situation whereby the members of UWO, the majority being mothers and housewives, with minimal knowledge and education about economics, started interrogating the 'economics and politics of apartheid militarism' – an obvious example of a transformative consciousness from female to feminist. During that period R1 million was spent daily on the war in Namibia. The slogan, 'Bread for people and not for profits' linked the struggle to broader political and specifically class and labour issues. It also made the links between the personal and the political, and the private and the public. The increase in bread prices was also seen as an attack on children's health:

> We must make our voices heard in defence of our children's health and future (UWO pamphlet, 1985).

This illustrates how the political (spending of public funding) links to a personal position (motherhood), which challenges a political situation (government's legitimacy). The majority of Black mothers were extremely poor. The government for which they had not voted had arbitrarily increased the basic cost of living. The majority of the UWO members were domestic workers. They saw the disparity in their lives and in the lives of their employers. They had to pay the same for food and yet were earning 'starvation wages'. They also came to the understanding and realization that it was not their fault that they were poor, but rather that their poverty was the result of the prevailing socio-economic system; again an example of female consciousness being transformed into feminist consciousness.

Many other campaigns had similar outcomes. Two other campaigns that also started with the concerns of mothers for the welfare of the families were: the KTC (informal settlement) Housing Struggle and Marching against Rent Increases in New Crossroads. These two campaigns concluded by directly challenging the government. Women illegally occupied the area in Guguletu (NY78) opposite the KTC Bazaars where they built their shacks. Many of these women came with their children from the rural areas to join their husbands and partners in the city. Every morning the police destroyed the shacks, and with the help and support of UWO women, the women rebuilt them again. This occurred several times, sometimes with increasing violence and brutality on the part of the police. However, after a while, the repeated defiance by the women, and their ability to organize forced the authorities to declare this area a legal informal settlement. This was seen as a direct triumph for UWO and the women of KTC, many of whom then joined UWO. As the majority of these women were from the rural areas, it was their first experience of political organization after living most of their lives under tribal and traditional structures.

In response to demands by residents (the majority of these were women) from Old Crossroads for decent housing, women were resettled in a newly developed area named 'New Cross' (i.e. New Crossroads), opposite KTC. When they eventually occupied the newly built houses in New Crossroads, the rents escalated dramatically. This was contrary to the agreements made by the local authorities with the women. Women marched against this and for years they did not pay any rent as they could not afford it. Eventually a compromise was made that suited the New Crossroads women. As this type of protest and defiance by women continued, these 'mothers' in UWO demanded, through their pamphlets, motions and actions that the apartheid government resign (UWO, 1984b). It has to be emphasized though that not all members were biological mothers and that often women were addressed by members in their speeches as 'We as Women and Mothers'. It also has to be noted that the defiance through these years increased. The first few protests and marches were characterized by apprehension, fear and a degree of timidity. However, the women became more defiant and brave, challenging police at all levels; they understood and gradually demanded their rights as citizens of South Africa. There were various incidences when some mothers were adamant that they would never march and protest, however, they later initiated defiance activities – again showing how over time motherist activities were transformed into feminist activities.

Women and Mothers in UWO and UWCO as Political Agents for Mobilizing Communities into the UDF

It was characteristic of the organization (UWO) that women worked alongside men in the broader struggle. A slogan from the Women's Charter (1954) of the Federation of South African Women states: 'We stand shoulder to shoulder with our menfolk in a common struggle against poverty, race and class discrimination … until we have achieved our freedom.' This slogan was readily adopted by UWO (1984d). UWO members were instrumental in forming organizations like Parent, Teacher Associations (PTA) in 1981, the Western Cape Civic Association (1982) and the United Democratic Front (UDF) in August 1983, a national broad anti-apartheid front with diverse affiliates.

As a result of its existing infrastructure, UWO members were central to the formation of UDF area committees in the Western Cape. The three women on the UDF executive were all UWO members. It is important to note that UWO had no outside funding and that the rent for the office, the salary of the office administrator and all campaigns and media were paid for by members' subscriptions and fundraising. For the first few months of its existence the UDF shared the UWO office.

Generally, the effect of the UDF on the UWO was positive and a catalyst to many community activities. However, the challenge that confronted the UWO was working with a fast-paced male-dominated coalition. In the UWO general council, the UWO representative to the UDF stated: 'UDF must be led by its affiliates, not the other way around' (UWO, 1984b). The relationships with the UDF and its other affiliates, revealed the contradictions women experienced. Theoretically, women's liberation and national liberation for citizenship are complementary. However there were tensions around which issues were to be prioritized, and a demand for women to work in all of these structures. In many areas it was women who initiated civic organizations but the men who were the leaders. Women were the ones who carried the burden of domestic labour as well as doing the political groundwork. Most of the joint protest marches were initiated by women. Some UWO branches ceased to function as their members became leaders in the civics while others prioritized UDF activities, like in Mitchell's Plain and Macassar. Other members took up leadership positions in the trade unions. In UWO council it was stated that we had not lost members, but that rather we had broadened 'the struggle'. The reality was, however, that the UWO was weakened as an organization.

The UDF advised the UWO to amalgamate with the township-based Women's Front (WF) as they had similar constitutions. This amalgamation took place on 22 March 1986, and the United Women's Congress (UWCO) was formed. In the 1985–1986 period there were the most violent confrontations between activists (including many school pupils and students) and police. Many women, both political leaders and grassroots members were imprisoned and tortured during the state of emergency that was declared in some magisterial districts in 1985 and nationwide in 1986. However, one of the greatest mobilizing factors was the response to police brutality towards youth and children, again kindling maternal instincts or motherism. As a result many new branches of the United Women's Congress (UWCO) in Cape Town were established through mothers mobilizing after their children had been detained and tortured.

UWCO had a varied programme of action looking at women's and national liberation. As part of the UDF, UWCO spearheaded the One Million Signature Campaign against the tricameral government. UWCO was one of the most broadly representative women's organizations in the UDF consistently raising issues around sexism and patriarchy. The UDF stood for four main principles and any organization that wanted to affiliate to it had to adhere to these four principles – democracy, non-racism, non-sexism and a unitary South Africa. It needs to be categorically stated that the UDF did not always function in a non-sexist way and UWCO was usually the lone voice protesting about this.

This tension between ways of working in mixed organizations of women and men was sometimes prevalent. At specific times this was raised. There were also cases of sexual harassment and even violence against women. At one stage there was a disciplinary hearing and the alleged guilty man was expelled from the UDF. In this journey towards citizenship which women assumed would be attained once South Africa was democratic and free from sexism and racism, women learnt many lessons. A UDF assessment workshop in the Cape Town region illustrated to UWCO members that building non-sexism was not always seen as a priority by male comrades. A central question at a Cape Town Regional workshop was: 'To what extent does the UDF in its workings promote non-racialism, non-sexism and democracy?'

This was discussed in groups. When a male comrade stated that it was women's own fault that they were oppressed, women, strategically, kept quiet. Another male comrade responded by explaining the complexities of patriarchy. During the plenary discussion the chairperson cut the discussion on non-sexism short as 'there were time constraints'. However, immediately after that when democracy was discussed in a non-gendered way the chair had no time problems. In the Woodstock UDF area committee, discussions around sexism and the contradictions between what male leaders said in public and how they behaved in their private lives, were often seen. Both men and women felt it was important to raise these problems but because of the sheer pressure of work, there was never time to strategize about doing so. Thus, even within these progressive structures, that were working and demanding a new and democratic South Africa – i.e. full citizenship for all – women did not have substantive equality.

Women within the UDF were not complacent. The UDF Women's Congress (UDFCO) was launched in Cape Town on 25 April 1987 because of the need for UDF women to assert themselves within the UDF structures. Although not very active, the resolutions it took are important statements indicating the problems women have within mixed progressive organizations. Many of the UDFCO resolutions sought to address the sexism women experienced within the democratic movement.

Noting that:
Sexual harassment of women comrades by male comrades is not unheard of;

Believing that:
The national struggle against racism and exploitation will not be a victory unless it is also a victory against sexism;

We therefore resolve: to eradicate sexism from the ranks and to promote a vision of a non-sexist future South Africa amongst progressive organisations. We believe that the future emancipation of women is dependent on the level of participation of women in the struggle as a whole (Extract from the UDF Women's Congress Resolutions, Cape Town, 1987).

It must be emphasized that throughout this period, as much as women were increasingly in the public space demanding political equality, the private space of family and relationships within the household generally remained the same. Women, exhausted after a whole-day workshop, often bemoaned that they still had to cook and that the house would probably be in a mess when they returned. The concern about the blatant political injustice (public) took precedence over the social relations within the home and family (private realm). Despite some utterances challenging the inequality within the family, the gendered division of labour within the home was never a primary area of contestation. For example, Dora Tamana's famous speech, 'You who have no houses, Speak... Women and men must share housework ...' (UWO, 1981, p.3) seems to have fallen on deaf ears. Even after marathon 9-hour meetings women still had to cook the dinner or do the ironing.

In UWO/UWCO there were attempts to balance women's public needs and national needs. Whereas women were in the streets protesting and doing political work (initially the prerogative of men), men seldom did 'women's private work' in the home. Occasionally men took charge of child minding, e.g. when UWO first had its national conferences, men were responsible for the child-minding and the catering. Interestingly, this was mostly done by white men.

One general council reported that the Masincedane Branch (an informal settlement next to KTC) had to get the permission of their husbands before they could meet. This, however, was only true in the beginning. After a while women as mothers challenged their husbands and emphasized that they were now living in the urban areas and they would not be dictated to by 'tribal' authorities and customs of the rural areas. Women often expressed this ambivalence – they readily accepted and respected their culture, but they were critical of the double standards – certain practices for men and others for women. This too was something new and radical in parts of the community. There had been earlier times when some of the women would not have dared to disobey the male leaders if they tried to prevent the women from meeting.

Similar gender dynamics were experienced in Wynberg branch, where most women were Muslim. There was fierce opposition from their husbands to their wives' public roles. The Muslim women also experienced a radicalization. They questioned the customs and tradition and then studied the Qu'ran and the Shariah laws. Through this they learnt about the power they have as Muslim women – a shift from their maternal roles and female consciousness to a radicalization to feminist consciousness. Later, with the formation of the UDF, men joined their wives on the platforms and in the streets in anti-apartheid protests (personal interviews for PhD dissertation).

Race and Class

In this struggle for citizenship, even though white women obtained political rights, they were still subjected to patriarchal relations. Some white women members of UWO believed that the potential attainment of citizenship for women across racial boundaries would come through identifying with grassroots women's and anti-apartheid struggles. White women, although never in large numbers (never more than 10 per cent of the membership), were therefore always part of the grassroots women's organizations, fighting for non-racism and democracy. A central tenet for UWO was that all women, irrespective of race and class, work together: 'Building non-racialism is not an easy task. But for UWO it is a priority because we believe that South Africa belongs to all who live in it ...' (Barrett et al., 1985, p.242).

With the formation of UWO in 1981, the invitation to the UWO launch was extended to all women. It was called by women, to unite, and invited all women to join. During the open session of the first conference all women were invited to speak. The majority of the women spoke about poverty, housing, pass laws, unemployment, etc. Of course, not all women present had first-hand experience of these issues. However, the need for unity prevailed. One speaker's words: 'Here we are all of one colour' (UWO, 1981), captured this spirit.

However, at a later stage, most of the UWO/UWCO rhetoric refers to the 'triple oppression of women'. This indicates some development despite Wells's statement that motherist movements are static and not political (Wells, 1998, p.253). According to the analysis of United Women's Organisation, women were oppressed as workers, as women and as blacks: class, gender and race oppressions intersect. The 'triple oppression' was much criticized as being 'theoretically vacuous' (Wells, 1991), and 'triple oppression' has become 'rhetorical commonplace' (Walker, 1990, p.2). The members of UWO found it was a crucial mobilizing tool and created the awareness of the differences and similarities amongst women. Together, women classified as African, coloured, Indian and white discussed their varying degrees of oppression and the intersectionality of race, class and gender.

At a much later stage, post-1988, other categories like geographic location urban/rural, ability/disability, religion and sexual orientation were included. With the awareness of the rights of lesbian women, they experienced a change in perception of women's roles; it was not 'inevitable' and 'natural' for all women to become mothers but that women had choices in this. This was thus also an evolution of a feminist consciousness.

Federation of South African Women – FSAW (Western Cape Region)

In accordance with the national mandate to relaunch FSAW, UWCO initiated discussion and consultation with other women's organizations. In August 1987, the FSAW was relaunched in Claremont Civic Centre, Cape Town. It succeeded in 'broadening out' the struggle. It was commonly understood that most affiliates of FSAW subscribed to the Freedom Charter, which was drawn up by the Congress of the People in 1956. New affiliates included Rape Crisis (mostly white feminists at that time), Bellville Gemeenskap-Organisasie (a coloured, mainly religious community group) and coloured working-class organizations like Atlantis Women's Group. Other affiliates came from religious groups. The FSAW also developed a close working relationship with Black Sash (Women's Issues Group). Black Sash was not able to affiliate as their constitution prevented this. Because women were from different organizations with different political perspectives, they focused on campaigns that would unite and promote the position of women. An example is the October 1988 'Take Back the Night candle march' to protest violence against women. In 1981 the majority of the members of UWO/UWCO admitted that violence against women was an important battle but not a priority; seven years later they realized that it was an integral part of national struggle.

This once again illustrates how the changes took place in the understanding and struggles of motherist movements in the development towards a more feminist struggle.

Even though organizations like Rape Crisis and Black Sash were not characteristically motherist, the common slogan used in mobilizing meetings still argued that 'we as mothers need to unite for the good of our children and the future South Africa'. A memorable reference which highlighted the stark racial polarization was when Albertina Sisulu, the then Patron of the UDF, addressed a public meeting in the Cape Town City hall. As speaker at the End Conscription Campaign (EEC) meeting, she appealed directly to white mothers: 'It is your sons in the SADF army who are going to the townships to kill our sons. As mothers in South Africa we must stop this violence' (1988). This demonstrates that 'motherism' is also powerful in its ability to appeal across race.

FSAW filled the gap when UWCO functioned underground. A state of emergency was declared in October 1985 in Cape Town. After this, UWCO, UDF and many other organizations were not allowed to meet. Most of the executive of UWCO were either in detention or 'on the run'. Ironically it was also during this time of extreme repression that the Langa branch relaunched with 300 members. Tension mounted as repression increased, not only because of the political situation externally but also internally in the organization. Members with boyfriends or partners in the police were not trusted. Anxiety and distrust intensified when a venue intended for a meeting was surrounded by police as only a handful of people knew about the venue. At times there was almost general paranoia about the *impimpi* (police informer). The increased militancy in the Western Cape brought more demands and challenges to women. Often women who had just been released from detention were expected to address meetings, even when they did not feel emotionally strong enough to address meetings. They were almost coerced to be strong as the struggle needed and demanded it. 'They were the cadres!' Women as mothers had to be martyrs for the struggle; the struggle's needs and the needs of the comrades were also more important than their personal needs.

Another change in the women's and mothers' activities was the movement towards underground activities. Initially mothers took to the streets in defence of their children. Later they harboured children 'on the run' from the police, including young people active in the underground army. There were times these mothers hid the young cadres including their arms. At later stages mothers themselves were smuggling and hiding weapons. Many of these mothers ended up being part of the underground movement where their tasks varied from procuring passports and documents for people leaving or entering the country illegally to being engaged in actual armed conflict. This transition from peaceful protests to illegal underground military activities once again illustrates the transformation from female consciousness to feminist consciousness.

With the increase of detention of women activists, FSAW took up the campaign to demand the release of women political prisoners. One of the activities was a women's religious service. For most women present this was a very revolutionary experience. The liturgy was composed especially from women's perspectives. This service was a very new experience for the majority of women, most of whom were religious. The majority was Christian and some were Muslim and Jewish. This first encounter with anything vaguely resembling feminist theology was perceived as radical. Women were confronted directly with the patriarchal nature of their religions. Religion was something very private and sacrosanct to most and this experience for the 'mothers' was a gradually transformative one. The Women's Creed, a creed free of the traditional language portraying God as all male, was popularized in the following terms:

> I believe in God/who created woman and man in God's own image ... I believe in the Holy Spirit/ the woman spirit of God/ who like a hen/ created us/ and gave us birth/ and covers us with her wings (Women's Creed).

Amongst the most successful activities of FSAW were the annual women's cultural festivals celebrating women's culture and creativity. From 1988 to 1990 FSAW annually held two-day festivals with fêtes, women's poetry, plays, songs and dance, speeches and gumbos (dances to traditional African music). The Black Sash's play on the 'Special Branch', the South African Domestic Workers' Union's play highlighting the lives of domestic workers and UWCO's multi-media presentation of black women artists were particularly successful. The Festival was a way of bringing affiliates closer as well as encouraging women's organizations to participate.

At a festival planning meeting in November 1987 OLGA (Organisation of Gay and Lesbian Activists) applied to have a stall. Members enquired about OLGA and when the acronym was explained the next question was: 'What are gays and lesbians?' The answer was followed by silence. Lesbian women present deliberately waited for a response from the majority, heterosexual women. After a brief explanation about the choices and preferences that lesbian women make, one of the township women nonchalantly stated that there was no reason why OLGA should not have a stall and that they should be welcomed. No animosity or homophobia was expressed at that stage. Subsequently however, in 1988, when a lesbian member was detained and others, through this exposure, learnt that she was gay, some members of that branch wanted her censured. A discussion on this followed where the majority concluded that the organization stood and worked for the freedom of all, including lesbians and gays.

The lessons were many for the women who first joined the struggle because of their children. The FSAW planned the Women's First Cultural Festival because of political repression. Culture was used as a weapon but through the experience of the festival, women learnt the value of their own culture and their own cultural expressions. They had found their own voices and asserted them.

Similarly, it was the first time that gays and lesbian participants and issues were openly part of the mass democratic grassroots women's movement. Their participation led to their growth and women developed sensitivity around a previously 'invisible' issue. It seemed at that stage that women/mothers could identify with the oppression of gays and lesbians because of their own oppression. However, the issue around sexuality and sexual preference has still not been addressed openly and honestly in post-1994 South Africa, almost a decade after democratization. This remains a challenge. Theoretically, most South Africans are proud of the Constitution but homophobia still abounds.

One of the last workshops held by FSAW before it dissolved was to form the Women's Alliance, an even broader coalition. This was decided at a workshop held in 1991 at the University of Western Cape. It focused on strategies for taking the women's struggle forward. One of the proposals from the Women's Issues Working Group of the Black Sash was that the government be asked to ratify the United Nations Convention on the Elimination of All Forms of Discrimination Against Women (CEDAW). Many women had not heard about CEDAW at that stage. After the explanation there was a lively debate, not without tension, on how strategic it was to ask the present government, which the majority of affiliates saw as illegitimate, to ratify CEDAW. Even though CEDAW would have meant increasing the possibility of attaining citizenship for women, however limited, the majority of women, who incidentally were black, were adamant that it could not be done within the apartheid context. A new and democratically elected government would be pressured to ratify CEDAW. The South African government ratified CEDAW without reservations in January 1996.

Conclusions

Kaplan outlines her theory of how female consciousness can be transformed into feminist or political consciousness. Under specific circumstances, because of their exposure to various actions, women will move from their position and concerns as mothers and question the wider political motives. I contend that there has been a definite broadening of issues for mothers in the 1980 to 1990 period. As mothers who initially organized 'in the defence of' their children, their own experiences and contact with other women's organisation broadened their political insight to a broader vision than their own roles as mothers. They developed an awareness of the power relations in the family which upholds the sexual division of labour, and of sexism which is responsible for gender based violence. Contact with organizations like OLGA also raised awareness around sexual orientation. By the late 1980s the 'mothers' were including the intersectionality of ability and sexual preference in their analyses of oppression. This transition from a perception of themselves as mothers to an understanding of sexual relations being based on power inequalities, is indicative of a developing feminist consciousness. But this did not mean that in reality their lives were changed and they now have substantive citizenship. However, it is also clear that South Africans have still to confront their own homophobia in the reality and not be contented with only the theory. In theory according to the constitution, the citizenship of women and lesbians is protected. Today HIV/AIDS status adds another dimension to discrimination and the likelihood of exercising citizenship is limited through this disease.

The struggles outlined above also reveal how at various levels poverty in the home was linked to macro-economic issues, and that patriarchal power in the public was translated to the private too. This was translated into challenging the national budgets and the legitimacy of the then apartheid government. Violence against women became a major rallying point for women after a while and still continues to be one in the face of the appalling violence against women and children in South Africa. The awareness of the patriarchal nature of their lives within the home and religions was also challenged but minimally so. On the other hand it could be argued that as SA is in a transition, and that the struggle against patriarchy is still a very long and complex one. Many women today still do not acknowledge that their lives are dictated by patriarchy.

The dramatic increase in violence against women and children is particularly frightening and urgent resources, energy and action should be harnessed to counter this. But is there the political will to do this? The Gender Advocacy Programme (GAP) researched the obstacles which prevent the implementation of the Domestic Violence Act and found that the main obstacle was budgetary constraints. How does one confront the situation that there is no budget to implement the Domestic Violence Act but that Arms Deals cost the country billions? What does this say about the priorities of the government and about the presence and/or lack of power of women parliamentarians in these decisions? The Constitution makes provision for the socio-economic rights of all, albeit within the fiscal discipline. Much work has gone into creating a gender budget but this has been left out of the national budget in the past two years. Despite the controversy around the use of Nevirapine to prevent mother-to-child transmission of the HIV/AIDS virus, many women believe it can alter the quality of their lives and those of their children. This battle continues in the courts, the internet and the streets and hundreds of children are dying while the debates and theorizing continue.

But as much as it is government's role to create an enabling environment, women too have responsibilities towards realizing their full citizenship. At the Truth and Reconciliation hearings, in testimony after testimony women spoke about the pain and suffering of their husbands and children. Special women's hearings had to be organized so that women could tell their own stories and not those stories that affected them as wives, sisters, daughter and mothers. When the Commission on Gender Equality (CGE) lobbied political parties at their national conferences for support for the 50/50 campaign in 2002, mostly women disagreed with it. At the elections for many political and organizational institutions, it is often the women who vote for men as chairpersons and women as secretaries.

So what precisely is the nature of the citizenship that SA women have achieved? Citizenship also entails being part of drawing up policy and being involved in submissions to Parliament (Hassim, 1999, p.14). The reality of the average person, especially women, is far from this. Most people do not even know that they have these rights, nor do they have the ability to participate in this process if they so desired. Illiteracy amongst women is especially high compared to that of men.

CEDAW had been ratified by the South African government in January 1996 but the majority of women do not even know what it is. It is the task of the Commission on Gender Equality and other chapter 9 constitutional institutions to educate the South African public on this and related issues and to promote the constitutional principles. The CGE is also mandated to monitor the compliance to these international instruments but it does not have the capacity, both in terms of finance and person power, to do so. In 2002 it was the fifth anniversary of the South African Constitution and an ideal opportunity to popularize its content. There were major proposals for celebration by the Chapter 9 institutions to celebrate the 5th anniversary of the SA Constitution, but currently almost 80% of the population does not know the content of the constitution. These are some of the many serious challenges that face the CGE.

In the past South African apartheid policies and laws afforded white men full citizenship in South Africa, and because of patriarchy, white women minimally so. Today it seems as if the race factor has been altered. A small new black (previously disenfranchised) elite has been added to the privileged status of full citizenship: politicians, black and white, male and female government bureaucrats that the affirmative action have realized. But the majority of South Africans, women more than men, experience full citizenship on paper only.

The challenges are many: with the increased number of women in the executive and parliament, why is it that there has not been more meaningful and successful implementation of legislation for greater equality – i.e. that people's lives should really be transformed into full citizens? Zanele Mbeki challenged women at the National Gender Summit held in August 2001: 'Why have we not effectively used the powerhouse of women that we have in this country?' But do these women have substantive power to challenge and really effect meaningful change? Albertyn, Hassim and Meintjes (2002) refer to the politics of presence and the politics of power. Do women really have the politics of power? Women are present in the government and as much as the CGE sees the 50/50 campaign as a means of increasing women's representivity, the crux of the matter is that the numbers game is not enough. In the new South Africa we have public power for some, like women ministers, speakers etc. This challenges public power to a degree, but most women still suffer private powerlessness. This division is sustained by understandings of liberal citizenship which upholds the public/private dichotomy. Unless there is an understanding and commitment to seeing women as full citizens, changing the private/public dichotomy and treating women's nurturing qualities and care as integral to citizenship, there will not be transformation.

Notes

1. The editor is deeply grateful to Mikki van Zyl and Marleen van Wyk for their respective contributions in completing this chapter for publication.
2. Known generally as 'Influx Control' etc. According to the Population Registration Act of 1950 all persons had to be classified into one of the ethnic 'races'. All persons had to have identity cards on them at all times which had to be produced on demand. However, in the case of African people the pass or 'dompas' as it was derogatively known, had to be 'stamped' by a local authority whether or not the bearer was allowed in that area. Thousands of African people were arrested weekly. One of the reasons why there was since the beginning of the century, vociferous protests by women that passes be issued to them, was because the arbitrary arrests of women for pass contravention would be a threat to the family (Walker, 1982, p.28). It has to be noted that it was only in the late 1950s (1959) that the government was able to coerce African women into carrying passes. Women were not able to get jobs without passes.
3. Other maternalist processes of moving from the private to public realm could be anti-feminist, for example conservative women mobilizing and torching pro-choice clinics. Therefore a feminist analysis is crucial in assessing whether public activity by women based on maternalism is *feminist* political action.
4. See Amrita Basu (1995, p.12). There are also many references to the role of women as mothers in Latin America e.g. Mothers of the Plaza de Mayo in Chile.
5. See Leshabari (1994).
6. Both black women (Mothers of the Nation) and Afrikaner women (*Volksmoeders*) were mobilized around ideologies for issues defined by men supposedly on behalf of all. Neither group tolerated women starting to mobilize on issues that highlighted gender inequities or conflicts of interest between women and men i.e. that evidenced a feminist

inequities or conflicts of interest between women and men i.e. that evidenced a feminist consciousness.

7. Black Sash was an existing, predominantly liberal women's organization opposed to apartheid, which had started in 1955 (named the Women's Defence of the Constitution League) to hold silent protests about the government's disregard for the constitution (Davenport and Saunders, 2000, p.396). During the 1980s they were operating advice offices in many parts of the country to assist black people with bureaucratic and legal problems.

References

Albertyn, C., Hassim, S. and Meintjes, S. (2002), 'Making a Difference? Women's Struggles for Participation and Representation', in G. Fick, S. Meintjes and M. Simons, *One Woman, One Vote – The Gender Politics of South African Elections*, Electoral Institute of Southern Africa, Johannesburg.

Argosin, Marjorie, (1987), 'Emerging from the shadows: Women in Chile', The Barnard Occasional Papers on Women's Issues, Vol.2, No.3 (Fall), (pp.9-31).

Argosin, M., Kaplan, T. and Valdez, Terry (1987), 'The Politics of Spectacle in Chile', The Barnard Occasional Papers on Women's Issues, Vol.2, No.3, (Fall), (pp.1-8).

Barrett, Jane, Dawber, Aneen Klugman, Barbara Obery, Ingrid Shindler, Jennifer and Yawitch, Joanne (1985), *Vukani Makhosikazi: South African Women Speak*, Catholic Institute for International Relations, London.

Basu, Amrita (ed.), (1995), *The Challenges of Local Feminisms; Women's Movements in Global Perspectives*, Westview Press, Boulder, Colorado, Oxford.

Bernstein, Hilda (1975), *For their Triumphs and for their Tears*, International Defence and Aid Fund, London.

Besha, Ruth (ed.), (1994), *African Women: Our Burdens and Struggles*, Institute for African Alternatives, Johannesburg.

Brink, Elsabe (1990), 'Man-made women: Gender, class and the ideology of the *volksmoeder*', in Cherryl Walker (ed.), *Women and Gender in Southern Africa to 1945*, David Philip, Cape Town, pp.273-292.

Clayton, C. (1989), *Women and Writing in South Africa, a Critical Anthology*, Heinemann Southern Africa, Wynberg, Cape.

Davenport, T.R.H. and Saunders, Christopher (2000), *South Africa: A Modern History* (5th edn.), Macmillan Press, Houndmills, Basingstoke, Hampshire and London.

Dietz, Mary (1985), 'Citizenship with a Feminist Face: The Problem with Maternal Thinking', *Political Theory*, 13:1, pp.19-37.

Drew, Allison (1995), 'Female Consciousness and Feminism in Africa', *Theory and Society*, 24:1, pp.19-33.

Elshtain, Jean Bethke (1981), *Public Man, Private Woman*, Princeton University Press, Princeton.

Elshtain, Jean Bethke (1982a), 'Feminism, Family and Community', *dissent*, Fall 1982, pp.442-450.

Elshtain, Jean Bethke (1982b), 'Feminist Discourse and its Discontents: Language, Power and Meaning', *Signs*, 7 no.3, pp.603-621.

Elshtain, Jean Bethke (1983), 'Open Letter to Marshall Berman', *dissent*, Spring 1983, pp.250-255.

Federation of South African Women (1991), 'Fedsaw Disbanded – Newsnips', *Agenda*, No.9, p.41.

Fester, G. (1997), 'Women's Organisations in the Western Cape: Vehicles for Gender Struggle or Instruments of Subordination?' *Agenda*, No.34, pp.45-61.

Fester, G. (1998), 'Closing the Gap – Activism and Academia in South Africa: Towards a Women's Movement', in Obioma Nnaemeka (ed.), *Sisterhood, Feminisms and Power*, Africa World Press, Trenton and Asmara, pp.215-237.

Fester, G. (2000), 'Despite Diversity: Women's unity in the Western Cape', in Suki Ali, Kelly Coates and Wangui wa Goro (eds.), *Global Feminist Politics – identities in a changing world*, Routledge, London and New York, pp.11-27.

Gaitskell, D. and Unterhalter, E. (1989), 'Mothers of the Nation: A comparative analysis of Nation, Race and Motherhood in Afrikaner Nationalism and the African National Congress', in F. Anthias and N. Yuval-Davis (eds.), *Women-Nation-State*, Macmillan Press, Houndmills, Basingstoke, Hampshire and London, pp.58-79.

Gouws, A. (1999), 'Beyond Equality and Difference', *Agenda*, No.40, pp.54-58.

Hassim, S. (1999), 'From Presence to Power: Women's Citizenship in a New Democracy', *Agenda*, No.40, pp.6-17.

Hassim, S. (1993), 'Family, Motherhood and Zulu Nationalism: The Politics of the Inkatha Women's Brigade', *Feminist Review*, No.43, Spring, pp.1-25.

Hendricks, C. and Lewis, D. (1994), 'Voices from the Margin', *Agenda*, No.20, pp.61-75.

Kaplan, T. (1982), 'Female consciousness and collective action: The case of Barcelona', *Signs*, 7/3 Summer, pp.545-566.

Kaplan, T. (1992), *Mother and Representation. The Mother in Popular Culture and Melodrama*, Routledge, London.

Kaplan, T. (1997), *Crazy for Democracy: Women in Grassroots Movements*, Routledge, New York.

Leshabari, Sebalda (1994), 'The Concept of Motherhood as an Instrument of Women's Oppression. A Case Study of the Chagga tribe, Tanzania', in Besha, Ruth (ed.), *African Women: Our Burdens and Struggles*, Institute for African Alternatives, Johannesburg, pp.34-39.

Lewis, D. (2001), 'African Feminisms', *Agenda*, No.50, pp.4-10.

Lewis, D. (1993), 'Feminism in South Africa', *Women's Studies International Forum*, 16(5), pp.535-542.

Lister, R. (1997), *Citizenship: Feminist Perspectives*, New York University Press, New York.

Meintjes, S. (1996), 'The Women's Struggle for Equality during South Africa's Transition to Democracy', *Transformation*, 30, pp.47-64.

Meintjes, S. (1993), 'Dilemmas of Difference', *Agenda*, No.19, pp.37-42.

Ruddick, S. (1983a), 'Maternal Thinking' in J. Trebilcot (ed.), *Mothering, Essays in Feminist Theory*, Rowman and Littlefield, Maryland, pp.213-230.

Ruddick, S. (1983b), 'Pacifying the Forces', *Signs*, Spring 1983, No.3, pp.471-489.

Ruddick, S. (1989) *Maternal Thinking, Towards a Politics of Peace*, Women's Press, London.

Soiri, I. (1996), *The Radical Mother – Namibian Women's Independence Struggle*, Nordiska Afrikainstitutet, Uppsala.

United Women's Organisation, (1982), *Die Federasie: Vroue-Organisasie van Suid-Afrika*, United Women's Organisation and Social Research Agency, Woodstock, Cape Town.

United Women's Organisation Minutes, (1981), (1982), (1983), (1984).

Walker, Cherryl (1982), *Women and Resistance in South Africa*, Onyx Press, London.

Walker, Cherryl (1990), 'Women and gender in southern Africa to 1945: An overview', in Cherryl Walker (ed.), *Women and Gender in Southern Africa to 1945*, David Philip, Cape Town and James Currey, London, pp.1-32.

Walker, Cherryl (1995), 'Conceptualizing Motherhood in Twentieth Century South Africa', *Journal of Southern African Studies*, 21(3), pp.417-437.

Wells, J. (1991), 'The Rise and Fall of Motherism as a Force in Black Women's Resistance'. Paper read at Women and Gender in Southern Africa Conference, University of Natal, Durban.

Wells, J. (1998), 'Maternal Politics in Organizing Black South Africa Women' in Obioma Nnaemeka (ed.), *Sisterhood, Feminisms and Power*, Africa World Press, Trenton and Asmara, pp.251-262.

PART V
SEXUALIZING CITIZENSHIP

Chapter 10

Escaping Heteronormative Bondage: Sexuality in Citizenship[1]

Mikki van Zyl

The table was a large one, but the three were all crowded together at one corner of it. "No room! No room!" they cried out when they saw Alice coming.

"There's *plenty* of room!" said Alice indignantly, and sat down in a large armchair at one end of the table.

"Have some wine," the March Hare said in an encouraging tone.

Alice looked all round the table, but there was nothing on it but tea. "I don't see any wine," she remarked.

"There isn't any," said the March Hare.

"Then it wasn't very civil of you to offer it," said Alice angrily.

"It wasn't very civil of you to sit down without being invited," said the March Hare.

"I didn't know it was *your* table," said Alice. "It's laid for a great many more than three."

Lewis Carroll, 1946, *Alice's Adventures in Wonderland*, pp.76-77.

Introduction

Since democratization in South Africa in 1994 the *definition* of citizenship has altered radically for the majority of South Africans who were previously excluded from a primary criterion of citizenship in republican discourse – belonging to a nation-state. Through racialization, indigenous Africans were disenfranchised in the country of their ancestors and birth. In 1994 they were included in the liberal democratic achievement of the vote, bearing a tradition where 'the citizen' is signified by an 'abstract, ungendered individual who can lay claim to certain (natural) rights' (Gouws, 1999, p.55). Further nuances of 'othered' citizen-subjects emerge in more detail as rights in the Equality Clause of the Bill of Rights in the Constitution. These focus in a more textured way on historic exclusions:

Groups that do not conform to the universal norm established by the white, able-bodied, heterosexual male still represent 'the other' whose claim to citizenship is insecure (Lister, 2003, p.74).

Therefore the *claiming* of citizenship, for example through human rights instruments, emerges in a context[2] of people deeply divided by historical social relations, and is predicated on perpetuated dynamics of inequitable economic and political power. A person's rights are not unitary and are always balanced against other people's rights, set against a background of struggles for hegemonic dominance. Moreover, rights are expressed within a particular *rhetorical system* which is explicitly or implicitly subtended on an ethical base, reflecting values which have wider contextual references.

Sexual Citizens

Unravelling the notion of a 'sexual citizen'[3] is complex and contended, problematizing the underlying values of current concepts of citizenship in modern humanist democracies. It foregrounds issues raised by feminists in reconceptualizing the relationships between citizenship, rights, universality, difference, equality and culture. A useful frame for analysis is through interrogating international human rights discourses concerning sexual rights: a long tradition of struggle provides a context for understanding the social and theoretical implications of access to rights via sexuality and gender.

> This combination of 'sexual rights' as a contested concept, and the increasing usage of the language of citizenship in relation to sexuality, underlines the need for a critical analysis of its meaning and value as a concept (Richardson, 2000a, p.268).

In addressing the question *What concepts of citizenship underlie sexual rights claims in South Africa?* I argue that liberal concepts of citizenship are not only deeply sexualized, but are also constituted through gendered and racialized discourses. Following Richardson (2000a; 2000b), I develop the view that citizens are 'normatively constructed as (hetero)sexual subjects ... and that "excluded" citizens' consequently face inequities, (2000a, p.257). In order to make sense of the varied and intersectional inequities, I use a sex/gender-disaggregated notion of sexuality, but contextualize problematic concepts such as sexual *identities*, sexual *relationships* and sexual *practices*. I do not limit the meaning of sexual citizenship to rights to sexual expression, but more generally as the access to rights through a citizen's status in relation to their sexuality.

Further, I develop the idea of 'intimate' citizenship (Giddens, 1992; Plummer, 2003; Richardson, 2000a, 2000b; Weeks, 1998) through foregrounding the inseparability of the (so-called) public and private arenas. In this context the incorporation of the 'emotional as a central part of the political process itself' (Yuval-Davis, 2003, p.1) is salient. Drawing on Yuval-Davis's (2003) discussion about human security discourses, I extend Weeks's (1998) concept of sexual citizenship within a context of 'belonging'. This, in turn, bridges the divide between individual and community, and demands an understanding of how groups struggling for liberation succeed in getting political representation of their sexual rights. Finally, I apply the concepts developed about gendered sexual citizens to the definitions of sexual *rights* advanced by Petchesky (2000).

Claiming Sexual Rights

In this chapter I accept that not only is the concept of citizenship profoundly gendered and racialized (Lister, 2003; Young, 2000; Yuval-Davis and Werbner, 1999; Manicom, 2001; Gouws, 1999) but argue that it is also deeply (hetero)sexualized (Richardson, 2000a, 2000b; Cossman, 2002; Weeks, 1998). The recognition of (homo)sexual identities and same-sex intimate relationships as a Constitutional right has the potential radically to subvert heteronormativity: firstly through affirming habitational diversity; secondly by exposing the social construction of the public-private dichotomy; and finally, by underwriting values of social diversity it opens possibilities for transforming histories of 'othering'. To concretize my arguments, I briefly contextualize sexual rights within broader gender politics by referring to gender-based violence and reproductive rights, then proceed to focus on issues challenging heteronormativity, such as domestic partnerships and sexual rights under the 'sexual orientation' section of the Equality clause, Chap.2 S.9(3) and (4) in the South African Constitution (Act 108 of 1996). I note explicitly that claims to sexual rights are made from positionalities of social, economic and *rhetorical* privilege, and therefore represent sectional interests that may or may not be representative of a larger whole. Nevertheless, I conclude that South Africa is in the process of *formally* establishing values and principles in the *discourse* of citizenship, that reflects respect for diversity, and works to overcome the binarism implicit in hegemonic traditions of 'othering'.

Citizenship as Belonging

As was proven by apartheid, 'citizenship' can be a powerful exclusionary device for setting boundaries between centralized subjects and 'others' or 'outsiders'. Theorists have long engaged with the universality that promotes citizenship as a neutral abstraction where the 'citizen' is de-sexed, de-racialized and de-classed. Even the nation-state's autonomy in defining citizenship is being challenged through transnationalism and international human rights discourses, agencies and instruments (Lister, 2003, p.196). Yet the state as 'the regulator of a range of citizenship rights, including immigration, cultural, reproductive and sexual as well as social rights' (Lister, 2003, p.10) has the power of formal inclusion. How it defines the terms of membership, status, rights, obligations and the framework for participation can deeply influence people's everyday lives – that dimension of citizenship that resonates with the emotional, a feeling of belonging. Though 'belonging is a "thicker" concept than … citizenship' because it transcends 'membership, rights and duties', it is 'about the emotions that such memberships evoke' (Yuval-Davis, 2003, p.4). Belonging is a hegemonic construction which only becomes visible when threatened. For instance, the anti-apartheid struggle was articulated primarily as a politicized narrative of belonging (Steyn, Grant and Van Zyl, 2001). However, struggles of belonging can as easily be appropriated for exclusionary as well as inclusionary purposes – the current USA-driven rhetoric of global terrorism is mobilizing people around narratives of fear and threats to security, thereby petrifying boundaries around national collectivities rather than developing a culture of greater tolerance for 'others'. By contrast, through the lens of post-colonial feminisms, we can recognize and respect different positionalities – many feminists, especially in Africa, insist on recognizing the differences between women, while simultaneously being able to organize politically (*Agenda*, 2001, p.58).

Sexuality, steeped as it is in contexts of intimacy and emotion (Padgug, 1999, p.18), is easily relegated to the private sphere, where the hegemony of patriarchal familiality grounds it in heteronormativity – the biologically essentialist paradigm used to advance (a certain type of) heterosexuality as the only 'natural' form of sexuality. Upon this assumption is built a multitude of ideologies of exclusions and 'othering'. Rubin (1999) describes a hierarchy of sexual values in Western societies, ranging from 'the charmed circle' to the 'outer limits' (p.153). These sexual values function along the same exclusionary principles as ideological systems of racism, ethnocentrism etc. When sexuality transgresses the boundaries of heteronormative privacy through homosexuality (or any other marginalized sexuality), or enters the public domain through economic relations such as sex work, there are calls for state regulation of sexuality.

The struggle for equal sexual citizenship rights has been a history of challenging the terms of privacy around sexuality – the gender based violence movement wanted to expose abusive patriarchal family relationships, and conversely, lesbian and gay rights asserted the right to privacy of persons in consenting same-sex relationships. Cossman (2002) concludes that lesbian and gay rights struggles have succeeded in creating 'a modality of sexual citizenship ... in which sexual subjects are privatized, de-eroticized and depoliticized' (p.483). These struggles reflect the problematization of the public-private dichotomy that has been addressed by feminists in re-theorizing citizenship (e.g. Pateman, 1989; Lister, 2003). Struggles for sexual rights are deeply personalized, with the body and affective relationships as primary signifiers – both of which are deeply imbued with notions of safety, security and belonging. This understanding is fraught with ambiguity: on the one hand, there is a danger of reinforcing the rigid (gendered) bifurcation of the private and public spheres; and on the other, a politicization of the private which asserts the imbrication of both. However, these struggles for bodily integrity have contributed to the notion of 'sexual citizenship' (Lister, 2003, p.125). Thus it is through *claims* for 'sexual justice' by political groupings that concepts of sexual citizenship have been developed, showing how the 'universal' notion of citizenship is sexualized and founded on normative privatized, de-eroticized heterosexuality (Cossman, 2002; Richardson, 2000b; Weeks, 1998).

Gendered Citizenship

Citizenship in democratic systems usually confers on individuals' status, rights and obligations and circumscribes the powers of the state (Hassim, 1999, p.7). The primary inscription of citizenship in modern Westernized liberal humanist democracies is through ideologies of individualism, where the solitary 'good' citizen-subject enters a reciprocal relationship of rights and obligations towards the state. He (sic) may claim his rights, but is also enjoined to exercise agency in the polity. In scripting a 'universal' citizen, the manner in which citizenship constitutes that citizen is obscured – maintaining and perpetuating particular arrangements (of exclusion) which enhance the power and privileges of the normative 'universal' citizen.[4]

Another basic inscription is heteronormativity, which is written into the social institution of the (assumed) patriarchal family, with a male head of household mediating the relationship with the state for women and children (Lister, 2003, pp.72, 120). This articulation of gendered social relations[5] also upholds the gender division of labour, which in turn reinforces and maintains the public-private dichotomy in modern Western societies. Through these historical social articulations, female citizens are positioned pre-eminently in the private realm, in reproduction and caring roles, while males represent the 'real' citizens situated in the 'world' of 'worker' (earner) (Lister, 2003, p.167).[6]

Feminist scholars have contested the implicit gender relations built into modern liberal conceptions of citizenship, focusing extensively on how women are positioned as citizen-objects: problematized, marginalized, particularized, privatized, and biologized while certain men are positioned as the universal citizen-subject (Lister, 2003, pp.72, 120). But a sliding of the concept 'gender' onto a category of sexed citizens (women) tends towards reasserting the biological determinism which underlies the 'othered' positionality of females, and fails to account for the numerous instances where males are also 'othered', nor does it critically examine the subject positioning of men in the private, affective realm (Lister, 2003, p.136).[7]

> This broad understanding of sexuality as the 'private' involves other significant dualities, which while not simple translations for the general division into private and public spheres, do present obvious analogies to it … the sexual sphere is seen as the realm of psychology, while the public sphere is seen as the realm of politics and economics; … sexuality is the realm of 'nature', of the individual, and of biology; the public sphere is the realm of culture society and history. Finally sexuality tends to be identified most closely with the female and the homosexual, while the public sphere is conceived of as male and heterosexual (Padgug, 1999, p.17).

Universal citizens are heterosexual men who practise their sexuality in private (Cossman, 2002; Richardson, 2000a). Hence a mutual identification of women with bodies and the feminization of the private sphere elides into conceptions of a de-sexualized, dis-embodied (public) citizen. But if gender is conceptualized and scrutinized as hierarchical relations of power operating between historically and socially marked signifiers of masculinity and femininity, and 'resulting in exclusions and disadvantage' (Manicom, 2001, p.8), it allows us to be more inclusive of people's differing sexual positionalities, while opening up the discourse of men's (hidden) positioning in the personal. Lister (2003) calls for a de-gendering of the public-private split (pp.136, 141) – a 'disruption of its gendered meaning', while recognizing the dialectical relationship between them (p.197). While she perceives it as 'subversion, transcendence or critical synthesis of the original dichotomies' (Lister, 2003, p.9), others argue for a more radical and contextual re-conceptualization:

> We need a refusal of the fixed and permanent quality of the binary opposition, a genuine historicization and deconstruction of the terms of sexual difference. We must become more self-conscious about distinguishing between our analytic vocabulary and the material we want to analyse. We must find ways (however imperfect) continually to subject our categories to criticism, our analyses to self-criticism ... analysing in context the way any binary opposition operates, reversing and displacing its hierarchical constructions, rather than accepting it as real or self-evident or in the nature of things (Scott, 1999, p.65).

Sexual Citizenship

The focus on sexual *rights* emphasizes the embodied-ness of citizens, and exposes the private in public, making the sexual nature of citizenship visible (Lister, 2003, p.72), while providing insight into how sexuality is articulated within these gendered and gendering relations of citizen-subject and state.[8] But by re-inserting males into the equations relating to sexuality, I do not want to re-agglomerate the sexes with the male as 'universal' subject (Richardson, 2000a, p.256), but wish to extend the vocabulary of a gender-differentiated approach, which rearticulates the private-public divide by deconstructing the values associated with them, acknowledging how they impact on one another, and recognizing the changing nature of the boundaries between them (Lister, 2003, pp.120-121). The legal recognition of 'alternative families' in South Africa (e.g. *Domestic Partnerships* below) opens up and challenges the hegemony of the Western patriarchal nuclear family, but at the same time normalizes (and re-genders) other hegemonic discourses like the privatization of care.

Increasingly theorists around power, gender and sexuality have come to the conclusion that for democracy to succeed, recognition must be given to the profound interdependence of the public and private spheres. They contend that democracy cannot flourish only as a system of relationships to be upheld in the public sphere, but also needs to be enacted, maintained and reproduced in intimate relationships (Giddens, 1992; Connell and Dowsett, 1999; Parker, Barbosa and Aggleton, 2000, Plummer, 2003). They argue a rethinking of sexual ethics which focus on democratic, egalitarian social exchanges, sidestepping the good/bad normalization of sex by 'judging sex acts by the way in which partners treat one another, the level of mutual consideration, the presence or absence of coercion, and quantity and quality of the pleasures they provide' (Rubin, 1999, p.153). Most significantly, they propose a public model of democratic practice, based on affective egalitarian relationships.

Highlighting sexual citizenship is part of politicizing emotional and intimate relations, and contributes to de-gendering and confounding some of the mechanisms of women's exclusion from the polity (Yuval-Davis 2003, p.1). Jeffrey Weeks (1998, p.35) argues that the concept of sexual citizenship has arisen as a result of the current world focus on sexual subjectivity, using a general definition of sexual citizenship which includes all citizens, but in differentiated positionalities. These formulations of sexual citizenship contribute to exposing the fluidity of sexuality as well as the socially constructed dimensions of affective relations. Sexual citizenship is also about human security and autonomy, and intersects the personal and political on the body. What is most individual and one's own, becomes most public as it comes under public control. Cossman (2002) warns that 'sexual citizenship is a normalizing discourse ... a strategy for inclusion in the prevailing social norms and institutions of family, gender, work and nation' (p.486). A struggle for sexual rights faces the dilemma of at once trying to transform cultural conceptions as well as find 'a place at the table' (Petchesky, 2000, p.96).

A further distinction in sexual citizenship concerns rights struggles around sexual *identities* or *practices* (Richardson, 2000a, p.259) – for example the right *to be* a lesbian, or whether one be allowed to *practise* lesbian sex. These different forms of sexual citizenship give rise to understanding boundaries of community differently. But no matter how they are organized, their existence assumes membership of a group which is located 'outside' the norm, because they would not be constellated as separate or different if they were accepted as part of the social fabric. This raises the issue of cultural citizenship, for instance the right to see one's identity reflected in cultural representations, and to do so in safety. These in turn lead to questions of community relations and context, and in the face of histories of institutionalized and cultural violence against 'others', re-evokes human security as a central tenet of citizenship and belonging.

> Neither citizenship nor identity can encapsulate the notion of belonging. Belonging is where the sociology of emotions interfaces with the sociology of power, where identification and participation collude, or are at least aspired to or yearned for (Yuval-Davis, 2003, p.4)

Whether individuals feel safe and experience a sense of belonging, depends largely on their relationships with their community. Social networks anchor people's rights to find solidarity, or practise their cultures. This positions sexual rights struggles as struggles for *recognition* (in contrast to struggles for *equity* and *redistribution*) that are deeply imbricated with rights to dignity, and rights to public representation. Having a 'sexual orientation' clause in the Bill of Rights is a significant step for people identifying as lesbians and gays in South Africa towards defining a sexual citizenship which affirms (certain forms of) sexual diversity, and can begin to shape their sense of belonging.

Sexualities Politicized

> The realm of sexuality also has its own internal politics, inequities, and modes of oppression. As with other aspects of human behaviour, the concrete institutional forms of sexuality at any given time and place are products of human activity. They are imbued with conflicts of interests and political maneuver, both deliberate and incidental. In that sense, sex is always political. But there are also historical periods in which

sexuality is more sharply contested and more overtly politicized. In such periods, the domain of erotic life is, in effect, renegotiated (Rubin, 1999, p.143).

The political regulation of sexuality in Western societies was for centuries dominated by Christian interpretations of sex as inherently sinful, but that it was necessary for procreation within marriage. Erotic sex[9] became one of the boundaries of 'othering' in a hierarchical system of sexual value ranging from marital, reproductive heterosexuals (with the man on top) to homosexuals, polygamists and sex workers. Clearly these hierarchies are ordered differently depending on the time and the place. In many African cultures polygyny would fall closer to the centre than in the West, but in either cultures polyandry is likely to reside on the outer margins (Nelson, 1987, p.233).[10] The further people fall from the centre in this range of hierarchies, the more the individuals will be stigmatized: criminalized, medicalized, and demonized. Those whose sexual behaviour is closer to the centre will be rewarded with 'sanity, reason, respectability, legality, social and physical mobility, institutional support and material benefit' (Rubin, 1999, p.151).

In South Africa these hierarchies are also intersected with the hierarchies of value that are inscribed in racialization, sex-gender, nationality, ethnicity, religious chauvinism, age, physical or mental abilities etc. The transition to democracy and the Equality Clause heralded a major shifting of several boundaries around sexuality, many of which have been solidified through legislation during the last ten years, some which have remained the same as during apartheid, and some which are on the transformation agenda – of government institutions as well as social movements.

What is inescapable when dealing with sexual politics is how attempts at social regulation are inscribed on the human body, and play into gender ideologies of feminization in citizenship: 'particular, embodied, rooted in nature, emotional, irrational, subject to desire and passion' (Lister, 2003, p.71) etc. Foucault (1998) claims that sex is a political issue, because politics is about controlling life, and sex is about life.

> The 'right' to life, to one's body, to health, to happiness, to the satisfaction of needs, and beyond all the oppressions or 'alienations', the 'right' to rediscover what one is and all that one can be, this 'right' – which the classical juridical system was incapable of comprehending ... (p.145).

In this intersection between society and the individual 'body as social', oppression is written onto the body as experiences of objectification and 'othering', and forms the basis also for a collective mobilization for rights. The purpose of 'othering' is to dominate and exploit, and experiences within the categories of difference are co-constituent i.e. the oppressions of gender, class, race etc. should be treated as inter-related realities (Lerner, 1997, p.194).

> Gender, race, ethnicity and class are processes through which hierarchical relations are created and maintained in such a way as to give *some men* power and privilege over *other men* and *over women* by their control of material resources, sexual and reproductive services, education and knowledge. Such control over others is maintained by a complex weave of social relations among dependent groups, which offers each

group some advantages over other groups, sufficient to keep each group within the dominance system subordinate to the elite (Lerner, 1997, p.196, author's emphasis).

The categorization of difference 'imposes an altered reality and a different historical experience upon the person so designated', for example '"race", a social construct, exists on three different levels: (1) as a tool for dominance' – institutionalized racism '(2) as an historic experience' – experiential racism and '(3) as a distinguishing marker for the oppressed group' – resistance formation (Lerner, 1997, p.189). It is around these 'markers of difference' that gender and sexuality groups have mobilized around *identity* for sexual rights.[11] Through sharing experiences of objectification, people come to an understanding of common identity, and move to political action.[12]

Context – A Long History of 'Othering'

By the last decade of the twentieth century, South Africa had experienced more than 300 years of colonization and more than a hundred years of political organization and struggle by Africans (and political allies from other races) for equitable political representation in the land of their birth. By the time the non-racial liberation struggle had succeeded in bringing about a negotiated settlement in 1994, a dominant ethos of Eurocentric whiteness was firmly embedded within all the economic, political and social institutions.

The rights discourse which informed the Constitution had already been encoded in the Freedom Charter of 1955, reflecting a mixture of Western liberal democratic tenets (UN Universal Declaration of Human Rights, 1948) and some socialist economic principles.[13] It was a document which became a symbol for the 'will of the people', a rhetorical vision which subsequently became the cornerstone of South Africa's Constitution and Bill of Rights in 1996. The profound moral implications of 'people injured' inherent in the anti-apartheid struggle had succeeded in mobilizing people around the globe.

> The wellspring of cohesion, however, is the overwhelming sense of injury suffered by all as a result of one small group cruelly oppressing an undeserving majority (Steyn, Grant and Van Zyl, 2001, p.23).

Not only political, but many varieties of social movements supporting human rights had come out in support of The Struggle, including Western lesbian and gay organizations. In South Africa, the negotiations provided a unique historical moment for lesbian and gay organizations to seize the opportunity for the inclusion of 'sexual orientation' in the Equality Clause in the Bill or Rights.

During the 1980s, two non-racial organizations aligned with the anti-apartheid movement emerged in Cape Town and the Witwatersrand – Gays and Lesbians of the Witwatersrand (GLOW) and Organisation of Lesbian and Gay Activists (OLGA). During the period of negotiations before the drafting of the Constitution, these organizations used the irrefutable argument that human rights were indivisible, and through sophisticated lobbying succeeded in having the sexual orientation clause included in the interim constitution.

> Several minority political parties and right-wing religious groupings opposed the inclusion of the equality clause and began mobilizing for its removal from the final constitution. Gay activists responded by forming the National Coalition of Gay and Lesbian Equality (NGCLE) in late 1994 at a conference where 41 gay organizations from across South Africa were represented. The coalition's mandate and the basis for its political platform was to secure the equality clause (Jara and Lapinsky, 1998, p.52).

The coming out of several prominent anti-apartheid activists and their involvement in progressive gay organizations (OLGA and GLOW), together with the ANC's commitment to human rights and a constitutional democracy, led to the clause being included in the Bill of Rights. Women's organizations similarly had mobilized to ensure that gender equity would be formalized in the Constitution.

The Bill of Rights, and specifically the Equality Clause as a whole, emerged as a result of activism in the political movements (Hassim, 1999, p.6). The ongoing negotiation of the definition of those rights has continued mainly in a process of rhetorical struggles in the courts, and particularly the Constitutional Court. The fact that they are enshrined in the Constitution means that the terrain of struggle for rights has moved largely from the political organizations and movements to legal subjects.[14] Here equitable access[15] is governed not only by the inertia of hegemonic privilege and power which existed previously, but also by the emerging hegemony of 'power in the making' of states in transition.

Liberation struggles throughout the latter half of the twentieth century in Africa and elsewhere had the effect of massive mobilization of colonized and disenfranchised people into struggle movements which did not necessarily dissolve post-colonization. Though many activists were taken up in the new government, others are still active within other structures such as NGOs. The period of transition has been marked by competing struggles for hegemonic terrain.[16]

Comaroff (2001) discusses how the legacy of the colonial state in Africa resulted in 'alternative modernities' – competing modalities of 'governmentality, legality, materiality, and civility'.

> The two images of nationhood and political order – one based on the liberal ethos of universal human rights, of free, autonomous citizenship, of individual entitlement; the other assertive of group rights, of ethnic sovereignty, of primordial cultural connection – are, more than ever before arraigned against each other in struggles for the determination of the continuing present and millennial future of many postcolonies (p.64).

In Europe, Northern America and Australia lesbians and gay men had mobilized around homosexual identities to address the criminalization, medicalization and demonization of homosexuality (Van Zyl et al., 1999, p.43). Both political and cultural movements arose to fight for equal rights on a variety of bases – identities, conduct, recognition of relationships – which though contentious, have slowly and unevenly been recognized and incorporated into legislation (Richardson, 2000a, p.268). The lesbian and gay organizations in South Africa that attained public visibility since the 1960s until democratization, had predominantly male, white memberships, and though the Coalition now covers 'various class, race and gender groups ... [a]ffluent, white gay men are still ... the most influential, even if they are not in the majority' (Jara and Lapinsky, 1998, p.53). Therefore, if one chose, it would not be difficult to see the Coalition as representing sectional interests, and to equate lesbian and gay organizations with whiteness, as has happened in Zimbabwe and Namibia. Post-colonial states in Southern Africa are struggling to displace the centrality of white (masculine) Eurocentrism through nationalist discourses that attempt to reassert the rhetorical terrain of (masculine-defined) culture in Africa (Zegeye, 2001, p.3).

The Equality Clause

South Africa's transition to democracy provided a unique historical opportunity for marginalized groups to be recognized under the new Constitution. Political organizations had to act strategically and speedily. Women's organizations, lesbian and gay organizations and disabled people's organizations amongst others seized the moment to have their rights formalized in the Equality Clause in the Bill of Rights.

> (3) The state may not unfairly discriminate directly or indirectly against anyone on any one or more grounds, including race, gender, sex, pregnancy, marital status, ethnic or social origin, colour, sexual orientation, age, disability, religion, conscience, belief, culture, language and birth.

> (4) No person may unfairly discriminate directly or indirectly against anyone on one or more grounds in terms of subsection (3). National legislation must be enacted to prevent or prohibit unfair discrimination (Chapter 2, s 9, Bill of Rights).

Many of the categories listed above can be problematized, but as a broad collection they represent many of the concepts that have formed the basis of critiques about exclusions in existing interpretations of citizenship in modern democracies: five out of the sixteen are related to gender and sexuality, and six link to racialization. Hence, it could be argued that the Equality Clause in the South African Constitution represents a quantum leap in formal rights for previously excluded groups.

Sexual Rights

Whether one agrees with the conflation of gender and sexuality when Scott says '[s]exuality is to feminism what work is to Marxism: that which is most one's own, yet most taken away' (1999, p.60), sexual rights campaigns have centred sexual objectification as one of the primary sites for the subjection of women.

Sexuality first entered the international human rights discourse in 1993, when the women's lobby at the World Conference on Human Rights in Vienna tabled a 'Declaration and Programme of Action' for states to eliminate 'gender-based violence and all forms of sexual harassment and exploitation' (Petchesky, 2000, p.83). Later that year the UN General Assembly passed a Declaration on the Elimination of Violence Against Women, including 'physical, sexual and psychological violence against women' (Petchesky, 2000, p.83). The next year

(1994), at the International Conference for Population and Development (ICPD) sexuality was framed for the first time in a positive light, though incipient battle lines were also being drawn between fundamentalist religious and progressive (feminist) ideologies, which carried over into subsequent international arenas. Though issues of sexuality had to be acknowledged, undoubtedly due to the lobbies concerned with the consequences of the HIV/AIDS pandemic and the women's lobbies, the struggle over the rhetoric had only just begun. Neither at Cairo, nor subsequently at the Fourth World Women's Conference at Beijing in 1995, was 'freedom of sexual expression and orientation' affirmed, though the principle of 'self-determination, safety, and satisfaction in sexual life' was not limited to 'heterosexuals, married couples and adults' (Petchesky, 2000, p.84).

At Beijing a 'concerted media campaign' by the Vatican-led alliance set out to vilify concepts like 'reproductive and sexual rights' and 'diverse family forms' (even 'gender') through linking them to 'homosexuality, lesbianism, sexual relationships outside marriage, paedophilia, prostitution, incest and adultery' as well as blaming homosexuals for spreading HIV/AIDS.[17] This backlash from a patriarchal 'sex-phobic right wing' won against thousands of women and women's groups from more than sixty countries around the world who had signed a petition asking member states

> to recognise the right to determine one's sexual identity; the right to control one's own body, particularly in establishing intimate relationships; and the right to choose if, when, and with whom to bear or raise children as fundamental components of the human rights of all women regardless of their sexual orientation (Petchesky, 2000, p.88).

Though the assertion of positive rights for women continues to remain elusive in international human rights instruments, there have been many gains worldwide around *formalizing* negative rights (protections against violence and abuse). But Petchesky (2000) maintains that a principle of sexual rights has been entered into the language of women's human rights.

> This ethics postulates not only that women must be free from abuse and violation of their bodies (including their fertility and sexuality), but also that they must be treated as principal actors and decision makers, as the ends and not the means of population, health, and development programs. Moreover, through this ethics, this principle applies not only to states and their agents but to every level where power operates – in the home, the clinic, the workplace, the church, synagogue, or mosque, and the community (p.89).

She argues that the success in implementing negative rights (protection) around 'the worst horrors', derive from the positioning of women as victims in this paradigm, mirroring 'fundamental, patriarchal images of women as weak and vulnerable' (Petchesky, 2000, p.90). Framing sexual rights in positive terms would require

> two integral and interlocked components: a set of *ethical principles* (expressing the substance or ultimate ends, of sexual rights), and a wide range of *enabling conditions* without which those ends could not be achieved (Petchesky, 2000, p.91, emphasis in original).

She lists five ethical principles:

1. sexual diversity (diverse types of sexual expression – 'multisexualism'
2. habitational diversity (diverse family forms)
3. health (including sexual health)
4. decision-making autonomy
5. gender equality.

The South African Constitution operates as a powerful *enabling tool* even though it does not contain all these rights in the same formulations: sexual and habitational diversity could be contained within the 'sexual orientation' phrase; gender is contained by the Equality Clause (chapter 2, s 9); health is covered specifically by section 27 of the Bill of Rights; and decision-making autonomy could be inferred in a number of sections, especially those relating to 'freedoms'.

But these terms are rhetorical, and caught in the hegemonic struggle of the 'power to define'. Manicom (2001) problematizes the terms and processes by which 'gender' has been normalized in government discourses, questioning the 'levels of violence against and poverty amongst, particularly, African women' (pp.17-18). She concludes that government discourses on 'gender' should be contested, and that gender politics should be interrogated within the 'complex ... national, regional, global, racialised and class agendas' (Manicom, 2001, p.18).[18]

Though the first steps have been won through the enshrining of sexual rights in the Constitution, the struggle is far from over. The actual articulation of those rights still depends on positionality, agency, and the manner in which those rights are interpreted, negotiated and *implemented* or *practised* within the institutions of governance.

Contested Definitions and Identifications

In South Africa, the apartheid government imposed ethnicity from above through legislation and other sanctions, distorting all constituents of identity except race and ethnicity. The anti-apartheid struggle facilitated the formation of an identity unified around opposition to apartheid in

> ... a common assertion of non-racialism and anti-racism. To a certain extent it also unified South Africans in anti-colonialism, and perhaps a common 'Africanness'. The varied social and political movements that participated in the anti-apartheid struggle created a new identity by ... undermining ... notions of whiteness ... The radical inclusive definition of identity created by these movements formed the basis for many citizen-based checks on governmental authority in the new democratic dispensation (Zegeye, 2001, p.4).

The same dynamics of a broad – even internationalized – unifying rhetoric of struggle did not occur in the liberation struggles of Zimbabwe and Namibia. Hoad (1998) discusses how '[t]he anti-colonialist and nationalist discourse of the post-colonial ruling elites of Zimbabwe, Namibia and Swaziland contain an entrenched resistance to emerging gay and lesbian identities in their countries' (p.33). He analyses their positioning as straddling the paradox of being at once 'the vehicle for economic and cultural progress – as the agent of modernity', and 'custodian' of '(an imagined) pre-colonial past … the repository of tradition', which is characterized as 'monolithic and homophobic', and where homosexuality is seen as 'un-African', a 'Western decadent import' (Hoad, 1998, pp.33, 34). Phillips (2003) shows how criminalization of homosexuality in Zimbabwe was part of the colonial 'civilizing' mission – where discourses of sexuality were linked to sin and repression of desire, 'rather than the prioritizing of procreation and the making of social alliances' (p.164-165). To the extent that Western imperialism is responsible for a great deal of cultural imports, (including the monogamous heterosexual nuclear family!), (homo)sexual identities in post-colonial Southern Africa have distinct histories which are deeply interwoven with whiteness, racial identities and post-colonial nationalisms (Phillips, 2003; Hoad, 1998).[19] Though there is extensive documentation of same-sex sexual *practices* and *behaviours* in Africa pre-colonization,[20] *homosexual identity* as a distinct sexual category only emerged during and after colonization, much as it has been shown to have emerged historically in the West.[21] These have been met with increased homophobia, and the accusation of homosexuality as 'un-African' has amplified. Reddy (2001) characterizes it as struggles for traditional patriarchal hegemonic constructions of masculinity and femininity (p.83), simultaneously pointing out that '[r]espect for homosexuals is regarded as a "litmus test" for human rights in … democratic societies' (p.84). Ironically, given the wide range of *same-sex sexual behaviours* of indigenous Africans, it may equally be argued that *homophobia* is un-African and a Western import of 'colonial repression' (Reddy, 2001, p.83).

That still leaves the problem of identification – only those who 'come out' and identify as homosexual, could lay claim to the rights under the 'sexual orientation' sub-section. Patton (1999) quotes Zulu gay activist Machela about male-male sex structure that is 'part of a social/paramilitary bond of serious dimensions but is not considered "homosexuality"' (p.399). Speaking about 'widespread' female-female 'normative erotic relationships among Basotho women … (including cunnilingus) was not defined as sexual'. The researcher Kendall (quoted in Cock, 2003) found that the social category 'lesbian' was 'linguistically inconceivable' in Sesotho, since sex itself was not possible without a 'koai' (penis) (p.42). It is understood that identities are

> … open-ended, fluid and constantly in a process of being constructed and reconstructed as the subject moves from one social situation to another, resulting in a self that is highly fragmented and context-dependent … conflicting racial, ethnic, gender, class, sexual, religious and national identities are a reality. Hence members of a particular group do not all have the same concerns and viewpoints (Zegeye, 2001, p.1).

Given the Western origins of the sexual orientation clause, the struggles around identity are more likely to fall on the shoulders of those 'lesbians' and 'gay' men who seek an Africanized identity, and who are (still) marginalized by class, gender and race. What the clause has provided is a public 'space' where alternative interpretations of identities, interests and needs may be formulated.

State Regulation

> The concept of gender within governance discourses is implicitly hetero-normative and is constructed as distinct and separate from other axes of difference (Manicom, 2001, p.10).

The sexual citizen is written into the Bill of Rights in the language of anti-'discrimination', a signifier of historical 'difference' and marginalization. Gender is being inscribed through 'gender mainstreaming' in governance, and a tendency towards re-essentializing homosexuality. The Coalition strategically argued that 'sexual orientation is immutable – that the individual cannot change it' (cited in Cock, 2003, p.38). This strategy worked as the clause was accepted by some conservative political parties who could not argue for discrimination against a 'natural group' (SALRC, 2003a, p.43). Sexual citizens had been subject to different forms of social control in the past, mainly ranged along the 'hierarchy of sexual values' set out above. Through the contribution of strategic alliances like the Women's National Coalition and the National Coalition for Gay and Lesbian Equality, those boundaries have shifted during the process of transformation. The present nation-state is tasked with giving form to the rhetoric in the Constitution.

> Policy and administrative discourses require explicit and bounded categories; they cannot entertain nuance or instability ... they might bear little resemblance to the categories of identity that emerge from lives and meaning systems of different sectors of the population. The more extensive the institutionalisation of particular categories, the more difficult it is to 'keep difference alive' and to challenge the inevitable exclusions and misrepresentation that are effected by the designations (Manicom, 2001, p.12).

In the last eight years, many legislative remedies have been enacted to ensure compliance with the Equality Clause in the Constitution – some through new legislation, some through amendments or re-definition, and some through challenges in the courts. Below, I discuss the significant ones pertaining to sexual rights.

Sexual Citizenship in Action for Lesbian and Gay South Africans

Sexual rights fall into and across various arenas, interdependent, and implicated in each other – deriving meaning and value from each other in a common system of signification historically rooted in gender identifications and heteronormativity. The judicial transformations that are taking place have the power to disturb these hegemonies by re-positioning the historical 'other', or by consolidating old positionalities. The arenas which fall under the broad definition of sexual citizenship concern: gender based violence, reproductive rights, alternative families (habitational diversity), sexual orientation, sex work and public representations of alternative sexualities. However, due to lack of space, I do not discuss the last two, and only discuss the other arenas in so far as they pertain to lesbians and gay men.

Gender-based Violence

Sexual violence against women has been theorized as political violence by numerous authors (Brownmiller, 1976; Schwendinger and Schwendinger, 1983; Van Zyl, 1991, pp.66-77; Du Toit, in this collection). Muthien and Combrink (forthcoming 2003) contextualize it within the broad field of 'peace and security studies', and contrast hierarchical societies with partnership-based ones. In keeping with many modern democracies, South Africa has instituted various laws relating to gender based violence. The legislation relates to individual citizens' negative sexual rights, i.e. the protection of rights against sexual assault or abuse. Implicit is the notion of women as victims, and the masculinist elision, victims as feminine.

Though the South African state is one of the most important agents of change because it is 'both the result of the political transition and the catalyst and motor of transition' (Morrell, 2001, pp.20-21), it is also implicated in maintaining and reproducing the 'gender order'. Gender based violence is consequently a crucial category of analysis in current sexual citizenship as the extent and degree in South Africa (and Africa) of gender based violence suggests that it is systemic of our times[22] – post-coloniality, nationalisms and identities, culture etc. Bennett (2001) despairs when she contemplates

> 'finding the ears' to understand violence against African-based women. The prevalence of this violence, and the almost infinite variety of the forms of abuse to which survivors attest, suggest a level of gender-based hostility that is terrifying (p.88).

Other forms of gender based violence involve assaults against lesbians and gays (as part of 'hate' crimes) as well as domestic violence within same-sex relationships, which usually remain invisible under the cloak of heteronormativity that pervades gender based violence work. The need for disaggregation is apparent firstly because homosexuals are positioned differently in their communities, and may experience violence purely on the grounds of their alternative sexuality (Kwesi and Webster, 1997, p.91), but homophobia also means that avenues available to heterosexual women may not be available to them (Moothoo-Padayachie, 2004, p.81). The experiences of lesbians and gay men also need to be considered separately (see Herek and Berrill, 1992) as they are likely to be victimized according to their gendered positionality. Lesbians are raped by men who see their sexuality as a 'challenge to their manhood' and 'undermin[ing] of the established order of male dominance' (Kwesi and Webster, 1997, p.93). Gay men are frequently singled out as the most visible group for homophobic attacks in African nationalist discourses (Reddy, 2001, pp.84-85), and gay-bashing is well-documented in military institutions (see Conway in this collection and Van Zyl et al. 1999).

A major exacerbating factor in sexual offences relates to HIV infection. Due to cooperation between an active civil society sector and the government, over the last decade substantive formal reforms have been introduced in the judicial system in relation to gender based violence. But until processes can be found for transforming deep-rooted social attitudes and beliefs on the ground, most gender-based violence advocacy efforts will be directed at the justice system – law reform, law enforcement and victim support. But the victim-supportive approach will tend to reinforce historical gendered positionings of women and children as victims in need of protection, and men as 'unmasculine' when they are sexually victimized. The formal re-definition of the rape law as gender-neutral legislation on the one hand obscures the actual power dynamics of rape, and could reinforce the individualization of a political phenomenon, but on the other hand makes the social construction of gender violence visible by moving it out of biological essentialism. Therefore the continued participation of civil society organizations is crucial for ensuring a legal framework which upholds real equality and democracy (Samuel, 2001, pp.24-25).

Rights to Sexual and Reproductive Health

Subsuming sexual rights under reproductive rights perpetuates ideologies of heteronormativity that tend to essentialize women's reproductive roles and the sexual division of labour. Therefore, sexual and reproductive rights should be addressed as separate rights (Hlatshwayo and Klugman, 2001, p.15). Health has been a significant focus for discussions about sex and sexuality, especially in relation to HIV/AIDS[23] and gender-based violence. The basis for access to sexual rights for women is through control over their bodies and mobilization around health issues.

Health – AIDS Drugs In August 2003, after mass mobilization and several court cases, the South African parliament finally approved the roll-out of AIDS drugs to HIV-positive citizens through the health system, eighteen months later than promised. In December 2001 the Pretoria High Court ordered the government to provide anti-retrovirals (ARV) to all HIV-positive pregnant women after the Treatment Action Campaign (TAC) took them to court arguing that it was their constitutional right to health care. In April 2002, the Constitutional Court confirmed the High Court's decision and the government agreed to provide ARV as prophylaxis to survivors of rape and sexual assault (IRIN, www.irinnews.org/AIDSreport.asp?ReportID=2401&SelectRegion=Southern_Afri ca, accessed 7 October 2003). This process revealed the weakness in an enabling tool on its own – the Constitution. It was the mobilization of the TAC and the sustained and combined pressure by NGOs, international donors, some provincial governments and media criticism that pushed the government to fulfil its obligation to citizens as ordered by the courts. This emphasizes the importance of citizens' agency in accessing and claiming their rights.

Women's Control of Fertility Patriarchal backlashes against 'pro-choice' supporters were defeated in the Constitutional Court, but women's movements supporting women's autonomy in controlling their own fertility will need to continue mobilizing around the issue (Everatt and Budlender, 1999). Single women's and lesbians' access to sperm donors and *in vitro* fertilization was incorporated   in   the   legislation   in   1997   (Behind   the   mask,

www.mask.org.za/SECTIONS/AfricaPerCountry/ABC/south%20africa/south%20a
frica_015.htm. accessed 13 October 2003). It formally increases women's control
over their own fertility (those who can afford it), and potentially undermines
patriarchal ideologies of 'women as men's property'. The arenas of sexual and
reproductive autonomy for women are where patriarchal backlashes are most
evident, as they threaten to subvert the foundations of patriarchal control over
women.

In the international arenas conflicts around sexual rights have crystallized
around homosexuality and the rights to choose abortions, with right wing
American groups forming an 'unholy alliance' with fundamentalist African groups
(Haffajee, 2000,
http://www2.womensnet.org.za/beijing5/news1/show.cfm?news1_id=60).[24]   By
contrast, Amanitare – African Partnership for Sexual and Reproductive Health and
Rights of Women and Girls – was formally launched in Uganda in February 2000,
and articulates three fundamental principles and core values to achieving

> women's and girls' sexual and reproductive health rights in Africa. These are: the rights
> of all women and girls, regardless of citizenship, class, age, culture, religion, marital
> status, ethnic identity, sexual orientation and physical and mental ability, to:
> * Bodily integrity and sexual autonomy;
> * Sexual enjoyment and healthy reproduction;
> * Protection from the threat of death or disease as a result of their reproductive
>   functions, and to freedom from coercion, violence or punishment as a means of
>   controlling sexuality and fertility (http://www.amanitare.org/home2.html, accessed
>   27 September 2003).

Around these principles, core values affirming that 'every woman is an
individual who is entitled to enjoy full sexual and reproductive health and rights'
confirm positive sexual autonomy for all women in Africa.[25]

Domestic Partnerships

Discussion Paper 104, Project 118: Domestic Partnerships The potentially most
radical and transformative legislation to erode gender and heteronormative
ideologies is in the process of formulation at the moment (October 2003). The
South African Law Reform Commission's (SALRC) Discussion Paper (2003a) on
domestic partnerships formulates the arguments and ethical base for a proposed
Bill on domestic partnerships. Citing many reasons for, and instances of people
living in domestic partnerships ranging from economic conditions to legal reasons
to cultural choices, it is argued that the law can no longer ignore these relationships
(SALRC, 2003a, p.17). The Equality Clause in particular is cited as a motivation
for 'the development of family law towards a more inclusive and pluralistic
system' (SALRC, 2003a, p.44), highlighting the 'marital status' and 'sexual
orientation' aspects. The areas of legal concern that are singled out are: common
home and other property; maintenance; business interests; succession/inheritance;
insurance; insolvency; employment benefits (health care, housing, pension);
immigration and nationality; adoption and taxation. After considering the multi-

cultural context of South Africa as a post-colonial country trying to synthesize African and Western legal models, the Commission opts for a differentiated approach rather than a single statutory measure. The principles are that same-sex relationships be acknowledged by law; both same-sex and opposite-sex partnerships may come into being as private contracts with the option of registration; that benefits will be limited in unregistered partnerships but the Court may under certain conditions be approached for an equitable distribution of assets if they end (SALRC, 2003a, pp.334-335). Four legal options are proposed: marriage for same-sex couples; civil unions either for same-sex couples only, or for same-sex as well as opposite-sex couples; registered and unregistered domestic partnerships for same-sex or opposite-sex partners (pp.vii-xiv). Various combinations are discussed, and in the four proposed Bills the details for each are set out (SALRC, 2003a, pp.341-424).

These proposals profoundly affect values underpinning the ideologies of the patriarchal nuclear family: they make the economic dynamics of interdependence in affective relationships visible, lift out the assumptions of sex and sexuality, and put in place tools for attaining equity in intimate relationships. However, the notion of a 'partnership' consisting of a dyad has not been challenged in this set of proposals. But even this concept is decentred by other legislation regarding customary marriages (see endnote 10).

Sexual Orientation

The 'no discrimination against sexual orientation' section of the Equality Clause has resulted in a number of court cases which ended up in the Constitutional Court. Findings related to this provision have had a 'chaining out', affecting many other existing laws, and lifting out the implicit heteronormativity in legislation enacted before the 1996 Constitution. The judgments are important because not only have they changed the formal rhetoric in legal discourse around intimate partnerships, but in many instances have ensured significant de facto economic rights or benefits for significant others. Some cases were brought by individuals, while others were brought by the National Coalition for Gay and Lesbian Equality (now known as the Lesbian and Gay Equality Project).

Adoption Du Toit and another v Minister of Welfare and Population Development concerns the rights of same-sex life partners to jointly adopt children. The Child Care Act confined joint adoption to married couples, so only one partner was granted custody and guardianship rights. Their concern was that if anything happened to the guardian, the other partner who had co-parented would not have legal standing, and argued that they were being discriminated against on the basis of sexual orientation and marital status, nor was it in the best interests of the child. The judgment in the Higher Court upheld their argument which was unanimously confirmed by the Constitutional Court (The Lesbian and Gay Equality Project, http://www.equality.co.za/archives/landmarks/, updated 30 July 2003).

However, most state social workers responsible for adoptions apply a hierarchy of allocations. Believing that 'matching' parents with children by race, culture etc.

is 'best' for the children, people like lesbians and single parents are told they will have a 'special needs adoption', an 'unmatched' adoption, i.e. they 'will get a black baby' (Hilton, 2003, p.3). This criterion for state adoptions resonates with ideologies of racism, homophobia and biological familialism, and it appears that if there were not the current (over)supply of possible orphans outstripping demand for adoption, non-heterosexual families would not be selected, regardless of their parenting potential. Therefore, though the legislative basis is in place, the practices in the adoption institutions need to be more inclusive and respectful of diversity.

Conditions of Employment Several cases were concluded which ruled that marital benefits be extended to encompass same-sex or partners who were not legally married. One which was ratified in the Constitutional Court, confirmed that judges' same-sex partners were entitled to the same benefits as spouses. The Equality Project successfully instituted an action against the Minister of Finance for not providing same-sex partners of state employees with equal pension benefits to those of surviving spouses. A lesbian policewoman won a case against the Minister of Safety and Security in relation to 'spousal' dependency and benefits, while the Pension Funds Adjudicator (PFA) in two cases awarded full benefits to surviving same-sex partners, without necessarily being so directed in the deceased's will (The Lesbian and Gay Equality Project,
 http://www.equality.co.za/archives/landmarks/, updated 30 July 2003).

Parenting Two women were both registered on their children's birth certificates – making them 'legitimate'. One woman gave birth to twins after receiving an egg from the other which was fertilized by an anonymous sperm donor (GenderNews, 2002,
http://www.communitylawcentre.org.za/gender/gendernews2002/2002_2_update.p hp, accessed 6 October 2003). This ruling exposes and deeply disturbs the links between biological reproduction and its links to social organization, thereby undermining heteronormativity.

Immigration In 1999 the Constitutional Court ruled that 'foreign partners of homosexual citizens must be afforded the same immigration rights as married couples' (Gay Rights Info, 2003, http://www.actwin.com/eatonohio/gay/sacc.html, accessed 9 August 2003). Increasingly international instruments on refugees recognize gays and lesbians as asylum applicants for persecution on the grounds of their sexual orientation, and in South Africa the Refugees Act (130 of 1998) explicitly refers to 'sexual orientation' as a 'social group' with potential refugee status (Magardie, 2003, p.81). However, general homophobia in society, as well as amongst personnel in the relevant authorities, often makes it difficult for homosexual asylum seekers to 'prove' that they are homosexual or that they were persecuted. Magardie (2003) cites a case where brothers who overheard an applicant mention that he was gay, victimized him and 'expelled him from the family home' (p.83).

Sodomy Old apartheid legislation that discriminated particularly against gay men remained in the common law and on the statute books until the Minister of Justice was challenged by the National Coalition for Gay and Lesbian Equality that it was an infringement of their rights to equality, dignity and privacy. The Constitutional Court confirmed a High Court decision in favour of removing sodomy as an offence in all relevant legislation, with one judge (Sachs J) emphasizing the centrality of human dignity for citizens, and the importance of the court to uphold 'acceptance of difference in an increasingly open and pluralistic South Africa' (Lesbian and Gay Equality Project, http://www.equality.co.za/archives/landmarks/, updated 30 July 2003). With the removal of this legislation, the dignity of erotic sexuality was affirmed.

One of the biggest problems for citizens in claiming rights in respect of the legislation, lies in social homophobia and the need to 'come out' (identify) as a homosexual to benefit by the legislation. In particular, the mounting hegemonic cry of homosexuality as 'un-African' is disturbing, as it resonates with the entrenched Western traditions of 'othering' – vide colonialism and its consequent establishing of binary hierarchies of domination and subordination. These ideologies are deeply antithetical to respect for human diversity.

South Africa is justifiably proud of being the only country in the world to include sexual orientation in its Bill of Rights. The domino effect of this provision on legislation has already resulted in deeply transformative rhetoric regarding the values underlying positive sexual rights.[26] It confirms sexual diversity and diverse types of sexual expression, it is an affirmation of erotic sex, alternative family forms and domestic arrangements, and through affirming people's dignity also extends their freedom of choice and autonomy. Even though many people may not identify as homosexual, the sexual orientation clause has reserved a public space for the expression of alternative cultures of sexuality. In particular, it has opened up a space where women may assert control over their bodies, though this space will have to be held against rising discourses of 'traditional' patriarchies (Rankhotha, 2004).

Conclusion

To confront the enormous task of transformation which has scarcely begun, we need to take cognizance of the gains and keep re-thinking and re-working the base. We need to understand the power of the state to be transformative, but also its need for rigidity.

In this chapter I examined the concept of sexual citizenship, and how positive sexual rights have been bolstered by the formal rhetoric of the South African Constitution, the courts and through legislation. Through processes of negotiating definitions of sexual rights, we are simultaneously reinterpreting cultural meanings and practices, thereby displacing traditional views of family, marriage and kinship (Richardson, 2000b, p.115). I have also shown how important ongoing mobilization is for changing historically entrenched discourses of 'othering' into discourses of diversity. Examining the influence of mobilization around gender and sexual rights in South Africa contributes to feminist critiques of Western constructions of citizenship: it shows how agency and participation (Lister, 2003, pp.26-27; Hassim, 1999, p.16) help to shape the rhetoric of democracy, and highlights the importance of bridging individualized notions of citizenship with acknowledgments of how rights are borne by groups. It also demonstrates how community mobilization has the power to gain hegemonic ascendancy and, as McEwan has noted (2001, p.56) help us see democracy as a process.

It is within the fluidity and vibrancy of social and political movements that tendencies towards homogenization of citizens, essentialization of issues and marginalizations can be problematized and continually reworked. It is through mobilization that political development of citizens as *agents* can occur, issues can be kept alive and rescued from institutionalization where they become 'the domain of technocrats and professionals' (Skinner, 2000, p.82). And yet, caution must be exercised so that those groupings and their own hegemonies are continually deconstructed and disaggregated – made transparent about who is representing whom. One must not lose sight of the positionalities of privilege which empower people to claim rights.

While women's rights have been formalized in myriads of ways, many black South African women are marginalized out of citizenship, suffering the worst burdens of poverty, in spite of the socio-economic rights written into the Constitution. They are also subject to the harshest gender violence, yet have least access to the institutional mechanisms that are supposed to protect them, and are most affected by HIV/AIDS. Access to justice and substantive equity has proved to be merely a dream for many South African women – citizenship remains confined to a vote.

To claim rights around sexual orientation, Westernized identities of homosexuality have to be adopted, while Africanized behaviours and practices continue to be marginalized and people ostracized from homophobic communities. Differing claims to sexuality such as bisexual, queer, transgendered have been marginalized from the margin. Hegemonies in construction around sexual rights in South Africa need to work the margins to bring sexuality out of the closet – public, erotic and political.

> Society does not simply construct sexuality, society is constructed sexually. Once this is accepted we cannot be content with images of moulding, regulating, controlling. We must think of sexuality in terms of historically dynamic patternings of practice and relationship, which have considerable scope and power (Connell and Dowsett, 1999, p.190).

At the same time, the South African Constitution has shown itself as a powerful enabling tool. Once certain values have been affirmed in the discourse of citizenship, they generate other discourses, perpetuating those values in other loci through a rippling out of meanings. The 'sexual orientation' phrase has been a crucial seme[27] for decriminalizing the sexual activity of 'sodomy', for instigating a process where 'marriage' is being radically redefined, shifting concepts of sex from the biologism of reproduction to include sex for pleasure, challenging the sexual hierarchies of intimate relationships, and reformulating the heteronormativity in traditional family forms. People with HIV/AIDS can finally access treatment – a significant gain in socio-economic rights.

By participating in the discourses of governance, as pressure groups or through 'mainstreaming', definitions are constantly being renegotiated. Through these synthesizing processes, the chance of developing a 'human rights culture' in the future becomes a possibility. It requires a notion of *agency* that is at once personal, individual, but also collective.

> Cultures are fluid and change over time and they are constructed to some extent by persons (mostly men) in social power, such as tribal chiefs. In fact, the assertion that 'human rights' and 'equality' are western concepts is somewhat complicated by the history of colonialism and slavery, where human rights were denied to the Other, for example women, black people and anyone else perceived to be different (Bohler-Muller, 2002, p.89).

In this chapter I have shown how mobilization by the 'other' has power to influence the definitions of values that are articulated through enabling tools like the Constitution. It contributes to the project of feminist citizenship, stressing the need to eschew biological determinism, to put men's hidden history into gender politics and to reinscribe the body as a sexual agent into politics. It shows how sexual citizenship is fuller than status, membership, rights and duties, nor can it simply be equated with identities, that it is about emotions and the politics of belonging (Yuval-Davis, 2003), where a person can feel safe and secure and powerful in her body. Sexual citizenship provides the nexus where everyday emotions – fears, hopes, love – enter the political arena.

Notes

1. I am very grateful to Oliver Phillips for reading and commenting on this chapter.
2. The *definition* of citizenship must also be seen as a 'contextualised concept'. 'Vocabularies of citizenship' and their meanings vary according to social, political and cultural context and reflect different historical legacies. Citizenship is expressed in 'spaces and places' (Siim quoted in Lister, 2003, p.3).
3. The ambiguity in the term 'sex' reveals its ideological heteronormativity, where the biological distinction between female and male is also used to refer to sexual intercourse. Mostly I will use 'sexual' to refer to how the cultural construction (both *constructing* and *constructed*) of sexuality is written into a person's body – knowing that these constructions are fluid – never totally rigid, but nor are they entirely open.
4. The argument of universalization has also arisen in feminism where the category 'woman' has often concealed racial, sexual and other differences (Richardson, 2000b, p.113).
5. The meaning I ascribe to 'gender' is not reducible to the category 'woman', but recognizes it as 'a system' of hierarchical social 'relationships that may include sex (male/female), but is not directly determined by sex nor directly determining of sexuality' (Scott, 1999. p.59).
6. The early Marxist-feminists, in particular Zillah Eisenstein, Heidi Hartmann, Ellen

Malos, Annette Kuhn and AnnMarie Wolpe, (to name but a few) politicized women's domestic and reproductive labour as 'work'.

7. See a discussion of how 'gender' has become a *floating signifier* (my terminology) in Manicom (2001, pp.6-21).

8. Some discourses of citizenship emerging from 'maternalism' have also shifted away from the biological essentialism by emphasising 'an ethic of care'. See Tronto, 1987 (cited in Lister, 2003, 102). It would also be seen as one of the elements of *ubuntu,* a basic tenet of communitarian African philosophy, which can be characterized as 'I am because we are' (Van Zyl, 2002, p.9).

9. I prefer to use 'erotic' as a term for sex-for-pleasure, as it does not signify as a binary to procreative sex. It implies that there is equity (e.g. through consent), unlike rape which is oppression. Vassi uses the term 'metasex' to cover everything that is not heterosexual intercourse for procreation (1997, p.71). Giddens invents the term 'plastic sexuality' which is 'decentred sexuality, freed from the needs of reproduction' (1992, p.2).

10. The Recognition of Customary Marriages Act 120 of 1998, recognizes the customary law 'traditionally observed among the indigenous African peoples of South Africa' (s 1.ii). Marriages by one person to more than one spouse is each regarded as a valid marriage (s 2 (3) & (4). In July 2003, after three years' deliberation, The South African Law Commission submitted a report for a draft Bill on the recognition of Muslim marriages to the Minister for Justice and Constitutional Development (SALRC, 2003b). Both pieces of legislation are aimed at ameliorating the position of women in customary marriages, but within the bounds of patriarchal hegemonies which support polygyny, but not polyandry. Buried in the gender-neutral terminology 'polygamy' used in the laws, is the assumption that men may have multiple wives, but a woman will not be entitled to have multiple husbands. The recognition of polygynous marriages radically decentres Western Judaeo-Christian notions of monogamy, while affirming values of African and Muslim traditional patriarchies. I have not come across texts which discuss 'polyandry' when referring to 'polygamy', revealing the universalized, male-centred construction of the term.

11. The boundaries between collectivities are often also exclusionary – for example, because many lesbian and gay movements did not easily accept other sex/gendered identifications, bisexual, transsexual and transgendered people cohered under the label 'queer'. Though boundaries clarify identities, they may perpetuate inequalities; and though coalescing boundaries might be strategic to overcome inequities, stigmatized groups may remain hidden through false generalization.

12. See Fester's chapter in this collection on the politicization of women in maternalist movements.

13. The Freedom Charter demanded a non-racial, democratic system of government, legal. social, economic equality and equal access to education for all. It affirmed that South Africa belonged to all its inhabitants, and urged for nationalization of national assets, and land redistribution (Davenport and Saunders, 2000, p.404).

14. A 'legal subject' includes individuals as well as various legal associations classified as 'juristic persons' such as certain organizations, churches, political parties etc.

15. See particularly Hassim (nationalism), Gouws (equity), McEwan (women's rights), Chirwa and Khosa (poverty) in this book for further elaborations on differential access by groups to claim rights.

16. For example, globalization and the government's GEAR (Growth, Employment and Redistribution) policy have resulted in a widening gap between the historical Struggle tripartite allies, the ANC (African National Congress), SACP (South African Communist Party) and Cosatu (Congress of South African Trade Unions). In a research paper on gender activism in SA in the 1980s, (forthcoming) I show how people are

'educated' into political activism and take it on board as part of their identity. Though many are now working in different milieus, they continue doing 'political' or human rights related work for equity – though many activists have been absorbed into the new government institutions, others are still 'struggling' around contentious issues such as poverty, HIV/AIDS, labour, land redistribution etc.

17. See Treichler (1999, pp.357-386), for an analysis of how Western medical discourse on AIDS perpetuates homophobia. Though she focuses on medicalization as the primary terrain for stigmatization, the mechanisms of signification in 'othering' could equally well be applied to fundamentalist religious discourses, i.e. demonization.

18. See also in this collection Manicom on women's political agency, and Gouws on gender mainstreaming.

19. Ideology is apparent not only by what is said, but also what is not said. Currently there is a tendency in the emerging discourses on African feminisms to return to the master (sic) narrative of an essentialized and naturalized heterosexuality which is *not spoken*, especially in discourses foregrounding maternalism and family.

20. See for example Amadiume (1987), Shepherd (1987), and Murray and Roscoe (cited in Cock, 2003, p.41) who show that same-sex intimate behaviours were traditionally practised in almost every African society.

21. Two of the most cited authors for the historicization of homosexuality in the West are Foucault (1992; 1998) and Weeks (1981; 1999).

22. Many examples of violence against women show its endemic nature in current South African society. See Goldblatt and Meintjes (1997, pp.7-18) for sexual violence and the Truth and Reconciliation Commission (TRC). More currently, Wood and Jewkes (2001) say that gender based violence is a 'common feature of young people's sexual relationships' (p.318) in a study in the Eastern Cape, which is supported by findings in other studies elsewhere.

23. See Meerkotter in this collection.

24. The American religious right and some African government representatives who oppose a move to enshrine gay rights in the conference outcome document claim that Western feminists are directing the discourse away from issues such as poverty, which are Third World women's 'real' concerns. Unfortunately these discourses are reminiscent of whiteness and Western tendencies to 'othering', dualism and oppression. Respect for diversity requires a decisive move away from these tendencies. Equally, discussions on poverty should not only focus on distribution (which keeps global economic power hierarchies intact), but on overcoming mechanisms of appropriation, especially as facilitated by globalization.

25. They are that sexual and reproductive rights are central to: the realization of women's Human Rights ...; [to] every aspect of women's and girls' lives ...; to economic development, human rights, the advancement of civil society, democracy and the rule of law; ... bodily integrity and autonomy in decisions concerning their sexuality and fertility; social, cultural and religious interpretations, practices and norms (including customary law) which impinge on the rights of women and girls to full citizenship; ... adequate, affordable, accessible, and quality reproductive health information and services that protect them from the threat of death or disease; ... laws and policies which undermine, constrain or allow for limitation and violation of sexual and reproductive rights; ...[women's] self determination and must be recognized as full citizens with guaranteed political and social participation and legal protection in all matters concerning their sexuality and reproduction.

26. By 10 September 2003, around 35 pieces of legislation had been changed since 1994 (Lesbian and Gay Equality Project, 2003, http://www.equality.org.za/archive/202/achievedsa.php, updated 10 September 2003).

27. A linguistic term signifying 'a unity of meaning' (Oxford University Press, 2002).

References

Amadiume, Ifi (1987), *Male Daughters, Female Husbands: Gender and Sex in an African Society*, Zed Books, London.

Amanitare (2000) 'Principles and core values', http://www.amanitare.org/home2.html, updated 3 July 2003, accessed 27 September 2003.

Agenda (2001), 'Interview: "Talking about feminism in Africa", Elaine Salo speaks to Prof. Amina Mama', in *Agenda*, No.50, pp.58-63.

Behind the mask, 'South Africa: legal and policy reform 1997 to 1999' (http://www.mask.org.za/SECTIONS/AfricaPerCountry/ABC/south%20africa/south%20africa_015.htm., accessed 13 October 2003.

Bennett, Jane (2001), '"Enough lip service!" Hearing post-colonial experience of heterosexual abuse, conflict and sex wars as a state concern', in *Agenda*, No.50, pp.88-96.

Bohler-Muller, Narnia (2002), 'Really listening? Women's voices and the ethic of care in post-colonial Africa', *Agenda*, No.54, pp.86-91.

Brownmiller, Susan (1976), *Against Our Will: Men, Women and Rape*, Pelican Books, Harmondsworth.

Carroll, Lewis (1946), *Alice's Adventures in Wonderland*, New York, Random House.

Cock, Jacklyn (2003), 'Engendering Gay and Lesbian Rights: The Equality Clause in the South African Constitution', in *Women's Studies International Forum*, Vol.26, No.1, pp.35-45.

Comaroff, John L. (2001), 'Reflections on the colonial state, in South Africa and elsewhere: factions, fragments, facts and fictions' in Abebe Zegeye (ed.), *Social Identities in the New South Africa: After Apartheid – Volume One*, Kwela Books, Cape Town and SA History Online, Maroelana.

Connell, Robert W. and Dowsett, Gary W. (1999), '"The Unclean Motion of the Generative Parts": Frameworks in Western Thought on Sexuality', in R. Parker and P. Aggleton (eds.), *Culture, Society and Sexuality: A Reader*, UCL Press, London, pp.179-196.

Cossman, Brenda (2002), 'Sexing Citizenship, Privatizing Sex', in *Citizenship Studies*, Vol.6, No.4, pp.283-506.

Davenport, Rodney and Saunders, Christopher (2000), *South Africa: A Modern History* (5th edn.), Macmillan Press, London and St Martin's Press, New York.

Everatt, David and Budlender, Debbie (1999), 'How many for and how many against: private and public debate on abortion', *Agenda*, No.40, pp.101-105.

Foucault, Michel (1992), *The Use of Pleasure: The History of Sexuality Volume 2 (L'Usage des plaisirs*, trans. Robert Hurley) Penguin, Harmondsworth.

Foucault, Michel (1998), *The Will to Knowledge: The History of Sexuality Volume 1 (La Volonté de savoir*, trans. Robert Hurley) Penguin, Harmondsworth.

Gay Rights Info (2003), 'South Africa Constitutional Court: Homosexual Issues', http://www.actwin.com/eatonohio/gay/sacc.html, updated 29 March 2003, accessed 9 August 2003.

Gender Update, (2002), 'Court recognises women as legal parents in landmark decision', compiled by Raygaanah Barday from http://www.sundaytimes.co.za/ 4 November 2002, http://www.communitylawcentre.org.za/gender/gendernews2002/2002_2_update.php, accessed 6 October 2003.

Giddens, Anthony (1992), *The Transformation of Intimacy: Sexuality, Love and Eroticism in Modern Societies*, Stanford University Press, Stanford, California.

Goldblatt, Beth and Meintjes, Sheila 'Dealing with the aftermath: sexual violence and the Truth and Reconciliation Commission" in *Agenda*, No.36, pp.7-18.

Gouws, Amanda (1999), 'Beyond equality and difference: the politics of women's citizenship', *Agenda* No.40, pp.54-58.

Haffajee, Ferial (2000), 'Beijing +5: Uneasy bedfellows fight sexual rights', 8 June 2000, http://www2.womensnet.org.za/beijing5/news1/show.cfm?news1_id=60, accessed 27 September 2003.

Hassim, Shireen (1999), 'From Presence to Power – Women's Citizenship in A New Democracy', *Agenda*, No.40, pp.6-17.

Herek, Gregory M. and Berrill, Kevin T. (eds.), (1992), *Hate Crimes: Confronting Violence Against Lesbians and Gay Men*, SAGE Publications, Newbury Park, London, New Delhi.

Hilton, Karin (2003), '"Alternative normalities": Interracial adoption in "alternative family" structures', unpublished essay, Institute for Intercultural and Diversity Studies of Southern Africa (iNCUDISA), University of Cape Town.

Hlatshwayo, Zanele and Klugman, Barbara (2001), 'A sexual rights approach', *Agenda*, No.47, pp.14-20.

Hoad, Neville (1998), 'Tradition, modernity and human rights: an interrogation of contemporary gay and lesbian rights' claims in Southern African nationalist discourses', in *The right to be: Sexuality and sexual rights in Southern Africa, Development Update*, Vol.2, No.2, Quarterly Journal of the South African National NGO Coalition and INTERFUND, Johannesburg, pp. 32–42.

IRIN PlusNews (2003), 'South Africa: Chronology of HIV/AIDS treatment access debate', 19 August 2003, UN Office for the Coordination of Humanitarian Affairs, http://www.irinnews.org/AIDSreport.asp?ReportID=2401&SelectRegion=Southern_Afr ica, accessed 7 October 2003.

Jara, Mazibuko and Lapinsky, Sheila (1998), 'Forging a representative gay liberation movement in South Africa', in *The right to be: Sexuality and sexual rights in Southern Africa, Development Update*, Vol.2, No.2, Quarterly Journal of the South African National NGO Coalition and INTERFUND, Johannesburg, pp. 44–57.

Kwesi, Busi and Webster, Naomi (1997), 'Black, lesbian and speaking out', in *Agenda*, No.36, pp.90-93.

Lerner, Gerda (1997), *Why History Matters*, Oxford University Press, New York and Oxford.

Lesbian and Gay Equality Project (The) (2003), 'Landmark cases archive', http://www.equality.co.za/archives/landmarks/, updated 30 July 2003, accessed 7 August 2003.

Lesbian and Gay Equality Project, (2003), 'Lesbian and Gay Equality in South Africa: What has been achieved?' http://www.equality.org.za/archive/202/achievedsa.php, updated 10 September 2003, accessed 8 October 2003.

Lister, Ruth (2003), *Citizenship: Feminist Perspectives* (2nd edn.), Palgrave Macmillan, Basingstoke and New York.

McEwan, Cheryl (2001), 'Gender and citizenship: learning from South Africa?' *Agenda*, No.47, pp.47-59.

Magardie, Sheldon (2003), '"Is the applicant really gay?" Legal responses to asylum claims based on persecution on account of sexual orientation', *Agenda*, No.55, pp.81-87.

Manicom, Linzi (2001), 'Globalising "gender" in – or as – governance? Questioning the terms of local translations', *Agenda*, No.48, pp.6-21.

Moothoo-Padayachie, Nitasha (2004), 'Lesbian violence explored', in *Agenda*, No.60, pp.81-86.

Morrell, Robert (2001) 'The Times of Change: Men and Masculinities in South Africa', in Robert Morrell (ed.), *Changing Men in Southern Africa*, University of Natal Press, Pietermaritzburg and Zed Books, London and New York, pp.3-37.

Morrell, Robert (ed.), (2001), *Changing Men in Southern Africa*, University of Natal Press, Pietermaritzburg and Zed Books, London and New York.

Muthien, Bernedette and Combrinck, Helene (forthcoming 2003) 'When Rights are Wronged: Gender-Based Violence & Human Rights in Africa', in M. Bahati Kuumba and Monica White (eds.), *Transnational Transgressions: African Women, Struggle and Transformation in Global Perspective*, Africa World Press, Inc./Red Sea Press, Inc. 24 pages.

Nelson, Nici (1987), '"Selling her kiosk": Kikuyu notions of sexuality and sex for sale in Mathare Valley, Kenya', in Pat Caplan (ed.), *The Cultural Construction of Sexuality*, Tavistock Publications, London and New York, pp.217-239.

Padgug, Robert A. (1999), in R. Parker and P. Aggleton (eds.), *Culture, Society and Sexuality: A Reader*, UCL Press, London, pp.15-28.

Parker, Richard, Barbosa, Regina Maria and Aggleton, Peter (2000), 'Introduction: Framing the Sexual Subject', in R. Parker, R.M. Barbosa and P. Aggleton (eds.), *Framing the Sexual Subject: The Politics of Gender, Sexuality, and Power*, Berkeley, University of California Press, pp.1-25.

Parker, R., Barbosa, R.M. and Aggleton, P. (eds.), (2000), *Framing the Sexual Subject: The Politics of Gender, Sexuality, and Power*, University of California Press, Berkeley.

Pateman, Carole (1989), *The Disorder of Women: Democracy, Feminism and Political Theory*, Cambridge, Polity Press.

Patton, Cindy (1999), 'Inventing "African AIDS"' in R. Parker and P. Aggleton (eds.), *Culture, Society and Sexuality: A Reader*, UCL Press, London, pp.387-404.

Petchesky, Rosalind P. (2000), 'Sexual Rights: Inventing a Concept, Mapping an International Practice', in R. Parker, R.M. Barbosa and P. Aggleton (eds.), *Framing the Sexual Subject: The Politics of Gender, Sexuality, and Power*, University of California Press, Berkeley, pp.81-98.

Phillips, Oliver (2003), 'Zimbabwean Law and the Production of a White Man's Disease', in Jeffrey Weeks, Janet Holland and Matthew Waites (eds.), *Sexualities and Society. A Reader*, Polity Press, Cambridge, pp.162-173.

Plummer, Ken (2003), 'Intimate Citizenship and the Culture of Sexual Story Telling' in Jeffrey Weeks, Janet Holland and Matthew Waites (eds.), *Sexualities and Society. A Reader*, Polity Press, Cambridge, pp.33-41.

Rankhotha, Charles Sylvester (2004), 'Do traditional values entrench male supremacy?' in *Agenda*, No.59, pp.80-89.

Reddy, Vasu (2001) 'Homophobia, human rights and gay and lesbian equality in Africa', in *Agenda*, No.50, pp.83-87.

Richardson, Diane (2000a), 'Claiming Citizenship? Sexuality, Citizenship and Lesbian/Feminist Theory', *Sexualities*, Vol.3(2), pp.255-272.

Richardson, Diane (2000b), *Rethinking Sexuality*, Sage Publications, London, Thousand Oaks and New Delhi.

Rubin, Gayle S. (1999), 'Thinking Sex: Notes for a Radical Theory of the Politics of Sexuality' in R. Parker and P. Aggleton (eds.), *Culture, Society and Sexuality: A Reader*, UCL Press, London, pp.143-178.

Samuel, Sharita (2001), 'Achieving equality – how far have women come?' in *Agenda*, No.47, pp.21-33.

Schwendinger, Julia R. and Schwendinger, Herman (1983), *Rape and Inequality*, SAGE Publications, Beverly Hills, London, New Delhi.

Scott, Joan Wallach (1999), 'Gender as a Useful Category of Historical Analysis' in R. Parker and P. Aggleton (eds.), *Culture, Society and Sexuality: A Reader*, UCL Press, London, p.75.

Shepherd, Gill (1987), 'Rank, gender, and homosexuality: Mombasa as a key to understanding sexual options' in Pat Caplan (ed.), *The Cultural Construction of Sexuality*, Tavistock Publications, London and New York, pp.240-270.

Skinner, Caroline (2000), 'South-feminist perspectives on gender justice and governance in Africa', *Agenda*, No.43, pp.79-83.

South African Law Reform Commission (SALRC) (2003a), Discussion Paper 103, Project 118. Domestic Partnerships Vol.1, South African Law Reform Commission, Pretoria.

South African Law Reform Commission (SALRC) (2003b), Media Statement by the South African Law Reform Commission Concerning its Investigation into Islamic Marriages and Related Matters (Project 59), http://www.law.wits.ac.za/salc/salc.html, accessed 7 October 2003.

Steyn, Melissa, Grant, Terri and Van Zyl, Mikki (2001), *THE END. Deferred: How fantasy themes shape experiences of return for 'The Struggle' exiles of South Africa*, Cape Town, iNCUDISA, UCT.

Treichler, Paula (1999), 'AIDS, Homophobia, and Biomedical Discourse: An Epidemic of Signification', in R. Parker and P. Aggleton (eds.), *Culture, Society and Sexuality: A Reader*, UCL Press, London.

Van Zyl, Mikki (1991), 'Invitation to Debate: Towards an explanation of violence against women', in *Agenda*, No.11, pp.66–76.

Van Zyl, Mikki, De Gruchy, Jeanelle, Lapinsky, Sheila, Lewin, Simon and Reid, Graeme (1999), *The aVersion Project: Human rights abuses of gays and lesbians in the South African Defence Force by health workers during the apartheid era*, Simply Said and Done, Cape Town.

Van Zyl, Mikki (2002), 'Peace in Africa', *Annual Report 2001*, Quaker Peace Centre, Cape Town, pp.5-9.

Van Zyl, Mikki (forthcoming 2004), 'Dis-Closure – Activists Remember Sexuality Struggles in Gender Organizations During the 1980s in Cape Town', in Neville Hoad, Karen Martin and Graeme Reid (eds.), *Where were you in the Eighties?*, Natal University Press, Durban, 20 pages.

Vassi, Marco (1997), 'Beyond Bisexuality' in Carol Queen and Lawrence Schimel (eds.), *PoMoSexuals*, Cleis Press, San Francisco, pp.70-75.

Weeks, Jeffrey (1981), *Sex, Politics and Society*, Longman, London and New York.

Weeks, Jeffrey (1998), 'The Sexual Citizen', *Theory, Culture and Society*, 15(3-4), pp.35-52.

Weeks, Jeffrey (1999), 'Discourse, Desire and Sexual Deviance: Some Problems in a History of Homosexuality', in R. Parker and P. Aggleton (eds.), *Culture, Society and Sexuality: A Reader*, UCL Press, London, pp.119-142.

Western Cape Network on Violence Against Women (2003), 'Submission to the Parliamentary Portfolio Committee on Justice and Constitutional Development, for the Sexual Offences Bill 2003', personal email 16 September 2003.

Wood, Katherine and Jewkes, Rachel (2001), '"Dangerous" Love: Reflections on Violence among Xhosa Township Youth', in Robert Morrell (ed.), *Changing Men in Southern Africa*, University of Natal Press, Pietermaritzburg and Zed Books, London and New York, pp.317–332.

Young, Iris M. (2000), *Inclusion and Democracy*, Oxford University Press, Oxford.

Yuval-Davis, Nira (2003), '"Human security" and the Gendered Politics of Belonging',
(forthcoming) as 'Transversal Politics and the situated imagination', *International
Feminist Journal of Politics*, Centre for the Study of Women and Gender, University of
Warwick, url:www2.2arwick.ac.uk/fac/soc/sociology/gender/events/symposium/yuval/,
last updated 9 May 2003, accessed 7 October 2003.
Yuval-Davis, Nira and Werbner, Pnina (eds.), (1999), *Women, Citizenship and Difference*,
Zed Press, London and New York.
Zegeye, Abebe (2001) 'General Introduction' in Abebe Zegeye (ed.), *Social Identities in the
New South Africa: After Apartheid – Volume One*, Kwela Books, Cape Town and SA
History Online, Maroelana.

Statute and Case References

Refugees Act, Act 130 of 1998.
South African Constitution, Act 108 of 1996.

Carmichele v Minister of Safety and Security and another 2001 (4) SA 938 (CC).
Du Toit and another v Minister of Welfare and Population Development and others 2002
(10) BCLR 1006 (CC).
J & B v Home Affairs.
Minister of Health and others v Treatment Action Campaign and others 2002 (5) SA 721
(CC); 2002 (10 BCLR 1033 (CC).
*National Coalition for Gay and Lesbian Equality (NCGLE) and another v Minister of
Justice and Others* 1999 (1) SA 6 (CC); 1998 (1) BCLR 1517 (CC).
*National Coalition for Gay and Lesbian Equality (NCGLE) and another v Minister of Home
Affairs and Others* 2000 (2) SA 1 (CC); 2000 (1) BCLR 39 (CC).
Satchwell v President of Republic of South Africa and another 2002 (6) SA 1 (CC); 2002 (9)
BCLR 986 (CC).

Chapter 11

A Phenomenology of Rape: Forging a New Vocabulary for Action

Louise du Toit

Introduction

South Africa's 'world record' rape rate relegates its women and children to second class citizenship. This degree of violence shows that South Africa is not yet the fully democratic society it hopes to become. Paradoxically, it is also true that the transition to democratic rule gave new scope for raising the problem of rape as a citizenship issue.[1] In this chapter a conceptual grid is placed on the phenomenon of rape assisting in the formulation of the values underlying rape, and the kinds of harm it inflicts. Although connotations of the term 'rape' implicitly contain a moral judgement of the action to which it refers, it is still necessary to spell out both what is wrong with rape and *what rape is*. In 'forging a new vocabulary' for rape in our own context, I will make clear the link between rape and citizenship. It will be argued that rape ought be framed as a citizenship issue, because of its political and public nature, in opposition to those in society who persist in trivializing rape on the assumption that it is personal and private. The understanding of rape as a 'private' event, is very often facilitated by our morally conservative societies where sexuality *as such* is often still regarded as both shameful and private. Part of what this chapter therefore illustrates is that sexuality and the ways in which it is played out are political issues. This would imply that rape lies in the extension of how we politically and publicly shape our sexual identities as women and as men.

Rape, according to my working definition, is any form of forced or coerced sex. By this I do not mean to imply that rape is not about power; the long-standing debate in feminist literature seems to assume that one must choose between an understanding of rape as either sexual or power abuse. This is a false dilemma; rape is the violent abuse of power in a sexual way. The fact that the violence takes a specific, namely sexual form, does not make it more private or less harmful than any other form of violation or attack. Rape is a matter of political and public concern, because politics is about who has power over whom, and rape (and its threat) is one of the multiple ways in which people with penises wield power over people without penises. Men humiliating other men through rape seem to simply transfer the logic of 'female rape' to that of 'male rape', where the male victim is humiliated precisely because he is being 'feminized' – treated like a woman. The rape of a woman is thus paradigmatic.

Below I list and discuss some of the specific harms, injuries or damages of rape and the impact of these harms on women's citizenship, through a 'close reading' or a 'phenomenological' analysis of the event that is rape. The use of the term 'phenomenology' implies here that the (inter-)subjective experience of rape rather than statistical or quantitative (i.e. 'objective' or 'external') data about rape will form the main focus of my concern here. The approach I follow in analysing rape will partly be based on Elaine Scarry's phenomenological analysis of torture (Scarry, 1985), implying that rape is akin to, and can be understood as analogous to torture.[2] Of course one can also point to many differences between these two phenomena, and they should be kept distinct in a conceptual sense. Nevertheless, *reading rape as torture* helps one understand at least some elements of rape better. One of the important analogies between rape and torture lies in the way in which the systematic instilling of fear or terror in a clearly defined section of the population translates into power-political gain for another section of the population. Women's and children's[3] realistic fears of sexual violence from men in general, helps to create and sustain a clear gender hierarchy *within* South African citizenship. The paradoxical nature of women's citizenship is a well-known theme within feminist scholarship internationally.[4] In South Africa, as elsewhere in the world, these well-documented formal problems surrounding women's full citizenship status are exacerbated by the *high levels of fear* women experience in their everyday lives. In South Africa, the more general 'African' or continent-wide disillusionment with formal liberation[5] takes various forms, but perhaps none so striking as the gap between women's formal citizenship status and gender equality on the one hand, and women's actual oppression on the other.

Men are by far the main perpetrators of both violent crime in general, and of rape in particular; the victims of rape are almost always female.[6] There is little or no distinction concerning the category of woman singled out for rape. It is not uncommon to hear of seventy-, eighty- and ninety-year-old women being raped, nor of infants and babies as young as a few months old being raped and sodomized. Women and children in this country are taught from early on not to trust anyone, especially not strange men. But the crisis in social trust affects more than just the horizontal relationships of citizens amongst themselves. The government's response to rape, and the actual rape statistics also ensure that women lose faith in the government's sincerity in taking rape seriously and protecting women against its lethal threat. Smith records the following events (2001, pp.284, 301-302):

- In December 1999, President Thabo Mbeki began querying rape statistics.
- In February 2000, the Minister of Safety and Security Steve Tshwete and Minister of Justice Penuell Maduna were interviewed by Bob Simons of CBS 60 Minutes. 'They jokingly asked Simons: "You have been here for more than twenty-six seconds. Have you seen anyone raped in that time?' in reference to a much-quoted statistic that a woman is raped in South Africa every 26 seconds.
- The Commissioner of Police, Jackie Selebi, told ABC's 20/20 in April 2000: 'Most South African women who report rape are lying'.

- And more recently, in February 2002, a magistrate from Pretoria passed an outrageously light sentence on an eighteen-year old rapist who had raped a five-year old girl. The reasons she gave for this was firstly, that the young man had his whole life in front of him (!) and secondly, that the five-year old was no longer a virgin when she was raped, which must cast some doubt on her character.
- In Cape Town a father who raped his daughter was also given a lighter sentence than usual, because he was perceived not to pose a threat to the broader community.

The authorities will inspire little trust in women and children if these are their typical responses to rape.

Rape Understood as a Form of Torture

Understanding rape as analogous to torture places rape firmly within the realm of political crime. This would imply firstly that rape should be regarded as a political as well as a personal crime; secondly that rape is seen as a crime affecting its victims' human rights and citizenship status, rather than being relegated to a 'woman's problem' like pregnancy and childbirth; thirdly that rape, like torture, is a crime that may affect men as well as women; and fourthly that rape (like torture) is officially illegal but officially tolerated, so that masculinity and the male-biased or male-dominated public sphere themselves become implicated in the perpetuation of the crime.[7] The choice to compare rape with torture should also be understood against the backdrop of the Truth and Reconciliation Commission (TRC) and its exposure of state criminality under the apartheid regime. The activities of the TRC and the moral outrage that flowed from its findings are still very much alive in the imaginations of South Africans from all walks of life. The TRC and the new Constitution have managed to create a broadly based moral consensus among South Africans about the accountability of the state to its people. It is within this political-historical context that I find it appropriate and necessary to link rape to torture to make the argument that rape or sexual oppression should be taken at least as seriously as racial oppression and state-sanctioned use of torture. A comparison with torture will thus hopefully serve to convince people to take rape more seriously, as a political crime.

There is however a further reason for the analogy between rape and torture – it also facilitates the understanding of rape as an *inter-subjective phenomenon* or traumatic event – an understanding of rape that is denied or underplayed as long as we persist in seeing rape one-sidedly as 'something bad or unfortunate that happens to women' rather than as something bad that 'men do to women'. Antjie Krog noted that during the TRC trials, men did not use the word 'rape' when they testified, speaking instead about 'being sodomized, or about iron rods being inserted into them'. She comments on this: 'In so doing they make rape a women's issue. By denying their own sexual subjugation to male brutality, they form a brotherhood with rapists which conspires against their own wives, mothers and daughters' (Krog, 1998, p.182). According to Krog's interpretation, the term 'rape' is reserved exclusively for *women's sexual subjugation,* and thereby becomes sexist in its meaning. Also, the *legal definition* of rape used in South Africa makes it technically 'impossible' for a man to be raped, which contributes to the understanding of rape as something that happens to women.[8] The law limits the definition of rape narrowly to 'intentional unlawful sexual intercourse with a woman without her consent',[9] i.e. the law states that only women can be victims of rape; thus, that rape is a gender issue. On the other hand, however, by not acknowledging the possibility of male 'rape', or by limiting the more severe punishment for rape to the raping of *women*[10] the law may actually inadvertently contribute to perpetuating the idea that rape is 'a women's issue' and *therefore* not worthy of serious *political* consideration.[11] Describing rape in terms of torture then, will hopefully contribute towards piercing the veils of sexist and overly privatized understandings of rape which deny its power-political dimension.

It is important to ask exactly how and why rape has become such an accepted, almost banal, part of the everyday lives of South African women. How do we maintain a sense of moral outrage and injustice in the face of the institutional 'normalization' of rape? And which vocabulary can help us all (women and men) to de-familiarize and re-sensitize ourselves to the phenomenon so that we can see clearly what needs to be done about it? Some of the worst injuries of rape will now be analysed in terms of the following themes: silence and shame; (self-)betrayal; false motive; and performance. Finally, the impact of these elements of rape-as-torture on women's citizenship will be summarized.

Silence and Shame: Rape as a 'Dirty Secret'[12]

It is notoriously difficult to speak about rape. Charlene Smith[13] strongly believes that the only way to overcome rape, both individually and socially, is 'through the mouth', through speaking about it. She believes one of the main problems with speaking out is that survivors 'feel deeply that sense of malaise which I ... call "shame"...' (2001, p.104). Smith describes the silence of shame associated with being raped as follows:

> Within that dark and fearful room are dozens of women and children, many are people you admire, who sit in silence, believing they are alone despite the claustrophobia of their overwhelming presence (Smith, 2001, p.42).

She calls this paradoxical place of claustrophobic isolation 'the rapist's prison' (2001, p.42). Women don't speak easily or openly about rape because they fear that they will be ostracized by their families and communities. But why is rape associated with shame and silence? Firstly, it seems to be extremely difficult to talk or write about rape and torture, just as it is difficult to articulate intense physical pain.[14] But other indicators show that the silence is associated less with the personal pain and more with the aspect of social shame. In the second place then, many people believe that there is a disturbing link between rape and pornography (Everywoman, 1988). The prevalence of pornography makes it difficult to recognize rape for the sexual terrorism that it is. This is because it is argued that pornography naturalizes sex as violent and violence as sexy. It is therefore not surprising that audiences respond to accounts of rape as if they were pornography. A study of South African rapists revealed that only 5.9% gave sex (i.e. lust, or desire) as the *reason* for committing the rape (Burchell and Milton, 1991, p.487). This indicates clearly that hurt, punishment and humiliation of the woman rather than sexual gratification must be the driving force behind rape. It does not, however, explain *why* it is that violence against women and children takes the form of *sexual* violence with its own particular form of humiliation.[15] Charlene Smith (2001) describes her experience of rape being turned into pornography by a masculine readership:

> After writing about a woman gang raped in front of her children and who now has HIV, a number of male callers to the *Mail and Guardian* insinuated that my writings about rape suggested I had a boring life and 'just needed a good fuck' (p.201).

Language, Plato had already noted, is a *pharmakon*, in that it can act as either a medicine or a poison. The point made by Derrida (1978), who expands on Plato's ideas, is that language is not so firmly under our control (whether we speak or write) that we can *make sure* that it acts as a remedy rather than as poison (pp.101, 121). Language, words and concepts are far too 'slippery' and 'treacherous', giving us only a tenuous grasp on reality; they can easily turn around and poison us or our audience, betraying our best intentions and conveying meanings we never intended. Scarry (1985) also acknowledges the double-edged nature of language. Although she believes (as does Smith) that the articulation of torture (rape) is essential for its political representation and therefore for political action to curb or stop it, she is very much aware of the fact that language *articulating* torture can be used to *hide* the pain of it, to turn torture into something that it isn't. She says

> [t]his verbal sign [of the 'weapon'] is so inherently unstable that when not carefully controlled[16] it can have different effects and can even be intentionally enlisted for the *opposite* purposes, invoked not to coax pain into *visibility* but to push it into further *invisibility*, invoked not to assist in the *elimination* of pain but to assist in its *infliction*, invoked not to extend culture but to dismantle that culture (Scarry, 1985, p.13, author's emphasis).

This is of course precisely what the *Mail and Guardian* readers did when they interpreted Smith's attempt to expose the pain of rape as pornography which essentially hides or denies the pain. The pain and humiliation suffered are dwarfed or disguised by, and serve to enhance the pleasure of the pornographic male gaze. Further on I argue that *the act of rape itself* has an inherently pornographic or performative dimension.[17] It is therefore very difficult to write accurately about rape without one's writing itself becoming (or being read as) pornography. By reading a rape ordeal as pornographic text, these male readers by implication assist the original rapist(s) in acknowledging and perpetuating their 'work' as 'production work', like a pornographic shoot. However, the moral blame for this is shifted onto the survivors and activists who are accused of 'creating' the pornography that the men simply passively enjoy. The attempt to represent an *experience of female pain* with the aim of fighting or stopping it, is hijacked by an audience who reads it (apparently innocently) as a *spectacle of male pleasure.*[18]

A second reason for the difficulty in speaking about rape relates to the ways in which guilt is often *internalized* by women – with a survivor internalizing the rape as *her* shame, partly because of a pervasive mentality which views women's sexuality as a scandal and a shame *per se*, and partly because of the paradoxical nature of humiliation itself. Stoltenberg (1990) records a typical case of a woman who, several years after being gang-raped at the age of fourteen, recalled:

> I felt like I'd brought out the worst in these men just by being an available female body on the road. I felt like if I hadn't been on the road, these men would have continued in their good upstanding ways, and that it was my fault that they'd been lowered to rape me ... I forgave them immediately (p.27).

This deep sense of shame and complicity, of unintended but indisputable initiation of the action, has an analogue in torture: the shame or self-betrayal that torture aims for is the 'confession'. According to Scarry (1985), the *structural* function of the confession is to *invert* the moral universe of torture. The confession both absolves the torturer from responsibility and confers responsibility for the torture on the prisoner – it is regarded as providing the ultimate justification for anything 'unpleasant' that's happened. The confession 'credits the torturer, providing him[19] with a justification, his cruelty with an explanation', while it 'discredits the prisoner, making him rather than the torturer, his voice rather than his pain, the cause of his loss of self and world' (Scarry, 1985, p.35). In this way, the prisoner is turned into his own biggest enemy, and his final physical breakdown is encoded as a *betrayal*: 'in confession, one betrays oneself and all those aspects of the world – friend, family, country, cause – that the self is made up of' (Scarry, 1985, p.29). This is of course a blatantly false construction: by the time the prisoner 'confesses', he no longer *has* a world to be faithful to – that has already been destroyed by inflicted suffering. Even if false, though, the 'acting out' of both rape and torture seems to create a sense of profound shame in the survivor. In the face of death, the tortured or raped person is forced *to enact a performance of betrayal of the self*, to actively inflict damage on his or her own self-respect and dignity to the extent that his and her sense of personal coherence, their 'world', and their view of themselves as moral agents in that world are shattered. This happens through being reduced to bodily (sexual) existence in a public display which denies the existence of their subjectivity, agency, spirit – reduces them to the state of victim. The demise of one's world is acted out so that it becomes a reality to both prisoner and victim, rapist and raped. Something about the self and its place in a morally ordered world, its habitat, its 'ethos', its control over its own vital interests is lost – often irrevocably so. If voice embodies the presence of a self integrated within a meaningful world, then voice is precisely what is destroyed during rape and torture.

A third reason why it is so difficult to give voice to rape, is closely linked to the first two: humiliation is inherently paradoxical. In his detailed analysis of humiliation, Avishai Margalit (1996) conceptually links humiliation as psychological cruelty to torture as physical cruelty. Humiliation is for Margalit distinct from shame or embarrassment, in the sense that humiliation involves injury to one's self-respect rather than to one's self-esteem or pride. Self-respect is respect for the self based on the mere fact that one is fully human, whereas self-esteem is respect for the self based on achievement. To humiliate someone is thus different from insulting that person – humiliation has the specific sense of excluding someone from the human commonwealth *by treating her as less than fully human*, thereby injuring her respect for herself as fully human. Humiliation means to act in such a way that one's actions and/or words indicate a lack of concern for the other's vital interests in controlling *what properly belongs under their control as fully human creatures*. The phenomena of sexual abuse, rape and torture are paradigmatic examples of humiliation in Margalit's terms. This is so both because of their being inextricably linked to physical cruelty or the threat of physical pain and death, as well as their denial of a person's vital interest in control over her own body and sexuality.

The inability to speak about rape is thus related to injured or wounded self-respect. Margalit's paradox of humiliation gives a further clue to understanding a woman's sense of complicity in rape. Humiliation is paradoxical because it succeeds in damaging the self-respect of a person, i.e. that respect which is properly due to *oneself* simply on the basis of being human (Margalit, 1996, pp.115ff.). Margalit explains the paradox by saying that if the rejection of oneself by another is based on sound reason, then one should re-evaluate one's life or actions, but if it is based on an untruth which one knows to be a lie, then one should in theory be able simply to resist or reject that attempt to injure one. In actual fact, however, our self-respect seems to be a rather fragile, thoroughly social or relational construction. Our respect for ourselves and for others springs mainly from our being socialized into respectful habits and attitudes, from having been systematically treated as fully human by someone important and close to us. Also, whom we acknowledge as fully human or as belonging to the human commonwealth, depends a lot on who is acknowledged as such by our formative communities. In other words, our very conception of 'the human' is shaped by society. This is why it is logically possible for an individual, a group or a whole society as such to seriously injure people's *self-respect* by consistently or systematically treating them as less than fully human. I submit that the South African society is perilously close to treating its women and children as a less than fully human category through its callous response to rape.[20] Treating a woman *as if* she had no vital interest in controlling her own body and sexuality, in fact often leaves her seriously disempowered to do so in future. The actual act of removing a woman's or child's power over her most intimate self translates into her believing that she never had full control to begin with, and/or that she will in future never have complete control.[21] An essential part of the raped woman's selfhood – the control over her own body – was disowned and placed in control of another for as long as he wished. He had absolute control, not only of her sexuality, but also over her life or death.

What is more, humiliation is contagious, as discussed by Margalit (1996, p.32). If someone is treated with disrespect in the presence of another person who identifies with that person's social positioning, like age, colour or sex, the latter might feel indirectly humiliated by association.[22] The fact then that women are raped on a large and seemingly uncontrollable scale without the authorities taking a strong stand on all policy levels, translates for ordinary South African women into pervasive fear, systematic (contagious) humiliation, and incapacitation. Large stretches and innumerable pockets of space in every woman's and girl's living environment are physically inaccessible or dangerous to her, so that her agency is seriously curbed. She forms the habit (and teaches it to her daughters) of fearing men and to always look out for and avoid situations that may put her in danger. She lives out on a daily basis her fear of being raped, of being both physically and mentally tortured, of being punished for her womanhood. She lives an imposed identity of the sexually vulnerable simply on the basis of being female. Her very body becomes conspicuous to her, the *reason* for which she may be tortured and killed. In such a society as we have become, a woman objectifies her own body; she lives her body as a corpse, i.e. as a potentially offensive object that may lead to the obliteration of her self. It is vitally important to remember that the fear of rape is never the fear of 'only' rape – inherent in the act of rape is the threat of death itself, and this is so, even without the added (realistic) fear of contracting HIV/AIDS. In response to all of this, a woman becomes self-conscious and docile, and fears that she may inadvertently invite male aggression through bodily dress, composure, or gesture. *She is careful not to provoke male disapproval or anger in most situations.* This seriously erodes *all* her considerable rights under the new Constitution.

A fourth reason for the difficulty in speaking about rape relates to all the above, but merits a discussion of its own. It relates to the ways in which sexual identities are constructed in our society and elsewhere. Because masculine sexuality is constructed as acquiring, initiating, active and virile, and feminine sexuality as passive, receiving, responding and void of a desire of her own, sex itself is understood as masculine aggression, as one-sided action, as colonization or invasion; in short, as something *men do to women* (or other men, or children – people less powerful than themselves). '[T]he act of prevailing upon another to admit of penetration without full and knowledgeable assent so sets the standard in the repertoire of male-defining behaviours that it is not at all inaccurate to suggest that the ethics of male sexual identity are essentially rapist' (Stoltenberg, 1990, p.26). If women are deemed to be vague or ambiguous about what they want, men must feel assured that all women want or need (lack) what men 'have' to 'give' to them. Masculine sexuality is seen as 'naturally' assertive and female as 'naturally' yielding. According to MacKinnon (1989), 'men are systematically conditioned not even to notice what women want ... Rapists typically believe the woman loved it' (p.181) and '[i]t is not only men convicted of rape who believe that the only thing they did that was different from what men do all the time is get caught' (p.174). A man is therefore not a *real* man if he isn't sexually aggressive, or at least strongly assertive. And a woman is not really a woman if she doesn't yield, give in, drop her defences, because that is what women *do* – they put up a little resistance but *everyone knows* that all of that is merely pretence, intended to test the strength of the man's desire.

These *are* men's and women's sexual identities respectively, and if they should deviate, they would be regarded as monstrous, sexually speaking.[23] If this is how we popularly view male and female sexual identities, then it becomes very clear that the rapist is not an exotic stranger, a half-crazy criminal, but in actual fact a very banal, all-too-familiar figure. We could also call him the policeman of male sexual ethics. He enforces the law which stipulates that it is right to rape; wrong to be raped, and right to be male; wrong to be female (Stoltenberg, 1990. p.28). Carolyn Craven (in MacKinnon, 1989) speaks of the man who raped her as follows:

> Stinky [her rapist] seemed to me as though he were only a step further away, a step away from the guys who sought me on the streets, who insist, my mother could have died, I could be walking down the street and if I don't answer their rap, they got to go angry and get all hostile and stuff as though I walk down the street as a ... that my whole being is there to please men in the streets. But Stinky only seemed like someone who had taken it a step further ... he felt like an extension, he felt so common, he felt so ordinary, he felt so familiar, and it was maybe that what frightened me the most was that how similar to other men he seemed. They don't come from Mars, folks (p.171).

MacKinnon (1989) argues that the wrong of rape has probably been so difficult to define 'because the unquestionable starting point has been that rape is defined as distinct from intercourse' and 'for women (and men, and courts) it is difficult to distinguish the two under conditions of male dominance' (p.174). She argues that when sexuality is constructed in this way, and if sex is understood as something men do to women, then the questions about force and consent in the legal context of rape largely lose their meaning. Maybe this also accounts for the fact that only about 8% (less in the case of children) of reported rape cases in this country lead to convictions.[24] This is why, '[m]ost women get the message that the law against rape is virtually unenforceable' and that, from women's point of view, 'rape is not prohibited; it is regulated' (MacKinnon, 1989, p.179). Sensible women would conclude that either they have not been raped (because they could not prove it in court) or that they have been raped but dare not risk a 92% chance of losing their case in court. This risk is even more pronounced seen in the light of evidence that women are most often raped by men whom they know (i.e. not complete strangers) and are therefore likely to meet again after having 'lost' their cases.[25] Additionally of course, '[u]nder a patriarchal state, the boundary violation, humiliation, and indignity of being a public sexual spectacle' lead women to feel that they are raped a second time in court (MacKinnon, 1989, p.179). Often women have to face their attackers in court and bear their grins and sneers, reliving and retelling their account of the rape to a hostile audience.[26] The courts seem to force the rape victim into playing the role of a live pornography star to a largely male institution, the script being her actual past trauma. On top of all this, she is required to 'prove' something ridiculous: it is as if a robbery victim has to *prove* that he was not engaged in philanthropy when his wallet was forcibly taken from him.[27]

(Self-)betrayal

The popular notion that women 'ask for it' is based on the false assumption that rape is motivated mainly by (virile, male) sexual lust, which *women* incite by their demeanour, dress or conduct (Burchell and Milton, 1991, p.487). Women, we are made to believe, create lust in men and then deny them satisfaction. This, it is then argued, *justifies* or rationalizes force. 'Consent in this model becomes more a metaphysical quality of a woman's being than a choice she makes and communicates' (MacKinnon, 1989, p.175). If the prisoner's self-betrayal is embodied in the final confession (cf. Scarry), then the self-betrayal of the rape victim entails the many ways in which she is understood to have consented to the act. As has been indicated, the whole notion of consent, so central to legal definitions of rape, becomes a hollow notion if we concede to the ways in which sexual identities are structured under patriarchy. The idea of a woman's consent (submission) as the female version of male initiative or demand, is flawed in the sense that it assumes that women are free to make their own sexual choices, and that the men who initiate and the women who respond are equally powerful in that situation. The idea is flawed on both counts. Women's 'consent' following on men's 'initiative' is also *assumed* when we believe that all women ultimately initiate men's interest in the first place – women are always the *first movers*. The higher the rape rate in any given society, and the higher the levels of official and social tolerance of rape, and thus of women's fear, the less power do all women in it have over any particular sexual encounter. If the *failure rate* of our country's policing and legal systems to punish rape is any indication (92% of reported rapes do not lead to convictions), then a woman currently has very little chance to enforce her 'no' to sex in any given situation. If she is raped, she has only an 8% chance that her 'no' will have legal and official backing.

Smith (2001) describes her fear of death and her extreme effort in trying to keep calm at knifepoint in order to save her life and not alarm the rapist. Only hours after the rape, she received the following comment from an officer of the sexual offences unit:

> It's a shame that you did not fight back. He would have beat the shit out of you, but we would have had great pictures and a strong case. He would have gone away for years longer. But because you did not fight, a judge could say it was consensual (pp.32-3).

The 'great pictures' of her scarred body (if not corpse) would have removed the inevitable doubt about the possibility of her consent. This then is the way in which the moral universe of rape, like that of torture, is turned upside down, inverted to the point where the rapist is absolved from guilt, because it could be shown that the survivor had 'participated in' or had 'facilitated' or had 'at least not actively resisted' her own rape[28] – and that therefore no rape took place.

There are many versions of this 'betrayal' or 'consent'. Women are often accused of 'looking for it', of asking to be raped if they dress in a certain way, walk in certain places at certain times, or if they walk in a particular manner, talk to men in any of a variety of ways, and so on. This kind of thinking effectively silences survivors of rape, convincing them that they have betrayed themselves and their loved ones in 'allowing themselves' to be raped. Of course, this accusation is only levelled at the 'lucky ones' who actually survive. The occurrence of murder after rape is so common that women have very good reason to do anything they can just to stay alive. 'Anything they can' is sometimes incredibly much: women might be forced to perform oral sex with rapists, to masturbate themselves, to allow their children or husbands to watch, to be sodomized and gang raped, to be penetrated with other objects than penises, to offer up their children to be raped, to participate in pornographic talk. All of this, Smith notes, will contribute to a rape survivor's feeling of guilt and shame, her feeling of having *contributed* to or *caused* the atrocity. She also comments that women forced to experience either forced masturbation or orgasm 'have the highest rate of suicide of all rape survivors' (Smith, 2001, p.89) due to a heightened sense of complicity. Rape victims often report feeling dirty afterwards – a feeling that must be understood on both a physical and a mental level – not only may the woman be infected with a sexually transmitted disease, she is also likely to feel polluted from being 'drawn into' unwanted and unloving sexual proximity i.e. from being an (unwilling, but undeniable, to her mind) accomplice in the crime of supreme humiliation of herself. The self-betrayal experienced by the survivor of rape is further intensified by her community and society at large, when she is made to feel responsible for betraying them, too. Turning the moral universe back on its feet, we must say that *she is betrayed by them*, however, in as far as they doubt her reality.

The atmosphere of silence surrounding rape at the TRC was partly created and partly reinforced by the ways in which rape featured in both the apartheid regime and the freedom struggle, as well as by the inability of the TRC to deal with this properly. Antjie Krog (1998) writes that a very small number of women activists were willing to testify to the TRC about rape and that they were extremely reluctant to name the rapists (p.182). Women were raped by policemen as well as by comrades and prison wardens during the virtual civil war of the 1980s. One activist explained:

> A group of six guys and myself in Sebokeng decided to form an organization to keep the senior comrades busy all the time. We rape women who need to be disciplined. Those who behave like snobs. They think they know better than most of us. And when we struggle, they simply don't want to join us (Krog, 1998, p.181).

This is a political organization which sets itself the task of 'disciplining' or punishing women using rape to do so, in the name of the freedom struggle. Women who did not join the struggle were punished with rape, and women who did join the struggle were punished with rape.[29] Another woman did not want to testify about being raped by comrades because 'the day [she] became involved in the struggle, ...[she] fully understood the consequences of it' (i.e. that she had to endure being raped by 'her' comrades?) (Krog, 1998, p.181). Soldiers and policemen also raped women accused of being part of the struggle. As in the case of torture, the woman/survivor is set up as the guilty party, with the soldiers/comrades supposedly being 'forced' to act as they do, because of whatever it is that they assume or imply *she* has done. Her sexual humiliation is presented as the predictable outcome of her political betrayal. In these ways then, women's sexual humiliation during the struggle was acknowledged as such by neither of the two opposing regimes, and still today is not allowed into public and political discourse. Men's biggest shame – their abuse of women – inverted cruelly into women's biggest shame, was finally left untouched by the reconciliatory efforts of the TRC. The inevitable effect of this is that women's silence, along with their sexual abuse on a large scale, is still not a political priority of society at large, and seems set to be perpetuated for a long time to come.

False Motive

In torture, the false motive for torture (information gathering) sets the torturer up as the vulnerable party with a special need that only the prisoner can fulfil. Similarly, in rape, the rapist likes to understand himself as vulnerable to the desire created in him by the woman. But ironically, the pretended vulnerability of both torturer and rapist serves also to cover up a *real* vulnerability or need – the actual motive for the torture and the rape. In the case of torture, it is the *threatened*, the *unacknowledged* or *contested regime* that *needs* and resorts to torture. This is the case because torture facilitates the translation of the prisoner's pain into the power of the regime. The false motives for rape might include the legacy of apartheid, the male urge factor or women's imagined sexual power, the punishment of women, the militarization of our male youth, and culturally entrenched attitudes towards women and their role. All of these 'motives' probably are contributing factors to the high rape rate, and they all contain *some* truth. However, over and above all these popular causes listed, there is another very important motive for rape, which emerges clearly from the analogy between rape and torture.

The 'real' or hidden vulnerability of the rapist is the contested nature of his masculine identity. According to Vogelman (1990), 'men rape primarily to bolster their masculine pride and feed their desire for power. This is largely attributable to the rapist's need to live up to society's ideal of masculinity ... [and] his objectification of women' (p.197). Whatever the rapist's precise understanding of the ideal of masculine power or privilege, he is enormously frustrated in that ideal. That is why the presence of an 'other' person (mostly a woman or girl) is needed – her *female, sexual* pain and humiliation as incontestably real is needed to be objectified and then denied, in order that it may be translated into the (fiction of the) 'incontestable' reality of his manhood. In South Africa there are clearly many factors contributing to threatened masculinities, but whatever the reason for the individual man's vulnerability, it seems that all rapes share this same structure of a threatened and contested regime – that of 'true manhood'. If men were in need of sexual satisfaction, they could make use of sex workers. But the motive for rape is not sexual need but the need for a spectacle of power which would give substance to 'make up and make real' (Scarry, 1985, p.21) a contested and fragile masculine sense of self. One of the most enduring myths surrounding rape is that *real* men are always sexually ready, and that a *real* man 'punishes' a woman or 'puts her in her place' with his male 'weapon' (a weapon that she forever lacks), the penis. This myth is belied by Smith's (2001) observation that rapists in fact often struggle with erection – the moment that they have orchestrated to perform and display their maleness, is precisely the moment in which many of them come to lack that epitome of male control (pp.5, 70). This is indicative of their real vulnerability as men.

This understanding of 'what rape is for' is also borne out by the fact that many (any) substitutes for the non-obeying penis are often used to perform the rape. Men penetrate with their fingers, with bottles, rods, with anything that can hurt the woman as much as the penis is *supposed* to. Even our legal definition of rape plays into the myth of the virile male – rape is by definition penile penetration of the vagina (Smith, 2001, p.159). Rape can take many forms, but its logical structure is such that the suffering, the fear and the agony of the raped woman must give substance and form to the rapist's sense of *masculine* identity (often identified purely as superiority over women) that he feels is contested or denied by society at large. Stoltenberg (1990) argues in a similar vein that '[t]he disintegration of the victim's sense of self is … a prerequisite for the integration of the rapist's sense of self' (pp.28-29), and that rapists often report that they felt 'better' after committing rape, that the rape itself was stimulating, exciting, enjoyable, and fun. This shows that the violence of rape takes on a *sexual* form of humiliation and torture – it is the *sexual* identity of the rapist which is at stake, to which the agony of the survivor must attest, and make real. This is then why rape also shares with torture its sense of being a performance, a stage, a theatre or a 'production room', all of which is discussed under the next heading.

Performance

In Scarry's description of torture, she explicitly and firmly places the phenomenon of torture in the context of 'the making and unmaking' of the world (or worlds[30]). She makes it clear that torture is used to 'make' the world of the torturer and to 'unmake' the world of the prisoner, and that these two phenomena are interdependent. The insecure or contested reality of the torturer must be given 'flesh'; it has been 'made up' and must now be 'made real' *through the prisoner's loss of world* – his confession, which is his acknowledgement that his world, his truth, his self and voice, are all but lost. Torture is thus primarily aimed at whoever may be in doubt regarding the existence of the regime's power. Smith talks about the 'static coldness' and mechanical nature of rape as one of the particularly repugnant aspects of rape, it being divorced of all humanity and decency, of privacy and intimacy. These aspects or dimensions of rape could be understood as a function of it being a performance, an essentially imagined activity, however real and banal the pain and suffering of the prisoner/survivor may be. According to Scarry (1985), in the torturers' idiom, the room in which the brutality occurs (the torture room) was called the 'production room' in the Philippines, the 'cinema room' in South Vietnam, and the 'blue lit stage' in Chile. She says, 'built on [the] repeated acts of display and having as its purpose the production of a fantastic illusion of power, torture is a grotesque piece of compensatory drama' (Scarry, 1985, p.28). The same is true of rape.

In South Africa, 75% of those who report rape to the police have been gang raped by three to thirty perpetrators (Smith, 2001, p.189). Lorna Martin (quoted in Smith, 2001) records in her 1999 rape homicide study that

> ... the dynamics of gang rape appear to be related to camaraderie and male bonding. There is often a ritualistic aspect. The focus of the rape is not the survivor but the assailants themselves in watching and taking turns. The woman is merely the vehicle for the interaction of the men amongst themselves (p.235).

Gang rape in its explicitly theatrical structure reminds one a lot of torture's cinematic nature, but gang rape is not unique in this regard. Rapists often find it important to have (male) onlookers or spectators. This phenomenon seems to fit in with the idea of rape as a kind of torture, where manhood (as the torturer's regime) is contested and has to be 'proven' or made alive through a spectacle of sexual pain and humiliation, translated into a spectacle of masculine power. The fact that so-called male sexual power (associated almost exclusively and obsessively with the penis) has to be assisted with various 'props' is conveniently glossed over. The theatre of rape allows the penis to appear as the splendidly isolated protagonist of that whole small world – *all of the world*, for the duration of the 'play of rape'. Everything works together to create the spectacle of phallic power. This illusion is created, even if the woman's body acts as the very stage without which there would have been no 'world' in which the phallus could have appeared as protagonist in the first place. *Her* sexual, moral and personal disintegration forms the unacknowledged stage, décor and material background to *his* drama of sexual rebirth.

Rape can thus be understood as theatre, with the woman's body providing both the stage and props, as well as possibly the antagonist, opposition that the protagonist of phallic power has to conquer in order to rise victoriously. With reference to Irigaray (discussed in Diprose, 1994, p.36), in rape more than anywhere else, man's autonomous identity, his manhood, his separateness from the (m)other, is ironically and obscenely 'played out' at the expense of woman. In rape more than anywhere else, does woman appear in the role of the 'envelope by which man delimits himself', is she reduced to *nothing but* a womb, a bag, a box, a container which provides man with a place, a self, a voice and a world. But the precondition for this 'creative' exercise is that woman has to be robbed of *her* place, self, voice and world, which by their very existence would, according to this logic, threaten the man in his manhood. The existence of woman can however, through the transformative and world-dissolving power of rape, be turned into the raw material man needs to build 'his' world, 'his' truth.

If extreme bodily pain reduces the prisoner to raw bodily existence, and if his world is destroyed to the exact measure that his body enlarges to fill his universe, then in rape, something similar happens. In rape, the woman's body comes to fill her universe and destroy her world,[31] her body itself turning into her enemy and into the rapist's weapon.[32] Through societal prejudice about women's complicity in rape, through being faced with death and complying with the rapist's demands out of fear of death, and through extreme sexual humiliation, the woman or child is brought to a point of profound self-alienation and intense self-hatred. A rift is torn open between her will or desires, her deepest intentions and fears on the one hand, and her actions on the other. As in torture, the person being raped often loses control of her bodily functions:

> During rape, women are in such a state of terror that they have little or no control over bodily functions. Some may laugh hysterically, others weep, some urinate or even defecate, some experience acute vaginal dryness, while increased adrenalin in their bodies causes some to orgasm ... The woman's body betrays her and appears to succumb to the rapist, even as her mind may remain aloof (Smith, 2001, p.90).

During and after rape and torture, victims experience an acute loss of control over their lives, their bodies, their voices. This loss (also a bereavement) is essentially a loss of world and of a prior, integrated sense of self. This loss is at least partly brought about by the final loss of control over speech and body functions. In losing control over one's body functions, one is reduced to infancy, and therefore also to a pre-linguistic state. These losses are all *required* by the rapist/torturer for his own purposes: 'It is only the prisoner's steadily shrinking ground that wins for the torturer his swelling sense of territory ... [torture and rape] are the unfurling of world maps' (Scarry, 1985, p.36). And this loss of world, this final betrayal of the self and this absence of voice earns the person in pain not compassion but contempt. This is also true of both rape and torture. The suffering of such deep losses is exacerbated and prolonged for both types of survivor if their suffering remains unacknowledged and unavenged by the world at large.[33] Smith calls her experience of rape an experience of loss and bereavement and acknowledges that she needs someone to *mourn* with her, especially in the light of society's indifference and incompetence in dealing with her claim for justice. The loss of self and world[34] is thus in both rape and torture accompanied by a loss of voice, by a loss of agency and self-extension which is carried or embodied by the ability to speak and more especially, to be *heard*.

The Impact of Rape on Women's Citizenship

I have argued that rape in South Africa should be regarded as a political problem, related to gender oppression and clear masculine power objectives. This means that we need to find *political solutions*. As long as circumstances make it *reasonable* for women to conclude that it is useless to report rape, then I would contend that the state and its structures are complicit in sustaining and perpetuating a culture or social ethics of rape which systematically humiliates and paralyses far more than half of its population (if we count all women and children). Like the lynching of slaves and the torture of political enemies, the rape of women should be understood as systematic and deliberate control through fear: '[f]rom prehistoric times to the present, rape has played a critical function. It is nothing more or less than a conscious process of intimidation by which all men keep all women in a state of fear' (Brownmiller, 1976, p.34). As MacKinnon (1989) phrases it, '[t]o be rapable, a position that is social not biological, defines what a woman is' (p.180);

womanhood is defined by vulnerability to rape. Women's vulnerability to sexual violence is interwoven with their more general vulnerability and oppression: women are more likely to be poor than men, to contract HIV/AIDS, to be illiterate or have low levels of formal education, and to become prostitutes. Women also occupy the lowest paying jobs *and* do the bulk of caring work, with little or no compensation. For most South African women, including the male 'wives' of prison inmates, intimate and personal subjugation epitomized in sexual servitude is closely linked to subjugation on all other levels of existence. Rape and its associated forms of violence such as battering, kicking and killing, embody the ever-present threat of punishment for imagined or real insurrection and disobedience to male authority.

Government's failure to respond effectively to the HIV/AIDS crisis and to systemic violence against women forces new loads of caring work onto families, translating into even more unpaid and unrewarded work for women, and even children, some of whom form families without any adult support. There exists a vicious circle between women's private sphere vulnerability, and their vulnerabilities in the public and political levels.[35] The question that women should pose to our government is the following: exactly how much money do you *save* by keeping South African women and children in a state of perpetual fear and servitude? In other words, what is the value of work done by women and children, out of fear of male punishment, compared to the work done in some other countries by networks of social security? And what are the likely long-term *costs* to our society of allowing this state of fear to persist? One of the most obvious prices we are paying is that our households, where our future citizens are being raised, are paradigm examples of inequality, subjugation and fear. This is far removed from the ideal formative environment for democratic citizens embodying democratic virtues. Neither girls nor boys are socialized into roles that promote democratic citizenship (cf. Okin, 1989). A further, and related problem, is that our social order is held in place not by trust and mutual support, but by the most intimate, and therefore the most damaging, forms of structured violence. Through the sexual division of labour, women are mostly responsible for the caring work in society, the work that fosters relationships and supports children, the aged and the sick. Sometimes it is being done by women forced into caring roles through sexual subjugation and domination. We should look very closely and critically at the ways in which men in South Africa manipulate the meanings of both clusters culture/tradition/religion and liberation/democracy/citizenship to keep women in their un-political, domestic roles. Keeping women in private roles simultaneously means keeping them out of proper and full citizenship, where citizenship implies, at the very least, substantially more freedom of choice, more personal control and more agency, than most South African women enjoy at the moment. In the light of the above, it is absolutely crucial that a strong new national women's movement be cultivated that would ensure that gender issues such as rape and women's associated second class citizenship become issues of national priority instead of retaining its current back-seat position.

Notes

1. Neither the 'survival' tales of the nationalist government nor the 'liberation' stories of the struggle forces before 1994 allowed for rape to surface as an issue of political or national importance. The statistics seem to show a sharp rise in the rape rate after 1994 – this should more likely be interpreted as the 'normalization' of statistics in a climate of greater political stability and as an indication of women's determination to make the new democracy work for them. In other words, I read the rise in reported rape not as in indication of more rapes, but of a higher level of reportage, based on women's political expectations. In any case, rape statistics are notoriously controversial and unreliable in the final instance. The SA government's continued moratorium on crime statistics places a further obstacle in the way of anyone who tries to get an accurate picture of the situation.

2. The South African Law Commission (September 1999) at least once called rape 'sexual terrorism' and a crime 'akin to torture' (Smith, 2001, p.73). Jean Améry and others (in Brison, 2002) have also suggested that rape and torture as phenomena can serve to illuminate each other.

3. Under 'children' I include both boys and girls, although girls are more frequently singled out for rape. In sub-Saharan Africa, six times more girls than boys are infected with HIV, *and this is mainly because of rape.* Charlene Smith (2001), the South African journalist who wrote *Proud of Me*, a first-person account of rape survival, and a book I will draw on heavily for this chapter, says '[t]he rape of children in South Africa is endemic' (p.85).

4. Pateman (1988), Okin (1989), Young (1990), Sevenhuijsen (1998), MacKinnon (1989) and Yuval-Davis and Werbner (1999) represent some of the highlights within this debate. Using other starting points African and other marginalized women have started to criticize western or northern conceptions of citizenship.

5. For an example of this argument, see Tsenay Serequeberhan's *The Hermeneutics of African Philosophy* (1994) in which he draws heavily on the work of post-colonial authors Franz Fanon and Aimé Césair. Serequeberhan follows his predecessors in framing the colonial and post-colonial dilemmas in exclusively masculine terms.

6. According to the legal definition of rape, viz. 'forceful penetration of a vagina by a penis', only women can technically be raped, and 'rape' where penetration is not effected by a penis, and the orifice is not the vagina, is called 'sexual assault', and carries a lesser penalty. In this chapter I shall however follow the broader understanding of rape as sexual violation, which would include all forms of coercive sex.

7. Some feminist scholars established links between rape or other forms of sexual violence and torture, either as part of wars, or as part of domestic relations (Petchesky, 2000, quoting Copelon, 1994).

8. A new gender neutral sexual offences Bill has been drafted, but not yet been enacted by August 2004 (for more details, see Van Zyl, this collection).

9. This formulation has been debated and criticized on many counts. On the one hand, limiting the victims of the crime of 'rape' to females, makes the gender implications explicit, while using 'sexual assault' would make it gender neutral, and lose the sexist i.e. political nature of the crime.

10. The phraseology of the rape law as it stands also implies that adults ('women') are the main target of rape. That might still be true, but in this the law also seems to fail or disregard the high levels of child abuse and child rape.

11. The background to the paradoxical role played by the law in this instance is of course

the much more fundamental question about the proper role of the law in society. Depending on whether one sees the law as playing a more descriptive role or a more prescriptive, utopian role, one will probably argue for a narrower or broader definition of rape, respectively.

12. Talking about the rape of her mother to Charlene Smith, a young American woman used the words 'dirty secret'. She was raped while the father was away on a business trip, and the daughter was in the house. For ten years this event was considered 'a dirty secret' and never discussed openly with the daughters. The young woman wished for such a conversation because 'somehow, when your mom gets raped you fear it will happen to you too. I need to know we can cope' (Smith, 2001, p.107).

13. Charlene Smith is a well-known South African journalist who was raped and who subsequently used every opportunity to speak about rape and HIV publicly. Many other first-person accounts of rape from the west share this conviction about breaking the silence and the personal and social need for speaking out. Both the need for, and the difficulty of speaking about having been raped are recurring themes in first-person narratives of rape victims, especially in the light of a general audience that fails to listen empathically. (See References section for more first-person accounts.) It must be noted that rape may be experienced and its victims reach resolution in many different ways. It is also known that many rape victims have remained silent for many years about having being raped, therefore it is reasonable to suppose that some may never speak about it, nor feel the need. Until women who choose silence find the space to break it, it is impossible for us to know what their needs are.

14. 'Intense pain is language-destroying', says Scarry (1985, p.55).

15. I regard the sexual nature of rape to translate into a specific form of intense humiliation which depends on turning the essentially and paradigmatically private into public spectacle. More about this below.

16. Scarry seems to think, contrary to Derrida, that verbal signs can be controlled to convey the meanings we want. But the main point is that she is highly conscious of the danger inherent in language to obscure precisely that which it is meant to convey, and that this is especially true of language employed to convey pain.

17. This will be motivated by the detailed analysis of rape as theatre and performance in a later paragraph.

18. Catherine MacKinnon (1989) speaks of split reality with regard to rape, so that many rapes involve 'honest men and violated women' (p.183).

19. I will follow Scarry's exclusive use of masculine terms for both 'torturer' and 'prisoner' while discussing her exposition of torture, well aware that both torturers and the tortured may be of either sex. In my discussion of rape, however, I will use the masculine for the rapist or 'torturer' and the feminine form for the survivor of rape, thereby making the gendered (and consequently political) nature of the crime explicit.

20. Of course, in the recent past South African was infamous for its systematic humiliation of black people. Whether or not the systematic humiliation (some say emasculation) of black men 'resulted in' or 'helped create' the violent society we now find ourselves in, whether in other words we are experiencing a kind of 'revenge' taking the form of rape, is much debated, but inconclusively so. Such an interpretation would in any case account for only a minority of all rapes, since proportionally many more black than white women are raped, and white men also rape.

21. If this happens systematically enough, then women (and men) come to see sex as something *men do to women*, and the notion of female 'consent' loses all effective power. After being raped, many women have difficulty in distinguishing between sex

with and without their consent. They do not experience their own 'yes' or 'no' as essential to the nature of the act; in fact, they come to see their own will or desire or lack of these as all equally ephemeral and unreal. More generally: if one's point of view (on anything) is systematically ignored, never asked for, or belittled when forthcoming, one will very soon cease to even form an own view, opinion or perspective. I believe this is the experience of the majority of South African women when it comes to sex.

22. There is a strange process of 'othering' which sometimes takes place inside the vulnerable group. For example, women who fear rape need to believe that it happens to women who are *not* like them i.e. whores, sexually promiscuous women, women who wear short skirts etc. They *need* to believe this, in order to make themselves feel safe(r), and that rape can't happen to them. In this way they also participate in blaming 'other' women for rape by perpetuating the construction of categories of 'women asking to be raped'.

23. 'Monstrous' sexual identities are of course routinely associated with gay and lesbian sexualities. Sasha Gear (2002), a researcher at the Centre for the Study of Violence and Reconciliation writes in an interesting article, 'Sex behind the bars' in the *Mail and Guardian*, how equal or mutual sexual relationships between men are punished by prison gangs in male prisons, whereas 'marriages' or unequal sexual relationships are tolerated as part of prison culture. These latter relationships mirror stereotypical heterosexual relationships, with the 'wife' or 'wyfie' being the sexually submissive and available, usually younger male, and the 'husband' being the sexually and otherwise dominant one demanding both domestic and sexual services, and providing protection and coveted items in return, for the 'wife'. Masculinity is equated with male sexual dominance and sexual hierarchy, even with violence and rape, and sexual equality (even amongst men) is frowned upon as an abomination. Within the hierarchy there are clearly-defined gender roles kept in place through naked intimidation and especially threats of rape, even if these are all played by men in the prison. The wifely role is clearly marked as despicable, reserved for only the most vulnerable of prison inmates.

24. The South African government's moratorium on giving out rape statistics makes it difficult to situate arguments about rape as a crime within an empirical context. In a study conducted in Cape Town (Maconachie and Van Zyl, 1994, pp.57-58) with 159 women, 30 had reported sexual assaults to the researchers, twenty of those had spoken to a friend or family member, seven had reported to other available services, and only 3 had reported to the police. In 2000, there were 52 975 rapes reported nationally to the police. Fifty-four per cent went to trial, and 8% secured convictions. Of those 55% were committed by more than one offender, 25% by 'gangs' and 50% were accompanied by injuries. The crime statistics reinforce myths that women are raped by strangers. Of the women who had reported spousal abuse in Maconachie and Van Zyl (1994) 50% also reported sexual assault and rape by their partners.

25. 'Proving' a rape case in a criminal court is difficult since the burden of proof is 'beyond reasonable doubt'. Where you often have one person's word against another, this burden is hard to make. The social interpretation of a court case where an alleged rapist is 'not guilty' then creates the presumption that the rape didn't happen. However, it is merely that the case could not be proven 'beyond a reasonable doubt'.

26. This process known as 'secondary victimization' has been described by many feminist scholars (Clark and Lewis, 1977; Hanmer and Saunders, 1984; Stanko 1985; Van Zyl 1989).

27. This is an analogy adapted from MacKinnon (1989, p.180).

28. The existentialist point that we are 'condemned to be free' and thus *always* free to

choose, does not invalidate the notion of *degrees* of freedom from force, with important moral, political and legal implications. I want to argue that an option between certain death now, and rape now and possible death later, is no real choice, and that therefore no woman can logically be blamed or held accountable for submitting to rape (see also Clark and Lewis, 1977; Hanmer and Saunders, 1984; Stanko 1985; Van Zyl 1989).

29. There is a lot of 'double-talk' when it comes to reasons given for rape: here clearly the intention was to punish, and rape is mostly understood as punishment when meted out to men, or in the context of war. At other times, however, rape is regarded as something that all women 'really' want or need, and that it should then really be experienced as pleasurable.

30. Although the 'outsiders' to torture can see that one can logically and coherently speak of the existence of more than one 'world', the logic of torture seems to be that there *can only be one world*, one truth, and one objectivity. That is why the prisoner's version of reality and truth has to be destroyed in order to give credence, reality, and flesh to the torturer's inverted world. Elsewhere I have referred to MacKinnon's similar notion of 'split reality' in the experience of rape. The 'life' of the regime is thus parasitic on the 'life' of the prisoner: as long as he has a non-life, the regime can be proven to have a life – that non-life, that living death, *is* the proof of the existence of the contested world, according to the twisted logic of torture and of rape.

31. Just as every object in the torture room turns for the prisoner into a weapon directed against himself, and the world of everydayness is transformed into the 'world' or non-world of torturing pain, for the rape survivor also the 'everyday' world is transformed into the unbearable. Smith could not return to the bathroom in her home where the rapist overpowered her, she got rid of the bed she had been raped on, and repainted the whole house. She suggests that one either move house altogether, or sell, burn and give away as much as one can of anything that reminds you of the rape (Smith, 2001, p.54).

32. Scarry (1985, p.47) describes how not only the displayed weapons and the room itself and the 'everyday' objects in the room are all transformed into enemies of the prisoner, but even his body itself. The prisoner is forced to experience himself as the agent of his own annihilation, and his body as the agent of his agony. This leads to self-hatred as much as hatred of the enemy, to self-alienation and self-betrayal.

33. Smith tells of an eight-year old whose bitterness at being raped seems to have been largely overcome by the knowledge that her community had killed the rapist. This is not meant to serve as a plea for the death penalty for rapists, but to make the point of how crucial it is to the recovery of the survivor of rape that the rape be acknowledged publicly as a serious loss, that she be treated with respect and dignity, and that rapists effectively and swiftly be brought to justice and seen to be aptly punished. Ideally, it should be treated as a crime against the community.

34. Scarry makes it clear how the torturer draws the whole world of the prisoner into the torture room either physically or through allusion – especially the loved ones, the political ideology, the home of the tortured. He does this in order to effectively kill them off – he brings them into the presence of pain so that the pain may kill them off or transform them into the prisoner's enemy, as everything else is killed off or transformed through the pain. Smith, in her discussion of rape, suggests that something similar happens there: she says that her family have been raped too, and she repeats that the spouses and partners of rape survivors are also 'raped' to the extent that they are rendered 'emasculated' or powerless – especially powerless to help her restore her world.

35. Susan Moller Okin (1989) helps us to understand the vicious circle operation between

women's private or household inequality and their public or political inequalities. See especially the chapter called 'Vulnerability by Marriage' from Justice, Gender, and the Family. In this book, she regards the gender-structured and unjust institution of marriage is enough to systematically render women vulnerable within a male dominated society; she does not focus on women's further vulnerability created by sexual violence.

References

Améry, Jean (1980), *At the Mind's Limits: Contemplations by a Survivor on Auschwitz and Its Realities* (transl. Sidney Rosenfeld and Stella P. Rosenfeld), Indiana University Press, Bloomington and Indianapolis.

Assiter, Alison (1999), 'Citizenship Revisited', in Nira Yuval-Davis and Pnina Werbner (eds.), *Women, Citizenship and Difference*, Zed Books, London and New York.

Brison, Susan J. (2002), *Aftermath: Violence and the Remaking of the Self*, Princeton University Press, Princeton and Oxford.

Brownmiller, Susan (1976), *Against our will: men, women and rape*, Penguin, Harmondsworth.

Burchill, Jonathan and Milton, John (1991), Principles of Criminal Law (2nd edn.), Juta, Kenwyn, South Africa.

Clark, Lorenne and Lewis, Debra (1977), *Rape: The price of coercive sexuality*, Women's Educational Press, Toronto.

Copelon, R. (1994), 'Recognizing the Egregious in the Everyday: Domestic Violence as Torture', *Columbia Human Rights Law Review*, 25, pp.291-367.

Derrida, Jacques (1978), *Spurs: Nietzsche's Styles*, Chicago University Press, Chicago.

Diprose, Rosalyn (1994), *The Bodies of Women: ethics, embodiment and sexual difference*, Routledge, London and New York.

Estrich, Susan (1987), *Real Rape*, Harvard University Press, Cambridge, Massachusetts and London, England.

Everywoman, (1988), *Pornography and Sexual Violence: Evidence of the Links*, Everywoman, London.

Foucault, Michel (1986), *The History of Sexuality Vol.2: The Use of Pleasure* (transl. Robert Hurley), Penguin, Harmondsworth.

French, Stanley G., Teays, Wanda and Purdy, Laura M. (eds.), (1998), *Violence Against Women: Philosophical Perspectives*, Cornell University Press, Ithaca and London.

Gear, Sasha (2002), 'Sex behind the bars', in *Mail and Guardian*, October 25 to 31, 2002, p.19.

Gordon, Margaret T. and Riger, Stephanie (eds.), (1989), *The Female Fear*, The Free Press, New York and London.

Hamilton, Edith and Cairns, Huntington (eds.), (1961), *Plato. The Collected Dialogues: Phaedrus*, Princeton University Press, Princeton.

Hanmer, Jalna and Saunders, Sheila (1984), *Well-Founded Fear: A community study of violence to women*, Hutchinson, London.

Krog, Antjie (1998), *Country of My Skull*, Random House, Johannesburg.

Maconachie, Moira and Van Zyl, Mikki (1994), *Promoting Personal Safety for Women: Women set an agenda for policy formation*, Human Sciences Research Council, Pretoria.

MacKinnon, Catherine (1989), *Toward a Feminist Theory of the State*, Harvard University Press, Cambridge, Massachusetts and London, England.

Margalit, Avishai (1996), *The Decent Society*, (transl. Naomi Goldblum), Harvard University Press, Cambridge, Massachusetts and London, England.

Okin, Susan Moller (1989), *Justice, Gender and the Family*, Basic Books, USA.

Pateman, Carole (1988), *The Sexual Contract*, Polity Press, Cambridge.

Petchesky, Rosalind (2000), 'Sexual Rights: Inventing a Concept, Mapping an International Practice' in R. Parker, R.M. Barbosa and P. Aggleton, (eds.), *Framing the Sexual Subject: The Politics of Gender, Sexuality, and Power*, University of California Press, Berkeley, pp.81-103.

Sanday, Peggy Reeves and Gallagher, Ruth (eds.), (1990), *Beyond the Second Sex: New Directions In the Anthropology of Gender*, Goodenough University of Pennsylvania Press, Philadelphia.

Scarry, Elaine (1985), *The Body in Pain: The Making and Unmaking of the World*, Oxford University Press, New York and Oxford.

Scherer, Migael (1992), *Still Loved by the Sun: A Rape Survivor's Journal*, Simon and Shuster, New York, London, Toronto, Sydney, Tokyo and Singapore.

Serequeberhan, Tsenay (1994), *The Hermeneutics of African Philosophy: Horizon and Discourse*, Routledge, New York and London.

Sevenhuijsen, Selma (1998), *Citizenship and the Ethics of Care*, Routledge, London and New York.

Smith, Charlene (2001), *Proud of Me: Speaking out against Sexual Violence and HIV*, Penguin, Harmondsworth.

Stanko, Elizabeth A. (1985), *Intimate Intrusions: Women's experience of male violence*, Routledge and Kegan Paul, London.

Stoltenberg, John (1990), *Refusing to be a Man*, Fontana Paperbacks, Great Britain.

The South African Law Commission, September 1999, available at http://www.gov.za/documents/99sublist.htm.

Tomaselli, Sylvana and Porter, Roy (eds.), (1986), *Rape*, Basil Blackwell, Oxford and New York.

Van Zyl, Dine (2001), *Slagoffers*, Tafelberg, Kaapstad.

Van Zyl, Mikki (1989), 'Rape Mythology' in *Women Represented, Critical Arts*, Vol.5 No.2, pp.10-36.

Vogelman, Lloyd (1990), *The Sexual Face of Violence: Rapists on Rape*, Ravan Press, Johannesburg.

Young, Iris Marion (1990), *Justice and the Politics of Difference*, Princeton University Press, Princeton.

Yuval-Davis, Nira and Werbner, Pnina (1999), 'Women, Citizenship and Difference', in Nira Yuval-Davis and Pnina Werbner (eds.), *Women, Citizenship and Difference*, Zed Books, London and New York.

Index